Yellow Tavern and Beyond

From
Family Letters and Journals

Dorothy Francis Atkinson

HERITAGE BOOKS
2019

HERITAGE BOOKS
AN IMPRINT OF HERITAGE BOOKS, INC.

Books, CDs, and more—Worldwide

For our listing of thousands of titles see our website
at
www.HeritageBooks.com

Published 2019 by
HERITAGE BOOKS, INC.
Publishing Division
5810 Ruatan Street
Berwyn Heights, Md. 20740

Heritage Books by the author:
King William County in the Civil War, Along Mangohick Byways
Yellow Tavern and Beyond, From Family Letters and Journals

International Standard Book Number
Paperbound: 978-0-7884-4131-8

DEDICATION

Dedicated to the honor of

Grandpa Tom Francis and "Aunt Sally" Anderson

TABLE OF CONTENTS

FOREWORD

In recent years Civil War historians have looked with increasing frequency at the war's impact on the home front, particularly in the South. Every county in the Confederacy endured its share of hardships, both with economic suffering and the diminution of the male population through battle casualties. Appreciating the ordeals of those wartime communities is of fundamental interest. It also opens an important window that will help us understand the daily stresses that plagued Civil War soldiers and influenced their morale while they fought, often far from home.

Hanover and Henrico counties, which wrap around the Confederate capital city of Richmond on its northern and eastern sides, afford two of the best possible case studies. Both counties contributed a very large number of units for Confederate service. That alone is not unique, but the repeated presence of the contending armies on Hanover and Henrico soil brought those places into the national limelight. Several of the greatest battles in American history occurred there. Only Spotsylvania and Dinwiddie counties, farther north and south of Richmond respectively, can lay claim to equal significance in Virginia's military history.

The patriotic fervor with which this area embraced the Confederacy is especially notable. Nearly every church in Hanover had a ladies' sewing society or a soldiers' aid organization. Citizens of both counties donated huge sums, both individually and collectively, to arm, clothe, and feed their soldiers. As the young men banded together into local organizations and offered their services to the state, they chose remarkably uninventive names. There were the Hanover Grays and the Henrico Grays, the Hanover Light Dragoons and the Henrico Light Dragoons, and self-named companies of artillery for each county. Eventually Hanover County fielded at least nine separate companies, a significant achievement for a county that numbered only 3,700 white males of all ages in the 1860 census.

In that final national survey before the war, the census taker found 17,000 individuals in Hanover County, and 24,000 in Henrico. Slaves accounted for approximately sixty percent of those population totals. When the armies arrived in 1862, they collectively brought nearly one-fifth of a million men to the largely rural environments of Hanover and Henrico. Two years later they numbered 150,000 fighting men. The impact of that presence on the citizens and on the landscape, exclusive of the destructive battles, is almost incalculable.

Dorothy Atkinson brings a special perspective to *Yellow Tavern and Beyond: From Family Letters and Journals*, which in essence is the Civil War history of the community where she grew up. The Yellow Tavern area and a wide swath around it no longer survive in any meaningful historical way. Like much of the rest of Henrico County, it has been robbed of its character with seemingly endless miles of commercial development that renders it virtually indistinguishable from the suburbs of Washington, D.C.

The number of folks who saw that region before its obliteration is dwindling. Mrs. Atkinson knew the descendants of the wartime families that populated the area. She roamed the farms and absorbed the atmosphere of the place. She recollects the years before World War Two, when as a young girl she helped her father in the annual decoration of the J.E.B. Stuart monument on the Yellow Tavern battlefield. One could look south in those days, out across the battlefield and over the ground crossed on May 11, 1864, by Union general George Custer in his climactic charge. Today that same vantage point offers nothing more than a bleak view of two interstate highways.

Mrs. Atkinson's book conveys the story of this region during its grimmest years. Using a diverse collection of first person sources – many of them not otherwise available – she follows the area's families through the course of the war. Hanover and Henrico soldiers saw combat on all the war's legendary battlefields in the east, including in the deadly woods around Dunkard Church at Sharpsburg and at Cemetery Ridge during Pickett's Charge at Gettysburg. The staggering human cost of Civil War battles is well known, yet those memorable places achieve fresh meaning when seen through the eyes of just a few of the thousands of affected families.

The strength of *Yellow Tavern and Beyond* is in its neighborly tone. Mrs. Atkinson has devoted equal attention to local soldiers, to their loved ones in war-torn Henrico and Hanover, and to the community they called home. In the process she has thrown vivid new light onto a desperate era in one of Virginia's most historic regions.

Robert E.L. Krick
Glen Allen, Virginia
October 2005

ACKNOWLEDGEMENTS

This project has been the work of generations. To each who participated, I am profoundly grateful. It began with my grandfather, Tom Francis, his three brothers, and their brother-in-law, Charles Terrell who left home to serve in the 15th Virginia Regiment. Out of their concern for those they left behind, they wrote letters telling of their experiences. Some of them did not live out the war, but their letters have been cherished by the women in the family and passed down as tangible records of their personalities and the times in which they lived. In these letters, often written in the dialect of Virginians the words spelled phonetically, this generation, who never knew them, can still hear the fellows speaking.

As children we were aware that grandmother, Lucy Ann Cross Francis, had saved letters and that our aunt, Cora Francis Bowles who lived with us, had them safely tucked away in a tin box. After her death, we began to read the letters and my sister, Otelia Francis Bodenstein, began to transcribe them. Then we learned that our great aunt, Emeline Josephine Francis Terrell, whose husband had died from his wounds, had also saved letters. Her granddaughter, the late Martha Terrell Durham, was kind to let us copy those letters. Upon the death of our dad's first cousin, Fannie C. Cross, who had served as a surrogate grandmother to us, we found that she had saved letters written by her stepbrother, Mahlon Terrell who had died as a prisoner of war. The last to come to light were letters written by Jimmie Gray, who was killed at Nance's Shop. They were saved by a sister, our great aunt Betty Powell Gray Cross, rescued from destruction and copied by her grandson, Tom Scott.

Tom Scott gave us his aunt Catherine Cross's recollections and allowed us to make a copy of the Peterkin typescript. The late Maggie Davis Bowles allowed me to copy her cousin Creed Davis's "The Slashes of Hanover." James Thomas

Francis gave us a copy of the Joseph Park Thomas Memoirs. Ruth Cross Hawthorne brought me a copy of her great grandmother's notes entitled "Some Troubles of the War." This was written by Mary Elizabeth Francis Davis, my grandfather's sister.

One day the late Patsy Taylor walked into the University of Richmond Library, where my sister Kathleen was working, with the journal of Blanche Norment Powell, her husband's relative who with her family lived at "Melrose" during the war. My sister told her that our mother had lived there as a child. Patsy made copies of the journal for us. On another day Martha T. Lupton called me from Virginia Beach to tell me that her family, that of John Spotswood Mosby, had witnessed Jeb Stuart's fall at Yellow Tavern. She has graciously shared her family history and pictures with me.

I am grateful for the help and encouragement of my sister, the late Lucie Francis Samuel and her daughter Marjorie Samuel Becus, and that of my sisters, Otelia Francis Bodenstein and Kathleen B. Francis, who pushed, critiqued, and proof read my manuscript. Leland Terrell, now in possession of the Terrell letters, has allowed me to make references to them and his parents, the late Lily and Lewis Terrell, clued me in on later happenings. My cousins, Tom Scott and his wife Betty, and Betty Gray Scott Faber, have shared their family's pictures and recollections with me. My cousin Mark Cross allowed me to collaborate in his research on the Cross family and also sent me pictures.

Friends Jayne M. Massie, Lois Cumber and her mother, and Marian Litchfield Lauterbach have shared their family recollections as well as Lillian Baughan Baldock those of her grandmother Mary Anderson. Bob Ehrhart gave me material by DeWitt Clinton Gallahar and Wesley Brannan brought me material on the Haws of Haw's Shop. Kenneth Miller helped me understand the Battle of Brandy Station.

The staff at the Pamunkey Regional Library – Mae Taylor, Myra Cramer, and Ann Long – helped me obtain books and material, as also did the staff of the Henrico County Library and the Virginia Baptist Historical Society Library. Kim Sicola at Meadow Farm Museum has obtained copies of pictures for me.

My patient editor, Robert E.L. Krick, shared his copy of the Mordecai diary and his maps and collected material on the Yellow Tavern area. Julie Krick, Bob's wife, has modified old maps for current application. Sam Craghead urged me to use my material and helped ready it for publication. The meticulous Shelby Griffin, of Virginia Beach, has done the index. Bray Young served as my faithful photographer. Many young friends pulled me out of the pitfalls with my reluctant computer: Char Arthur and her son Will, Chris Stevens, Jon Jones and his wife Alexx, Lea Ann Pauli, Lisa Wilkerson and her father Kenny, my nephew Patrick Becus, Ernest and L.T. McAllister, Jr., Keith Lauer, and my pastor Justin Williams.

I am grateful to my tried and true publisher Craig Scott for his confidence in the readability of Yellow Tavern and Beyond!

Thanks folks. I couldn't have made it without you.

Dorothy Francis Atkinson

INTRODUCTION

Settlers in Henrico County, Virginia, had been concerned about the safety of their women and children since before the establishment of Richmond. It was frontier land. The Indians and the elements were both unpredictable. William Byrd set up a trading post on the south side of the James at the Falls but was reluctant to raise his children there. Byrd moved his bride, the widowed Mary Horsmanden Filmer, into a stone house built by his uncle Thomas Steppe which was similar to the one still standing (2004) on East Main Street in Richmond. There William Byrd II was born.[1]

Byrd was often away on expeditions into the unknown countryside, leaving Mary and the boy for weeks at a time. An Indian uprising killed three of Byrd's servants and an overseer for Nathaniel Bacon among many others. Bacon had set up a trading post on his quarter just across the river adjoining land also owned by Byrd. Later Brook Avenue came to bisect this area. When Governor Berkley refused to give protection, Byrd and his neighbors turned to Nathaniel Bacon for security. William Byrd chose to send his wife and son to England.[2]

Returning to the lonely house on the James when some of the Indian threat had subsided, Mary bore William four more children: Susan, Ursula (called "Little Nutty"), Mary, and a son Warham who died in infancy. William II was sent back to England at the age of eight years to be educated under the watchful eye of "Father Horsmanden." The girls were also schooled in England. During this time the James River flooded and the water came up on the first floor of the stone house. Byrd built his wife a more pretentious house, "Westover" in Charles City County. There the colonel died in 1704 at the age of fifty-two, Mary having preceded him in death by five years. He had been a trader not only in tobacco, furs, and other commodities, but also in slaves.[3]

Troop movements through Virginia during the American Revolution led by Washington, Lafayette, Cornwallis, and Tarleton had to use what once may have been no more than Indian trails: in Henrico County the Brook Road which led north out of Richmond, the Mountain Road to the northwest from the Brook through the Chickahominy Indians' campgrounds to Louisa County, and the Three Notch Road westward from Richmond to Charlottesville. In Northwestern Hanover County they used the Ridge Road between the Little and South Anna rivers. On the latter, Elizabeth Carter Berkeley had been entrusted with the sacred silver from Fork Church for safekeeping. When Colonel Banastre Tarleton's dragoons demanded that she hand it over to them, it has been said "she defied them with a pair of scissors."[4]

By the end of the 18th century, the threat to the peaceful countryside was not from the natives or the British, but the Blacks and their descendants who had been brought over to be the servant and laboring classes. In 1859, Colonel Robert E. Lee took a young lieutenant with him to stem an insurrection led by John Brown at Harper's Ferry. The young man, Jeb Stuart, later rose to be a major general in the Confederate cavalry. As a battle raged along the fields and gullies beyond Brook Bridge north of Richmond, Virginia, on May 11, 1864, Confederate General J.E.B. Stuart received his mortal wound and the name of an abandoned ordinary, "Yellow Tavern," entered the annals of history.

The area called Yellow Tavern cannot be located on any modern map. It can be defined by the action that took place there, along the roads that passed through, the railroads that encircled it, and by the lives of some of the families who lived there during the 18th century. It is my intention in this treatise to try to look at the strife through the eyes of the women as they wove the threads of their lives and those of their loved ones through events that transpired. I will use as my locale the 25 mile radius from the tavern on Brook Turnpike to the west, north, and east through Henrico County and into Hanover County.

During the Civil War the roads stretched out from the wrist of Richmond's northern defenses on Brook Road like the fingers on a left hand. The thumb – Wilkinson's Old Road - would point toward the Meadow Bridges over the Chickahominy River and the Virginia Central R.R.; the pointing finger - Telegraph Road- to cross the Chickahominy into Hanover County and on to Fredericksburg; the middle finger - the Ashland Road to cross the R. F. & P. Railroad at Kilby's Station and the ring finger - the Mountain Road to Louisa County. The little finger - Hungary Road - pointed to a spur of the R. F. & P. Railroad at the coal pits.

Across the fingertips of this hand, to the north in Hanover County, there are three roads that mark the boundary of a triangle formed by the two railroads. The Peaks and Ashcake Roads move west below Ashland from Hanover Court House to Beaverdam and the Ridge Road moves westward from Hanover Junction to Fork Church.

Chapter 1
SPARKS FROM THE FORGE

Yellow Tavern was like a grand old lady, her many windows look to the west, reflecting the sun setting on a way of life. Her opening and closing doors appeared to be listening for the changing sounds, her chimneys sucking out the warmth of complacent comfort. The white-barked aspen trees between her and the much traveled road flickered and turned their leaves, the fronts green and the backs silver.

Her guests had left the famous Eagle and Bell taverns in Richmond near Thirteenth and Main streets at first light that morning. The swaying stagecoach had rocked over and around the many gullies made by the creeks and springs yet to be conducted to the James. It passed by or through the yet to be fenced capitol grounds where cattle grazed. May and Jimson weeds grew in profusion and young boys pricked their fingers on the chinquapin bushes. The stage made its way across the muddy or dusty broad (later Broad Street) to where the western farmers brought their produce into town to possibly the head of the turnpike at Brook Avenue. This would take them over Bacon Quarter Branch and by Butchertown where livestock were slaughtered.[1]

After nine miles northward, the stage arrived at a tavern at the terminus of Brook Turnpike. The fee of twenty-five cents per vehicle plus six cents per wheel had been paid at the toll house at Brook Hill, just before Brook Bridge. The General Assembly had given the Brook Turnpike Company permission to construct the turnpike from Richmond to Dabney Williamson's tavern at or near this location. A survey of the land was filed with Henrico County and a thirty-foot road was authorized using "timber, gravel, earth or stone" purchased from adjoining land owners for its upkeep. The first turnpikes were covered with long heavy planks nailed to log crossties.

These quickly deteriorated, rotted, or broke under heavy loads and would float in torrential rain. After five or six years the timbers were replaced by crushed stone.[2]

It is not known who built the fifty foot-long tavern that stretched here along the stage road. The basement was of brick; the upper story was frame with a porch running the full length. An extension reached from the back, with racks, lean-tos and stalls for weary horses. Many taverns had sprung up where the right fork led to Hanover Courthouse and Fredericksburg and the left fork to Louisa County and the mountains. They often changed hands and their names reflected new owners. Someone had painted this one yellow and that name stuck with her long after her demise.[3]

At one end of the basement, the still sleepy travelers sided up to the bar for their morning eye opener. At trestle tables, the tavern wenches, most probably black women hired from the neighboring plantations, brought them the hearty fare. All this conviviality was presided over by the jolly tavern keeper and his equally rotund wife. Papers brought in on the stage were passed around and the men turned their attention to what lay ahead of them: problems of the young republic, sales of land and goods, and listings of runaway slaves.

The women had been left behind to tend to the household affairs: the feeding, clothing, and medical care of both black and white constituents, and the education of the children. Certainly the wives were not far from the men's minds as they wondered how they were dealing with an obstinate house servant or an unruly farm hand. In a quiet moment they could hear some of the local children who had been sent to the tavern owner for instruction as they recited their lessons, their youthful soprano adding to the melody of voices.

Still fresh in the men's minds was the recollection of the aborted Gabriel's Rebellion. In 1800 Gabriel had been a slave at "Brookfield," the Prosser plantation which they had just passed on the right side. Perhaps men of the same ilk may be mending the stage wheels across the pike. What did the Blacks talk about as the anvil rang, the sparks flew, and when there were no white men nearby to listen? What worries and nightmares did the women of both races have as they remembered what had transpired? Few of the Blacks, men or women, in the early years of the republic learned to read and write, whether slave or free. We can only surmise from the court records how the black women of Henrico and Hanover felt toward the condition of servitude and how the white women reacted to the threat of servile rebellion.

There had been an attitude of trust between the races along the Chickahominy in the 18th century. Monthly passes for the Blacks, needed elsewhere, lapsed into quarterly or less frequently. Restrictions on travel were lightened. They were allowed to assemble on Sunday afternoons and holidays for religious services and barbecues at Brook Bridge.[4]

Gabriel Prosser had learned to read and write. He was born the same year, 1776, as his master's son, Thomas H Henry Prosser. Patrick Henry was a friend of the family, having defended the elder Prosser from being ousted from the Virginia House of Delegates. The war for American independence had been fought and won. Ideals of freedom had been fought over in the French Revolution and they spread to the West Indies.[5]

The elder and more lenient Thomas Prosser had died in 1798, leaving 22 year-old Thomas Henry in charge of about fifty slaves. The next year Gabriel, Solomon, and Jupiter (a slave on Nathaniel Wilkinson's farm) were in Henrico Court for stealing a hog from Absalom Johnson, a white overseer who had rented a part of Wilkinson's land. Catching them in the act and during the fight that ensued, Johnson lost part of his ear to the more skilled fighter, Gabriel. For stealing a hog the penalty was whipping, but attacking a white man was a capital offense. Gabriel's life was spared "by benefit of clergy", the fact that he could recite a Bible verse. He was branded in the hand. Johnson had him back in court before the year was out, declaring that he felt threatened. For this Thomas Henry Prosser had to post a promissory note of $1000.[6]

By 1800 Gabriel was six foot two or three with strong arms and shoulders from working at the forge both at home and hired out in Richmond. Both he and an older brother Solomon had been so trained and were able to fashion tools, knives, and other equipment. Freedom and rebellion could be more readily discussed in the city with those who had read of the uprising in the Caribbean under the slave Toussaint Louverture. Gabriel began to feel that the white and black artisans of Richmond and other cities might join the slaves in a revolt against their agrarian masters and mercantile bosses. At Sunday barbecues at Brook Bridge or Prosser's spring, and at gatherings at meeting houses, he began to collect the pledges of his fellow blacks, and sent out those who could travel to recruit in nearby counties. At the same time they were fashioning and collecting knives and weapons.[7]

An opportunity for a planning meeting came on August 10 when William Young gave permission for one of his slaves to have a funeral for his young daughter and he obliged them by leaving home that day. Gabriel and other Blacks slipped down to the spring and discussed plans for the uprising. Final plans were announced that the Brookfield slaves would on August 30 first kill Thomas Henry Prosser and Absalom Johnson and then join those coming from the surrounding counties at Brook Bridge. Leaving 100 men at the bridge, 100 would go to Gregory's tavern to pick up the weapons stored there, then split up to fire the warehouses at Rockett's Landing in Richmond. They would capture the unguarded powder at the penitentiary, and hand out guns at the capital to the city slaves. Gabriel did not mention that he might take Governor James Monroe hostage while they awaited word of the success of fellow insurgents in Petersburg and Norfolk.[8]

But torrential rain that Saturday night caused Brook Creek to flood, making roads impassable and bridges unusable. Pharaoh, a slave from "Meadow Farm," rain soaked and weary and possibly thinking about his wife and child, returned to the farm on the Mountain Road and talked to an older Tom who had not been involved. The young master, Mosby Sheppard, was in his office. The two slaves told him of the plans and he immediately set out to alert his neighbor William Mosby and the local militia "troop of horse." The uprising had been postponed to the next day, Sunday, and no insurgents were seen along the Brook. William Mosby returned home wondering if the alarm had been false but a female house servant came to him to verify it.[9]

An unknown slave arrived at John Mosby's home with the word that the news was out. Prosser's Ben rushed back to "Brookfield" with the alarm. By afternoon of the 11th many whites had converged on the plantation, but Gabriel and others had fled. Governor James Monroe upon receiving word that afternoon had the arms removed from the capitol to the unfinished penitentiary and called out the Nineteenth and Fourth regiments. Mosby Sheppard was a member of the latter. By September 1, six insurgents were in the Richmond jail and others were being rounded up. Gabriel was not caught until September 24. John Minor, a traveler from Fredericksburg to Richmond in October, found the road still lined with guards and many soldiers in the city.[10]

The conspirators were tried before five to seven "gentlemen justices" whose decision had to be unanimous. It was a special court for slaves called "oyez and terminer," with no jury and from which there was no appeal except to the governor. Other Blacks including their families were not allowed in the courtroom. The sentence of hanging was often carried out the next day. Families were allowed to retrieve the bodies, customarily buried at night by torchlight. The owner was paid the determined value of each slave. Someone observing must sign the certificate of death. This was often young Mosby Sheppard from "Meadow Farm."[11]

Four of Prosser's slaves were hung on the Richmond gallows at 15th and Broad streets: Solomon, Martin, Frank and – when later caught – Gabriel. Two of Prosser's men: Peter, a mulatto and Tom were executed at a tavern Prosser had bought not long before, just north of the city. There their lives were snuffed out by a rope over a tree limb. Though not so intended, their families lived close enough to witness the ordeal. This was also true of Jupiter and Sam, owned by Nathaniel Wilkinson in the area of present day Wilkinson Road, and William Young's man Gilbert (living in present day Lakeside). Young's William was taken to the crossroads at Four Mile Creek. Other families living in the area (those of Judith Owen's Michael and John Mosby's Will just north of "Brookfield") had to travel to downtown to fetch the bodies.[12]

There must have been rejoicing in their families when seven bearing Biblical names: two Daniels, Absalom, and Emmanuel were acquitted and John, Jacob, and Peter were pardoned. The lives of Prosser's elderly slave and Williamson's Lewis were spared, but the grief of the families must have been immeasurable when they were transported out of the state. The Virginia legislature called upon the governor to purchase the slaves Tom and Pharaoh who had alerted Mosby Sheppard. They were given their freedom.[13]

Among the black women in the early years of the new republic, few in servitude could either read or write. To date no written account has come to light from white or black women concerning Gabriel's Rebellion. We can only surmise from court records the trauma in the upper Chickahominy community. Gabriel and his cohorts did not recruit women, although they must have been at some of the gatherings. Daniel Egerton says of Nanny, Gabriel's wife, that her owner, birth date, place of residence, or names of any children are unknown. The chances are that they were married by the custom of jumping over a broom three times. She was probably younger that he by two or three years and was not charged with the conspiracy.[14]

We can speculate that young Nanny lived nearby and may have seen the brawny Gabriel at the integrated services at the nearby Hungary Road Meeting House where the Reverend Richard Courtney was preaching at the time. Or perhaps she had come on an errand to the blacksmith shop and watched as he worked at the sounding anvil, the sparks flickering in the shadows. Certainly she could later see the tension building up in her husband as the conspiracy was planned. It was brought out in the trial that Nanny had tried to make one recruit. Some of the black women went to the barbecues, others refused to go. Gabriel was hung on the city gallows at 15th and Broad streets. The chances are that Nanny lived too far away to get there.[15]

White mistresses, some widows, as well as masters and overseers were to be targets of the uprising. Living in the area were: Elizabeth Sheppard at Meadow Farm; Anne Prosser at Brookfield; Judith Owen who lived between them; the new widow of Jacob Smith; Mary Jones; Jane Clarke; and Anne Parsons. Some of these hired their slaves out to Richmond where even those who could not read the local papers could have heard liberty discussed. Anne Prosser, still grieving over the loss of her husband two years before, now would grieve with the stricken families left on the plantation, both young and old. Had she pampered Gabriel and taught him along side Thomas Henry? Certainly they had played together as children. Thomas's sister Elizabeth was much older and had married the year after he was born. What had gone wrong that their own people had turned against them?

Just up the Fredericksburg road from Anne Prosser, on Turner's Run, lived the Owen family. Judith Owen had apparently inherited the slaves from her husband Hobson's estate. An 1817 accounting of his estate shows her still owning six slaves totaling $1,830.00 in value. One of these was a man Ned. Michael had been hung for his part in the conspiracy. Ned had testified against them. Roger Gregory, Jr. lived adjoining some Owen land across the road. Gregory's slaves Billey and Charles had been hung.[16]

There is ambivalence between the actions of some slaves to strike for freedom at any cost and those who acted to protect their owners or turned to testify against their fellow Blacks. James Sidbury has concluded that young Mosby Sheppard must have been more lenient on his slaves than some of his neighbors. Although he never manumitted any slave, he was permitting his Gabriel to buy his freedom over a period of six years. He would allow Pharaoh to buy things on credit and later to buy his son from another man. Pharaoh and Tom worked the 135 acre farm with three other slaves. Sometimes Mosby would leave Tom in charge.[17]

The widowed Elizabeth Sheppard lived at Meadow Farm on the Mountain Road with her unmarried sons, Mosby and Philip. She had five daughters: Mary, Elizabeth, Susannah, Lucy, and Nancy – one or more girls still unmarried and living at home. Was it for the Sheppard women that Pharaoh changed his mind and came home in the dripping rain to give the alarm? Or was it for his wife and son's sake? After Tom and Pharaoh were given their freedom, Elizabeth Sheppard was adamant that the Sheppards be compensated $500.00 for each. Pharaoh is shown later serving as Mosby Sheppard's overseer.[18]

There were no young children in the Prosser home at the time of the rebellion. Thomas Henry would marry Lucy Bolling Hylton at St. John's Church on June 15, 1801. The next year Lucy gave birth to a son which they named Albert. There would be three more children. Albert was of school age when Thomas Henry Prosser served as captain of a cavalry troop during the summer of 1814. The farm having been sold to Benjamin Sheppard, the family left the neighborhood shortly thereafter to settle in Mississippi. Lucy and Thomas Henry were saddened by the death of two children in 1823 and then Lucy died soon thereafter. Albert had been trained as a doctor when he met a sudden death at the age of 24. Thomas Henry left only one heir, a son Daniel, in 1839.[19]

****

Brook Turnpike was a main thoroughfare into and out of the capital city. The need for more and better roads became more obvious during the War of 1812. The Brook Turnpike Company was organized in 1812 for travel from Richmond to Dabney Williamson's, just north of Brook Run. Horses, mules, and horned cattle passing through incurred a charge of three cents each. A turnpike to the coal pits at Deep Run, in Henrico to the west, had been built earlier. Within a few years, the line was extended to terminate Brook Turnpike at Ground Squirrel Bridge over the South Anna, connecting it to points north. By 1829 a connected line of stages ran along the Atlantic, passing through each state capital from Maine to Savannah, Georgia. Those that carried the mail had to pay no tolls. Postage varied according to the distance traveled, the number of sheets, and it was paid by the addressee.[20]

Oliver Holmes, in his *Stagecoach East,* has described the evolution of the stagecoach from the "Jersey Wagon" of Revolutionary times to the more commodious yet still bone rattling vehicles of the nineteenth century. It started out as a virtual box-wagon with four benches across. There were four stakes on each side supporting the roof and leather or canvas sides that could be closed in bad weather. The driver was seated on the outside, six to twelve passengers inside, trunks strapped on the back. The mailbags were carried under the seats or between the passengers' knees with the smaller luggage. Through the years the wagons became more oval and coach-like and were suspended on leather straps. The patrons entered through doors on the side and sat facing each other. The outside was painted yellow or red with emblems and lettering as desired.[21]

Chapter 2

A SENSE OF COMMUNITY - 1860

The community that is Yellow Tavern has not been a visual entity. It would tend to blend into Richmond where the county courthouse was located. The city acted as a magnet not only for its commercial but also for its institutional development. Gabriel's thrust for the Blacks' freedom had been toward the city.

An attempt was made by the Virginia Baptists in the 1830s to establish a seminary on 240 acres at Brook Tavern Farm. The students were to work on the farm for three hours a day in partial payment for their school expenses. They soon voiced their dislike of the way the food was prepared and the high cost of their board. They began to neglect the manual labor required. It was concluded that the site was not suitable, being too far from the public road, "scarcely perceptible to strangers who traveled the turnpike." There was more land than was needed. By January 1835, the land had been sold and the seminary moved to the Columbia building west of Richmond to become Richmond College and later the University of Richmond.[1]

The Williamsons of "Brook Hill" had tried in the early 18th century to have a parish church built nearby only to lose out to William Byrd's land on Church Hill (St. John's) in 1741. The family attended Monumental Church, six miles away in Richmond. They also helped to establish St. Paul's Church in Richmond. In 1860 Emmanuel Episcopal Church was built at "Brook Hill," home of Mary Amanda Williamson and her husband John Stewart. Neighbors had helped build Brook School (ca. 1785), which was used as a free or union church.[2]

The nearest established church to "Brook Hill" may have been Slash Church on the stage road just over the Chickahominy in Hanover County. The Reverend Patrick Henry, father of the orator, served many years as its pastor. After the Revolution the congregation moved to Hanover Court House and Slash Church became a union church. The Baptists, Presbyterians, Quakers, Methodists, and Disciples of Christ used the facilities, predominately the latter two. It was bought by the Disciples of Christ in 1842 and the Methodists built Lebanon Church nearby.[3]

Lebanon Church, on the Hanover Circuit, was built on land purchased from Samuel LeMay and his wife Sally for the sum of "Fifteen Dollars, good and lawful money of Virginia." It burned before 1860 and was rebuilt. Even then it was "not lathed and plastered, a mere shell of a house … The seats were rough … the room divided into two equal parts, one for the ladies and girls, and one for the men and boys."[4]

Union churches were the norm throughout the sparsely settled area and were first called meeting houses. Blacks were not allowed to have churches of their own in rural areas until after the Civil War. One of the earliest meeting houses was built in 1775 on Mountain Road at the bridge over the South Anna River. Through the years it was called Ground Squirrel Meeting House, Ground Squirrel Christian and Calvary Christian Church. At the beginning of the Civil War it was still a small brick building.[5]

Not far away, in 1776, the dissenters from the established church, John Waller, Samuel Harris, and James Read, organized a Baptist Church which they called Chickahominy Church. The first pastor was John Clay, father of the senator. A frame church 40 feet by 12 feet was built near a "grand old spring." In 1833 the name was changed to Bethlehem after the congregation had been divided by the teachings of Alexander Campbell. The records show a membership of 331 in 1854 – 133 whites and 248 "colored." Some were free Blacks. Many of the whites were owners of slaves. Families from both sides of the Chickahominy, in Henrico and Hanover counties, attended the church. Throughout the years the church has been called Winns Baptist for the family that gave the land.[6]

Other churches in lower western Hanover served as union churches and had many black members. Among these was Taylorsville Baptist which originated in a protracted meeting near Hanover Junction in 1841. They met in a brush arbor while a small frame church was being built. When that building no longer would accommodate them, they held services at Fork Episcopal Church for three months while a brick structure was built in the current style with a balcony for the slaves. The frame church was moved a few miles away to be used as a Sunday School and later became Elon Baptist. Elon used components from the Beaverdam Meeting House to complete its construction.[7]

Bishop Francis Asbury started a Sunday School at St. Peter's Methodist Church on Mountain Road in 1786. A Methodist minister of the Virginia Conference, the Reverend George Nolley, was instrumental in building a union church in Slash Cottage in 1853. It was called Ashland Free Church and was used by Baptists, Episcopalians, and Presbyterians as well as Methodists. It stood on the present site of the Masonic building on England Street. The Baptists met here until they built a brick church on the railroad in 1859.[8]

Some churches had to discontinue their services when armed forces were close by, but Mt. Olivet Baptist, west of Ashland, continued in operation. The only references in their records for those years are a list of those serving in the "Southern Army" and notations that James C. Butler was killed in the battle at Sharpsburg and Marcellus C. Lowry died "in some Yankee prison."[9] It was these scattered churches that gave Yellow Tavern a sense of community while the people faced the disruptive war years.

****

An 1853 map of Henrico County tells that there were 2,369 free Blacks in the city of Richmond and 1,268 in the county. There were 9,927 slaves in the city and 6,782 in the county. The white population ran 15,274 city and 8,552 in the county. The census taker in 1850 for western Henrico visited 960 domiciles, which included 140 separate households of free blacks and mulattoes. Among them the most common surnames were: Johnson, Smith, Cooper, Harris, Jackson, Freeman, Jones, Hill and Cousins. There were 60 solitary surnames, either living alone or with a white family.[10]

The farms in Henrico were valued at over two and one half million dollars. They had horses, milk cows, working oxen and other cattle, sheep and swine. Their fields produced potatoes, peas and beans, corn, buckwheat, hay, and garden vegetables. Their animals produced wool and meat for the slaughter houses. Beehives furnished honey. Education was available in the county and city at two colleges, twenty public schools, and 23 private ones.[11]

The census taker was instructed to record the profession, trade, or occupation of all males over the age of fifteen. Even in a predominately rural area there was a surprising diversity. In Hanover he listed painters, bricklayers, shoemakers, millwrights, a bridge minder, comb makers, plough makers, fishermen, hatters, musicians, cabinet makers, coopers, millers, merchants, storekeepers, paper makers, a "jack of all trades" and a superintendent of the poor house. Among the professions there were doctors, lawyers, sheriffs and constables, commissioner of the revenue and other county clerks, preachers and teachers. He even slipped in that two of the teachers were women. Sixty-five women had real estate in their own name. Two of these women had control of two of the largest farms in the county. The doctors' land holdings averaged $5,000 in value.[12] The chances are that the census returns in rural Henrico were comparable to Hanover's.

Western Hanover did not have as many free Blacks and mulattos as western Henrico. The 1850 census taker listed one hundred and ninety six. Among these the surnames were: Winston, Harris, Smith, Maxfield, Hogg, Davis, Dandridge, King, Freeman, Bryce, Query, and Tyler. Less than 50% were under 21 years of age and two were 100 years old. They were living in fifty-seven separate abodes and only three households had their own real estate. About half of the white farmers did have real estate of their own. .In western Hanover there were fifty-one overseers. We can see listed conductors, engineers, agents, hotel keepers, tavern owners, and a bar keeper.[13]

****

Travel through Yellow Tavern changed from horseback to four wheel vehicles, from the lowly farm wagon to the more commodious coach moving in stages to allow respite for the animals and passengers alike. They could "pike along" in the bouncing vehicle until they came upon a bar or pike across the road. There they must pay toll in order to proceed farther. They encountered the first collector at Bacon Quarter Branch or the present Rennie Avenue, the second at Brook Hill. The road was moved to the west because the Stewart family complained of the dust. By 1854 the old yellow tavern was no longer in use. It may have been replaced by Turner's Tavern at the intersection of Mountain (Louisa) and Telegraph or Fredericksburg roads.[14]

Many travelers had come through the area. Some stopped at the Hanover Tavern in Hanover Court House, others at Merry Oaks Tavern near Slash Church, or T.E. Wheeler's Hotel (later "Walkerton") on the Louisa Road where there was a large stable to exchange horses. The singer Jenny Linn may have stayed in one of the taverns during a snowy December night in 1850. Lafayette came by boat to Richmond in 1824. During the festivities or soon afterwards, a local family (Cross?) bought a set of wooden bottom Hitchcock chairs decorated in his honor.[15]

The stagecoach in passing over dirt, stone and planked roads from Richmond to Washington took thirty-eight hours. It passed through Hanover Court House, Bowling Green in Caroline County, and stopped overnight in Fredericksburg. The next day it met the steamboat at Aquia Creek on the Potomac River. Later when the stage went directly to the creek, the passengers spent the night on the boat and travel time was reduced to twenty-four hours.[16]

Piking along was not fast enough. For a couple of decades businessmen had been pushing for railroads to be built for the movement of people and produce. None would pass through Yellow Tavern, but one to the west and one to the east were built. Nicholas Mills, a resident of Richmond with Hanover connections, was the president of the Petersburg Railroad. Mills envisioned a feeder railroad from Richmond to the steamboats on the Potomac. He engaged Martin Robinson to do the surveying and the Richmond, Fredericksburg, and Potomac Railroad was chartered in 1835 by the General Assembly of Virginia with the stipulation that no other railroad would run parallel for the next thirty years. With its terminus at 8th and H (or Broad) streets, it proceeded out the wide country road before turning north into the county. In Henrico it crossed the Mountain Road, the Chickahominy into Hanover and moved on through what would become Ashland to Taylorsville.[17]

The first rail lines were as problematic as the early planked stage routes. William E. Griffin in his story of the first 100 years of the R.F. & P. R.R. has written that the tracks were flat iron strips, one half inch thick and two inches wide which were nailed to crossties twelve inches square, seven feet long and five feet apart. When the fragile strips would break, they would pierce the wooden floors of the coaches and injure the passengers. These intruders were called *snake heads.*[18]

Six wood burning engines were ordered for the new railroad, five of them coming from England. They weighed five to six tons and were powered by high pressure steam. An artist's rendition of an 1830's train shows a four wheel engine (two small wheels in the front) with a narrow stack, three bag or wood carts, and three passenger carriages resembling stagecoaches. They came to have one car for horses, covered cars for produce and merchandise, and longer ones for timber and wood. Passengers paid six and one half cents per mile. Freight was ten cents per mile for light and valuable cargo, cheaper for other commodities. And of course they carried the mail.[19]

The first trip from Richmond to the South Anna River in 1836 was a festive occasion with the governor of Virginia, the mayor and other dignitaries among the 160 passengers. Awaiting them was plenty of wine and liquors and dinner at a steam sawmill. Soon alternate trains were running for passengers and freight, leaving Richmond at 9 a.m. and 1 p.m. and the North Anna at 7 a.m. and 4 p.m. They were advertising that horses and carriages could be transported between Washington and Blakely, North Carolina in two days. The unheated coaches had no screens on the windows, allowing some of the smoke from the whale oil lamps to escape but more cinders and sparks to fly in.[20]

Residents of the inland counties with no outlet by water to markets had, during the fall and winter months, driven their hogs and cattle along the old Indian trails, purchasing corn to feed them along the way. Using 400 slaves, some of whom were purchased and others hired, tracks were laid from Taylorsville to Fredericks Hall in Louisa County in 1837. The trains operated by the R.F. & P. under a Louisa Railroad charter. It was not until 1851 that the railroad, known as the Virginia Central, was allowed to cross the R.F. & P. lines with tracks of its own to come into Richmond. Edmund Fontaine of Beaverdam was the second president of that railroad.[21]

Accommodations became more comfortable. There were separate compartments with red plush sofas and glass doors for the women. The men had crosswise seats with mahogany backs and cushions made of the "best black haircloth, well stuffed." The coaches were fitted with glass paned windows that could be hoisted and worsted curtains. A passenger could breakfast in Taylorsville at 6:15 a.m. and be in Charlottesville by 1 p.m. In 1837 the trains were running daily with sixteen cars for passengers and freight. By 1847 there were separate freight trains. They transported wheat, corn, tobacco, hogs, sheep, bacon, butter and lard, fish, dry goods, groceries, and fertilizer.[22]

****

Tentacles of rebellion stretched out along the roads and the turnpike from Brook Bridge. In the years to come armed forces, in attempts to rectify the explosive situation would move in and out of the capital city along these very roads and rails which encircle Yellow Tavern.

Daniel, owned by the Williamson family living just south of Brook Bridge, had been acquitted of participation in the rebellion. Fifty years later, John Stewart, having married a Williamson daughter and moved to "Brook Hill," longed to improve the quality of life in that community. He at the age of 16 had come over from Scotland with his brother, Daniel, to work for their uncle, a tobacco merchant in Richmond. By 1841, they had prospered enough to not only pay off their father's debts in Scotland, but to also to take on the mortgage of the Williamson estate, "Brook Hill." John Stewart and Mary Amanda Williamson had three daughters at the time of the Civil War: Mary Amanda, Isobel (called Belle), and Marion. A multi-leveled mansion with many porches had been built around the 18th century house. The park-like grounds stretched to the turnpike. Mrs. Stewart remembered walking down as a child with her mother to watch the thrice weekly Washington stage go by. The toll keeper's house was built at Brook Hill between 1825 and 1840.[23]

In assembling a history of Emmanuel Church, Marion Peterkin brought to light some correspondence between her father and the Reverend Richard H. Wilmer, an intimate friend living in Bedford County whom he was urging to become the first minister of Emmanuel Church. Marion said that her father yearned "to do something in his day and generation for the betterment of and Christlike uplift of his neighborhood." Stewart was aware of some selfishness on his part for having the minister as his pastor, but expressed as his main desire "to show my love and gratitude to Him who has done so much for me, by bringing His blessed gospel to be preached to the poor, black and white, around me." The Reverend Wilmer came be their minister. He was allowed to have services for the Blacks within the body of the church and a balcony was reserved for the Blacks, both bound and free.[24]

Marion Stewart Peterkin, in her recounting of life at Brook Hill, mentions that "Uncle Nelson" made and mended their shoes. The United States census for 1850 shows three free Blacks living with the Stewarts. The overseer was William Lindsay, from Scotland. Their housekeeper was Lindsay's sister, Mrs. Lizzie Drever. The first sexton at Emmanuel Church was known as "Uncle Lucius" Randolph. He served there until his death sixty years later.[25]

Mrs. Peterkin recalled some of the families living within walking distance of the church. "Above the Brook was Dr. Shepherd [sic], the Powells, Atkinsons, Paleskes, Warwicks, Darracotts, Kings, Vass, Hilliards, Warrens and Col. Lucius Davis' family. South of the Brook, Stewarts, Chamberlaynes, Youngs, Mordecais, Lyons, Terrels [sic] Gooches, Carters, Redds, Ladds, Beveridges, Taylors, Burtons, Storrs, Fords, Waltons." Among those attending her church, she remembered with affection hoary headed Grandfather Robert C. Williamson and "old Dr.Shepherd [sic], a fine old gentleman of the old school, with snow white hair, holding his prayer book outstretched as he walked with stately tread from his carriage (which had steps that let down) up the aisle with his delicate wife beside him."[26]

Chapter 3

FAMILIES AND SLAVES

As war looms on the horizon, let us look at some of the slave holding families in the Yellow Tavern community: the Cross family, the Sheppard family, the Francis family, the Powell family, and the Mordecai family.

Much of the acreage where Brook Turnpike branched off to Turners Run along the Fredericksburg Road had been owned by the Owen family. There were many slaves. The will of Dr. William Owen, probated in 1775, expressed the wish that families be kept together. Also he was concerned that if those slaves taken over by his daughters be treated imprudently they should be hired out to someone who would be more humane.[1] Richard Cross bought some of this land in 1849; with it apparently came the slaves.

The Crosses lived at Falling Creek in Hanover County. Richard had already bought some acreage in 1839. Now he moved across the Chickahominy, leaving his twin brother Nathaniel on the farm in Hanover. He and his wife, the former Catherine Snead, may have lived for a while in the old Owen mansion on Turner's Run. By 1849 there were six children (Thomas, Mary Jane, Joseph Finch, Lucy Ann, Robert Nathaniel, and Bettie) and they were living in a house near the center of the farm. Lucy Ann Cross saved the letters written to her during the Civil War. She also saved A Catechism for Families and Sabbath Schools Designed also for Oral Instruction of Coloured Persons.[2]

This Cross farm in Henrico reached from the Ashland plank road to the Fredericksburg road. It consisted of 303 acres and was surrounded by numerous farms of the Sheppard family. Richard Cross died in 1857 and was buried in the family graveyard which would overlook the battlefield of Yellow Tavern. His estate was settled in 1860. There was no will. Dr.

John M. Sheppard, a neighbor living at "Meadow Farm," served as the administrator. It appears there were only three children left at home: Nathaniel, Lucy, and Bettie, who took her father's name, Richard, for her middle name at his death. Dr. Sheppard listed the total value of the ten slaves as $5,200.00. The slaves Oscar and William (Buck Owen), apparently adults or nearly grown, were valued at $800 each. Margaret Jane, valued at $900, may have been the cook. Then there was Mary and her child James, Kitty and her child Catherine. Martin, Fountain, and Eliza were possibly still children. There is no record of the sale of the slaves. It is known that at least Buck and Kitty stayed with the family.[3]

A survey of Richard Cross's 303 acres shows that Catherine received a widow's dower of 75 acres, four of the children 42 to 44 acres each, and Lucy Ann received 54.2 acres. The plot shows the house built in two sections and the graveyard on the east side. Since there was no will everything had to be sold. The total sales came to $1,160.45 - $250.05 from the neighbors and $910.40 from Mrs. Cross. Everything in the house and farm had to be assessed and put up for auction on December 10, 1857. There were five tables - three pine tables, one mahogany and one walnut, - one cabinet, twelve Windsor chairs, a rocking chair and six old chairs (possibly the solid bottom Hitchcock chairs decorated in honor of General Lafayette's last visit to the United States and Richmond in 1824.) Also the house had curtains. Also shown were two barrels wool, one spinning and one winding wheel, and dining equipment - crockery, knives, forks, spoons, white plates and colored plates, waiter and tea set. From the kitchen there were: cooking pots and pothooks, a brass kettle and a tea kettle, earthen jars, buckets and trays, a barrel and a lot of old boxes. Among the linens there were: three pairs of sheets, a blanket, counterpanes, towels, and table cloths.[4]

The widow had to bid on the things she needed to garden and keep the farm in operation: axes, grubbing and weeding hoes, cutting blade, forks, spades, rakes, ploughs, cultivators, guano sieve, horse cart and body, carryall and harness, cart gear, bridles and saddles, and hogsheads. She purchased the animals: hogs, sows and pigs; white cow, red cow. spotted heifer, bell cow and calf, old bay mare, young bay and colt, thirteen sheep - some better than others, plus the peas, fodder, and shucks to feed them. She paid $2.00 for a lot of chaff (for whatever use that was?). The neighbors came to buy the surplus farm products. George Hopkins bought the barrels of Irish potatoes, Robert Melton the stack of blade fodder. The hay went to a Mr. Lucas and John Mosby, the straw to T.O. Burton, Alfred Winston and James Francis. The corn was sold to six neighbors: Mr. Lucas, Mr. Burton, Mr. Melton, Mr. Winston, Benjamin R. Perkins, and Reuben Garnett. Mr. Lucas also bought a plough.[5]

Dr. Sheppard had been making sick calls at the Cross home for the last twelve years. He assisted Catherine in either a miscarriage or a still birth in 1849 and the woman Kitty during her pregnancy and at her delivery on January 27, 1857. There were calls on the children, both white and black, dispensing medicine and pills. Richard Cross had asthma. There were frequent visits to see Richard in 1845 and then again almost daily starting in March until his death May 11. Dr. Sheppard's account book shows that for his day visits he charged $2.00. For his night visits, whether it was for an adult or child, black or white, it was $4.00. Services rendered (probably delivery of a child) was always $10.00[6]

Richard and Catherine Cross's eldest son Thomas was no longer living. Their second son, Joseph Finch Cross, was a bricklayer. He and his wife Frances, the former Mrs. Eddie Crew from Ohio, were living in Henrico in 1860 near his sister Mary Jane and her husband William H. Davis. Frances Cross had four daughters: Georgie by her first husband, George Terrell; Eddie and Eugie, by Eddie Crew; and a baby Fannie, by Joseph Finch Cross. She had two step-sons: Mahlon Terrell and Dr. Albert H. Terrell, who lived on the road to the Meadow Bridges. Dr. Terrell served patients south of Brook Run.[7]

Mosby Sheppard, the liberator of Tom and Pharaoh, married Mary (Polly) Glen Crenshaw and they had seven children, three boys and four girls. Eleven years younger than her husband, Polly continued to live at Meadow Farm after his death in 1831. Like Elizabeth before her, Polly took over the role of matriarch. Their third son, John Mosby Sheppard, graduated from the University of Pennsylvania in 1840, purchased the farm from his mother in 1843, and began practicing medicine in the community in 1845, setting up his office in a small house in the yard. Polly Sheppard died in 1851 and is buried across the Chickahominy in Hanover along with their daughter Elizabeth DuVal and her two small children on land that may have been inherited from Mosby Sheppard's brother Philip. This cemetery adjoins the John Francis home place.[8]

Dr. Sheppard married Virginia Ann Young in 1846. Their first child, Alexander Hamilton Sheppard, was born the next year. By the time the war started, there were eight children: another boy - Mickleborough named for Virginia's father; Helen Virginia, 12; Nannie Mosby, 9; Mary Elizabeth, (Lizzie), 8; Susan Ann, 6; Isabella (Belle), 4; and Maria Louisa (Lula), 3. Mrs. Sheppard, using the office as a schoolroom, is said to have seen to the education of the children and perhaps some of the management of the farm while the doctor was making his calls. In 1855 fifteen slaves had been brought to Meadow Farm from the estate of Mickleborough Young. They were Henry, Thilman, Campbell, Herman, and Peter - adult males; Elizabeth (with her child Jordan), Maria and Louisa - females; and Julia, Sarah, Bob Hill, Malinda, Nancy, and Ginny - children.[9]

****

The John B. Francis farm, across the river, stretched along the road from Winns Church to Kilby Station on the R.F. & P. railroad. John B. Francis had died in 1846, leaving his 296 acres to his wife, Jane Mildred Terrell, and their children. He stipulated that each of the children should receive at least two years of schooling. Their story and a half house has since been cut down to one story. His brother, James G. Francis, owned almost 300 acres not far away, on the Mountain Road in Henrico.[10]

After the death of their mother, it fell to Charles (Buck) Francis, now 24 in 1860, to put the farm up for sale and also the seven slaves. The oldest brother, James, 34, who was already farming the land, bought out his brothers' and sisters' shares, also a bed and a black girl, Sarah Jane valued at $625.00. If not already married, James would soon be marrying the widow Sarah Harris and they would need help in raising their children. Buck was living with them, possibly helping with farming with his black man Henry, bought from the estate for $850.00. He also bought a bed for $2.50. Their sister Martha Jane's husband bought in the black girl Eliza for $505.00, a clock and a bed for $10.00. Their brother-in-law, John J. Davis, took the woman China with her children, Elizabeth and an infant, for $1,735.00. Tom bought the black man Montgomery for $750.00, thereby keeping all seven slaves within the family. Sam, still underage, received only stock and a guardian was appointed for him. At the beginning of the war, Tom and Sam were living in Richmond and studying the carpenter's trade.[11]

Mary Elizabeth Francis (Liz), 37, and her husband John J. Davis lived along the Elmont Road to the east. John J. had two children by a previous marriage and served as a father figure to the Francis brothers during the war. He had Mollie and younger daughters by Liz. Nearby lived her sister Jo (Emeline Josephine, 26) who had married Charles Terrell. To the west lived Jo and Liz's aunt Ann, her husband Joe Carr Terrell, their son John David and daughter Planne, now teenagers, and the Francis siblings' grandmother Mary Henley Thompson Terrell. Grandfather David Terrell had served in the war of 1812 for fourteen days - four days shy of the prerequisite for a widow's pension. The Terrell and Francis families had married cousins, making for multiple pains as they shared their wartime experiences in many letters. Jo's husband Charles was the son of Joseph Z. Terrell and his wife, the former Martha Washington Harris. Charles had three sisters: Mollie Goodwin. Ann or Nannie, and Barbara. He had four brothers: John, Joseph, William or Billy, and Nicholas, who would all serve in the war. There were a few slaves who were shared among the families as the need arose. The letters that passed between showed their constant care and concern.[12]

****

Dr. John Norment Powell, his wife Mary, and their three children - Junius, John and 14-year-old Blanche - lived at Melrose, a few miles east of the tavern. The farm stretched to the swampy Chickahominy. In 1861 there were forty-two slaves, twenty males and twenty-two females. Dr. Powell jointly owned nearby "Solitaire" with Captain George Pulaski. The chances are that the two farms were worked together. The two storey slave quarters stood just to the rear of the framed Powell dwelling. .It is possible that the cook, 25 year-old Harriett, and her girls lived over the separate kitchen. Always there must have been two of them underfoot. Leati age 1 and Clara age 4, with Georgie age 6 or 8 carrying the food back and forth to the big house. The house servants Agnes the seamstress, and Mary Susan, 18, may have slept in the big house. There were also two unrelated teenagers, Crissy 15 and Lucy 13.[13]

Within the quarters there appears to have been at least six family groups:

1. Adam, the carpenter, 40; Adelaide, his wife, 38; and sons William 12, Peter 5 or 6, and Lindsay, 1.
2. William, the team driver and messenger, about 40; his wife Felicia, 40; and children: Marcia14, Billy 13, John 12, Albert 5 or 8, and Kitty, 4.
3. Emmeline, 28 or 39, and her daughters: Margaret 12, Rose 11, Grace, 4 or 5, and Frances 3.
4. Eliza, 28 or 30, with her 4 year-old Laura and a month old baby.
5. A family group of three brothers and a sister: Bob 25, Davy15, Ben13, and Jenny 14.
6. Brothers: "Little Charles" 20, Hiram, 25 or 26.

There were five males supposedly unrelated: Joshua, the foreman and seeds' man, Moses the carriage driver 37; Bob 25 or 26, considered "quite valuable for farm work;" Tom about 50 and called an "ordinary farm laborer;" George, a mulatto about 43 years and usually hired out. After the war, Mrs. Powell wrote that Joshua had been an excellent farm hand. Adam was very valuable; William extremely valuable; and Bob quite valu-able. She referred to young Wilson, Peter, and Lindsay as quite likely. Among the women, she called Felicia and Agnes very valuable. Mary Susan was very competent and young Margaret and Rose were very likely, smart or bright, Jenny and Lucy she considered likely and smart.[14]

****

In the 1860s the area where the Baptists had tried earlier to have a seminary lay the farms of the Mordecai and Young families, who were friends and neighbors of the Stewarts at "Brook Hill" and the Powells at "Melrose." Jacob Mordecai had brought his family from North Carolina to settle six miles from Richmond on "Spring Farm," where Gabriel's cohorts had congregated. To a small country house, apparently two rooms up and two down, he added two large rooms with an entry way. The Young property, "Westbrook," was on the north side. The two farms stretched from the R.F. & P. Railroad to the turnpike. Rosina Young and Augustus Mordecai were childhood sweethearts and when they married he built "Rosewood" overlooking a beautiful rocky millpond. Her brother John continued to operate the grist mill and generally kept an eye on Rosina and her four young children; William, John, George, and young Augusta, after Augustus died in 1847 at the age of 41.[15]

Apparently the slaves on the two farms intermarried. Augustus Mordecai's sister, a spinster, Emma, came to live at "Rosewood." In her journal she speaks of Cyrus working the farm, George driving the wagon, Deborah the seamstress, and the "maidens" – Lizzie, Mary, and Georgiana. Cyrus daughters Martha and Caroline lived with the Young family. Little Fannie was very distressed when Cyrus came for his daughters at the end of the war.[16]

****

There were households in the Hanover area, stretching from the environs of the Pamunkey River to Hanover Court House through Ashland to Beaverdam, whose fathers and sons participated in the conflict but whose womenfolk's observations are not available at this time. These households, some of modest means and others more affluent, included the Edmond Fontaine family at "Beaverdam;" the Wickham family at "Hickory Hill" near Hanover Court House, the family operating the tavern at the courthouse, and the Winstons at "Courtland," the Prices nearby at "Dundee;" the Newtons and Pages at "Summer Hill" and "Westwood" on the Pamunkey River, the Pollards at "Williamsville;" and the Haws at Haw's Shop.

Haw's Shop was surrounded by large farms with large families. There were two churches - Salem Presbyterian, whose membership had moved up from the defunct Hanovertown, and Enon Methodist, which had begun in a Temperance Hall. The settlement embodied a post office, a school, a foundry and machine shop, and a grist mill. The farmers raised the finest quality wheat which was marketed in Richmond and shipped it as far as South America and Australia. They had learned from the renowned agriculturist Edmund Ruffin to use green sand, marl, and oyster shell as fertilizer on their fields. George Watt, of "Springfield", had patented the Centre Draught Plow. He was manufacturing it and other farm equipment in Richmond and advertising it in the Richmond Enquirer in 1846. The Watt and Haw families intermarried. By 1860. John Haw, of "Oak Grove," was operating the foundry at the crossroads from Hanovertown, Hanover Court House, Old Church and Richmond. It was known as Haw's Shop, but has since taken on the name Studley for Patrick Henry's birthplace there.[17]

Joseph R. Haw has written that on a Sunday one might see at Salem Church coaches drawn by four horses from "Dundee" - Dr. and Mrs. Lucian Price with their daughters Lizzie and Nannie, the English Governess (Miss Louisa Webb), and the girls attending the school at their house; from "Williamsville" - Dr. and Mrs. Pollard and daughter Ellen; from "Buckeye" - the widow Pollard "with her charming curly-headed girls;" the Winstons from the courthouse area - Bickerton Winston, wife, and daughters Margaret and Janey of "Signal Hill" ("Lindley") and William O. Winston, wife, and daughters Betty and Sally of "Courtland." Following close behind came the young men on horseback.[18]

Nathaniel Cross, twin brother of Richard, had stayed behind on Falling Creek. He married Nancy Mitchell Davis and there were twelve children. He died at the age of 40 when the oldest child was 21 years. According to a nephew who knew the family well, the family "had to scuffle for a living from the very beginning." Their small farm just outside of Ashland "was very poor and by almost super-human energy and industry on the part of her sons and daughters, Aunt Nancy not only kept her house in order, but improved her farm and I think never knew what it was to owe a dollar." She was "spare built" with a "quick nervous temperament and the Davis light hair, big nose, and red complexion and could crack a joke with the best of them." Her children came to own their own farms around Ashland, were known as "paragons of honesty and thrift .., and respected as the best citizens." Six of her sons would go to serve in the Confederate Army: Joseph Franklin, James Henry, William Thomas, Richard Hardin, Nathaniel Adolphus and Harry Oliver Cross.[19]

Fear must have spread along the upper Chickahominy when in 1858 word of Abraham Lincoln's *House Divided* speech passed from family to family. "I believe," he had said, "this government cannot endure permanently half slave and half free."[20]

Terrell family letters in the late 1850s and 1860 do not speak of national discord. Instead there is concern for the physical and spiritual health of family and neighbors, black and white, elderly and young. Examples include one of Jane Mildred Terrell Francis saying, "one of the black children" is not well, and Mr. Waldrop "has lost his other old negro." One Sunday in 1859 six Negroes and four or five whites were baptized at Winns (possibly in the nearby Chickahominy River or Thomas's millpond). Jo Terrell expressed the wish that her brother Tom would be baptized since "he says he has had a hope ever since Sam (their youngest brother) was converted."[21]

Chapter 4

CLEAR AS A BELL - 1859 – FEBRUARY 1862

John Brown and his cohorts took Harpers Ferry on October 18, 1859. They killed the gentle old mayor, the railroad agent, and a farmer as he walked through the town carrying a gun. They had taken George Washington's great–grand nephew from his home, taken General Washington's pistol and the sword given him by Frederick the Great. Colonel Lewis Washington's slaves were armed and set to guard him. Also they took thirty Methodists on their way home from a revival. To one of the first captives at the armory, Brown said, "I came here from Kansas. I want to free all the Negroes in this state. If the citizens interfere with me, I must only burn the town and have blood." Governor Wise of Virginia called out the local militia. By the time they arrived, Colonel Robert E. Lee, Jeb Stuart and some marines were already there and Brown and his men had barricaded themselves in the fire engine house. Wise and the Richmonders returned home.[1]

A month later, after the insurrectionists were tried and convicted, the governor received a telegram informing him that 500 armed men were marching from Wheeling to rescue John Brown. The tocsin on the capitol grounds was sounded as a signal for the militia to gather. Within three hours, the newly formed Richmond Howitzers, some still without uniforms, had assembled and were sent to the armory to pick up their arms. They boarded the R.F. & P. R.R. for Washington and the B. & .O. train for Harpers Ferry. They stayed two days and nights, returned to Richmond, only to be sent back by the governor on November 24.[2]

In December 1859, Mrs. Frances Cross, wife of Joseph Finch Cross of Henrico County received a letter from a Isaac Lewis of Harrison County, Ohio (about 60 miles from Wheeling, West Virginia.) Apparently Lewis, a neighbor of Frances Cross when she had lived out there with her second husband, Eddie

Crew, had heard rumor going around that some of the people in that area were making plans to break John Brown out of jail. Lewis wrote:

> I am sorry that Gov Wise has made such a fool
> of himself & Old Virginia about the rescue of John
> Brown no body I am confident Seriously
> entertained such an idea – nor do any considerable
> number justify this foolish unjustifiable raid but
> there is general sympathy for himself afflicted family
> his fellow prisoners & their families for the trouble
> they no doubt honestly though mistakenly brot on
> themselves & the sufferers in Harpers Ferry – We
> think Slavery a great curse to all concerned but we
> do not think Browns the right way to labour for its
> end – Truth is stronger than the Sword and is mighty
> & will prevail peacefully when the right time comes –
> The Slaveholders & their families are our neighbors
> & fellow men as well as the Slaves in a humane &
> Christian Sense – and us do not favour doing evil
> that good may come of it.[3]

The militia was quartered in the basement of the Presbyterian Church until after Brown's execution. With them, although not a member of the Howitzers, was John Wilkes Booth. It has been said that his face turned pale when the trap was sprung and he called for a stiff drink of whiskey.[4]

Since the Federal Militia Act of 1792, men between the ages of 18 and 45, with a few exceptions, were liable for militia duty and required to attend an annual muster. The men enrolled in the district in which they resided. Residents of Charles City, New Kent, Hanover, and Henrico counties, and the city of Richmond made up the 4th Division, 2nd Brigade under Brigadier General Thomas Pearson August, who would be later colonel of the 15th Regiment Virginia Volunteers. The 74th Regiment Militia consisted of men from Hanover County and the 33rd Regiment of men from Henrico County. These were known as the "line militia." The Militia Act of 1860 made a provision for the training of armed and uniformed volunteer companies which were attached to the line regiments and drilled with them at the annual muster. The 74th Regiment had a muster in Ashland on May 12, 1860. There were 300 to 400 men attending, including the Volunteer Hanover Troop (Cavalry) and the Hanover Rifles. Colonel N.A. Thompson was in charge.[5]

Following Lincoln's inauguration in March 1861, Fort Sumter fell to the newly formed Confederate States of America. Virginia seceded from the union on April 17 and its militia took the arsenal at Harpers Ferry the next day. Four days later the quietness of a Sunday in Richmond was broken by the ringing from the bell tower. The sound of the tocsin was relayed across the city by the tolling of church bells. The *USS Pawnee* had been sighted ascending the James River. It was thought to be loaded with marines for the invasion of Richmond Newly assembled troops, some still unarmed, were sent eastward to Rockett's Landing. Spectators flocked to the hills overlooking the river. It proved to be a false alarm and the soldiers returned to their camps of instruction around the city.[6]

In May, Jo Terrell had a very endearing letter from her mother-in-law, Martha W. Terrell, possibly after some family discord, saying:

> We must both try and have enough of the love of God in our hearts to overcome assaults remembering this our warfare to fit us to dwell in the presence of God clouds and s(t)orms may rise but take holt of the promise I will never leave nor forsake thee be patient and forebearing and in every conflict …he will not put more on us than he will give strength to bear.

Mother Terrell had been visiting on the cars (train) and was concerned that little Johnny had been sick. She wrote Jo not to let him cry too much with the bowel complaint, and if he got worse to let her know and she would come help nurse him.[7]

By July 3, Jo's mother, Jane Mildred Francis, was quite ill "with something like Cholera Morbus" and two doctors, Dr. Terrell and Dr. Thompson, were visiting her. Jo's sister-in-law, Mollie Goodwin Terrell, wrote, "She labors under such a complication of diseases I feel very uneasy about her, sometimes she seems better and then worse so we can hardly tell how she is." Mother Francis died before the year was out. She was buried beside her husband, John B. Francis, in the Sheppard-Francis cemetery in Hanover County, southwest of Ashland. Mosby Shepard had died in 1831 and is buried there.[8]

****

Emma Mordecai wrote a letter from Richmond to a niece on Friday, March 26, 1861. She mentioned the tears on men's faces when the ordinance of secession was passed, "even those most anxious for the event could not unmoved break the ties which bound them to the dear old Union." She told that President Davis would be in town the next day with Vice-President Stephens, General Beauregard, Colonel Lee, General Johnston, and "others composing our Council of War!!" While she was writing, her niece was practicing playing the Marseilles.[9]

Virginia's governor, John Letcher, sent out a call for volunteers. Emma Mordecai's April 21 letter told of the distress among the mothers of the volunteers. Her nephew George Mordecai was "crazy to join a company." His brother Johnny was already a member of one at the university (Virginia), was probably on duty at Harpers Ferry, but had not been heard from. Their brother Willie was a member of the militia. The boys' mother, Rose, Emma said, although at first "crazy for secession," with the final news, was experiencing "weighted feelings as all must." Their 85 year-old blind grandmother felt the right thing was being done and had been busy scraping lint for bandages while her daughters were making shirts for the soldiers.[10]

Emma's major concern in her April 21, 1861 letter was for what one of her brothers would do. Alfred Mordecai had finished at the top of his class at West Point, served nearly forty years in the military and had been to the Crimea with George McClellan. When war loomed on the horizon, he was busy at Troy, New York, in the manufacture of six-pounder gun carriages and caissons for delivery to Washington. He appears to have been with Major Robert Anderson at Fort Sumter when it fell. His request for a transfer to another part of the country was denied, whereupon Alfred tendered his resignation, but never, in spite of the family's constant urging, turned to the cause of the South.[11]

Charles H. (Buck) Francis and thirty-three others enlisted in Richmond on April 23rd to form the Ashland Grays. From Buck's neighborhood went: Charles and Chastain Taylor, to serve as lieutenants and Charles and Thomas Buchannon. St. George Tucker served as their captain. Camp Hermitage, their camp of instruction, was at the fairgrounds on West Broad Street (where the Virginia Science Museum is now located.)[12]

Buck Francis's initial weeks at Camp Hermitage were filled with such confusion that he could scarcely write. However, he wrote short notes to his sisters and niece, Mollie Davis, signing them "I remain yours until death." He had not received the hen that Mollie had sent him, but did respond to her request that he pray for her with, "I will try God has said ask and you shall receive Seak [sic] and you shall fine [sic] knock and the doors of mercy shall bee [sic] open unto you this we should all do." The men would walk into the city at night for entertainment.

Back at camp they slept in tents that leaked during a hard rain.[13]

In a reunion address after the war, J. Staunton Moore, of Company B, 15th Virginia Regiment, remembered how they marched from the fairgrounds to Rockett's Landing on the James to board the *Glen Cove* for their trip down to Williamsburg. Their route took them along Main Street where men and ladies lined the street, waved handkerchiefs and strew flowers before them. It all seemed like a picnic. As they pulled off from the wharf, all the men rushed to one side to wave goodbye, causing their boat to careen into the *Patrick Henry.* One soldier fell overboard but was pulled out of the water uninjured. Landing after dark, one of the fellows located a stream while others got a fire going for coffee. The next morning they found boiled tadpoles mixed with the coffee grounds. That night they slept rolled up in their blankets on the campus of William and Mary College. After that some of them bedded down in the library. A Mrs. Morrison presented the 15th Regiment with a battle flag made up of the blue and white from her wedding gown.[14]

Buck Francis and other men from the Ashland area were in Company E – the Ashland Grays of the 15th Virginia Volunteer Regiment. Others from the area were in Company C, the Patrick Henry Rifles and those in Company I, the Hanover Grays, were predominately from the Old Church and Mechanicsville area. Many Henrico men were in company A, the Henrico Grays, and Company D, the Henrico Guard. They were under Colonel (later major-general) John B. Magruder, who was known as "Prince John." His headquarters were at Yorktown and his men ranged from Williamsburg to Hampton.[15]

Men were being organized into artillery units. George Washington Nelson, of Hanover, organized a company of light artillery at Hanover Junction and drilled it at Beaverdam. Among them was Nicholas Terrell, son of Martha W. Terrell. The Hanover Artillery left Verdon on the Virginia Central Railroad for Richmond. They found the Patrick Henrry Rifles already drilling at the fairgrounds. One of these artillerists was Henry Robinson Berkeley, called Robin, who lived near Fork Church, northwest of Ashland. He had attended Hanover Academy, founded by Lewis Coleman, who would later head the Morris Artillery. Robin said that they had been quartered in the old Trinity Church. The day after their arrival in Richmond they were mustered into the service of the state of Virginia and then two days later were sent on the old steamboat *Curtis Peck* down the James River to Jamestown. Later the Hanover Artillery was disbanded and many of the men from Hanover were transferred to the Ashland Artillery.[16]

The lawyer, George Wythe Randolph, a grandson of Thomas Jefferson, developed a volunteer militia in Richmond known as the Richmond Howitzers. Before the war he had fitted them with naval howitzers, although at Harpers Ferry they were only furnished with Springfield muskets and later with other guns. After the Pawnee incident they were divided into three companies. There were a few Henrico and Hanover men in each company. They drilled on the campus of the Baptist College, using six-pounders brought down by the cadets from Virginia Military Institute. First they had to scrub off the thick Virginia mud collected on the way from the institute. Junius Powell, from “Melrose,” was a cadet at VMI and appears to have joined the Howitzers at this time. He was put in the First Company along with local men Charles Pleasants, John Drewry, William Tatum, Thomas Whiting, and the famous writer John Esten Cocke. Assigned to the 2nd Howitzers were: Mahlon Terrell (stepson of Frances Cross), Samuel Hawes, Wallace McRae, Lebbeus Timberlake, Milas Gardiner, and the artist William Ludwell Sheppard. The battalion was given their tents, stores and wagons and went into camp at Howard’s

Grove on the Mechanicsville Turnpike. They were not there long before they were transferred to Chimborazo Hill where they could overlook the James River.[17]

On May 6 some of those who would be assigned to the 2nd Company went by way of the York River R.R. to West Point where they were served sturgeon, ham and eggs, beef, biscuits and coffee by the local tavern keeper. Then they were transported on the steamer *Logan* down the York River to Gloucester Point. Off shore on May 7 they fired their rifled Dahlgren gun at the steamer *USS Yankee* which had chased the *Logan* the day before. This may have been the Commonwealth of Virginia's first shot of the war. Confederate shore batteries came to their assistance before the *Yankee* pulled away.[18]

****

The men of the 15th Virginia waited to be called into battle, having heard that 5,000 Federal troops (Butler's) had landed at Newport News, only thirty miles away. The Confederate rations consisted only of coffee, bacon, and ship's crackers. Many were sick, including Buck Francis with a headache for several days and William Snead in the hospital for four days. Some in the regiment went to the river to throw up embankments and one soldier drowned himself. Buck had written to his sisters, Liz and Martha, receiving no answer. In his letter to Sister Jo, he asked that all "remember me at a throne of grace, and if we never meet on earth no moor [sic] I trust that we will meet in heaven."[19]

Buck's letter to their brother James described the terrible times they had since leaving Richmond, but that letter has been lost. On June 14 he wrote to his sister Jo and her husband Charles saying, "I am so nurvus [sic] that I can scarcely write at all, but you must excuse it." He told of the recent battle (Big Bethel) twenty-five miles away. His company was not engaged but four companies of the regiment were. He had heard that only two of their men were killed while 200 of the enemy succumbed. Buck hoped that Charles would be successful that year in his crops.[20]

Joseph Park Thomas, a cousin of Buck Francis and the youngest of seven children on a farm near Ashland, before the war started had been in Richmond for four years studying the bricklayer's trade. There was no employment for him so he returned to the country where his father allowed him to cut wood on the farm. Using the "loan" of a "colored boy" he cut the wood and sold it to the R.F. & P. R.R. for two dollars a cord. On June 10, 1861, he joined many of his school mates in Buck's company at Williamsburg.[21]

On May 26 the entire 2nd Howitzers Company was sent to Yorktown. There on June 7 they learned that the enemy under General Benjamin Butler had come up the Hampton road from Fort Monroe and was fifteen miles from Yorktown at Big Bethel Church. The 2nd and 3rd Companies, under Colonel Randolph, and three companies of the 3rd Virginia Infantry (an early name for the 15th) under John Magruder joined Colonel Daniel Hill with the 1st North Carolina in the fighting around the church. Howitzer Lebbeus Timberlake, of Hanover, was one of the men who was praised for "utmost skill and coolness" in the operation. The news sent home after the limited action at Big Bethel must have intrigued the Henrico neighbors. John Mordecai went to join his brother George with the Howitzers on June 22. Along with him went Joseph Rennie who lived nearby.[22]

****

The first term of the Henrico Quarterly Court meeting in May 1861 had appointed white patrollers "to visit and patrol at least once a week all Negro quarters and other places suspected of having there unlawful assemblies, or such slaves as may stroll from one plantation to another without permission." They were to serve "for a term not exceeding three months" and were not paid. Free Blacks were required to register with the court. Much of the court time was spent in verifying each registrant as to name, probable age, identifying marks, and someone to testify that they were born free. As the war progressed and young men went in service, older men like James G. Francis of Mountain Road were called on to patrol as well as serve on jury.[23]

We can only speculate on the feelings in the Francis family that early summer of 1861 as the three brothers, still grieving over the loss of their mother six months before and the breakup of the family home, went to join Buck at Williamsburg, taking their brother-in-law, Charles Terrell, with them. The oldest sister, Liz Davis, began to jot down a list she entitled, "Some of the troubles of the war." She said that Buck had left home April 22, 1861, then Jim, Charles, Tom and Sam on August 17. She went on to say, "In 1860, Buck lives with me. And in 1861 lived with Jim until this awful war broke out, and they all had to go in service. Joe left by herself. And Sallie by herself. Mat was then living in Richmond but moved to the country in 1862." Tom and Sam as well as Buck were single. Jim, the eldest, was married to the widow Sallie Harris. They already had one daughter and were expecting another child soon. Sister Jo and Charles had one son and were expecting another child. Mat (Martha Jane) was married to James Jenkins.[24]

Joseph Thomas said that the three Francis brothers and Charles arrived in the Williamsburg area (King's Mill) about the time the 15th Virginia Volunteer Infantry was taken into Confederate Service and just in time to be sent down in sight of Hampton with General Magruder in early August. It was very hot and they marched through marshy country where there was nothing to drink but stagnant water with tadpoles in it.[25]

From his tent on an August evening, while others were lying around on their blankets, some talking, some reading their Bibles, Mahlon Terrell of Henrico wrote to his sister Georgie Terrell, from Yorktown. He sent his love to their brother Dr. Terrell and his family saying, "Tell Chapmo and Julia that Uncle Mallie wants to see them very much but do not know when he can as it is hard to tell what a day may bring forth everything seems to be uncertain." They were ordered to be out at light the next morning. "We may have a good fight this time." He also sent his love to Miss Betty Redd.[26]

****

Letters written that first fall of the war show the adjustments the men of the 15th Regiment had to make. Not only were they in and out of camp on picket duty, but the regiment, at least company E, was constantly on the move up and down the peninsula. Their letters were sent from: Camp Adams, near Cockletown - six miles below Yorktown, Young's Mill, and near Young's Mill. They wrote that they had moved five times since they left Camp Adams and expected to move again before too long. Orders would be given to cook two days ration to leave for a fight near Newport News only to be countermanded. The home folks were instructed to continue to direct their letters to Yorktown.[27]

There was a good deal of rain and they had colds from sleeping on wet ground. One of them wrote that there were twenty men in the company who were sick. All were not fully outfitted. They had need of their heavy boots, socks, drawers, and blankets from home. Charles wrote that he must find a girl in one of the nearby houses to launder his shirts. First he wished that his wife make his uniform then they heard there was someone in the Forest Grove Methodist Church neighborhood of Hanover who could make the lot.[28]

We can see the pathos of the women left at home with their small children. Jo had a second son and named him Joseph Washington. Their eldest was John James, called both Jimmy and Johnny. Sally named her son William James. Apparently Jo had the new baby blues. Charles was a concerned that she might put her friends to too much trouble and the thought was too painful to him. Perhaps, he wrote, she should let his mother keep the older boy for awhile. She should tell Montgomery (Tom's slave) to take care of everything on the farm, especially his mare. After folding the letter, he realized that he had omitted sending his love to her, so he added "my love to you particularly … in haste." Previously he had written her that General Magruder said, "The death of a wife or child is no excuse to go home." Apparently she had also asked if he was killed would his body be sent home. Someone wrote on the outside of the folded letter, "Give Syrup 4 oz of hart's horn" (medicinal ammonia).[29]

A letter from the frail cousin Martha Terrell to her daughter-in-law, Jo, told of her distress when her last son left home. She said, "Dear Billie started today I should not mind it so much if he was healthy… but to think how delicate he is … if justis [sic] had anything to do with it I think I ought to have one son to have remained with me as I had three in the army." Cousin Martha wrote that measles has been rampant at Beaverdam, had gone through the entire Terrell family. She said that her daughter Tommie's (Martha T. Snead) little boy had been quite sick first with dysentery, then measles but all were well at that time. Tommie had been with her since "Mr. Snead" went to join Charles' brothers Nick and John with the Hanover Artillery in Jamestown. Sister Nannie (Ann T. Yeamons) had named her little boy Joseph Benjamin to be called Bennie. He was four weeks old and his two little sisters were growing fast.[30]

Letters from the soldiers in the camps of the 15th Virginia Regiment seem to have had a better chance of reaching home in the early years of the war if they were sent in the care of a visiting neighbor. Jo Terrell received a letter in August 1861 and another letter in October delivered by Mr. F.A. Woodson. John J. Woodson had joined them in July. Apparently his mother had died a number of years before and only his brother Adolph, age 14, was left at home. Jo was the recipient the next week of a letter delivered by Mr. A.L. Deitrick. He and his wife Temperance were the parents of Theophilus Adolphus Deitrick, age 21, who had joined the regiment at Williamsburg in June. Waiting at home for first hand news were his sisters Jane and Henrietta, age 19 and 12, brothers Adam and William, age 17 and 14, and possibly his older sister Elizabeth, age 23. In September, Mr. William Lawrence and Mr. Luck returned to the neighborhood after visiting at Camp Adams and Young's Mill. There were two Lawrence boys from Hanover, William and Robert, in the 15th Regiment. The latter had enlisted the same day as Jo's brother Buck. Their mother was Sarah and they had three sisters, Frances, Elizabeth, and Keziah and two younger brothers, John and Warren, at home. Jordan Luck, age 25, had also joined the same time as Buck. He was the son of Robert and Frances Luck of Hanover and the brother to Sarah, Frances, and James.[31]

Mr. George A. Timberlake brought letters to the fellows in October. He may have been the father of James L., who had enlisted in Richmond as a corporal. John J. Davis and their fellow servicemen, James McAllister and John Gower, also brought letters from Camp in November and December.[32]

December and January was the time when help not needed in the house or fields was hired out. It also appears to have been a time when Hanover County was trying to fill out its quota for slaves to build fortifications. Charles Terrell wrote to his wife that the county had not given him anything but one shirt and not to let the Commissioner of Revenue get Montgomery because he has hired him on the condition that he (Charles) might still be in service. Cousin Joe Terrell wrote to Jo that his boy John would not be suitable to work outside, being small and needing someone to train him. Susannah was no longer available for her housework. Cousin Agnes had a girl named Hardenia whom Mr. John Davis had the responsibility of hiring out. It turned out that Jo could get Hardenia for $20 if she (Hardenia) was willing to live with her.[33]

Charles Terrell was in the Female Institute hospital in Williamsburg for six weeks with what started out as yellow jaundice. Whenever his father and the women in the family got a chance, they would send him a box. Other fathers from the neighborhood visited their sons in nearby camps. Butter, pickles, and wine would travel well. . Sometimes the cooked food that would not keep until delivery would have to be removed. Charles wrote that he had his jacket and coat mended while he was in Williamsburg. He had an oilcloth and a good pair of boots that he bought for $15. Jo sent him a quilt and also one for her brother Sam. There was some discussion as to which quilt was intended for Sam.[34]

Young Sam Francis, in spite of his somber name of Eli Samuel, wrote the friskiest letters with ever a thought of women and marriage. He had the dullest Christmas of his life having to stand "quarter picket" three times but did get to set up with two girls until bedtime on Sunday. Sam wrote to his sister that he supposed there would be a great many marriages that year (1862):

The Boys and Girls have seen how it is to be from

> each and they think this their only chance and they will make hay while the sun shines but I believe I will wait some time yet until I can look around and pick and choice [sic] and if I can't then I want to be a old Bachelor for I can do house business now and I wont ask them any odds for I can do my own business so you can tell them they will have to be kind and obedient to the Boys when they come back again if they want to get Married but some says they intend to get a wife just as soon as they get home.

Buck wondered what chance a "small soldier like myself" would have with the ladies back home.[35]

Sam wrote from Warwick County a couple of weeks later saying that they were having fun. It had been raining and the boys were as full of mischief as if it were a holiday. Even Charles was as wild as he could be. He said that they would "lie back and eat bull and flour bread and catch lice who would not be a Soldier it is a fine life." Sam told Sister Jo that the only thing they lack in camp life was "Shemales." He said, "Brother James seems to be troubled more than any one in camp he cant have his way enough that sets him back you know he is one that likes to have his way we have a great deal of fun with him just hear his view on war matters."[36]

As winter progressed into spring, Jo continued to send Charles his requests in the way of clothing. He said that he would not say any more about homes affairs other than she "must make them all stir you know … provisions are high and clothing shoes and everything of the sort." Two days later, when Mr. Williamson had not left with the previous letter, Jo's husband wrote that she needed to buy a cow. If it was true that Dr. Carver has died and there is to be a sale of his property, it might be her best bet to get one. She should try, he told her, for one that already has a small calf or will have one in the spring.[37]

Cousin Martha sent over some material for Jo to make Charles a pair of pants. Charles wrote that he was in no hurry for them and she could take a month or six weeks. By that time he would be sending by Mr. John D. Taylor some of his clothes that were a little out of order and could be straightened in an hour or two. Mr. John D. Taylor was the father of Charles and Chastain Taylor in Company E and possibly the postmaster at Ashland. Communications at that time were often sent by Mr. Lewis Kimbrough when he visited his eldest son, 18 year old Lysander. Mr. Kimbrough was superintendent of the poor house and would drop off letters or packages with Mr. Taylor. Charles had recently received Jo's letter, some shirts and sausage by Mr. George McAllister, father of James McAllister in their company. Charles sent back a box by Mr. Kimbrough. He said that he was in need of two more pairs of socks.[38]

A Mr. Thomas, possibly the father of Joseph Park, had made Charles a good pair of shoes and he was in need of another pair. He sent his wife his measurements, the length and across the instep, for Mr. Thomas to make "a strong pair of brogues [with] thick heavy bottoms." The weather had been quite bad with five inches of snow on the ground. Previously Charles had been concerned that his wife would sleep warm. He wrote that she should put on plenty of cover "for it is very bad to sleep cold." and he had "quite a good bedfellow a beardless boy he feels very much like a lady and he leans up to me like a sick kitten we sleep quite well this bad weather." His only objection to camp life was the vermin. He wrote, "They are as large as a wheat grain and breed faster than cinch bug."[39]

Jo Terrell received letters from Charles giving detailed instructions as to how she should continue the farming with the help of Tom's man, Montgomery. Such farming must have been mainly on a subsistence level. They raised cattle and hogs for milk and meat for the table, corn and oats to feed the cattle, hogs and horses. The animal's manure was used to fertilize the fields. The stables must be cleaned out every rainy day. No mention was made of tobacco or cotton being raised. The only commodities to bring in cash may have been the piglets not kept over to fatten and the rails split for the nearby R.F. & P. Railroad.

New land must be cleared each year for better crops. Charles' letter to his wife on January 13, 1862, told her to have the trees cut, split into wood and rails and the stumps grubbed and cut up. The logs should not be hauled to the mill until the weather improved. Jo is to get someone to haul them at "one half for the other." Charles wanted enough sawed into poles and rails to enclose the garden and yard. The remaining logs "were to be cut into one inch thick boards to be used on the stable, cow pen, and pigpen. He said that there should be plenty of time to get the fencing done before the small crop was put in. "Hurry up but do not let your business hurry you." and "check out the work yourself, not take anyone's word for it being done." Charles did not want his horse injured by abuse for she was too "fine a nag to be spoilt."[40]

Chapter 5

KANAWHA VALLEY AND MANASSAS - 1861

Back home in the Yellow Tavern area, more families were suffering withdrawal pains. Certainly Catherine Cross must have been more than reluctant to give up Nat, her last remaining son at home. Finch and his wife Frances were living away from home. Her daughter, Mary Jane Davis, and a new born son had died the previous year. This left Catherine with two daughters, twenty-three year old Lucy Ann and sixteen year old Bettie, who was still grieving over the loss of her father and now called herself Bettie Richard. There was no one to work the farm except the slave William (Buck) Owen. Did she ask her brother-in-law Martin Smith Bowles for advice? His son Lyndall was also talking about leaving. The widowed Fannie Hopkins at Walkerton was in the same situation. Her son George would be leaving her at home with only her two daughters, Delia and Josephine.[1]

But leave they did. Nat - just after his 20th birthday, George Hopkins, Lyndall Bowles and about twenty-eight others went to the Henrico courthouse in Richmond on May 9 to enlist in the Henrico Dragoons under Dr. Zachariah McGruder. Did Catherine, Lucy Ann, and Bettie Richard hear the rattling of the wooden planks on Brook Bridge when scores of new dragoons rode across it on their way to the camp of instruction in Ashland? Soon they would be serving under a neighbor who lived just down the R.F. & P. railroad tracks, Colonel J. Lucius Davis.[2]

Colonel Davis was born in Winchester, graduated sixteenth in his class at West Point, had lived in Texas, fought in the Indian wars, wrote a couple of manuals on military tactics, and was now 45 years old and farming in Henrico. He and his wife Elizabeth had five sons, three of whom would follow their father into what would become the 10th Virginia Cavalry. Their eldest son, James Lucius, Jr., attended the University of

Virginia and the Virginia Military Institute. Colonel Davis had in 1854 reactivated a county militia and renamed it the Henrico Light Dragoons. When Henry Wise was governor of Virginia, Davis served as his aide-de-camp, 1856-1860, and was with him at Harpers Ferry.[3]

Before the war, cavalry and dragoons were trained alike to fight mounted and dismounted, armed with pistol, saber, and carbine. Dr. McGruder had long been with the Henrico troop and was elected their captain on April 5, 1861. He also represented Henrico County in the Virginia Legislature. Within a few weeks the troops in Ashland were petitioning to be assigned to former Governor Wise and his legion in western Virginia.[4]

Each trooper had to furnish his own horse. It was a long 300 mile journey by horseback to the Kanawha Valley. Even if they could have gone by rail, the Virginia Central terminated at the Jackson River in Covington. From there the Kanawha Turnpike, present day U.S. Route 60, winds its way through the Allegheny Mountains, across Greenbrier County, past Lewisburg to Hawk's Nest, the junction of the New and Gauley rivers that form the Kanawha River. A few miles downstream that river is navigable into the Ohio River, thence making connection westward to the Missssissippi.

Former Governor Wise had dreamed of heading a partisan command since the days of John Brown's raid. President Davis sent him toward the Kanawha Valley in early June. In seven weeks he had gathered 2,850 men for Confederate service, plus the militia from nearby counties. The militia proved undependable, many having joined solely to protect their own homes. The Federals had come eastward through the Kanawha Valley to Charleston and held Cheat Mountain near the Staunton-Monterey Turnpike to Parkersburg. It was important that they be kept away from the Virginia Central

Railroad through Bristol and Lynchburg. General Robert E. Lee, as advisor to President Davis, rode on horseback on July 29 from Staunton through Monterey to assist Generals Henry R. Jackson and William W. Loring at Cheat Mountain.[5]

Wise with his legion advanced down the Kanawha River to Charleston, but by the time the Henrico Troop arrived they had retreated to White Sulphur Springs where Davis was joined by General John B. Floyd. Colonel Davis's cavalry of 500 men guarded the passes from Fayetteville to Summersville (up the Gauley River above Carnifex Ferry).[6]

Floyd was also an ex-governor. He had recruited his men from Southwest Virginia and was senior to General Wise. However, neither governor wished to cooperate with the other one. When Lee joined them in August, General Wise asked that the commands be separated. Troop advancement was made toward Carnifex Ferry on August 21 and the Henrico Troop was sent to support a small group at Dogwood Gap. After the fighting was over, they were used to guard the tops of nearby mountains. A letter from Secretary of War Judah Benjamin on September 20 instructed Wise to turn over all his forces to General Floyd and report to Richmond. Wise's Legion, under Colonel Davis, was not ordered to Richmond until December 4. Even then they took their time. Traveling by way of White Sulphur Springs, they were sent back on December 19 to push back a force near Lewisburg.[7]

General Lee wrote to his wife on October 7, "The bird [enemy] had flown & the misfortune was that the reduced condition of our horses for want of provender, exposure to cold rains in these mountains, want of provisions for the men prevented the vigorous pursuit & following up that was proper." Lee returned to Richmond in the latter part of October.[8]

Nat Cross had sustained an accidental wound in his hand in October. His great-grandson, Mark Cross, projects that this may have been what is called a "cook-off." A trace of gunpowder may remain in the barrel of the musket, only to explode when being reloaded, causing the ramrod to pass through one's hand. Nat remained with his company, possibly enjoyed Christmas with them on the Jackson River near Covington and came east with them before his disability discharge.[9] Certainly Mother Catherine was glad to see him. Although injured, he was home in time for the spring planting.

Thirty-nine year old Williams Carter Wickham lived at "Hickory Hill" on the much traveled road from the courthouse to Ashland. He had attended law school at the University of Virginia, served as a Hanover justice and a member of the Virginia House of Delegates. In the turmoil following John Brown's raid, Wickham organized the Hanover Light Dragoons in November 1859, although as a member of the Virginia Secession Convention he favored remaining in the union. After the fall of Fort Sumter he remained loyal to the Confederacy.[10]

Williams Carter Wickham was the son of William Fanning Wickham and Anne Carter of "Shirley" plantation. His father and Uncle Edmund Wickham had married sisters, Anne and Lucy. Anne received "Hickory Hill" as a wedding gift and Lucy got "South Wales?" Grandfather John Wickham of Richmond had represented Aaron Burr in his trial for treason. Father William Fanning represented the estate of Samuel Gist of Hanover, who left in his will the stipulation that all his several hundred slaves be freed and that his land provide their sustenance. By the time of Gist's death, newly freed slaves could not remain in Virginia. William Fanning was an astute and innovative farmer. By 1850, "Hickory Hill" farm had grown to 3,500 acres and by 1860 there were 275 slaves. Williams Carter Wickham was still living at home, with his wife Lucy and their two young sons.[11]

About forty men from Hanover were sworn into the Hanover Dragoons on May 9, 1861. Many of them were Williams C. Wickham's near neighbors and kin. They ranged in age from 18 to 43 years, leaving many sad families around lonely home fires. Some were older sons whose younger brothers would be joining the Hanover troop later, including the Timberlake, Nuckols, Sydnor, Wingfield, Nash, and Leadbetter families. The roads and rails between Ashland and Richmond were well traveled in the early 1860s. The dragoons, who had helped dedicate Henry Clay's statue in the Capitol Square in April 1860, now mustered at Richmond with the companies from Powhatan, Goochland, and Chesterfield counties, and the Governor's Mounted Guard of Richmond. They drilled at Camp Stuart in Ashland for two weeks before going on to be at Manassas in April and May 1861.[12]

Wickham's men assisted in the retreat from Fairfax Courthouse to Mitchell's Ford on July 17. Two Hanover men lost their lives at Flint Hill, the first battle of Manassas on July 21: Boldman Bowles was shot through the head and Edmund Fontaine, Jr., of Beaverdam, was shot through the body. His comrades said of young Fontaine, "He was the personification of the much-abused term - the Old Virginia Gentleman ... ready to defend his views with tongue or sword." Two more Hanover men were killed at Manassas when they pressed the Federal retreat: 34 year-old Philip Spindle and 24 year-old Richard Saunders. Lieutenant William Newton, of "Summer Hill" said that after crossing a swamp, some of the enemy was hidden by some bushes and a fight ensued.[13]

On duty as a surgeon with the cavalry at Manassas was John Boursiquot Fontaine. The 20 year-old doctor had trained at the Medical College of Virginia and in New York and practiced in Ashland before the war. One of the first of the wounded he examined that night was his brother, Edmond. He soon realized that his brother's wound would prove to be mortal.[14]

The volunteer cavalry stood picket duty in Northern Virginia for the remainder of the year and quartered for the winter in their log huts. A West Pointer, balding Beverly H. Robertson, of Amelia County, "with unsmiling eyes (and) a long moustache" was their commander. When they were organized with other troops into the 4th Virginia Cavalry in November 1861, Robertson was made their colonel and Wickham the lieutenant colonel.[15]

The First Company Richmond Howitzers, with possibly Mary Powell's son Junius, from "Melrose" east of Yellow Tavern, had been ordered to Manassas Junction on May 31. A member of their company, Frederick S. Daniel from Richmond, has recorded the lighter side of their experiences. He said that they left Richmond "on a long freight train at the Central, now Chesapeake and Ohio, railroad station" and were greeted at stations along the way by ladies with baskets and trays of refreshments and drinks of ice water and lemonade. They "landed on the hot plain of Manassas," parked their guns and pitched their tents, being among the first to arrive. Soon they "contracted a very strong habit of lying down on straw to read newspapers and novels, sent from home regularly, and to play cards."[16]

The Howitzers built the first, but never to be used earthen works on the road from Fairfax to Washington. The first action, a "light artillery duel" was on July 18 and the Howitzers did not fire a gun. There were visitors from Richmond, including General Lee. They saw General Beauregard in his "short sack coat and wearing a light colored felt hat." There was a heavy fighting on their left on Sunday, July 21. The "Rebel Yell" was heard for the first time as the enemy turned back toward Washington. The Howitzers started in the pursuit, but "encumbered with the enemy's wreck and plunder, cast-off equipments and material" and the approaching darkness, they were ordered back to their position around the battle strewn field. The next day, although dreary and rainy, they entertained visitors, tended to the wounded and buried the dead.[17]

Junius Powell had enlisted in April for twelve months. Sister Blanche Powell wrote in her journal in January 1862 that he was barely 18 years old and has been at Leesburg for five months. He wrote to his family that they were as comfortable in tents with plank floors as they would be at home. They can hear the Yankee band playing across the river. Twelve year-old Blanche pined for her brother saying, "How terrible [a] thing is war, under any circumstances now doubly so is this in this unnatural fratricidal civil war, now raging between two sections of our beloved country." Dr. and Mrs. Powell drove into Richmond to try to talk Secretary of War Judah Benjamin into granting Junius a furlough, but to no avail.[18]

During the latter part of 1861, other units, both cavalry and artillery were organized in Henrico and Hanover. Nat Cross's brother Finch could never quite seem to make up his mind which branch of service he wanted to be in or even whether he wanted to be in the service. There was a baby at home, so tiny and frail that they hadn't even given her a name. That summer he enlisted in the Morris Artillery along with his first cousins James Henry and Richard Hardin Cross, sons of Nancy and the late Nathaniel Cross. Later another of Nancy's sons, Nathaniel Adolphus, called "Doll," would join the Morris Artillery. Finch Cross did not stay long in the artillery having furnished a substitute in the person of George Foster. James Henry Cross later transferred to the 10th Virginia Cavalry to be with his brothers Joseph Franklin and William Thomas Cross.[19]

Young men from Taylorsville to Beaverdam, fellow students and members of the families of Morris, Coleman, Fleming, and Jones flocked in 1861 to join the light artillery. Edward Morris, a Hanover lawyer who had married Matilda Fleming, began recruiting as early as July 3, 1861. Three weeks later, Matilda's half brother, Lewis Minor Coleman, a former teacher at Hanover Academy on Ridge Road, took up the task of recruiting along with Hilary Pollard Jones, a fellow teacher. The next month Morris and Coleman consolidated their efforts, calling it the Morris Artillery for Edward Morris' initial efforts. By August there were nearly 100 men on the roll.[20]

The new battery moved to the Baptist College in Richmond to train with other batteries. They were under the instruction of Colonel Thomas Carter with the King William and Henrico artilleries. The Morris Artillery remained around Richmond until October 10, 1861, when the officers, men, guns, and their 57 horses were put on the Virginia Central Railroad to pass through the upper Chickahominy area to Gordonsville and then on the Orange and Alexandria Railroad to join their fellow artillerymen of the First Howitzers around Manassas. They detrained at Fairfax Station, their four guns, caissons, and four battery wagons having been brought on flat cars. Winter camp was at Centreville. Captain Coleman and Lieutenant Jones were strict in matters of discipline and were voted out of office in 1862. However, the army soon realized their value and later promoted them to higher office. By this time, Lieutenant Morris was 40 years old and had resigned.[21]

****

Henrico County, during the war years, was governed by gentlemen justices. Four men were elected from each of the four districts to make up what was called the County Court which met as a Quarterly Court in March, May, August, and October and as a Monthly Court in the intervening months.

The major difference was that the former used juries and the latter could hear cases without juries. They had oversight over the Blacks, the poor, the roads, the naturalization of immigrants, the licensing of ordinaries and licensing of ministers to perform marriages.[22]

Among those representing constituents in the northern part of Henrico County and living apparently outside the city were: Martin Lipscomb; George King, who lived close to the city; Robert Courtney, who lived at "Ridge Farm" and his neighbor B.W. Green; and Spottswood Waldrop, who lived at Yellow Tavern. Jacob Keesee was Commissioner of Revenue for the Upper District and Spottswood Waldrop was his assistant. George D. Pleasants, the sheriff did not live in that part of the county, but in 1864 John Spotswood Mosby, of Yellow Tavern did. Court sessions were held in the old courthouse at 22nd and Main streets in Richmond.[23]

The county court would appoint those who would serve at public elections. Early in 1861 Abner Milliard, A.D. Johnson, Nat King, L. Chamberlayne, James Oilman, and A.D. Storrs were chosen to oversee the voting at Barney Dickman's house on the Brook Turnpike. Anderson King, John W. Sheppard, William Taliaferro, P.H. Waldrop, Robert Melton, and Alfred Winston were chosen for the voting at Hungary Station. M.S. Bowles, John S. Walker, John N. Powell and John D. Sheppard were among those serving at Hungary Station in 1863.[24]

The minute books of the county court for 1861-63 show whites being brought to trial for permitting an unlawful assembly of slaves, selling ardent spirits to a slave without consent of his master, and permitting a slave not belonging to (person charged) on his property more than four hours at a time. Gibson Garber was fined $10 and cost of court for allowing his slave Tom to be at large and trading as a free man.[25]

There were surprisingly few charges brought against Blacks during this period. One slave, John, the property of Richard Lyne, was charged with severely cutting and wounding a white man. A Court of Oyer and Terminer (criminal) was opened. He was determined to be guilty and hung on January 2, 1863. If this had been a white man charged, the sentence would probably have been flogging. Aleck, the property of Warren Guy, a trustee for Mrs. Mary Hopkins severely cut and wounded William Kavanaugh. Aleck was sentenced to a flogging of thirty-nine lashes one day and thirty-nine the next day. James King, according to the 1850 census a free Black and one of six children of a mulatto man and a white woman, was charged with stealing a cow worth $400 from Mr. John Stewart. He was jailed, escaped, rearrested, and a Court of Oyer and Terminer opened.[26]

Keeping the roads open for the local citizens was one of the responsibilities of the County Court. However, they were used and abused by which ever army chose to pass over them. In 1861 money was appropriated for the extension and repair of a road northward from the city line to Cannon's Old Road. Later in the year, it was determined that the "hands of Joseph C. Burton, Gustavus G. Carter, and Richard J. Thomas" be assigned to work on the Old Cannon Road from the Brook Road to the land worked by Garland Hanes.[27]

Chapter 6
THITHER AND YON - 1862

With the beginning of 1862, life at "Melrose" seemed little affected by the war. Junius Powell was still with the Howitzers in their winter quarters at Leesburg. The younger boy Johnny was yet to enter Virginia Military Institute. Preparations were being made to send Blanche to St. Mary's, a very fine girls' school in Raleigh, North Carolina.[1]

At her mother's suggestion, Blanche had begun a journal. She wrote of the regular domestic routines, making trimming for collars and underwear, her mother exchanging recipes for making grape jelly and blanc mange. Mrs. Powell set four hens. She forgot to send to town for candles and that night Dr. Powell had to read the day's chapter from the Bible by a lighted wood knot.[2]

Dr. John N. Powell made daily trips into the city, bringing the local papers back with him in the late evening. There was frequent traveling back and forth: Blanche and her mother into town for dress fittings; neighbors and friends who would come to visit, sometimes staying for two to three days. Blanche with her friends would ride for pleasure and to the Sunday School at nearby Emmanuel Church. If the weather was bad, Blanche would wait and ride in the carriage with her family. Once the roads were so bad, she and her mother had to ride in the mule cart. There was to be a new minister, the Reverend Cornelius Walker, the Reverend Mr. Wilmer having been made bishop of Alabama.[3]

The cycle of life and death went on even among the very young. The Reverend Mr. Wilmer's young daughter died and was buried in the churchyard. Each Sunday School scholar was asked to walk by the grave and drop in a sprig of holly. The Powells went to visit a neighbor with a baby less than a week old and another with a two week-old girl having "a full suit of hair." There was grief over the death at the Exchange Hotel of the ex-president John Tyler, a member of the Provisional Congress of the Confederate States of America.[4]

It was a changeable season, some days so warm no fires were needed, others cloudy and then with rain that froze on the windows, followed by a wet snow. Blanche worried about the fellows in tents and her father got a promise from Secretary of War Judah Benjamin of a furlough for Junius, which did not come about. They heard on January 24 of the Burnside Expedition to Roanoke Island and wished that the ships be "sunk to the bottom of the sea." Then they heard with dismay on February 10 that Wise's Legion had failed to hold the island. The first segment of Blanche's journal ended on February 12 with the news that the Yankees had reached Murfreesboro, North Carolina, only a few days' march from Richmond. Also there was news that Governor Letcher was recommending that the militia be called out – all men 16 to 60. If that passed, Blanche's father would have to go.[5]

This meant that the enemy troops were too close and the departure for school was put off until the fall when Blanche begins her journal again. Her leaving had been quite imminent. Mother Powell was getting together her daughter's medical needs – a phial of liniment for chapped face or hands, spirits of turpentine for sore throat. She had baked cakes for a snack on the "cars" (train).[6]

The Richmond Light Infantry Blues was one of the oldest units in the area. It was one of the companies of the 19th Virginia Militia soon after Congress passed the militia act of 1792. They were called out during Gabriel's Rebellion in 1800, the War of 1812, Harpers Ferry, and when it was thought that the "Pawnee" was coming up to Richmond in April 1861. With O. Jennings Wise, son of Governor Wise, as their captain, they voted to join Wise's Legion in western

Virginia. By January 1862, as a part of the 46th Virginia Infantry, they too were back in Richmond.[7]

Upon General Wise's assumption of command of the North Carolina coast east of the Chowan River, he requested that his legion be ordered to him. The 46th Virginia was among those so assigned. Leaving Richmond on January 14, 1862, the Richmond Blues went to Petersburg and then to Nag's Head by way of Norfolk. In the attempt to hold Roanoke Island, Captain Wise fell mortally wounded while his father lay sick at Nag's Head.[8]

Sallie Brock (later Putnam), of Richmond, regarded Roanoke Island as the "key that unlocked all the northeastern portion of North Carolina and the rich back country in the rear of Norfolk and Portsmouth." She wrote of the pathos of young Wise's death saying that, upon viewing the body of his son at Portsmouth, the general cried, "My noble boy, you have died for me ... You have died for your father!"[9]

Miss Brock recorded that St. James Church in Richmond was filled to capacity for the Captain's funeral and the crowds stood outside in the mud and melting snow. Many more lined the streets or peered from their windows as the cortege passed by. It was moving to the sound of muffled drums, followed by the carriages with the family and officials. Old men of the Blues and all the military in Richmond marched with reversed arms to the burial in Hollywood Cemetery.[10]

****

The weather in January and February, 1862, was atrocious across the southland. While Sam and Buck Francis were writing home that there had been snow and rain for the last three weeks and, on February 16, the snow was five inches deep, the 56th Regiment from Virginia was experiencing like weather during the siege of Fort Donelson in Tennessee.[11]

Their Henrico neighbors in the 10th Virginia Cavalry had just emerged from under the capricious orders of General John Floyd in the Kanawha Valley when the Harrison Guard, Company K of the 56th Regiment, made up of men from the Old Church area of Hanover, came to his command in Tennessee. The company had been organized by the Reverend Dabney Carr Harrison, a kinsman of President Harrison, and the pastor of Bethlehem Presbyterian Church in Hanover. After his brother, Captain J.P. Harrison of Hanover was killed at First Manassas, the minister vowed to take his place.[12]

In late November 1861, the 56th Regiment men had been sent through Abingdon to General Humphrey Marshall's small force in southwestern Virginia and eastern Kentucky. In early January they were detached from Marshall's forces and sent to Bowling Green, Kentucky, to be in Floyd's Brigade under General Albert Sidney Johnston with the Central Army of Kentucky. General Grant was threatening the two Confederate forts, Fort Henry on the Tennessee River and Fort Donelson on the Cumberland River. Those forts guarded the "gateway to the western Confederacy."[13]

Two days after Grant's ironclads captured Fort Henry, the 56th was sent to help in the remaining fort's defense. Donelson was a stockade of fifteen acres on a bluff overlooking the river. The small town of Dover, with wharf, hospital, and supply depot, was within the outer defense line. Twelve large guns stuck out from the hillside to protect it on the river side, trenches and log huts lined it on the land side. The Hanover men, one of four Virginia regiments, were set to digging new rifle pits. For the time being Floyd was in charge. Generals Gideon Pillow and Simon Buckner, with regiments from Mississippi and Tennessee, served as his subordinates.[14]

The plan was to push the Federals back while Johnston withdrew from Bowling Green to Nashville and then join him by a land route. The spring like weather the Federals had experienced at Fort Henry turned to wind, rain and then sleet. They missed their overcoats which they had tossed away earlier. Floyd's men never had overcoats but used "horse blankets, pieces of carpet, and even piano covers." They held out in the fortifications from February 12 to 14, then that night, under the muffling of falling snow, they positioned for an early morning attack.[15]

The frail Captain Harrison had swung the pick with his men during the day to deepen the rifle pits. He had been sick during the night in the hospital in Dover but joined them at sunrise. Together they repeated the 27th Psalm:

> The Lord is my light and my salvation; whom shall I fear? The Lord is the strength of my life; of whom shall I be afraid? … Though an host should encamp against me, my heart shall not fear: Though war should rise against me, in this will I will be confident.

Then he led his men against the Federal right. By mid-day they had pushed them a couple of miles and "captured General Grant's headquarters' tent, 5000 small arms, and 7 cannons." To the Confederates' surprise Floyd ordered the men to retrace their steps. Soon Grant himself arrived, attacked them on their right, and the "gateway" was no longer open.[16]

General Floyd loaded his Virginians on the General Anderson at the Dover wharf. The steamer captain pulled off before all the 56th Regiment and the Mississippians could get on board. General Pillow had slipped away by land and Nathan Forrest had taken his cavalry across a swampy area. Buckner was left to surrender the fort. Captain Harrison had been wounded and died on the way to Nashville. Twenty-four of his Hanover men were taken prisoner. Enlisted prisoners were held at Camp Morton in Indianapolis. There Edwin Acre died of pneumonia in April and William Peace of typhoid fever in May. Both men were buried there. Lieutenant Patrick Clopton was sent to prisons in Ohio. None were exchanged before August. Sally Harrison never knew where her husband was buried. In March and April of 1862, those remaining in the Harrison Guards were back in the rain and mud around Abingdon, despondent because their commanders had let them down. They must have been more comfortable when they were back in eastern Virginia, on the James River and helped to defend Richmond at Chaffin's Bluff.[17]

****

Letters from Mary (Mollie) Goodwin Terrell to her sister-in-law Emeline Josephine (Jo) spoke of her concern for Jo during the "dreadful spell of weather." Mollie's sister Nannie Yeamans made frocks for Jo's older boy Jimmie. Jo must trim them with her serpentine braid. Little aprons will be forthcoming, also the (spinning) wheel which Mr. Yeamans has gotten for Jo from Richerson's, and later Jimmie's shoes also. Brother Nicholas Terrell, now home on furlough with typhoid fever, sent the boys some candy. All others were well except for colds. They have heard a report from a gentleman that their brother Joe Terrell is with the army in the west. This has caused great distress because the news is not good from that area. Mollie included with the things she sent by Warner (a slave?) a copy of the previous day's Dispatch telling of the death of General Felix W. Zollicoffer at Logan's Crossroads, Kentucky, on January 18.[18]

Mollie settled back into teaching in early 1862. That year she had a smaller school and hoped to regain her health and spirits. She wrote to Jo on March 5 telling that: Nick would soon leave for the camp on the Peninsula; Mother Martha had put the gobbler up in anticipation of Charles's leave but she believed it was more like "pooring" than fattening; there was much grief in Jo's Aunt Mary Hendrick's home over the death of Pattie's little girl; and she supposed that she had heard that Joe Mills (Terrell) had taken charge at Rockets and his mother, "old Aunt Henley"- Jo's grandmother, is also there. She closed the letter with, "Kiss the children for me and do not be despondent bear up under all troubles the best you can the darkest hour is always before the dawn from sorrows joys often spring and pleasure is all the sweeter after pain."[19]

Measles was rampart in the camp of the 15th Regiment. Tom Francis was quite sick, confined to his bed, and looked badly. The body of David Lambert was sent home to his mother Frances V. Lambert who lived near Taylorsville. His record says that he died of a "disease of the heart." Charles Terrell wrote home that David died of measles and "was an excellent soldier and well liked in our company." Two more in the Patrick Henry Rifles were expected to die. The sad news had come of Wise's Legion's defeat on Roanoke Island, and there was some talk that the 15th may be sent to North Carolina.[20]

A Yankee attack on Norfolk was expected as soon as the ground got hard enough for the troops to move. Sam Francis wrote that they had not expected an attack by water until Burnside arrived. Sam had about reconciled himself to the fact that they will have to serve until the war is over, that they will be turned over to the militia if they do not reenlist. Buck Francis wrote on February 17 that the Yankees had sent a flag of truce to Norfolk for the women and children to get out.[21]

The 15th Regiment came out of winter quarters on the first day of March, but Charles's furlough was not imminent. General George McClellan had his forces poised to start up the peninsula. "Prince John" Magruder was disgruntled because some of his men had been sent to Suffolk. He continued to shift the regiment between Yorktown, Bethel Church, and Young's Mill, instructing them to fight the enemy wherever they saw him. The line, "some of the prettiest batteries you ever saw," extended to the James River, the fortifications having been thrown up by 1,400 to 3,000 Blacks. Some of the men, including the Francis brothers and Charles Terrell, often had to be left behind because of yellow jaundice. James Francis apparently had not reenlisted but was expected to return with the militia. It was reported that the Merrimac had sunk three boats in one day and taken another into Norfolk.[22]

The men at Yorktown were offered a $50 bounty and a thirty day furlough if they would reenlist for two years or more. Charles Terrell had reenlisted and expected to get home in the early spring. It seems that "Parson" Edward Willis, later a pastor of Leigh Street Baptist Church in Richmond, was trying to organize an artillery or howitzer company. This appealed to Tom, Buck, and their friends because they could be riding instead of marching and would not have to stand guard duty. By mid-March they had heard that President Davis had called for 4,000 more men from the state. Those who were already volunteers could not change their branch of service. The Reverend Willis was made captain of Company A, 15th Virginia and later chaplain of the regiment.[23]

The 2nd Company of Richmond Howitzers was now on the peninsula. They had moved from Harwood's Mill to a place near Yorktown and had been on an expedition to sixteen miles below Young's Mill. On March 15 they expected every hour to be moved somewhere else. Mahlon Terrell wrote to his sister Georgie, that he had reenlisted for two years. On their reorganization they elected Lieutenant David Watson, of Southall's Artillery, as their captain. Mahlon is sure that sister Eugie will be upset with the "Malitia law…as the Capt. will have to go." He hoped that they did not feel "skird" in Richmond yet.[24]

Dabney Williamson, probably a Henrico neighbor, brought Mahlon "Miss Jennie's Arbortype" and he was keeping it close to his heart. Their brother Joe was home on leave and Mahlon wished that Georgie take particular notice of his clothes, obtain samples of cloth and make for him a couple of shirts like Joe's. The ones Mahlon has are getting ragged. Twelve days later he approved the samples that she had sent him and asked her to trim the shirts with small brass buttons the size of pistol bullets. By that time they expected a fight daily. The Yankees came within sight of Bethel Church but had not remained long.[25]

The Powells of Henrico would have been concerned about Roanoke Island and their daughter's prospective school in Raleigh. McClellan's strategic plan in November 1861 had been to take the island, then to move on to Goldsborough, New Berne, and Raleigh. However, after Burnside had secured Pamlico and Albemarle Sounds, and taken New Berne on March 14, McClellan's orders were changed to operate against Richmond via the lower Chesapeake.[26]

General McClellan arrived at Old Point Comfort on April 2. Five divisions of infantry, two regiments of cavalry, and some reserve artillery had already disembarked. Two days later he had 53,000 men and was expecting three more divisions. A private with his forces has described the scene. He said that they pitched their tents among the charred ruins of Hampton where the only building left standing was the Episcopal Church. They fried their bacon and ate their hardtack while the army mules ate their grain and hay out of the pontoon boats and tried to eat the boats as well. He said:

> The scene was a busy one. The red cap, white leggings, and the baggy trousers of the Zouaves mingled with the blue uniforms and dark trimming of the regular infantry-men, the short jackets and yellow trimmings of the cavalry, the red stripes of the artillery, and the dark blue with orange trimming of the engineers; together with the ragged, many-colored costumes

of the black laborers and teamsters, all busy at something. They set out to go up the narrow peninsula on a bright April morning under a warming sun with the trees just beginning to bud. The grass was green and the birds were singing. Before they arrived at the hamlet called Big Bethel, consisting of only a dozen houses, the rain was coming down hard and the passage along the soft roads had become extremely difficult.[27]

A map drawn up for General Erasmus Keyes shows the Warwick River running parallel to McClellan's projected march. However, the Confederate forces had built dams, making the river deeper and wider. The Confederate batteries and infantry guarded these dams well, especially at Lee's Mill. Although McClellan had 50,000 men there at the river, "Prince John" Magruder, by constantly shifting his men, convinced the Federal general that he was outnumbered. On April 16, after an artillery barrage, he did cross the river at Burnt Chimneys, but, upon being counterattacked, withdrew his men.[28]

The approach came as no surprise to Magruder's men. Apparently scouting parties had been in the area for weeks. The 15th Regiment was encamped behind the Yorktown-Warwick line at Camp Lebanon when not being shifted around. Buck Francis wrote from camp on March 19 that the regiment had gone to Bethel and had been on the move one in every three days for the last two weeks. Tom wrote to Jim on March 27 from camp that the enemy had been to their old camp along the road to Bethel on the previous night and there was fighting every day somewhere along the line. There was still talk about the exploits of the Merrimac. A week later orders to ship all the baggage to Williamsburg had been countermanded. By April 2, Sam Francis had been sent to work at Mulberry Point and the regiment had moved ten times since they left camp at Young's Mill.[29]

Artillerymen from Henrico, Hanover, and Richmond were well represented at Yorktown in the Howitzers, the Ashland, Hanover, Henrico, and Morris artilleries. Sixty percent of the Ashland Artillery was from Hanover. Captain Pichegru Woolfolk was the recruiting agent. Colonel E.P. Alexander described him as "jolly, careless, hospitable, sociable, & always fond of a laugh." However, he also said of him that he was "high-strung" and "fearless in the face of danger." Among those he drew to his company were: his short brother Sergeant James Woolfolk, with a cleft pallet and a dry sense of humor, and his six-foot tall brother Lieutenant Edmond Woolfolk, called Ned. Pichegru Woolfolk continued to recruit through December 1861. They were outfitted and drilled at the fairgrounds in Richmond as a part of the Reserve Artillery. Then they were moved in February 1862 over the seventy-five miles to Manassas to go into winter quarters. The weather was so bad that they had to build log houses with fireplaces. The horses trampled their hay into the mud. It must have been with great relief that the battery was moved to Yorktown.[30]

The Terrell brothers, John, Nicholas, Billy, and Charles were now all on the peninsula. On April 20 Charles wrote to his wife from Camp August that they had a fight every day somewhere on the line. Some of the enemy were killed but few of their men. They were expecting a tremendous fight and if the enemy "should pass here they will get to Richmond … (and) this will be the greatest fight ever fought." Charles sent her $40. In a May 1 letter he said he would send her the $125 owed him by the Confederacy when he got paid. She must send him the shoes and another pair of pants. Perhaps his father would help her to buy a cow so the children could have milk. He closed his letter with the admonition, "You must manage the best you can I do not know what to advise but plant all the Corn you can and put the new ground in [even] if it is late you ought to get it in easy enough."[31]

Chapter 7

AROUND RICHMOND – SPRING 1862

We can picture young Jimmie Gray, now 18 or just turned 19 years old, trying to convince his "Pa" that he should take either "Nellie" or "Fleet foot" and go with the cavalry. The Gray farm lay along the south side of the Chickahominy, adjoining the Cross farm. He had wanted to go with Nat Cross and Colonel Davis to western Virginia in 1861, but the women folks would not hear to it.

There was little to do on the farm in the dead of winter except to feed the stock and shoot squirrels. The hog killing had been done possibly before Christmas. On the first day of 1862, Jimmie presented himself at Henrico Courthouse in Richmond, was assigned to the Henrico Troop, and joined them in a few weeks in Petersburg. By May all of Davis's regiment, still part of Wise's Legion, was together on the lower Peninsula.[1]

The neighbors around "Brook Hill" and Emmanuel Church became increasingly alarmed as preparations were made for the defense of Richmond. The Parish Register shows that a picket station was established in March at Walton's shop (on the turnpike?) and everyone's passport was checked upon leaving Richmond. In April, the passage of Confederate troops from Manassas was disruptive to the Lenten services. Reverend Cornelius Walker had taken over as the new rector. The vestry left it up to him whether the worship service would include a prayer for the president of the United States should the Federals take over the neighborhood.[2]

The Sunday school superintendent, many of the teachers, and members of Emmanuel had gone into service, yet the attendance remained good. Soon officers and men stationed in the area began to attend the worship services. Lenten services proceeded in spite of the many troops moving through the area. Occupying the breastworks at Brook Hill in March was the Parker Battery. It was known as the "Boy Battery," its members ranging in age from 14 to about 21 years. Many were boys from the Richmond area. The battery would march every Sunday to services at Emmanuel Church to participate and sing in the choir. One member of their group, W. McK. Evans later wrote: "As it was not far to Richmond, after dark nearly every night, quiet good nights would be said and some boy would be lost in the hedges to find his way to Richmond, to see mother, and be back before roll call in the morning."[3]

Their major wrote that they had four guns made at Tredegar Iron Works in Richmond and which were as apt to explode at one end as the other. The battery did not stay long at Brook Hill but left to distinguish themselves at Sharpsburg.[4]

****

With losses in Tennessee and with McClellan posing a strike toward Richmond, the people began to look around for union sympathizers. Even children in their games called their playmates Yankees when they became peeved with them. The much beloved John Minor Botts, a former representative of Henrico County in the Virginia Legislature and the United States House of Representatives, had made no secret of his ardor for the union and his disavowal of any right to secession under the constitution. When martial law was declared by the Confederate Congress, Botts was the first to be gathered in its net.[5]

Early on Sunday morning, March 2, 1862, one hundred armed men appeared at the Botts home before he had gotten out of bed and took him off to a former Negro prison just north of Main Street, in Lumpkin's Alley, that later came to be called Castle Godwin. There he was held in solitary confinement in a room with neither table nor chair. Although he was allowed to supply himself with some furniture, others were not as fortunate, having to sleep on the floor with a wooden block for a pillow and "the ceiling for a blanket."[6]

John Minor Botts was a prolific letter writer and he now used his pen to protest to Confederate officials, citing the suffering of the families of those who, like himself, were being held without a trial. The trunks and desks were searched in his home. Having turned up no evidence, he was paroled after eight weeks and ordered to the interior of the state. His family was offered passes to accompany him. Later he wrote that at the time of his arrest he had already given up any hope of a peaceful settlement of the hostilities that he had watched ferment over the last thirty years and had retired to the country.[7] Further research may show that he put on the market at this time his farm at Half Sink on the Chickahominy or his house called Elba on the western edge of the city.

****

The 4th Virginia Cavalry began its move from the Orange and Alexander Railroad on March 28, toward the Peninsula, pausing for a few days in Richmond with the beginning of April. They set up camp halfway between Williamsburg and Yorktown. Elections were held the later part of the month. Beverly Robertson was replaced as colonel by Williams Wickham. The men considered Robertson as "very cross and contrary."[8]

It was a cold night on May 3 when General Johnston had his infantry begin to slip away from Yorktown toward Fort Magruder, leaving the cavalry to man the trenches and cover their retreat. During a countercharge concerning a Federal battery on May 4, Colonel Wickham sustained a saber wound through his side. But for the intervention of Daniel F. Ball, a teacher and musician, the colonel would have lost his life. Wickham stayed in his saddle until the enemy was repulsed.[9]

The next day, Captain William Newton, of "Summer Hill" in Hanover, was riding with Major W.H.F. Payne, now in charge of the regiment, when they came upon some Federals bearing a Virginia flag. The major, a native of Fauquier County and a student of Virginia Military Institute and the University of Virginia, was shot in the face and both men were taken prisoner. Newton returned to his troops in August, 1862, and the major the following September.[10]

The first action Jimmie Gray may have seen was when Colonel Davis's command "won great praise for its charge and in hand-to-hand battle with the Federal cavalry near Saunders' Pond," not far from Williamsburg. It was raining hard all day. Both Jeb Stuart and General Lafayette McLaws commended their action. This was about May 4 as Johnston retreated toward Richmond. By the end the month they were assigned to Stuart's command. Jimmie's neighbor, George Hopkins of "Walkerton" on the Mountain Road, was made captain of what was now Company I of the 10th Virginia Cavalry. Captain Zachariah McGruder had been reelected and promoted to lieutenant colonel but resigned because of ill health.[11]

A distant cousin of the Francis brothers, Joseph Park Thomas, was also a member of Company E, 15th Virginia Infantry. He wrote in his memoirs that when General McClellan began his march up the peninsula, General Magruder with his small army fell back to Lee's Mill, about half way between Young's Mill and Williamsburg where he was reinforced by General Johnston. They began their retreat toward Williamsburg on May 3. After a slight skirmish with some cavalry and artillery, they continued on past Williamsburg toward Richmond and could hear the "hot fight" on May 5, but were not sent back. The wagons with their equipment did not keep up with them. After two days, they were issued flour but nothing to cook it in. Joseph Thomas said that he had to utilize his oil cloth as a dough tray and cook the bread on the end of his ramrod held over the fire. They built their breastworks where Highland Springs is today and remained there until May 30.[12]

Charles Terrell called their location "Camp 5 miles below Richmond on Doctor Garnett's Farm." They watched the enemy burn homes of "secession men" across the Chickahominy Swamp in Hanover County. He said that the Yankees had "taken horses and committed several depredations on Property we do bad enough but I am afraid they will do worse a great many slaves have gone off from the neighborhood."[13]

****

In the latter part of May, the Federal and Confederate forces met near Slash Church in the northern fringes of the Yellow Tavern area. It was called the Battle of Hanover Court House by Yankee participants, but in the South is referred to as the Battle of Slash Church. In past years, the stagecoach had passed through this neighborhood on its way from Richmond to Fredericksburg. Patrick Henry had drilled the militia here in Revolutionary times.

Since 1840 travelers had taken the Virginia Central Railroad. The tracks ran northward from Atlee Station. A mile or so below Slash Church the line bore northeast by Lebanon Methodist Church to Peake's Station and Hanover Courthouse and then it turned northwest to Hanover Junction and Beaverdam. It was near this bend that the fighting took place. General George McClellan felt that this area must be kept open in order that General McDowell could reinforce him from Fredericksburg. Confederate generals were concerned that it be kept open for Jackson's men to come from the Valley.[14]

General Lawrence O'Bryan Branch's men, mostly North Carolinians, had moved down from Gordonsville through Ashland May 19-22 to an encampment at Slash Church. On May 26, Branch's assignment was the Virginia Central and Richmond, Fredericksburg and Potomac railroads. General Joseph R. Anderson and his men, mostly Georgia troops, were on their way from Fredericksburg. Already patrolling in the area near the courthouse were the local troops of the 4th Virginia Cavalry. Their colonel, Williams C. Wickham, was recuperating in his home, "Hickory Hill," near Hanover Court House, from the saber wound sustained at Williamsburg. One of McClellan's advance guard took him prisoner. He was soon paroled and exchanged by special cartel for his wife's kinsman, Lieutenant Colonel Thomas L. Kane, of the Pennsylvania Bucktails.[15]

There had been a gala wedding celebrated in November 1853 by the families east of Hanover Court House. William Newton of Tappahannock had married Mary Mann Page, the only child of John Page and Catherine Nelson of "Summer Hill" on the Pamunkey River. The nuptial ceremony was at Immanuel Church in the Old Church neighborhood. An unknown poet described how the neighbors gathered in rockaways, buggies, sulkies, and gigs. The moon was bright that night and the fellows and their ladies danced until daylight.[16]

Now eight and a half years later, Mary Newton was at home alone with their three small children, Willoughby, Lucy, and Landon when Colonel Richard Rush with his lancers, regulars, and some Zouaves, came up Pamunkey River to burn the bridge at "Wyoming," the home of the widow Henrietta Nelson, just above "Summer Hill." Mary Newton's father had died and mother Catherine had married Dr. William Brockenbrough of across the way. Captain Newton, of the 4th Cavalry with Williams Wickham, was still in prison from his capture at Williamsburg. Little Willoughby Newton was sent to the courthouse under the pretext of getting the mail but actually to alert the Confederates that the Yankees were in the neighborhood.[17]

Colonel Rush went as far as Crump's Creek, between "Williamsville" and "Woodberry" about four miles from the courthouse, before running into the pickets of the 4th Cavalry and turning back. Two days later Colonel William Grier of the 1st U.S. Cavalry got within three miles of the courthouse and determined there was a "considerable force" there. It appears that this was the same route by which Colonel Gouverneur Warren approached Slash Church the next day, May 27. The roads were muddy and the streams swollen and Warren did not arrive on the field until 3 p.m.[18]

That morning some of the Georgia men had been sent to repair the railroad at Peake's Station. Two North Carolina batteries and the 4th Virginia Cavalry were on the road by Taliaferro's mill when they heard that Federal troops were to their right. The fighting took place along the railroad at Peake's and the tracks toward Hanover Court House. General Branch was pushed back toward Ashland where he united with some of Anderson's men moving toward Richmond. The Federals encamped that night at Peake's. The next morning McClellan recalled his men back to New Bridge on the Chickahominy. He had destroyed the R.F. & P. railroad bridge at the North Anna and the track and telegraph lines at Ashland.[19]

The engagement at Slash Church was only six to seven miles from the Cross home on the Telegraph Road and probably no more than that to the Terrell and Davis homes below Ashland. Buck Francis in his letter to sister Jo Terrell on June 5 rejoiced that the enemy had left her neighborhood and sent word to "Sister" (Liz Davis) that he "thought she had more spunk than to run away from home."[20]

An article in the Richmond *Dispatch* a few weeks prior to this shows the ladies' concern for the safety of their area. Each had contributed to the Ladies Defense Association for the gunboat fund. The list included: Mesdames Henrietta Nelson ("Wyoming"), Peachy Pollard, Wm. B. Newton ("Summer Hill"). Wm. Brockenbrough ("Westwood"), E.P. Meredith, Carter Braxton, E.B. Compton, J.P. Smith. P. Tinsley ("Totomoi"), Martha Hundley, T.E. Meredith, Susan Hill, O. Winston ("Lindley"), Wm. Norment, Julia Norment; B.L. Taliaferro, Mary Haw ("Oak Grove"), M.E. Blake, F.E. Elliott, and S.E Cross. Also listed were: the Misses Kate Nelson, L.L. Nelson, E.E. Pollard ("Williamsville"), Mary Haw, Mary Clark, and B.L. Elliot. The writer of the article commented: "It will be seen that they [the ladies] do not forget they inhabit the land of [Patrick] Henry and [Henry] Clay." In this same newspaper, the fall of New Orleans, the late General A.S. Johnston, and the fall of Fort Donelson are mentioned.[21]

The fighting must have been quite frightening for those who lived along Mechumps Creek, southwest of the courthouse, and along the railroad. The elderly James Sutton lived at "Mount Pleasant" and had sent his two sons to study at William and Mary College. Mrs. Sutton was dead. There were seven daughters: Elizabeth, Justina, Ella, Sarah Jane, Frances Ann, Mary Ann and Mary Jane. All were probably there with their father during the war, although Ella may have already have married Colonel William Davis. Philip, the eldest would soon lose an arm at Seven Pines, and would eventually become a major. William would serve in the Richmond city ambulance corps. Fortunately William and Martha Dabney with their three daughters and young son had already moved from "Clay Spring," the boyhood home of Henry Clay. The Cardwells lived there and their son, R.J., joined the Confederate army while still quite young and would eventually become a Virginia Supreme Court judge.[22]

Doctor Thomas Kinney lived in the big house, "The Elms," at the intersection of the Peake's Road and the road to Taliaferro's Mill (now Georgetown Road). It may have been at this time that that house was used as a hospital. There are blood stains on the floor and marks where the beds were fastened down. William J. Jerrell and his wife Lucy lived just down the road (now #301) at "Oak Level." Their home too was used as a hospital. Arabella Jerrell was age 14.[23]

It is uncertain who was living at "Woodberry," on the River Road, that year. The next year John and Betty Taliaferro bought "Woodberry" and lived there with his mother, Ellen, age 62, and their sons, William, 17, John, 15, and Champ, 13. It appears that some time later William joined the Hanover Grays of the 15th Virginia Infantry. At "Williamsville" on the road to Haw's Shop, young Bernard Pollard and his sister Ellen lived with their parents Dr. and Mrs. George William Pollard. In a few months Bernard would join the Hanover Troop of Virginia Cavalry.[24]

Just east of the road that winds its way from Dr. Kinney's to Taliaferro's Mill was "Hilly Farm," the home of the Jones family. Laney Jones, age 25, was in service, also his brothers, William, 23, in the Hanover Grays, and Henry, 21, in the Ashland Grays. Left at home were the father Laney, Jr., 56, mother Martha, 50, and younger children – Margaret, 16, Peter. 15, and Westmore, 13. This land is thought to have been the glebe for St. Paul's parish and the Reverend Patrick Henry had lived there in a small house in the yard. The passage of troops on their way to the battle at Slash Church must have been frightening to these families.[25]

Since 1850, Bickerton Winston, his daughters Jane and Mildred, and his second wife Elizabeth, had moved back to Hanover from Henrico to "Lindley," a mile or two below the courthouse. They were possibly related to the family at

Winston's Bridge, on the Telegraph Road over the Chickahominy River. Some of the Federals made their quarters in the hall at "Lindley," with the Winstons virtually prisoners in their own house. After the war, their home came to be known as "Signal Hill." At Courtland, their cousins, Mrs. William O. Winston and her seven children, saw the Confederate guns set up in their yard in order to answer the Federal guns positioned on the courthouse hill. Mrs. Winston petitioned the Confederates to move their guns so the house would not be in the line of fire.[26]

Hanover Tavern during the war years was owned by Cleavers Chisholm and his wife Amizela. It consisted of twenty-seven rooms, three large stables with 100 stalls, an overseer's house, ice house, smoke house, separate kitchen, three slave quarters, and was surrounded by 252 acres of farm land. The Chisholms moved there in 1861 from Negrofoot in western Hanover. Amizela, a large, good natured woman with common sense, managed the hotel which was soon filled with refugees from the Eastern Shore. "Cleve," as she called her husband, was small, nervous, and a Union sympathizer. When the Confederate flag was raised across the road at the courthouse in February 1861, Chisholm refused to participate saying that secession talk was foolish and would be the ruination of the southland. Hence many of the neighbors refused to patronize the tavern.[27]

The Chisholms had five children, two sons - William and Julian, and three daughters – Conway, Bessie, and Lillian who was underage. Conway died in 1864, leaving the Chisholms two grandchildren to raise. Early in 1862 with McClellan coming up the peninsula, Margaret Wight, her husband, and daughter Ellen moved up from Charles City County to live at the tavern. Margaret Wight started a journal in January 1863 and recorded the events as they swirled around the old inn.[28]

During the battle around Peake's Station, General Wm. H. Emory, head of the Federal cavalry, made his headquarters at the tavern for three days. His men camped on the grounds and helped themselves to Cleve's corn for their horses in spite of his protest to the general. Chisholm had a fellow union friend living a mile or so away on the Virginia Central Railroad. Henry Cady, with an interest in the railroad, had come down from New York in 1853. With the start of the war, Cady had sent his family, with the exception of his son Jonny, a good friend with young Julian Chisholm, back north. Both boys planned to join the Union army, but Julian was conscripted in early 1863 to serve with the Hanover Troop.[29]

****

On Sunday, May 25, the body of George Vass, a cavalry man from Culpeper County was brought to Emmanuel Church. He had been killed while scouting near the Meadow Bridges. With the congregation remaining after the worship service, a funeral was held and the soldier became the first of many to be buried in the churchyard.[30]

Chapter 8

NOT SO COOL HARBOR – JUNE 1862

The fellows in the 15th Infantry below Richmond had missed the May 30-31 fighting at Seven Pines by moving to Fairfield the night before. It had been raining everyday and the Francis brothers had not been able to write home because their paper was too wet. Buck told his sister that he had been soaking wet twice. However, they were eating very well, getting loaf bread and bacon. Their adjutant, Randolph Harrison, was severely wounded when he was accidentally shot by their picket. Also General Joseph Johnston was wounded and R.E. Lee took over his command.[1]

Lee was concerned about how far the Federal forces might extend to the north and east and gave General Jeb Stuart the assignment to find out for him. Henry B. McClellan, Stuart's adjutant and cousin of General McClellan, wrote after the war of his experiences with the Confederate cavalrymen. He included a map showing Stuart and his 1,200 men leaving Richmond along the Brook Turnpike on June 12. They passed by Emmanuel Church, turned on the Mountain Road just past Yellow Tavern to go for a mile or so on the Mountain Road before entering what appears to be the Old Washington Highway. Starting out at 2 a.m. on the 12th under a bright moon, this route would have taken them by the Stewart home at "Brook Hill" and possibly, later in the day, the Francis home near Winn's Church. They continued along the railroad to the South Anna River and crossed back over to camp for the night at the Winston farm. That night Stuart went with Rooney Lee to visit his wife's relatives at "Hickory Hill and to talk to the recuperating Williams Wickham.[2]

Historians rely on John Esten Cooke's account of how Stuart looked that day:

> The gray coat buttoned to the chin; the light French saber balanced by the pistol in its black holster; the

> cavalry boots above the knee, and the brown hat with its black plume floating above the bearded features, the brilliant eyes, and the huge mustache which curled with laughter at the slightest provocation … the perfect picture of a gay cavalier.

Also Cooke described their cautious approach to Hanover Court House the next day:

> Its old brick court house, where Patrick Henry had made his famous speech against the parsons, its ancient tavern, its modest roofs, the whole surrounded by the fertile fields waving with golden grain – all this we looked on with unusual interest, for in this bird's nest … some Yankee cavalry had taken up their abode.[3]

Stuart surprised a picket post at Haw's Shop , according to an account by Joseph R. Haw. His men captured the vidette at "Oak Grove" and chased the company back to the regiment. They had been observed a half mile from the courthouse by scouts from the Federal forces at Old Church but were not confronted until they reached a defensible ravine at the meandering Totopotomoy Creek. Near there Captain William Latane and some Spotsylvania cavalry met Union cavalry head on and Latane became the only fatality among Stuart's men during the expedition.[4]

According to a letter written by Mary Brockenbrough at "Summer Hill," the local people were surprised at seeing Stuart's men in the area. There had been Yankees present every day for the last three weeks, either in large numbers or as pickets. Sitting on the front porch, Mrs. Brockenbrough saw someone approaching on foot whom she took to be a Yankee. It turned out to be the brother of the captain slain about three miles away. The "Westwood" farm wagon had been on its way to the mill and now bore Latane's body. The women folks immediately scurried John Latane into the house for his protection until they could get him off to the courthouse on the last of Mary Newton's carriage horses. The servant Aaron was dispatched to Old Church for Mr. Carroway (the minister) but the soldiers would not let Aaron pass. The next evening Captain Latane was buried in the graveyard there at "Summer Hill" with only the women and children present.[5]

Fitz Lee was given permission to destroy the cavalry camp at Old Church. Stuart had now determined the location of McClellan's forces. How was the best way to get his information back to his commanding general? Recent rains had made the South Anna no longer fordable, if he should try to retrace his route through Hanover Court House, so he chose to continue south and to approach Richmond from that direction.[6]

****

Mollie Goodwin Terrell wanted her sister-in-law to write all the details on when the Yankees were in Ashland, how she was situated, was she much alarmed, did she wish to come up and stay with them in Beaverdam? Mother Terrell had been uneasy every day and would have come down, but "there was so much talk of Yankees and deserters in the neighborhood & Father thought it imprudent (for) her to go that distance without some protector other than a servant." A great many slaves were leaving the Beaverdam area, although the fords of the river were guarded every night. Mollie was thankful that the enemy had not come through there as expected. Many families had left their homes and other refugees had come from counties above and below them. Mail could reach them only if sent by way of Richmond.[7]

The 1862 annual report of the Virginia Central Railroad tells that the Federals did little damage to the road itself. They did burn the South Anna Bridge and the trestles near Hanover Court House and Mrs. Crenshaw's farm. They occupied the railroad from the Chickahominy River to the South Anna River.[8]

During June Marion Stewart at "Brook Hill" estimated that between thirteen and fifteen thousand Confederates of the left wing of Johnston's army were stationed between Yellow Tavern and the Meadow Bridges. Their commander, General Gustavus Smith, had his quarters at her home. Branch's North Carolina men, who had participated in the fighting at Slash Church, had their encampment in the pine grove in front of the church. One of the officers sent word to Mrs. Stewart that a young soldier was "heart broken over having been refused a furlough." The next day she sent the boy some games and food by her children. But the officer sent them back saying, "Take them back to your mother. The boy is dead. He died of a broken heart." The soldiers attended church services in large numbers and showed respect for the grounds and cemetery, where the 17 year-old boy and others of their men were buried. The sun was setting on June 25 when the North Carolina men left to participate in the fighting around Richmond. Just a half hour before a neighbor's funeral had been held at the church. During the fighting in the coming days, the old Brook Church and dwelling house at "Brookfield" (the former Prosser home) were made into hospitals.[9]

****

General Lee was sorely in need of Jackson's help. It was generally thought that he was still in the Valley. Actually he was on his way eastward from Gordonsville on Saturday June 21 with his troops and had stopped at Frederick's Hall in Louisa, fifty-two miles from Richmond. His men went into bivouac with General Whiting's troops and Jackson made his headquarters at Nathaniel W. Harris's home. His adjutant at that time was Major Robert L. Dabney, of Staunton, whose brother was Captain Charles W. Dabney, a former commonwealth attorney of Hanover County.[10]

About sundown that Sunday, a courier with the 25th Virginia Infantry brought Jackson a message from General Lee in Richmond. Apparently the message said that the Federals were in control of Ground Squirrel Bridge. The general turned to his adjutant to find a scout who was familiar with that area. The courier, a Nuckols boy who had grown up in Louisa County, was tired from his long ride but, with the promise of a good supper and some sleep in a good bed, he agreed to return with Jackson. The boy later told his family that he was awakened at 2 a.m. on Monday morning. They had to change horses several times on the way to Richmond. One of these horses pressed into service was a "beautiful sorrel stud." The general left the courier on the edge of Richmond in what is now Monument Heights and told him to await his return. The young soldier said that Jackson returned with some other officers in about three hours and gave him a dispatch to take back to Frederick's Hall. Within less that an hour after the message was delivered the general's entire command was on the move to join Lee's army. Jackson stopped at Maxwell's place on the Mountain Road and bought the sorrel stud.[11]

Colonel Walbrook Swank has published the memoirs of Carter S. Anderson who was a conductor on passenger trains running between Richmond and Gordonsville during the war. He wrote poignant accounts of the enemy raids and the Central Railroad's efforts to keeps the lines open for the transport of men and supplies. Anderson was on one of the ten trains of eighteen cars each that brought Jackson's men to Beaverdam in the spring of 1862. The 1,500 to 2,000 men with their heavy muskets, clumsy shoes, and haversacks "climbed into and on top of the twenty box cars and work train flats" of each train. It was a harrowing ride as Anderson tried to keep the drunken engineer from running into the train in front of them. They had been instructed not to shout or blow their whistle.[12]

Carter Anderson remembered that Jackson returned to Mrs. N.W. Harris's home at Frederick's Hall a little late for breakfast. The general apologized saying that "he often took a moderate ride before breakfast." When the maid had gone to call him for breakfast, she reported that the bed had not been slept in and concluded that the general had slept on the floor and made up his own bed.[13]

General Lee's orders from his headquarters on June 24 were that Jackson should encamp west of the Virginia Central Railroad and communicate with General Branch's brigade at "Half Sink" (on the Telegraph Road at the Chickahominy) on June 26. Lee's plan for Jackson was to drive the Federals from west to east, uncovering the various bridges across the Chickahominy. Lee expected A.P. Hill, D.H. Hill and James Longstreet's men to join Jackson in an encirclement that would cut off the Federals from their supply base at the White House on the Pamunkey.[14]

The hungry, tired, and thirsty men marched from Beaverdam toward Ashland. The hot sun bore down on them on June 25 as they trod along tree lined roads where no air was stirring. There was a scarcity of drinking water in the Ashland area and they had to search for country wells. Their food was late in arriving. It was sunrise on June 26 before they were ready to leave Ashland. Soon the impeccably dressed Stuart and his cavaliers met the shabby and sleep deprived Jackson. The Macmurdo family of Ashland had invited Jackson to spend the night but he had left there at 3 a.m. The troopers turned east on Ashcake Road, passed near Merry Oaks Tavern and Slash Church to turn right at Peaks. They were hours behind schedule and A.P. Hill would despair of waiting for them.[15]

General Stuart with the 4th Virginia Cavalry and other mounted forces would be joining Jackson on his left to cut off the Federals from their supply base at the White House. Colonel Davis and the 10th Cavalry had been left on the Nine Mile Road.[16]

The Courtney Artillery (Henrico) answered Lee's call for assistance against McClellan around Richmond. Unlike Jackson's Infantry, who got to ride the rails to Fredericks' Hall, they had to pull their guns over the muddy roads from the Valley through Louisa County. Below Ashland they turned southeast on the Ashcake Road, to past Merry Oaks Tavern, cross the railroad, and then go over to Shady Grove Church and Hundley's Corner. The weather had turned hot and steamy and the men were drenched in sweat. After Jackson conferred with Lee at Walnut Grove Church, they moved on to Old Cold Harbor. They were able to appropriate some of the Federal guns to substitute for their less efficient ones.[17]

Excitement in Richmond on June 26 was intense. Judith McGuire, a minister's wife and a refugee from the occupation of Alexandria, has written of Stuart's return from his ride around McClellan with 175 prisoners, a number of horses and mules and how he must have gone within a few miles of her relatives at "Summer Hill" and "Westwood" and also near his own father-in-law, U.S. General Philip St. George Cooke, in the area. Now it was rumored "some great movement was on foot." There were large numbers of troops "waiting for orders to march against the enemy." She heard that General A.P. Hill had his men on "Strawberry Hill" (in Henrico) overlooking the Meadow Bridges. This had been her childhood home. At 3 p.m. June 26 the order was given to charge across the bridge. It was led by the 40th Infantry and Pegram's Artillery. The fighting was watched from every high building in the city that night.[18]

The Letcher, Courtney, and Purcell batteries included men from Henrico and Hanover counties. All three batteries participated in the 1862 fighting around Richmond with A.P. Hill's Light Division. Lieutenant McGruder and William Berry were both wounded at Mechanicsville. At Malvern Hill, Berry was again wounded and this time his leg had to be amputated. John Watkins carried the body of his 19 year-old brother Charles from the field. Their widowed mother wrote to the secretary of war that John, only in his 16th year, was now her sole support and comfort.[19]

There were other Hanover and Henrico men attached to the reserve artillery and directed by Hanover men: Major Hilary P. Jones, Major William Nelson, Captain R.C.M. Page, and Lieutenant James Woolfolk. During the Seven Days fighting, the Morris Artillery had four guns – two 12 pounder howitzers and two 3 inch rifled guns. Their shelling was "rapid and incessant" while they were subjected to enfilading fire from sharpshooters. The next day they were on the New Bridge Road. When they were relieved on June 30 and sent back to camp the men and horses were "much broken down." However, Lieutenant Woolfolk reported that with two exceptions the men had fought "with marked coolness and gallantry."[20]

Of concern were the families of the cavalry under Colonel Tom Rosser who later married Betty Winston of Courtland and commanded the 5th Cavalry and those of the 10th Cavalry under Colonel J. Lucius Davis. The dashing Tom Rosser, 6 foot two inches with wavy black hair, was serving with the artillery when he was wounded at Mechanicsville on May 24, 1862. He was appointed lieutenant-colonel of artillery a few days before being transferred to the 5th Cavalry. A native of Campbell County, he had moved to Texas at the age of 13 and entered West Point at the age of 20 and withdrew on April 4, 1861, two weeks shy of graduation. The Mechanicsville wound was the first of nine sustained during the war. He survived each wound, a good fortune not shared by his successors in the 5th Cavalry, Colonel Pate and Colonel Reuben Boston.[21]

In the early spring of 1862, Captain Henry Clay Pate of the Petersburg Rangers was given authority as a colonel by the Secretary of War to recruit an independent battalion containing men from all over the state. These men would be familiar scouts wherever they were sent. He brought together 900 men and they were organized on May 25. However, on June 23 these same men were turned over to Tom Rosser and designated the 5th Cavalry. Henry Pate was retained as lieutenant-colonel. They contained some men from Henrico and Hanover who had been transferred from the 3rd Virginia Artillery. Among them were: the Lipscomb brothers – Nicholas and Winfield - and John and Lemuel Quarles. Joseph and Spottswood Waldrop had joined them in Richmond on May 9, 1862 and Benjamin Quarles would join in August 1862.[22]

The Henrico Light Dragoons were designated Company I in the 10th Virginia Cavalry. They were under Captain George Hopkins from Mountain Road and were now members of Stuart's cavalry. The men had just returned to Richmond from North Carolina on June 26 and scouted for General Benjamin Huger's infantry in the White Oak Swamp on June 30. They were under fire from the Union gunboats at Curles Neck and arrived on the field at the close of the Battle of Malvern Hill. The dragoons were assigned to burying the dead from both sides, collecting the abandoned equipment on the battlefield, and guarding the prisoners.[23]

Andrew Harris of the Morris Artillery had been mortally wounded at the White Oak Swamp and died at his residence at Jones Crossroads in Hanover. His widow, Judith Ann, received $67.80 the next year. Andrew Smith was wounded at Malvern Hill and died in a Richmond hospital. As they faced the enemy on the James River at Coggins Point, John Brooks lost his sight in both eyes. Others from Hanover in the Morris Artillery had lost their lives due to sickness as their batteries moved from Centreville to the Peninsula and then up around Richmond. James Chisholm, who had enlisted the previous year at the age of 17, had died in February at Hanover Court House and was buried there. The same month Benjamin Butler had died of typhoid fever at Centreville and was buried at the home of his grandfather in Louisa. After they came to Richmond, Nathaniel A. Cross died in a Richmond hospital. Mother Nancy was paid $24.30 the following year. During July, John Baker died of meningitis and John Wiltshire of cholera.[24]

With the tragedy of Fort Donelson still vivid in their minds, the Hanover fellows of the 56th Regiment were back on home soil. They met the enemy in Hanover at the Battle of Gaines's Mill and fought well, capturing cannon and infantry. By the time the fighting was over at Frayser's Farm, their honor had been redeemed and McClellan was being pushed out of the Peninsula. Now they were under the direction of George Pickett and would so remain until the end of the war. However, the price of esteem was dear. John Martin from Hanover and Joseph Gathright from Henrico had been killed in action. Jarrad Jeffries would die of his wounds. William Talley was able to get Edward Longan to his home before he too succumbed. At Frayser's Farm, John Jones, though wounded in action, was commended for his bravery. By the time the fellows reached Gettysburg the following year, Jones had been made the captain.[25]

Private Joseph Thomas wrote of little action for the 15th Virginia Infantry during the seven days of fighting until they were involved at Malvern Hill on July 1. When they reached there they had been marching for twenty-four hours. Positioned in a ravine 1,200 yards from the Federal batteries, the regiment suffered seventeen killed, fifty-six wounded, and sixty-three captured. Major John Walker died in the arms of his brother, Captain Norman Walker of Company B. Colonel Thomas P. August was so severely wounded that he never returned to active service. Captain Emmett Morrison, of the Patrick Henry Rifles, assumed command. Emmett Morrison was from Smithfield and had attended Virginia Military Institute. They had fought that day under the shelling from the gunboats on the James.[26]

The fighting had been so severe on the Watt farm that the house was taken for a Yankee hospital. Grandmother Watt had been moved to "Oak Grove" at Haw's Shop on the morning of the battle. She was a widow over seventy-five years old and sick in bed. The elderly lady died a few months later. Father Haw decided that his foundry equipment was too valuable to risk confiscation and he sold it to Tredegar Ironworks in Richmond. Throughout the war, raids continued to pass through the village. Afterwards Joseph R. Haw wrote, "The Tidewater District, once so prosperous, was now prostrate in poverty."[27]

"Old Steady" was the family coachman at "Brook Hill." One day when raiders were nearby, Mrs. Stewart put him to driving the goat cart into the woods. On the cart was a wooden box packed with family silver. One of the children was seated atop the box. Mr. Stewart led the way while the other children ran behind. The box was left at a safe place in the woods. Other household silver had been sent to Richmond and put in vaults. On another day a servant hid some silver in an unused chimney. It was thought that the goat went to make a delicious stew for some North Carolina soldiers when one morning all that remained were the horns and the hooves.[28]

****

Conditions in the prisons in Richmond cast a dark shadow over the city that spread into the surrounding counties. Sympathizers, both men and women, led by a Church Hill resident, Elizabeth (Betty) Van Lew, called "Crazy Bet," strove to come to their rescue. She obtained permission from General John Winder, head of the prisons, to visit the men and often slipped messages for them in the split spines of books or the false bottoms of her food baskets. Betty Van Lew communicated with the Union generals, supplying them with information on troops around the city and making suggestions on how the prisoners could be freed. She and her mother secluded escaped prisoners in their home and those of their friends. The family had moved from New York. Father Van Lew was a slave holder and prospered as a hardware merchant. After his death in 1860, the women had freed all their slaves.[29]

Some Union officers were taken as hostages for thirteen Confederate privateers taken off the New York coastline. First they were held in Harrison prison, predecessor of Libby, and then transferred to Henrico County jail. Elizabeth Van Lew wrote in her diary that she visited them in their room which was "small with a doubly barred window in a thick wall letting in a sad light to make darkness visible. Aaron Burr had been confined in this room." Mrs. Van Lew had taken the family of the prison keeper in as boarders. She kept a room ready for General McClellan "with new matting and pretty curtains." When John Minor Botts was in jail in 1861, he wrote to Miss Van Lew for advice. On June 26, 1862 Mrs. Van Lew and Elizabeth went to visit Mr. Botts and his family in Hanover on the Mechanicsville Turnpike. There, she wrote in her diary, the windows rattled. They could see the flash of burning shells and hear plainly the roar of the muskets.[30]

But McClellan did not get into Richmond to use Mrs. Van Lew's guest room. After seven days he withdrew his troops to the James at Harrison's Landing. Lincoln would soon turn McClellan's command over to Pope.

Chapter 9
MARYLAND – FALL 1862

The families around Hanover courthouse must have felt more secure during July and August while Stuart and his cavalry encamped there. John Esten Cooke wrote of the "old shady yard of Hanover Court-House" where Generals Stuart and Hampton met to talk under the trees. He described the latter as tall of stature, face browned by the wind and sun, with dark side whiskers and a long mustache." He said that his eyes were brown, almost black, and his voice low and sonorous. Hampton wore a "plain gray sack coat of civilian cut, with the collar turned down; cavalry boots, large and serviceable, with brass spurs; a brown felt hat, without star or feather; the rest of his dress plain grey." Fitz Lee and his brigade left the courthouse in mid-August to join Jackson at Raccoon Ford.[1]

After the battle at Malvern Hill, the tracks, bridges and trestles had to be repaired for the soldiers to be hauled back to Gordonsville before General Pope became a threat. Colonel Fontaine, president of the railway, was urged to have the repair work done between Hanover Junction and Richmond. He instructed his master road carpenter, George R. F Thomasson, "to cut timber wherever he found it most convenient." Mr. W.F. Wickham, of "Hickory Hill," heard the "whack, whack, and whack" of the axes in some of his beautiful pine timber a couple miles east of the South Anna. The gentleman was irate and asked who had given permission to come on his land. Somehow the matter was worked out. By August the work was finished and, as Anderson said, "Our road was open and we did not let anybody walk back but gave them all a ride."[2]

General Lee, still in Richmond in August 1862, sent word to Longstreet to move his men on the Virginia Central to Gordonsville and for Generals Hood and Whiting to take their men to Hanover Junction. When it was clear that McClellan was leaving by way of the James River, Lee ordered all but three brigades to follow him by train to Gordonsville. Pope was already trying to disrupt Lee and Jackson's communication by railroad by sending Rufus King's Light Cavalry on a 40 mile trek on July 19 from Fredericksburg to strike the Beaverdam station. They burned the depot, the flour and ammunition stored there, and cut the telegraph wires. Returning to Pope, the cavalry claimed to have broken up several miles of track.[3]

President Peter V. Daniel of the R.F. & P. and Edmund Fontaine of the Virginia Central Railroad were complaining to Secretary of War Seddon and President Davis about the wear and tear on their equipment. They felt that slave labor should be provided for the repair and upkeep of the tracks and roadbeds. Their facilities and rolling stock was limited and already they were having to discontinue some schedules.[4]

Members of the 15th Regiment during July and August were stationed east of Richmond near the New Bridge over the lower Chickahominy. The soldiers were concerned about: the whooping cough back home, milk for the children, and their own clothing needs for the next winter. Early in August McLaws' Division alone of Longstreet's men stood guarding Richmond against the remaining McClellan forces. Toward the end of the month, they too were ordered north. The 15th Virginia was under Major General Paul J. Semmes and did not join Lee until after the Battle of Second Manassas.[5]

Liz Davis made a note that her brothers, Tom and Sam, and brother-in-law Charles Terrell came by her home on August 27. This was the last time that she saw Sam. The march northward took ten days. Charles Terrell wrote from camp near Leesburg on September 5 saying that he, Sam, and others had stopped by his father's home to eat dinner and that he had given them a ham to carry along with them. His sister Barbara wrote that they had fed thirty-six soldiers as they passed through Hanover. She and her sister Mollie Goodwin have been busy drying peaches.[6]

The 15th Regiment passed by the Second Manassas battlefield two days after the fight. They moved through Leesburg, forded the Potomac through waist-high water, and were stationed on the Maryland Heights while Jackson laid siege to Harper's Ferry. They moved to South Mountain on September 11 and two days later were positioned atop that mountain. Only the artillery with them were was engaged. During the fighting at Crampton's Gap they were on a line just above Brownsville. After the fall of Harper's Ferry to Jackson, the 15th crossed back into Virginia at the bridge there.[7]

It was in the early morning hours of September 17 when they forded the river at Shepherdstown and moved toward the fighting at Sharpsburg. The fighting had begun the day before along the Antietam Creek that runs southward to the east of Sharpsburg. McLaws' men were weary from night marching and hungry from diminished rations. About 11 a.m. Captain Emmett Morrison, directing the 15th, ordered them to leave their knapsacks and fill their canteens in order to move quickly into the fighting. They joined Longstreet's men on the left flank in an area between the East and West Woods, in a triangle that had its apex at the Dunkard Church. The Hagerstown Road threaded the triangle from south to north.[8]

Captain Morrison led them over a high-railed fence and into a field. Private Thomas said that the bullets were as thick as hail and men were falling all around him. Thomas was struck by a piece of a shell, taken to the rear, and it did not prove serious. The captain received a severe wound in his right shoulder and the command was turned over to the Reverend Edward J. Willis, captain of Company A. Willis "had his coat shot all to pieces, and did not receive a scratch." He had applied to be a chaplain in July 1861 and had been accepted in December of the same year. He served as such until elected captain of Company A during the Peninsula Campaign. It was said that he was one "who would fight with his men during the day and pray with them at night."[9]

The casualties from the Ashland Grays were: killed or mortally wounded - E.S. (Sam) Francis, William E. Roane, William A. Snead, John R. Baker and wounded - James Blackwell, William H. Harris, George W. Kelly, Andrew McDowell, William K. Woodson, and Robert J. Forloine. The latter was taken prisoner and held at Fort McHenry until paroled on the 27th. Roane and Snead died on the field; McAllister, Baker, Forloine, and Francis were taken prisoner. Other Hanover or Henrico men killed from the 15th Regiment were: William Winston of the Patrick Henry Rifles, Charles Keppler from the Henrico Grays and Ezekiel and John Talley from the Hanover Grays. The regiment remained quietly on the field the next day. They had lost 58% of their men and officers. Captain Willis appointed a sergeant major to start back to Virginia with the walking wounded. On the night of September 18-19, the Confederates moved back across the Potomac, leaving those too ill to travel in the enemy's hands.[10]

Thomas Totty and Charles (Buck) Francis stayed behind to care for the wounded. Sam Francis died the next day and Buck buried him very carefully beside a fence on the Elias Grove farm. John Talley, brother of Ezekiel Talley, died on the Lavinia Grove farm. Their father came and took his sons' bodies back home to Hanover. Christopher Cherry of the Patrick Henry Rifles, William Snead, William Wicker, John Baker, and William Roane of the Ashland Grays and George Otey of the Henrico Grays died of their wounds, the latter being only 17 years of age. Left back home to moan were: Margaret Winston, mother of William; Catherine Keppler, mother of 20 year-old Charles; Judith Roane, mother of William; and John Snead, father of William.[11]

Starting in 1872, the bodies of Sergeant Cherry and Privates Francis, Wicker, Winston, Snead, Jordan Luck (of Caroline County) plus two from the 32nd Virginia Regiment along with the 2,449 Confederate fatalities from the fighting at Sharpsburg were moved to the Washington Cemetery in Hagerstown, Maryland. The records show those from the 15th Regiment had been found in Mayer's field, below the Grove house, toward the canal, and under a clump of honey locust. The graves were well marked and the bodies in good condition. Those of Privates Snead and Roane were found elsewhere. The reburials continued until 1872, many unidentifiable. Major-General Fitz Lee spoke at the dedication of the cemetery in 1877. Otelia Francis Bodenstein stood near the grave of her great-uncle Sam Francis in 1965, the first the family knew of its location.[12]

Colonel S.D. Lee had taken the Ashland Artillery with him as he crossed the Potomac into Maryland at Williamsport on September 14. Those who had no shoes had the option to remain on the Virginia side with the wagons. After crossing Antietam Creek, the Ashland men and their guns formed a part of Longstreet's line on the left, on a slight elevation facing a cornfield. There they were subjected to long range guns both on that day and the next day in another position on the Hagerstown Pike near the Dunkard Church.[13]

In the heavy fighting on September 17, they were placed to fire over their own infantry, a battery firing, then moving back for another to take its place. Many men and horses were killed, causing guns and caissons to be left behind. Woolfolk's battery lost a 12-pounder howitzer and its limber. Later the captain was praised for his "distinguished gallantry." Among the Hanover men with him: William H. Jenkins received a gunshot wound in his left leg, was taken prisoner and held in prison until the next April, only to spend the rest of the war either in the hospital or on medical leave; Edward S. Bumpass sustained a thigh wound and remained on furlough in Hanover until December 5. Barbara Terrell heard from her brother Billy that nine of his company were killed or wounded. Captain Woolfolk was wounded in his hand and a cousin Genet was mortally wounded. She knew that her brother Charles was all right but had no news of his wife's brothers.[14]

Stephen Lee, upon his promotion to brigadier-general, turned his battalion over to E. Porter Alexander, saying. "Old fellow, pray that you may never have to fight another Sharpsburg! Sharpsburg was just Artillery-Hell." Colonel Alexander, a native of Georgia, had married Betty Mason of King George, Virginia. He and Captain Pichegru Woolfolk became fast friends. They were both kindly men. A couple of men from Woolfolk's battery had deserted before they arrived at Sharpsburg. They were brought before a court martial at Carmel Church. The first was a bounty jumper who had agreed to serve as a substitute for $1,000. The other had been arrested by a recruiter near his home, but had later walked a good ways from Castle Thunder to report back to his unit upon their return from Sharpsburg. Alexander believed the latter only guilty of a short visit home to his family or sweetheart and remarked to Woolfolk, in charge of the guard, that he hoped that he would escape before his scheduled execution the following morning. When dawn broke, neither prisoner could be found in camp.[15]

The 2nd Company of Richmond Howitzers was not involved in the fighting at Sharpsburg, but did engage the enemy cavalry and artillery on the return to Williamsport. Vivian Fleming has recorded that when they returned to Winchester he was met by his half-brothers Lewis and Robert Coleman with the news that their brother Willie had died of typhoid fever at VMI. The firing of the guns at Sharpsburg had made William Mordecai deaf and blackened his brother with smoke. That fall William was made Quartermaster sergeant and put in charge of the battery wagons as they combed the country for provender for the horses and mules. He wrote to his mother that they had plenty food and clothing. Dr. and Mrs. Powell visited their son in Winchester and heard of the Howitzers' experiences. Junius had been wounded but was not sick from it.[16]

Blanche Powell went back to Raleigh for the fall session at St. Mary's. Her journal covers her experiences from October 4 to December 4, 1862. There she met Augusta Mordecai from Henrico and found her to be very pretty. General Robert E. Lee's daughter was also a new student. We can see that Blanche is now growing up with her first dress with a train and her mending her own clothes. She is enjoying reading, dancing, and hearing her friends play patriotic songs like the "Battle of Manassas" and "Maryland, My Maryland." Blanche considered a sermon by her headmaster lambasting them as "being listless and indulged, caused by the peculiar institution," a real Yankee sermon. Yellow fever was rampart in nearby Wilmington. Food was scarce there because the food carts would not enter the city. There was also diphtheria and a classmate had lost a sister. The sight of the omnibus arriving to take some of the girls to the train made her homesick and she became despondent if a letter did not arrive from home every day.[17]

The Henrico Troop missed the fighting at Sharpsburg. They were on picket duty in Winchester when summoned to join Lee's forces and met him coming back across the river into Virginia. Joining Stuart, they demonstrated around Williamsport and in the vicinity of Martinsburg for several weeks before leaving with Stuart for his second ride around McClellan. Stuart chose 1,800 of the best mounted and efficient men 600 each from those under Fitz Lee, Wade

Hampton, and Beverly Robertson. The 10th Cavalry were under Hampton and the 4th under Lee. Two hundred of each group was to seize horses, the remaining to take leading citizens to trade for hostages once they had entered Pennsylvania.[18]

From the 10th Cavalry, Colonel Davis took Major J. Travis Rosser, from Petersburg, and regiment surgeon, Dr. Archibald Atkinson from Smithfield. Williams Wickham went with his troopers. They started from Darkesville, about 12 miles west of Harper's Ferry, to cross the Potomac below Mercersburg. At the ferry at McCoy, Davis detailed twenty-five dismounted men under Lieutenant H.R. Phillips from Franklin to wade across and locate the Federal picket. Then Stuart and his men headed northeast to take over Chambersburg. There they got some shoes and Federal clothing. That night the troopers from 10th Regiment slept in a "cornfield in the pouring rain" and heard the explosions from the destruction of the ordnance and depot.[19]

Stuart's cousin and adjutant, Channing Price, (also a cousin to the Price girls at "Dundee") wrote to his mother in Richmond that he got "a nice black overcoat, pair of blue pants, 1 dozen pair of woolen socks, pair of boots & various other little things as much as I could carry." Just a few miles from Gettysburg, Price heard that his "distinguished relative Col. [Richard H.] Rush with his regiment of lancers [6th Pennsylvania Cavalry] had just passed by on the way to Gettysburg on the look out for us and Genl Stuart."[20]

Williams Wickham had his men facing west at Chambersburg, fully expecting Stuart to retrace his route, however he was ordered to move toward Gettysburg. Again Stuart was making a circuit. Wickham crossed his men at White's Ford. There were 500 sharpshooters on a hill but a shot from Major Pelham's gun and charging cavalrymen dispersed them, allowing the troopers to cross to Leesburg in Virginia. According to Henry McClellan, Stuart covered eighty miles from Chambersburg in twenty-seven hours "although encumbered by his artillery and captured horses, and had forced a passage of the Potomac under the very eyes of forces which largely outnumbered his own." His only casualty was the wounding of one man.[21]

****

October, 1862, brought the greatest calamity to the Hanover Dragoons. Their captain William Newton, of "Summer Hill," was mortally wounded at Raccoon Ford on the Rapidan River. He was commanding the regiment and received a wound to the brain. Fitz Lee wrote, "He was an officer of extraordinary merit and promise, and his death is deeply felt and mourned." His troops wept that night at Brandy Station. David Timberlake, of Hanover, took over as captain.[22]

Sometime during 1862, Andrew Ellerson was wounded. John Sydnor was wounded on October 15, just about the time Stuart returned from his raid into Maryland and Pennsylvania. At Upperville on November 3, 1862, Colonel Wickham was wounded in the neck by a shell fragment. Charles Taylor was captured and paroled about that time. Alexander Jones was wounded in the face at Brandy Station that winter and held at the Old Capital Prison in Washington.[23]

****

Soon after Thanksgiving, Tom Francis wrote to his sister Martha Jenkins from a camp near Fredericksburg saying that they expected to be in winter quarters in a couple of weeks. They were standing picket duty along the Rappahannock. The river there was about 150 yards wide, with the Federal forces on the opposite side, close enough so they could talk back and forth. However, they were not allowed to shoot. Tom added to his letter, "We are expecting evy day for a fite pretty nigh all the sittersins has moved out to [of?] town for them (the Union side) to shell it."[24]

Two weeks later they were still there. The Federals had completed their pontoon bridges and had come across. Tom wrote to his sister Martha J. Jenkins of watching the fighting:

> I have been in a line of battle for five day we have had a great fite and have whip the yankeys badly we have drove them back a cross the river they went a cross in the night and our company was out on picket and as soon we found out that they was gone our company and too others had to advance on them we caught six of them our brigade did not get in the fight a tall but we was where we could see it all on the rite wing it was a pretty site to see them march up and fite they would stand a while and then they would run and our boys after some times they would march up on our scermishes and our boys would ly down and fite them some times the yanks would be too much for them and would have to run back to their redgerment some would get up and some could not one of redgerments hade their own fun in town when they ran the yankeys back they would run and hide behine the houses … our fellows would march up on them and they would jump out and run and our boys would kill them … our loss was small to what the yankeys was.

Tom wished Mat's husband, Dumps, would come up for Christmas, also Liz's husband, Mr. Davis.[25]

At Fredericksburg, on December 13 the artillerymen under the direction of Colonel R. Lindsay Walker were stationed on Prospect Hill. When the fog began to lift, they could see the approaching Federal lines and by noon were subjected to severe musketry fire. By 3:30 p.m. the Purcell Artillery had run out of ammunition and Zephaniah McGruder had been killed. McGruder was single and only 24 years old. His body was taken to Richmond, where the funeral was held three days later. The Daily Dispatch said, "No braver man has given his life for his country's cause, and none has passed more deeply regretted." A few months later, his father received $219.00 for his back pay. [26]

Among the students from Hanover Academy attracted to the artillery was Vivian Minor Fleming, from "Chantilly" near Beaverdam. He was the brother of Matilda Morris and half brother of Lewis Minor Coleman. Yet he joined, not the Morris Artillery, but the Richmond Howitzers with his mother's permission in August, 1862. His brother, George Fleming joined in October and became the aide to Lewis Minor Coleman, who by then was a lieutenant colonel in the First Virginia Artillery.[27]

The 2nd Richmond Howitzers had come from Guinea Station through darkness, mud, and over broken bridges to join Lindsay Walker on Prospect Hill. Vivian Fleming and his half brother Lewis Minor Coleman were among those wounded. Vivian was now 19 years old, with dark hair, eyes and complexion. That morning the brothers met in Vivian's tent, prayed and read Psalm 84 together. The elder brother said, "Vivian, I know you have marched all night and have had no breakfast. Here are two biscuits. Remember you are mother's baby. Take care of yourself and preserve the honor of the family. Goodbye." The boy gave one of his biscuits to a comrade. Lewis Coleman was mortally wounded that day. When he died in March at the age of 36 years, Lieutenant-Colonel Coleman left behind his wife, the former Mary Ambler Marshall, granddaughter of Chief Justice Marshall, and three children. Vivian was sent home on disability to his parents, Mary and George Fleming, sisters Sarah and Mary, maiden aunts Isabella and Maria Fleming at "Chantilly," an eighteenth century frame house in western Hanover. Vivian spent some time convalescing in Georgia before being made an ordnance sergeant. He later told his wife that his gun was the closest to the front that day. When the driver was killed, General Stuart encouraged the four remaining men to keep on firing. Their shot was said to have been the last fired in the battle.[28]

The 10th Cavalry was picketing the river crossings and was not involved in the fighting, whereas Williams Wickham and his men may have been used.[29]

Dr. Powell went down to accompany Blanche home on the train. It was late when they arrived in Richmond and Junius met them at the station. They found that several regiments had encamped in their neighborhood. Blanche though their cotton tents with log chimneys were very pretty. Two officers from the 2nd Mississippi went with the Powells home for Sunday dinner. That night Dr. Powell vaccinated everyone in the family for smallpox. Cannonading could be heard from Fredericksburg, over 45 miles away. The report from Richmond was that Longstreet had "repulsed the Yankees three times in their attempt to cross the Rappahannock River."[30]

Marion Stewart remembered that it was the Georgia troops which encamped in the Bentley's field near the church from October until the last week in December. She said that they behaved badly, cutting down the ornamental trees in the Emmanuel cemetery and Brook Hill grounds, breaking into the church where they kindled fires in the stove at night, and injuring property in the neighborhood. The church, in spite of the depressing circumstances, was decorated for Christmas. Marion too could hear the cannonading from Fredericksburg and said that even before they heard the results of the battle many of the trees had been cut down in front of the nearby fortifications constructed during the past summer and fall.[31]

While Tom Francis was still in Fredericksburg, he wrote to his sister Mat Jenkins of seeing one of the fellows who had been left behind in Maryland with their brother Buck. He told that James McAllister was mending also James Blackwell after nearly bleeding to death three or four times. All the fellows have been exchanged so Buck should be home soon. Tom expected that they would winter at Hanover Junction.[32]

There must have been both tears of joy and sadness when Buck returned to Liz Davis's home on December 20 with news of Brother Sam's last days. Buck had written to her on December 14 as he passed through Richmond, despairing of ever seeing her again. He was a few blocks from where their Brother Jim was staying but was not allowed to get off the train. Charles Terrell was still home on a sick furlough.[33]

On December 8, Junius Powell left "Melrose" on horseback to return to the Howitzers at Port Royal. Preparations proceeded for Christmas. Blanche helped her mother bake a pound cake. There would be a banner at Emmanuel saying, "Hail, Prince of Peace," with the letters entwined with periwinkle. There was much visiting back and forth between neighbors and relatives: the Delaplanes, Davenports, Sheppards, Smiths (refugees from Alexandria), Marshals, Atkinsons, Drewrys, and Powells. The farm hands were busy shucking corn and cutting ice from the river. Mother Powell's arm was swelling and Dr. Albert Terrell came to see about it.[34]

Tom Francis appears to have spent Christmas alone in camp with no visitors or letters, although he said that he wrote to everyone before Christmas without receiving a letter from any one. Two days after Christmas they had moved not to Hanover Junction but to the Chandler farm just north of Guinea Station on the R.F. & P. Railroad. They were getting plenty to eat and he had gotten a bundle of clothes from home brought by Hoffman. William Hoffman was a Wagoner in their regiment. The men were "having fine sport now snow balling."[35]

Chapter 10

CLOSE TO HOME – SPRING 1863

Blanche Powell opened her journal for 1863 with, "How many events happened the last year, all, the battles around Richmond, and Fredericksburg and the last Manassas fight besides a great many other important fights. Innumerable skirmishes, and at all the battles we had whipped the Yankees, and poor Virginia has borne all the burden of the war." She also wrote of the "news of a glorious victory that we gained at Murfreesboro, Tennessee, under General Bragg." Her father brought the news from Richmond on January 5 that a gale had come up and the *Monitor* had sunk, losing all her crew.[1]

The Powell family and friends went to Drewry's Bluff on a little steamboat. Blanche said that they passed through (?) one of the pontoon bridges, "had a very steep hill to climb at the Bluff" and "never saw such formidable fortifications" and the largest cannons she ever saw. There were many obstructions in the river and many iron clad gunboats. They did not go on to Richmond to see a nearly completed gun boat. She thought that all the Yankee army even with the help of England would not be able to take those fortifications.[2]

Ransom's division was camped near Melrose and they could see the campfire through the woods in the direction of Mr. King's home ("Level Green" farm) and Blanche thought they looked so pretty. About 18 or 20 men came to the Powell home for food and others came for provender for their horses. Some of General Hood's division was encamped along Brook Turnpike. Officers of the 4th Alabama Regiment, Colonels Jones and Perry, Major Coleman, and a very pleasant little adjutant whose name Blanche forgot, came to visit and she played the piano for them. (Did Blanche wear her new hoop skirt?)[3]

Young Johnny Powell stayed at home and Blanche attended a nearby school. Their application for a commission for Junius did not come through. He resigned from the Richmond Howitzers in October 1862. His record states that he was in the Signal Corps from 1862 to the end of the war. He appears to have spent some time at home. On the morning of February 22, they awakened to two to three feet of snow on the ground. Junius took his mother and sister for a ride in the sleigh. By the 27th, rain had washed all the snow away. There, unfortunately, her journal ends.[4]

****

Charles Terrell was concerned that the fellows might be paid while he was on furlough and appointed Tom Francis to receive his back pay. His wife worried that her brothers might not be getting enough to eat. Tom wrote that they were being fed twice a day and sometimes got five or six biscuits at a time. Besides this their neighbor Hoffman had brought them a bundle from home. His sister must not send any more socks since he now has five pair. They are "having a fine sport" in snow battles between the brigades there at their camp near Guinea Station.[5]

On February 15, the men of Corse's brigade and the 15th Regiment put their baggage on the R.F. & P. Railroad and started their march southward at 9 a.m. in heavy rain. They spent the night at Hanover Junction and the next day marched through home territory during heavy snow that continued for the next two days. Often one of the companies would have to go back a mile or so to prize the wagons out of the mud. By the night of the 17th, those in the lead were 11 miles from Richmond. The night of the 18th they camped five miles from the city (possibly near Brook Hill). The following day they marched along Brook Turnpike to Broad Street and then over Mayo Bridge into South Richmond. The citizens of the city lined the streets, cheering the men as they marched by and handing them food.[6]

Surely many in the Yellow Tavern area, if not kept in by the storm, must have watched or at least listened as two full divisions, almost 16,000 men passed by. The snow would have muffled some of the sound of the rumbling of the wagons and the trampling of feet along Brook Turnpike, over the Chickahominy and past the Cross farm. Lucy Ann Cross and her sister Bettie missed the wedding at Mr. Carter's home that week. An admirer of Lucy Ann, Richard Green of the 15th who was apparently on furlough, wrote that he had hoped to see them at the wedding and would call on her if ever he was in the neighborhood again.[7]

The Ashland Artillery had wintered near Hanover Junction. Mollie Goodwin wrote to Jo Terrell that Charles's brothers - Billy, John, and Nicholas - got home often, some almost every week. Their mother was still quite sick, hardly strong enough to sit up while the bed was made. She sent word for Charles to come by before he went back to the regiment. There had been many deaths from smallpox. Also typhoid fever had been rampant for the last six months where Mollie had been teaching, with one Negro woman dying. She spoke of "poor old Capsie's Lamentation for 'Nias but glad he is in service." Jo's grandmother (Mary H. Terrell) had gotten better and gone back to Rocketts.[8]

Although the 15th Regiment had moved south, neighborhood boys of the Morris Artillery were still at Milford. The artillery had moved around much of the winter, but always south of Fredericksburg and where they could find forage for the horses. Some of them had been at the Carter wedding. Lucy Ann received a very chatty letter from her cousin, James H. Cross, teasing her about Joe Fleming and sending regards from his brother, Dick Cross, and cousin, Bob Davis.

Apparently she had written to him to tease him about eating so many pies at the wedding. He asked to be remembered to the neighborhood girls: Miss Betty Gray, whom he saw dancing at the wedding; Misses Mat and Tena; Cousin Betty Sheppard; Lucy Ann's sister, Betty, and their mother. Bill Davis, of Hanover, had invited him and Bob Davis down to eat some young chickens.[9]

In March, 1863, Jo Terrell's oldest boy, Jimmy, was staying with his grandparents and Aunt Mollie Goodwin, who was teaching him his letters. She promised to give him a new book when he has learned them all, and has made him a pair of pants. His Aunt Barbara and her husband will take him home soon and also take his mother some beans and potatoes. Mollie's letter in March told what it had been like in the area of Beaverdam that winter:

> I believe everyone was looking for the Yankees last week
> even at the old Beaver Dam Depot, which little place has
> been alive with Camps and camp fires Soldiers &c there
> were at one time between 500 & 1000 soldiers there sent
> with broken down horses to rest and recruit but they
> have nearly all left now, I have seen soldiers from all
> different states south & some horrid looking affairs
> they were.[10]

Their young cousins, Plan and Charley Terrell, are attending school at Ben Smith's house. Mother Terrell was still quite ill, her thumb swollen again and the doctor feared the second joint would come off. All the family had bid a sad farewell when Charles went back from his furlough. His brothers would be leaving the area of Carmel (Church) as soon as the condition of the roads improved. Mollie wrote:

> Oh! I have enjoyed their occasional visits this winter
> so much we are expecting Billy here now. How often
> I ask myself this question, When they too shall
> have gone what will become of me? but only trust

> implicitly in that God that never faileth, he will sustain and enable me to bear all things that he sees are for good farewell Joe farewell, May God our father comfort your troubled heart and return your dear one safely back to your affectionate embrace, is the sincere wish of your aff. sister.[11]

****

Buck Francis wrote that they (the 15th Regiment) were three miles from Petersburg. It was uncertain whether they were going back to Fredericksburg or to Chaffin's Bluff. They had all had "rite bad colds" but were over them now. For some unstated reason Tom has been in the guard house. A letter from Charles twelve days later came from Ivor Station on the Norfolk and Petersburg Railroad, in Southampton County 45 miles from Petersburg. They had marched the distance over dreadful roads in three days to three miles from the Blackwater River, arriving safely but almost all with very sore feet. The Yankees were about 20 miles below them at Suffolk. Charles asked his wife to write often and to send his tobacco by John Wood, who was then at home.[12]

John Wood brought Buck a ½ quire of paper and $25.00 from Liz's husband, John J. Davis. Mr. Davis was considerably older than the Francis brothers and they seemed to look to him to handle their business affairs at home while they were in service. Often their letters included reference to the teenage daughter, Mollie. Buck had expected Mr. Davis to meet him in Petersburg a couple of weeks before but, on returning to camp, he found a letter telling him that his brother-in-law had fallen from a colt. Tom Snead came back to camp with $6.00 for Charles from his wife. He wrote back that she should not have sent it but within less than an hour he had bought a "ham of bacon." They had been drawing a ½ pound of bacon a day but it had been reduced to ¼ pound. Pontoon bridges were being constructed over the Blackwater River and an advance was expected as soon as they were completed.[13]

During April a sick soldier was staying in the home of Uncle Joe Carr Terrell, who had married the sister of Mother Jane M. Francis. Mr. Terrell was in the process of getting together money so James T. (Jim) Francis could pay a substitute. He wrote to Emeline that he thought he could get $400 to $600, possibly more and to tell James to find out whether a substitute would be acceptable. If so, he would get Mr. Davis or a reliable friend to come up there about it. There is no record of Jim ever finding a substitute. His discharge for being overage (36 or 37) was dated March 10, 1863, when the regiment was near Petersburg. It said Jim was 5' 9", with dark hair and eyes and was a farmer.[14]

Jim was needed at home to farm the nearly 300 acres. His father had died in 1846, leaving seven children. Jim, age 17, was the eldest. Their mother, Jane Mildred Terrell Francis, had turned over to him 30 acres before her death in 1859. Buck, 23 years old at the time, auctioned off the remaining land so the estate could be settled. Jim was the highest bidder. Of the seven slaves, he only bid in one, a female. He and his wife Sarah continued to live in the seven room family homestead. By this time they had two children: Mary Jane, age 4, and William, age 2. There were 80 acres of woodland, some ready to be cut for cord wood. The remaining land was arable and suited to corn, wheat, and tobacco. His service record shows the he was given $143.43 in back pay. The men were due $11.00 a month and his company had not been paid since August 31, 1861.[15]

****

A "Bread Riot" was staged in Richmond on April 2, 1863. A crowd of Dutch, Irish and free Negroes – men, women, and children – armed with pistols, knives, hammers, hatchets, and axes broke into and looted shops along Main Street. Thomas McNiven, an associate of Elizabeth Van Lew, said after the war that a lot of American dollars went into organizing the riots. He identified three Richmond city councilmen as loyalists: Richard O. Haskins, Richard E. Walker, and Larkin W. Glazebrooke. Haskins was a councilman for twenty terms, owned warehouses at Rocketts and had been in partnership with Libby before the war. Walker was from Buckingham, became a typesetter for the Richmond *Enquirer*, and captain of the home guard. Glazebrooke was a Hanover native who owned a flour mill in Manchester and part interest in Haxall Mills. He was elected to city council in 1857 and, in spite of being a Union Democrat and against secession, was re-elected throughout the war years. When the monument to General A.P. Hill was erected at the intersection of Laburnum and Hermitage roads in Richmond after the war, the spy network would hold its annual reunion at the base of the statue.[16]

It had been General Joseph Hooker's intention to "harass and menace" General Lee from the west and south with Brigadier General George Stoneman's cavalry before confronting him across the Rappahannock. But there was a heavy rain on April 14 and Stoneman could not get all his wagons and artillery across the river and turned back. Then with the beginning of May, he and Hooker struck at the same time. Stoneman destroyed tracks, depots, and water coolers along eighteen miles of the Virginia Central Railroad before arriving at Thompson's Crossroads on the South Anna River. From there he dispatched the 1st Maine and the 1st Maryland cavalries down the South Anna to destroy the bridges, the 2nd New York to the bridges over the Chickahominy, the 1st New Jersey to the canal aqueduct at the junction of the James and Rivanna rivers, and the 12th Illinois to Ashland.[17]

It was Sunday, May 3. when the 12th Illinois under Lieutenant Colonel Hasbrouck Davis struck at Ashland, cutting the telegraph wires, destroying the track, two work trains, and two locomotives – the *Thomas Sharp* and the *Nicholas Mills*. They intercepted a train of wounded Confederates from Fredericksburg and paroled them before moving on to spend the night at Hungary Station, a few miles west of Yellow Tavern.[18]

Judith McGuire and her husband were visiting their children in Richmond during the Stoneman raids. She later wrote that the enemy had arrived at 3 in the afternoon. The engine of the train was confiscated and the parolees were told that they could walk to Richmond. The Ashland ladies ministered to their needs the best they could. Soon the cavalrymen made off with all the horses in town and a few of the "servants."[19]

While Stoneman was threatening Richmond, President Davis was ill with an inflammation of his throat and eyes. His wife, Varina sat by his bedside and read to him as they waited to hear news from Chancellorsville. The tocsin kept echoing the alarm. Mary Chestnut came with word that she had heard that the Yankees were within forty miles of the city. But, no, General Arnold Elzey had just brought word that they were really only three miles away. Mary dropped to her knees, praying loudly. The two women sat up all night, serving refreshments to the officers as they brought reports to the sick president. With the arrival of morning, Davis got up and with a loaded pistol set out to defend the city.[20]

War clerk John Jones recorded in his diary on May 3 of concern in Richmond that the enemy (Stoneman) had cut the railroad at Trevillians, had reached Ashland and destroyed the depot there. A Mr. Davis brought word to the War Department of the night's events in Ashland. He rode the eighteen miles into the city in an hour and a half, causing his horse to die from exertion. A lad of sixteen years by the name of Shelton came in from Hanover later in the day. He said that 1,500

Federals had foraged their horses on his father's farm and there were possibly three times as many more in the neighborhood. He had been taken as prisoner that morning but had escaped on a United States horse, apparently the one left in exchange for his father's "blooded steed."[21]

The tocsin was sounded for the men in the city, mostly old ones and employees of the government, to assemble in its defense. They quickly organized and marched to the batteries. Clerk Jones said that his son Custis "got a musket and marched with one of the companies." The Honorable James Lyons, a former member of the Virginia Senate who lived at Laburnum, said that the soldiers had come within a mile of his house. In a few days, Dr. Powell came in from Melrose bringing news that he had sent his young son on his finest horse to a neighbor's house on an errand. The boy had come upon "some Yankee Dutchmen" who brandished some pistols and took the horse, but they allowed the lad to return home.[22]

Marion Stewart recounted that when the raiders got within a mile of their house, Captain Byrne, a Irishman who had lost his leg fighting for the Confederacy and was staying with them, somehow managed to get a horse, hid, in the woods, then rode to Richmond with the alarm. The raiders were estimated to be between seven or eight hundred men. Many passed through the yard at "Brook Hill," others by the road to the Meadow Bridges. She thought that they seemed to be in almost as big a hurry to be on their way as the neighbors were to see them leave. They had "committed no improprieties beyond stealing some horses."[23]

Brigadier General David Gregg was able to destroy wagon bridges down the South Anna River through the Ground Squirrel Bridge on the Mountain Road. But he found the railroad bridges well manned by artillery and infantry. Colonel Judson Kilpatrick reached Hungary Station in Henrico on the

R.F. & P Railroad. There he burned the depot before moving to the outer defenses of Richmond. Finding a small battery in the fortifications, he captured a few men and then moved on to the Meadow Bridges. There he crossed the Chickahominy River, burned the bridge and ran a train into the river before proceeding on to Gloucester. Some damage had been done, but the railroad bridges were still intact.[24]

Someone has said that the ubiquitous presence of George Stoneman's men in the area for several days achieved little. Perhaps it was because the men were worn out from their long rides and too much was attempted at night.

Chapter 11

JOY AND SORROW – CHANCELLORSVILLE 1863

In the first five to six months of 1863, there was an intermingling of joy and sorrow on the personal, private, and national stage, with weddings in January and May and sickness and death stalking the roads of the Yellow Tavern area. Also entering the area was a native Marylander and his cohorts of Confederate persuasion.

Mrs. Judith McGuire, while residing in Ashland, wrote in her diary on January 19 that Colonel Bradley T. Johnson had been staying in the cottage with them for some days. He was the nephew of Bishop Johns of the Episcopal Diocese. Judith found him "as bright and agreeable in private as he is bold and dashing in the field." Colonel Johnson in the early days of the war had organized a company at Frederick City to help prevent the passage of Union troops through Baltimore. He and his company joined Stonewall Jackson at Point of Rocks and assisted him until the First Maryland Regiment was disbanded in August 1862.[1]

Johnson's wife, a native of North Carolina and close friend of Hettie and Constance Cary of Richmond, was a staunch supporter of the men under her husband. With the organization of his unit, in ten days time she secured rifles and cartridges for them from her native state and tents, blankets, and camp equipage from Virginia Governor John Letcher as she passed back through Richmond. At their encampment at Centreville that winter, she and the Carys contributed to their entertainment.[2]

Colonel Johnson offered to continue under Jackson and as acting commander of his second brigade at Second Manassas and did so well that Jackson recommended his appointment as brigadier-general. At the time he was at Mrs. McGuire's cottage, he was serving on a military court in Richmond. His promotion was not approved until June 28, 1864. By that time he had played a very important role in reconnaissance of the area around Yellow Tavern. He had assembled the Maryland Line, consisting of infantry, artillery, and cavalry, established a camp called Saint Mary's at Hanover Junction, and proceeded to carry out his assignment to keep communications open between General Lee and the capital city.[3]

Winter cabins were built at the junction. The colonel's wife and her sister, Mrs. Saunders, oversaw the construction of a "neat little" structure for a chapel. Among those who came to conduct services there was the Reverend Mr. Peterkin from Richmond. Mrs. Johnson continued to see that the soldiers were properly attired and entertained. There were parties, balls, and concerts, one of the latter raising $500 for a camp library.[4]

The nearness of the enemy seemed to bring on a spate of weddings. In the neighborhood, John Fontaine, of Beaverdam and the Hanover Dragoons, courted and wed Elizabeth Price of "Dundee," near Hanover Court House, in January 1863. General Stuart and his aide Heros Von Borcke rode the forty-five miles from their winter camp for the wedding. On May 23, a special train was furnished to bring Fitz Lee and his officers to the courthouse area for the wedding of Tom Rosser to Betty Winston at "Courtland." The grounds were well lit and there was an abundance of apple brandy served in the hall. Following the ceremony, there was dancing until daybreak. Between the two ceremonies came word of the death of Elizabeth Price's cousin Channing Price when he was accompanying Stuart in the Wilderness as his aide-de-camp. A shell fragment struck him under his knee. Not realizing that an artery was severed, Price continued to ride until his boot began to fill with blood. No surgeon was nearby nor did anyone have a tourniquet. His brother Tom met him at a house about a mile away. Channing died during the night from loss of blood.

After that Stuart furnished a tourniquet to each member of his staff.[5]

On the following day at Chancellorsville, Stonewall Jackson was fired upon by his own men. Surgeons and tourniquets were available, but his arm had to be taken off and he died of pneumonia a few days later at Guinea Station, beyond Hanover Junction.

Ham Chamberlayne of Henrico had been made an adjutant on General Lindsay Walker's staff. When Captain William Crenshaw resigned his commission in April, 1863, to become purchasing agent for the Confederate government, it appears that Chamberlayne was put temporarily in charge of the Crenshaw Battery. He found the company disorganized and lacking in discipline, but he soon assured his mother that he was "ready for the field with four Napoleon 12 pd. guns and ninety odd men." They left their winter quarters near Bowling Green and trudged through the rain and mud back to Fredericksburg and Hamilton's Crossing.[6]

Chamberlayne is shown to have been in Crenshaw's Battery on May 3 when they, Letcher's and Purcell's batteries along with Captain Richard C.M. Page's Hanover men fired upon Hooker at Hazel Grove, near Chancellorsville. Corporal James Beer and Captain Davidson were killed and their bodies returned to Richmond. The captain was said to have been the most fearless of men and loved by the entire command. Beers, a native of Connecticut who moved to Richmond, was remembered as "the finest gunner in the battery and fought like a Turk."[7]

The Second Richmond Howitzers were with Jackson when he turned toward Catherine Furnace. However, he left them on the hill to hold off an infantry attack. That night they caught up with him. Although they were recipients of severe fighting, they had only four men wounded. After Jackson and Stapleton Crutchfield were wounded, their colonel, J. Thompson Brown, was made chief of artillery under Stuart's command. William Mordecai wrote home to his mother, "The death of our beloved leader (Jackson) fills the army with grief but not despondency."[8]

When Hooker crossed the Rappahannock at Kelly's Ford, Stuart sent Colonel Lucius Davis to hold the Raccoon Ford over the Rapidan River. Some of Davis's men were taken prisoner. As Rooney Lee pursued Stoneman to the James, men of the 10th Cavalry missed the fighting at Chancellorsville. Some of them were at Louisa Court House later when the train passed through bearing Stonewall Jackson's body.[9]

For a few days there was no mail at Ashland. The people had been frightened and had lost their slaves, horses, and mules. Due to a lack of communication between Hooker and Stoneman, the raid had little or no effect on the fighting morale at Chancellorsville. The rails had been repaired so that the train bearing the slain general from Guinea Station on the Virginia Central Railroad stopped in Ashland on May 10.[10]

Mrs. McGuire recorded that almost every lady in Ashland visited his funeral car with flowers. While in Richmond a couple of days later, she heard that Colonel Hasbrouck Davis, who had led the raid on Ashland a few weeks before, had lost a leg near Tunstall (in New Kent County). She wrote, "So may it be!" General Lee was passing through Ashland by train on May 18. Others with him ate at the hotel, but Lee joined the McGuires for breakfast. His "very long and painfully gray" beard brought forth the comment that it made him "look too venerable" for his years. The general "pleaded as his excuse the inconvenience of shaving in camp."[11]

****

In the meantime Buck, Tom Francis and Charles Terrell were having varied experiences in the area of Suffolk. Buck had been left on the Blackwater River, some twenty miles from the action, in charge of the wagons. He was visiting around and sitting up with a dying lady and helping to bury her. Also he was falling in love with first one girl then another. He wrote that he would "have two strings to my Bow so if one will not tie the knot the other will."[12]

General Montgomery Corse had stationed the 15th and 30th Virginia Infantry on the extreme right across the White Marsh Road, adjoining Dismal Swamp, and facing the Federal entrenchments to the south of Suffolk. Tom and Charles stood picket on the outward post two or three times a week, in a slash where they had "to get on a tussock to keep out of the water." Half of the area was covered with water and they were hard put to find a dry place big enough to lie down. Joseph Thomas wrote of their foraging and being in several hot skirmishes. On May 1, he said, they had been throwing up breastworks and in line of skirmish for three weeks, sometimes shooting going on all day. Several in the regiment had been wounded or killed. The day before they had been alerted to the possibility of their joining General John Bell Hood who was one mile to their left.[13]

When Marion Stewart spoke of Hood's men coming through the area, the chances are that they included General E.M. Law and his Alabama regiments. They had fought with Jackson at Sharpsburg and Fredericksburg and assisted in Virginia through Second Cold Harbor. John Cussons, a native Englishman who had fought Indians in America and traveled as far as California, was a captain in the 15th Alabama Regiment and one of General Law's trusted scouts. This intrepid man probably had his closest call in a duel during the siege of Suffolk. When it was reported to the general that the 55th North Carolina Regiment had been slack in facing the enemy, John Cussons denied that he had anything against the North Carolinians but stood behind the fact. The North Carolina officers, under Colonel John Connally, challenged Captain Cussons and his fellow scout, Captain L.R. Terrell (no relation to the Terrells from Hanover), to a duel. Major Alfred H. Belo represented the Carolinians and faced Cussons. Two shots were fired by each Belo and Cussons from Mississippi rifles, one going through the captain's hat and one grazing the major's neck. Then word came from another part of the field, where Connally faced Terrell, that the offensive words had been retracted. The duel was called off.[14]

Major Belo's account was that upon arriving at the fortifications on the Nansemond River, gunboats from the river and stationary batteries were firing on the "Old Fort." The Federals had taken the fort and they met the Confederates leaving. His men had marched fifteen miles that day and their approach was voluntary. The major said that Cussons was known to be a "dead shot." The two had "no personal feeling, had never met before and never met again," although they "had much communication and hope for a meeting." No shot had been fired by either Colonel Connally or Captain Terrell. A few weeks later, when Connally reported the incident to friends and families back home, there was great relief that there had been no deaths or injuries. One of the major's friends said that she knew Belo "had a hankering for fighting a duel" and hoped this would satisfy him. He went into newspaper publishing in Texas after the war and in his memoirs told of one occasion how he tried to discourage an associate in the use of newly acquired dueling pistols.[15]

William C. Jordan was with the 15th Alabama Regiment at Suffolk and on the Blackwater River under Cussons in May 1863 and does not mention the duel. He wrote in his memoirs, "Captain Cousins (sic) would come in from a scouting expedition and report the condition and the position of the enemy and sometimes enter their lines. He was a very remarkable character." Jordan also spoke of leaving the Blackwater area under Cusson's command. His regiment appears to have followed a similar itinerary to that of Pickett and his men from Suffolk to Gettysburg and on to the end of the war. But he did not mention Captain Cussons again.[16]

Longstreet was having second thoughts about the practicality of trying to take Suffolk and was giving attention to the second alternative of gathering food in the area when word came from Lee to join him near Fredericksburg. It took five days to march through the rain back to Petersburg. By that time the battle of Chancellorsville was over and Jackson was dead. Charles Terrell wrote from Petersburg, "The march has knocked me up all most entirely I feel quite unwell today." His letter was sent by a slave named Sam, who cooked for them in camp and must have known the area of Hanover. Emeline wrote back the next day, sending him five dollars and insisting that he come home immediately to get well.[17]

Conditions at home must have made Charles quite anxious. Emeline wrote that the Yankees had been within a mile of their house, but came no farther than the bridge. William Winn's Negroes had camped for two nights on their place and she was quite uneasy. She has been to see her sister Liz whose constitution, according to the doctor, has "entirely given away." Liz's stepson, Bill Hardin Davis, returned home half starved and bringing terrible news of the battle. Emeline rejoiced that her husband and her brothers had not been at Chancellorsville although she had heard that almost certainly they would be. She advised him, since he was sick, to get a pass and "fall out" when they came through the neighborhood.[18]

Aunt Ann (Mrs. Joe Carr Terrell), living near Beaverdam at "Oak Level," wrote graphically of their fright. They had expected the Yankees for three or four days. All the Confederate soldiers had gone. People had been running and hiding. Some families lost all their horses and many of their "negroes." She, although suffering from a heart and stomach ailment and often giddiness in the head, still tried to keep her spirits up. Jo's grandmother, Mary Henley Terrell, age 77, was well and would be coming up from Rocketts soon. Ann Terrell mentioned that Cousin Martha was quite ill, but fortunately none of her sons was injured at Chancellorsville. From the Ashland Artillery – Peter Luck had been killed and John Mosby had been blown away by a shell while he was lying down with some of his men. She was distressed at the news of Jackson's death.[19]

Mollie Goodwin Terrell wrote on May 25 that the Yankee raid and the battle at Fredericksburg (Chancellorsville) had been too much for her mother's "already debilitated system" causing her mind to give way and "she is now as helpless & imbecile as a child." In her saner moments, Mother Terrell would say, "Charles, Charles, name ever dear to me!" Cousin Ann was there to sit up with her that night. Mollie expressed her frustration and pain:

> Joe this is truly a world of trouble. I've thought I had seen trouble in its worst form before this! but now I feel that I am in the severest of all affliction, I pray that grace & strength may be given me to bear up under this and other dispensations of the allwise Creator, who doth all things well! I shall try to 'be patient in tribulation" though I never felt the pressure of such a burden on me before!

Her mother died ten days later, just a few weeks shy of her 56th birthday. She had married Joseph Zachary Terrell in her 20th year, borne him thirteen children, losing three boys and a girl in their infancy or early childhood. Mollie Goodwin was her eldest. The chances are that Charles was at home. There were no letters from him during these weeks.[20]

The mail when it did go through, whether by train or hand delivery, might be in an envelope with the following inscription and a picture of a soldier on horseback:

Bright banner of freedom with pride I unfold thee;
Fair flag of my country, with love I behold thee
Gleaming above us in freshness and youth;
Emblem of liberty, symbol of truth;
For the flag of my country in triumph shall wave
O'er the Southerner's home and the Southerner's grave.[21]

The Ashland Artillery under Captain Woolfolk and Colonel Alexander had been with Jackson at Chancellorsville. One day the general saw one of his sergeants with a new rubber coat. Upon learning that he had gotten it from a row of knapsacks left by a regiment that had passed on down the road, the general ordered the fellow put under "close arrest for stopping to plunder on the battlefield." The captain considered the man an excellent gunner and persuaded the colonel to allow him to return to duty. Alexander often wondered what would have been his and the man's fate should Jackson have survived his wounds.[22]

The artillery battalion had gone with Jackson by Catherine Furnace as he turned Hooker's flank on May 2. Alexander said that at the sound of the bugle for them to charge, deer, turkeys, and rabbits preceded them out of the woods. The Ashland Artillery followed the Federals to the U.S. Ford over the Rappahannock and they were put to digging rifle pits. The next morning they found that they were being fired upon from an unexpected direction. Hooker had slipped across the river and had his artillery covering those yet to cross. The colonel took all his battalion to within a few miles of Fredericksburg except for Woolfolk and his men who were left in the pits until they could withdraw in darkness.[23]

During the fighting at Chancellorsvile, Bettie Alexander and her daughter had boarded with an elderly couple named Wortham, near Carmel Church and overlooking the Mattaponi River. General "Parson" Pendleton came to baptize the little girl. When they could hear the guns, little Bettie would say, "Hear my Papa shoot Yankee, Boo!" Squire Wortham had gotten misinformation that the Confederates had lost the battle and was making preparations to take his wife and boarders into Richmond when they received word that all was well. The Ashland Artillery encamped at Milford after the fighting and the colonel moved his family to live with the widow Woolfolk, mother of three of his artillerists. Room and board was $100 a month, half the colonel's salary, and his promise to watch out for her sons.[24]

Prisoners from Chancellorsville came along Brook Turnpike and stopped for the night at the Old Brook Church on their way to Richmond. It was probably about this time that young Belle Stuart walked out to the road early one morning, as she later recounted to her nephew, "When suddenly she looked toward the north and as far as she could see the road was blue with Yankee soldiers marching toward Richmond." Thinking the city must have fallen; she rushed back to the house and brought others of the family to see the sight. Someone noticed that they carried no rifles and that there were Confederate guards walking beside them.[25]

Chapter 12
BRANDY STATION – JUNE 1863

Jimmie Gray's company in the 10th Cavalry was near Culpepper Court House on May 13. He wrote that they were faring better, the men getting one half pound of bacon a day and the horses fed more fodder. Some of the horses were getting fatter but not his. He wondered if perhaps his brother Pomp could bring the other horse when he came. Fellows from the neighborhood were back and forth on leave. Bunny (Borney) St.Clair and Henry Priddy would probably stop by with the news. Joe Waldrop was looking better than he ever saw him. William Huffman would be coming as a substitute from Hanover. The records show that he served for Taylor Huffman.[1]

In November the 10th Virginia Cavalry had been placed in a brigade under Rooney Lee and sent to Fredericksburg to watch the enemy there. They were in Beaverdam in February and on picket duty along the Rappahannock in April. When General Ewell moved his troops away from Fredericksburg, the 10th Cavalry was in the right place to be involved in the battle at Brandy Station. The Federal cavalry surprised them on June 9.[2]

There were at least a dozen conflicts at Brandy Station from 1862 through 1864. There a little country store on the stage-coach line in Culpeper County advertised its fresh brandy in the days before the Orange-Alexandria Railroad was built. With the coming of war, both armies and their supplies would pass through there during the back and forth campaigns between Washington and Richmond.[3]

John Minor Botts had purchased a farm in the fall of 1862 and moved there with his family in January of 1863. It soon became evident that he had made an unfortunate choice of locality in which to farm. It was near Brandy Station. Both sides would encamp nearby in the winter and fight over the land in the spring and fall. Part of the fighting on June 9 took place on John Botts' land.[4]

Botts was an independent spirit, was against secession, even jailed for eight weeks in Richmond for his views. He had been released from jail on the condition that he move some distance away from the city. Botts had formerly owned land in Henrico County, perhaps it adjoined "Half Sink" on the Telegraph Road. Jimmie Gray and Nat Cross may have run rabbits on to his land from the Gray and Cross homesteads across the road.[5]

Botts wrote that he "had hardly grown comfortably warm in the house before General J.E.B. Stuart came in with his whole cavalry force, took possession of every part of my premises (of 2200 acres), except my house, yard, and garden, turned his horses loose to graze in every field, to the exclusion of my own stock." Stuart put no restraints on his command. They shot the hogs, stole the horses, and when they moved on took some of the Botts' cattle with theirs. When he was finally reimbursed for some of his loss and went to Richmond to replenish his herd, a rumor was spread that he had gone there for other than marketing reasons.[6]

General Alfred Pleasanton had taken over from General Stoneman the command of Hooker's cavalry and proceeded to threaten General Lee's forces as they approached the Rappahannock. Henry McClellan wrote that General Stuart reviewed the brigades of generals Fitz Lee, Hampton, and W.H.F. (Rooney) Lee on the broad fields which lie between Brandy Station and Culpeper Court House. Two weeks later there was another review, this time including twice the number of horsemen, two more brigades having arrived from the valley. General R.E. Lee, though invited, had been unable to attend. The parties were over and many of the guests had returned home when Stuart staged a third review, this time for his commanding general, on June 8.[7]

Having sent all his wagons to Culpeper, Stuart spent the night of June 8 under a fly tent on Fleetwood Hill, overlooking Brandy Station and close to the Rappahannock River. Rooney Lee's brigade was two miles from Fleetwood to the north on the Hazel River. Beverly Robertson's brigade was three miles behind him, on John Minor Botts' farm. W.E. (Grumble) Jones and the artillery were between Stuart and the river, and Hampton was further south, across the railroad. Emory Thomas has written, "The division was well placed for marching – but not for fighting," which is what Stuart's men intended to do on June 9. The Federals came across the river the next morning at 4:30 through the "hovering fog" at Beverly's Ford. These were the men of General John Buford's Division.[8]

The fighting around St. James Church was apparently well contained until word came at 8 a.m. that more Federals had crossed downstream at Kelly's Ford and were threatening Fleetwood Hill. These were men of General David Gregg's Division. R.E. Lee watched from the cupola of the Barbour house one half mile away. Rooney Lee's men were charging on the flank to the north around 3:30 p.m. when he received a thigh wound. That afternoon as General Lee rode out, he met his wounded son being carried to the rear.[9]

The Hanover Dragoons were assigned to outpost duty around Chancellorsville. Colonel Williams Wickham had announced his candidacy for the Confederate Congress, representing the area around Richmond. He was elected by a great majority without ever leaving his troops to campaign. During the fighting at Brandy Station, they were south of the railroad and confronted cavalrymen around Stevensburg. It has been called their darkest day of the war. Coming to the assistance of the

2nd South Carolina Cavalry, they had just come out of thick woods onto the Stevensburg Road when the Federals charged them. The two Confederate units were pushed into each other. Many of the Carolinians ran without firing a shot. Wickham was able to rally a few men to capture a few Federals before they crossed back over the Rappahannock at Kelly's Ford. Fifteen men of the 4th Cavalry had been wounded and twenty-six captured including Sergeant Walter Wingfield of near the Hanover Courthouse. Wingfield was held in the Old Capitol Prison for two weeks before being released.[10]

General Lee wrote to his wife that that he had seen Rooney that night and was glad that neither the bone in his leg nor the artery had been injured. Their son spoke of going to "Hickory Hill" for his recuperation. In a later letter that day, the commanding general wrote that he was sending his son there where "you will now have him with you for a time, and I shall look for you to cure him very soon and send him back to me."[11]

Jimmie Gray's letter to his sister Betty told of his unit's involvement:

> We have had the hardest cavalry fight yesterday we have had since the war began. The bugle sounded yesterday morning about sunrise for us to saddle and we had just enough time to saddle and galloped off about a mile from camp and met with the Yankee sharpshooters in an open field. Supported by cavalry and artillery Col. Davis deployed his sharpshooters on the hill and held them in check until evening when we charged. Col. Davis and Gen. Lee (W.H.F. "Rooney") led us in. Gen. Lee was wounded at the head of our column. We then rallied and charged them again and Col. [Solomon] Williams who after Gen. Lee was wounded took command of the Brigade, was killed and then Col. Davis took command and

> drove them over the river. Our regiment had about 70 men killed and wounded and captured about 50 prisoners. Our company had one man killed named [Louis] Otterburg and six wounded … Sargent [Joseph] McGruder was slightly wounded in the shoulder. Geo. Waldrop slightly in the shoulder and Walter Pruett mortally in the breast. Lucian Thomas was slightly wounded in the arm, just bruised it a little. Lieut. [James] McDowell had his horse killed under him. Tell Pa not to say Col. Davis will not fight again and never to say the 10th Va. will not fight, for we broke the charge of the Second U.S. regulars and the 5th regulars too. The prisoners belonging to the Second said they have been in service seven years but never were handled so well before. The Second is Gen. Lee's old regiment… I think I killed one Yankee and maybe more. I don't think the Yankees lost a great many in killed and wounded.[12]

Nat Cross appears to have missed the Battle of Brandy Station. If questioned later by Mother Catherine, he may have responded, "Don't you remember? I came by here about that time on a detail with Ed Schemerhorn and Corporal Joe Mann?" The roster shows that he was present with the regiment when Stuart made his third ride around McClellan. Lee was expecting Stuart as "his eyes and ears" to meet him near Gettysburg.[13]

Back home there had been reports toward the end of June that the Federals were near Shady Grove Church and the Meadow Bridges. Local forces were sent out from Richmond. These were replaced by General Micah Jenkins and his South Carolinians. They spread out across "Brook Hill" farm and Emmanuel Church grounds to the rectory gate. There they stayed until the end of August, often attended the Sunday worship services. The rector was asked to speak to their vesper services.[14]

When Lee moved north into Pennsylvania, Corse's brigade of General George Pickett's Division was left behind to keep his supply line open for him. For a while they led a very leisurely life at Hanover Junction. Then it was reported that the enemy had landed forces on the Pamunkey River. Joseph Thomas recorded that they marched down into King and Queen County, then back again. Just when the locals could have helped defend the area around their own homes, most of Corse's troops had been sent to Gordonsville. They had set out on foot, only to be picked up by the "cars" to arrive there on the morning of June 26. On June 28 and 29, when the Federals struck the South Anna bridges, the 15th Virginia Infantry was returned by train to the Virginia Central station in Richmond. They marched to the Osborne Turnpike in eastern Henrico County, only to be returned to Gordonsville on July 1. The lines of communication were down between Richmond and Lynchburg.[15]

Two companies of the 44th North Carolina Regiment under Lt. Colonel Tazewell Hargrove had been sent to General Corse's assistance at the railroad bridges. Colonel Samuel Spear and his 11th Pennsylvania Cavalry, in retaliation for the threat to their native state, burned the quartermaster depot at Hanover Court House and one bridge over the South Anna River before returning to their supply base at the White House. Although they had not been completely successful, they did have with them as prisoners about 100 men, including Colonel Hargrove, and Rooney Lee.[16]

There are at least two accounts of Rooney's capture, both told by members of the 11th Pennsylvania Cavalry. The first, written by William Shirley in 1884, told of meeting a colored man and asking if there were any "Rebs" ahead of them to which the man replied, "God bless you all; General Lee is just ahead." The Federals replied that could not be because General Lee was marching north. The fellow said, "But, I knows him. I was his slave. It's de young man; de cavalry General, William Fitz Hugh Lee, and his colored man is driving his coach with two bob-tailed horses." The second account, by W.B. Troy, reported that they followed the old man and "found the general at his country seat." Troy said that they put the wounded officer on a mattress in the family carriage and continued to the White House.[17]

Actually Rooney Lee was at "Hickory Hill," the home of his wife's relatives, the Wickham family. With Rooney on that day were: Mary Custis Lee (his mother), Agnes and Mildred (his sisters), Rob Lee (his younger brother), William F. and Anne Carter Wickham and two of their grandchildren, and Charlotte, Rooney's wife. Charlotte's father had died before she was born and her mother died when she was very young. Her grandfather, Williams Carter of "South Wales," had taken the young Charlotte on as a ward. Apparently she spent a great deal of her time also at "Hickory Hill." Rob has recounted that Rooney was staying in the office. When they heard that the Yankees were at the gate, Rooney told him to flee with the horses across the river (to "North Wales" in Caroline County). But Rob watched from the limbs of a fir tree while the Federals drove away with his brother.[18]

Colonel Spear and his men bivouacked for the night on Mrs. Henrietta Nelson's farm, "Wyoming," just across the Pamunkey River from Hanover Court House but in King William County. The Widow Nelson was very much perturbed when she saw that happening, but she became elated when she learned that Rooney would be spending the night in her house. She, her daughters, and the servants got together the best supper they could from their meager fare and she gave Lee her best room for his quarters for the night. Sergeant Stephen

Tripp of the 11th Pennsylvania Cavalry posted a guard at the door while he slept in the adjoining room.[19]

R.E. Lee wrote to his wife from Hagerstown, Maryland, on July 12, telling of his concern for the "injuries done the family at "Hickory Hill" & particularly that dear old Uncle Williams [Charlotte's grandfather] should be subject to such treatment." He had earlier written from Williamsport of his concern for Charlotte and Cousin Anne and that he "had not expected that he [Fitzhugh he called him] would have been taken from his bed & carried off." Rooney remained in prison at Fort Monroe and later at Fort Lafayette (in New York) while negotiations were in progress for his exchange for Federal prisoners held in Richmond. By the time of his return to his troops in March, Charlotte had died and he never got to see her again, although his brother Custis had offered to take Rooney's place while he visited her death bed.[20]

The Federals returned on July 3 for another attempt to complete the destruction of the bridges. This time their purpose was to cut the communications line at Ashland. There they destroyed one bridge, railroad tracks and equipment, and took away the telegraph instruments. General George Getty made his headquarters at Hanover Court House and Mrs. Nelson's wooden bridge was burned to the water's edge. Uncle Williams Carter's place was ransacked. He was hit over the head and died from his injuries.[21]

Chapter 13
GETTYSBURG – SUMMER 1863

Lee was moving his men into Pennsylvania. General Richard Ewell with the 2nd Corps had gone toward Carlisle. General Hill was with 23,000 of the 3rd Corps between Chambersburg and Gettysburg. Lee himself was traveling along with Longstreet's 14,000 of the 1st Corps. Pickett's division of 5,000 men had been left to protect the rear and the trains at Chambersburg. Lee ordered General Ewell to bring his corps of 23,000 back to Cashtown. Ewell's and A.P. Hill's men were subject to severe fighting on July 1.[1]

Edward Stackpole, in his book *They Met at Gettysburg,* has written, "The town of Gettysburg nestles in a small valley surrounded by low ridges and hills, with the South Mountain range looming on the horizon 10 miles to the west." Lee's headquarters on June 28 was near Chambersburg on the Gettysburg Pike. General George Meade had taken over from Joe Hooker. Longstreet's scout brought Lee word that the Army of the Potomac "was not only unexpectedly alive and kicking under a more worthy commander, but was actually moving rapidly forward in such a way as to constitute an acute danger to the widely dispersed Army of Northern Virginia."[2]

The artillerists of Crenshaw and Letcher batteries, serving under Colonel E. Porter Alexander and General A.P. Hill, had first moved northwest from Fredericksburg to Winchester and then on to Pennsylvania. Their experiences can be traced in Ham Chamberlayne's letters home to his mother, formerly of "Montrose" in Henrico. He wrote that their horses were in a deplorable condition. Ham led a contingent of twenty-six men into Millerstown, west of Gettysburg, on June 28 to obtain fresh mounts. It was a Sunday and he found the horses tied outside a church. Striding into the worship service, Chamberlayne promised the startled parishioners that they would be reimbursed when a peace treaty was signed by the governments of the United States and the Confederacy.[3]

The relief was short lived. Not many miles down the road they ran into a strong force of enemy cavalry. Ham and six other artillerymen rode into the Federals, covering the others' escape. Chamberlayne and three with him were taken as prisoners. While Willie Pegram and his other gunners fought in the melee at Gettysburg, Ham Chamberlayne languished in the prison at Fort Delaware and later at Johnson's Island until he was exchanged a year later.[4]

For the Ashland Artillery, the march to Gettysburg was beside ripened wheat fields and along dusty roads. Positions in the front of the line were coveted. Pichegru Woolfolk and another captain argued and challenged each other to a duel. It was scheduled for July 2; however, by then their batteries had been called into action against Federal infantry. Starting at 1 a.m. they marched under moonlit skies to arrive at Gettysburg around sunrise to water and feed their horses about a mile west of Seminary Ridge. Ashland Artillery's two 20-pounder Parrots were held in reserve. Before the day was out, seven of the Ashland Artillery, including the captain, were injured and one missing. Captain Woolfolk had sustained a right shoulder wound during a "gallant evening charge." This injury kept him out of active fighting for the remainder of the war while his brother James led the battery. Four of the wounded Ashland gunners were taken prisoner. Three would be released the next March, Samuel Mills, Richard Mason, and Josiah Perkins. Joseph O. Moody would die at Fort Delaware the next February and be buried at Finn's Point on the New Jersey shore.[5]

It had been decided that Thomas Ellett was of sufficient maturity to take command of the Crenshaw Battery. His appointment came through on July 3, the very day that he was wounded at Gettysburg. It was November 2 before Ellett was back with his battery to take over the command he would hold until the end of the war. Up until July 1863, the Crenshaw, Letcher, and Purcell batteries had fought with 10 pounder Parrots, 12 pounder howitzers, even a 6 pounder smoothbore. Each battery had had twelve to eighteen serious engagements. There would be twenty-two to twenty-five more battles. Before the war was over, they were possibly the most heavily used units in the Virginia artillery. The Letcher Battery was bereft of their beloved Captain Greenlee Davidson who had been mortally wounded at Chancellorsville on May 3.[6]

The Courtney Battery, sometimes called Captain (William) Tanner's Battery which contained some Henrico men, had been in the Second Corps since the days of Jackson in the Valley. With the reorganization they were assigned to the battalion of Colonel Hilary P. Jones (of Hanover). They had been left to protect Fredericksburg when Lee moved to confront Hooker at Chancellorsville, and were called on to help at Hazel Grove. Tanner's Battery participated in the second battle at Winchester in June before moving on with Early to the east of Gettysburg. They were used along the Heidlersberg Road on July 1 and the York Pike on July 2, where they suffered few casualties themselves and did not know that on a nearby hill the "Boy Major," Joseph Latimer, had been mortally wounded. When they were escorting the supply wagons back to the Potomac, Thomas Haskins was taken prisoner at Waterloo (Rouzerville, PA).[7]

In the summer of 1863, the 2nd Howitzers were back in the area of Sharpsburg. They camped at Chambersburg on June 24, then moved on toward Carlisle. Two days later they reversed their march, arriving at Gettysburg after the fighting had ceased on July 1. The next morning they were positioned west of the town. The fighting commenced about 4 p.m., lasting until dark settled in. That night they slept among the unburied bodies of the enemy. The retreat on July 5 was made in driving rain. Sergeant Mahlon Terrell, the assistant to the regional quartermaster, and five others in the company were taken prisoner as the Federals approached from the rear. Terrell's record shows that he was taken at Waterloo, Pennsylvania, and sent to Point Lookout Prison in Maryland.[8]

It is unfortunate that a letter written after Gettysburg by James Cross to his cousin Lucy Ann Cross is not extant. He was among the wounded in the Morris Artillery and was escorted back to Richmond possibly by her brother Nat and his fellow cavalrymen. The gunshot wound in his knee was treated in a Richmond hospital. Perhaps, before he returned to duty in January, he got to visit her a number of times and they discussed the grief of Jane Browning and her children over the death of her son John at Gettysburg, and that the Stone family had brought the bodies of Benjamin and Joseph Stone back to Hanover for burial. Apparently the body of Thomas Woody was never recovered from his burial in the field.[9]

There were others that James Cross and Lucy could have talked about. Had he heard that Benjamin Hazelgrove and Charles Woody were back in service or that William Chapman had died of measles at Fort Delaware? Perhaps they discussed that Zephaniah Rice had been exchanged, and that William Toler, who had been left behind to nurse the wounded prisoners, had also been exchanged. Marcellus Lowery and Joseph Pleasants were still at Point Lookout prison in Maryland.[10]

Their Hanover neighbors in the Harrison Guards were under General Pickett in the first wave that crossed the Emmitsburg Road and climbed the hill on Cemetery Ridge. Pickett on his coal black horse watched "in the orchard at the Cordori house within musket range of the Federal position on the ridge." One hundred and fifty men and General Lewis A. Armistead went over the wall. They captured the guns, but the Federal infantry was rallied and the general, with his hand on one of the disabled cannons, was fatally wounded. There, beyond the wall, many of his men remained unsupported until taken captive. Among them were six Hanover men and their captain.[11]

Three of the new prisoners had also been taken previously at Fort Donelson: Edward Kelley, William White, and William Wood. White died at Fort Delaware and was buried at Finn's Point in New Jersey. Peter McGee was captured while serving as a nurse to the wounded. Their beloved colonel, William Dabney Stuart, a cousin of J.E.B. Stuart, was mortally wounded and would die at his home in Staunton on July 30.[12]

Wickham's men were among those Stuart had taken around Meade into Pennsylvania. When the fighting began, they were on the extreme left flank. It had been supposed that the Confederates were in control at Carlisle, but when General Chambliss got there he found Union men. The 10th Virginia Cavalry, led temporarily by Colonel Lucius Davis, made contact with elements of Lee's command on July 2. Stuart sent word for them to remain in the saddle all night. Davis replied that the men and horses were exhausted. The horses grazed and the men devoured the sheep they had captured .The troopers got their first night's rest in weeks. The next day they engaged Federal cavalry near Rummel's barn. The 10th Cavalry had one killed, nine wounded and two taken captive that day.[13]

While escorting the Confederates back to Virginia, Colonel Davis's horse was shot in the head, subsequently falling on him. The colonel was badly bruised, sprained his ankle and was taken prisoner. The 10th Cavalry lost three officers at Hagerstown and had seven men wounded and eight others captured that day. Davis was sent to Ft. McHenry, Johnson's

Island and Point Lookout prisons. During the next three weeks, two other men – John White and Leonidas St. Clair – were taken prisoner as they rode on Lee's flank toward Fredericksburg.[14]

The artillery also accompanied the wagons and the wounded back to Williamsport. There they were met by General John Imboden with a new supply of ammunition. They set up camp a mile or two from Hagerstown, hoping to cross the river the next morning, but it was too swollen with the heavy rains. On July 13, the Potomac was low enough for some to ford at Williamsport. Others built pontoon bridges across the river at Falling Waters. Colonel Alexander said that they had marched during the night three miles on "awful roads, in mud & dark, & hard rain … [but] were still some distance from the bridge at sunrise."[15]

Augusta Mordecai and her brother George were in Richmond on Sunday morning July 12 visiting their Aunt Emma. The news coming in from Gettysburg was depressing and George was most cast down. He had not considered that any army in the world could defeat Lee's. The news coming in later in the day stated that Lee had retreated and was being pursued. The Richmond Howitzers had been in the hottest of the action. The Mordecai brothers and their McCarthy friend (Julian) from Richmond were safe. Emma saw the slightly wounded coming into Richmond that night. Some of them had been put in ambulances, but the greater number of them were walking. They heard at "Rosewood" that the generals Early, Imboden, and Breckinridge, with their corps, would "liberate our 35,000 prisoners at Pt. Lookout. A very hazardous enterprise."[16]

It is from the diary of John B. Jones, a clerk in the war department, that we can learn what was transpiring at the Powell home "Melrose" during the summer of 1863. He wrote: "My good friend Dr. Powell, almost every week, brings my family cucumbers, or corn, or butter, or something edible from his farm. He is one in ten thousand! His son has been in sixteen battles – and yet the government refuses him a lieutenancy, because he is not quite twenty-one years of age. He is manly, well educated, brave, and very qualified."[17]

John B. Jones, a man in his fifties, lived with his wife and three or four children in a rented house in Richmond. Their two sons, Custis and Thomas, served under Custis Lee in the Department Battalion and were called out by the ringing of the tocsin in the Capitol Square in Richmond. The older daughter, Anne, was often away teaching and the younger one, Fannie, was at home with her "fat cat" which also had to be fed. Jones, in his small garden tried to raise potatoes, yellow tomatoes, speckled lima beans, cabbages, red peppers, and turnips. In the fall and winter, Dr. Powell brought him apples, persimmons, sorgum molasses, and rutabaga turnips.[18]

Buck Francis wrote home from Winchester on July 15 that they had marched 100 miles in six days. It was raining and they waded through water most of the time. Charles Terrell was sick, had been left behind at Gordonsville and perhaps was already at home. The fellows in the regiment had heard about the reversals at Gettysburg and feared they would have suffered the same had they been there. Buck was having dreams about what might be happening at home.[19]

On September 5, Buck Francis wrote that they were back in camp in Orange County and he had finally heard from home. Things were so quiet there that it was hard for Buck to realize a war was on. He said that they were amusing themselves by catching rabbits. Charles had returned to camp bringing four chickens, three of which he kept for himself. He also brought Buck a piece of his sister Barbara's wedding cake to sleep on. Buck said that he couldn't dream of any girls because his bed was so hard. There had been an "excellent meeting" (revival) in their regiment with twenty-seven converts, their brother Tom being one of them.[20]

Barbara also wrote of the revival saying that her brothers Nick and John had been baptized and expressing her wish that Charles would be also. She spoke of her "good companion" – her new husband, Mr. Johnson she called him – and that she has been busy making wine, making preserves and drying peaches. She said that sugar was high but Mr. Johnson said that it was as cheap as anything else and she also wrote that Father Terrell had a (feather) bed and stead for Jo if she would send for it. Brothers Nick and John Terrell were home a short time and Barbara sent her letter by Nick, who has been made a sergeant.[21]

Nick and John Terrell's captain, Pichegru Woolfolk, was sent back to Caroline to recuperate from his wound and to recruit more men. It became the responsibility of his brother James Woolfolk to sign the requisitions for twenty-three more horses, "twenty-eight pairs of shoes, eight shirts, and one hat." In August Colonel Alexander took his daughter and pregnant wife Betty to near Milford to stay with the mother of the Woolfolk brothers.[22]

It is in a letter from Jimmie Gray, in Orange County, to his sister on September 22 that we learn that revivals were being conducted by three ministers: a Rev. McCartney, a Rev. Boggs (Charles H., a Methodist from King William County), and the chaplain in the 10th Cavalry Rev. Taylor (James B., a Baptist from Henrico).[23]

Captain Hopkins of Yellow Tavern had been on disability leave since March because of his eyes. He offered his resignation in August. Apparently Lieutenant James McDowell had recovered sufficiently from his wound at Brandy Station so he could take over the command of the

Henrico Dragoons, although McDowell's disability continued to plague him throughout the war. There was another cavalry battle near Brandy Station on October 11, with mainly the 9th and 13th Cavalry regiments under Chambliss being engaged. Others in the 10th Cavalry Regiment were left to support the artillery.[24]

John Minor Botts unashamedly entertained officers from both sides in his home. All were made welcome except General Stuart and a Captain Randolph who commanded troops stationed on his farm. The fighting was within a stone's throw of Botts' doorstep. He took over twenty men, both Union and Confederate, into his house for treatment and buried some of the dead. Stuart instructed his adjutant Major Reid Venable to have Botts arrested, taken to Richmond, and not to "allow him to annoy General Lee, but keep him as a prisoner of state." However, he was taken no farther than Culpeper and soon released.[25]

Theodore Garnett, of Hanover, an aide to General Stuart, wrote:

> The green fields and lovely meadows which are here spread out in magnificent expanse in front of John Minor Botts', Kennedy's and Wise's [farms] were once more, and for the last time I believe, made the scene of hostile encounter. Charge after charge was made in rapid succession, battery after battery brought into action, until the whole available force was joined in an awful fray.[26]

According to Jimmie Gray, there was a review of cavalry in November which was attended by General Lee, Governor Letcher, and "all the big generals." Jimmie felt that such an affair was a waste because one man was killed and three others "badly hurt by their horses falling." Five days later he wrote of the urgency that his horse "Fleet Foot" should arrive before his present horse broke down completely. He had asked his Pa to send it by Tom Sheppard when he returned to camp.[27]

The Botts family household was made up mostly of women. Timothy O'Sullivan, a photographer of the ilk of Mathew Brady, took a picture of them on the porch of their home in Culpeper County. It shows the burly John Minor Botts, a younger bearded fellow, and four either young or frail women. Botts wrote that after his arrest and the fighting on his farm, his daughter "has been ill of nervous typhoid fever ever since." Theodore Lyman, an aide to General George Meade, talked to a niece at the Botts home the next spring at the time of a Union review there. He found her a "dwarfish little woman of middle age, who seems a great invalid. She was all of a tremor, poor woman, by the mere display of troops, being but nervous and associating them with the fighting she had seen round the very house."[28]

On September 9, Williams Wickham had received his commission as brigadier general in Fitz Lee's division. He first participated in the Bristoe Station Campaign and later in the Mine Run Campaign. The death of Captain W.B. Newton, of "Summer Hill," on October 11, was much lamented. David Timberlake, of Atlee Station, took over as captain. John B. Fontaine was made Stuart's assistant medical director. The general commended him for his efficiency during the fighting in November when all the wounded as well as those killed had been removed from the fields. By the end of the year, Major Fontaine had been made the cavalry medical director.[29]

The Confederate cavalry had been divided into two divisions with the Henrico Dragoons, still under Chambliss, also being placed under Fitz Lee and participating in the fall campaign. In December Fitz Lee took them through a sleet storm into the Valley in the pursuit of Averell's Federal raiders and then back over frozen ground to camp in Orange. Jimmie Gray wrote to his family that some of the men had frozen feet but he was fine.[30]

That fall Captain Tanner of the Courtney Artillery was so seriously wounded at Bristoe Station on the Orange and Alexandria Railroad that he had to be taken from the field. A few days later he was taken prisoner at Warrenton, having been too badly wounded to be moved when the army withdrew. He was sent to Fort Delaware and Point Lookout prisons, exchanged in December, but never able to return to his battery. Royal Ford, of Henrico, was wounded during the Mine Run Campaign. Lieutenant Benjamin Maxwell, also of Henrico, was put in charge of the battery. He was of medium height with light complexion, auburn hair and hazel eyes. In late December, he took them into winter quarters at Fredericks Hall, where they built log cabins for themselves and shelters for their horses.[31]

Chapter 14

TENNESSEE – FALL 1863

It is possible that the Terrell brothers were given a few days at home as Alexander's Battalion marched through the area on their way to Richmond and Petersburg. When they passed through Louisa Court House, the colonel left the troops for five days to spend a delightful time with his wife Bettie in Mrs. Woolfolk's home in Milford, just a few hours by rail to Petersburg. His artillery had been designated to go with General Longstreet to assist General Braxton Bragg in Tennessee.[1]

Alexander wrote that the Federals had taken Cumberland Gap and the only rail route open to them was through the Carolinas and Georgia. The horses were put in stock cars, the guns on flat cars while most of the men and officers rode in box cars. They passed through Weldon, Wilmington, Kingston, Sumter, and Augusta – 852 miles in about 182 hours, arriving too late to take part in the Confederate victory at Chickamauga. Alexander and his staff got to share a delicious supper with his sister in Atlanta. The colonel received a telegram from home saying that Bettie had given birth to twins on September 21. Mother and children were doing fine.[2]

Three regiments of Corse's Viginia brigade, the 15th, 29th, and 30th, not having been involved at Gettysburg, were again detached from Pickett's division and sent to Eastern Tennessee and Western Virginia They marched to Richmond with the division, making camp one night near Emmanuel Church. Many of the fellows "ran the block" when they passed near their homes. Others were given a few hours off on September 13 to visit family and friends. Reverend Walker was asked to speak to some of Longstreet's troops near "Brook Hill." It was the last service held in the old Brook Church. By this time it was only a shell of a building, consisting of the walls, flooring and roof. The next July a campfire was built too close and the old timbers went up in flames.[3]

These infantrymen were sent to the assistance of General Samuel Jones, a Virginian commanding Georgia and Florida troops in the Department of Western Virginia. His headquarters was in Dublin, Virginia, and his major responsibility was the defense of the Virginia and Tennessee R.R. and the salt and lead mines. Knoxville had fallen to General Ambrose Burnside on September 2. General Jones received word on September 9 that the garrison at Cumberland Gap, under General John Wesley Frazier, had surrendered. Burnside marched up the Holston River with a force estimated at 30,000 strong. Jones was sick with diphtheria and had to remain at Abingdon for five or six days.[4]

This area can be likened to a right hand reaching up to grab the heart of the South. The thumb points toward Kentucky, West Virginia, and Ohio. The forefinger from the eastern slope of the Allegheny Mountains (Cumberland and Clinch mountains) points to the valley beyond the Blue Ridge. Through the valley itself are the fingerlike streams and rivers that make up the 140 mile Holston River as it flows southwest from Virginia into the Tennessee River west of Knoxville. There along the Virginia and Tennessee R.R. the Virginians were engaged from Bristol and Abingdon nearly to Knoxville. At the same time Grant and Sherman moved to the elbow at Chattanooga.

Charles Terrell's letter from Zollicoffer (Sullivan County in east Tennessee) told of a pleasant trip "all the way in the cars." On the way, he wrote that they had met a good many of his old acquaintances and they were fed plenty of beef, flour, and fruit. The crops looked good along the way. They had found themselves surrounded by the enemy (probably cavalry scouts). Charles wrote that there had been a fight on a Sunday in which they were able to push the Federals six miles with no losses among the Confederates. Word had come, he said, that General Bragg had whipped the enemy and "gained a great victory."[5] Was this at Chickamauga? Zollicoffer is not on our current maps. It was a few miles into Tennessee and six miles west of Blountsville.

Corse's brigade reached Zollicoffer on September 20. Jones ordered them to remain there with a field battery in strong position. The enemy was at Blountsville and tried to turn the Confederate left. The Federals were forced back to Blountsville and retired to Carter's Station, where they were met the next day by some of the same Confederates. Burnside sent word "to warn the non-combatants along the railroad … he would probably fire on the villages." During an artillery duel with one of the Confederate batteries, Blountsville was fired upon and the best part of the village burned. Jones said that his force was too small to hold Carter's Station and Zollicoffer, so he retired to the latter. Burnside burned the bridge at Carter's Station before he moved back toward Knoxville. Upon an urgent request from General Lee, Jones returned Corse's brigade to Virginia.[6]

Buck Francis found his first trip to Tennessee very enjoyable. However, he wrote that he would never take a wife from there because the women were all so ugly. They dressed the body well but wore no shoes or socks. While they were back in Virginia, Tom Barnet got a 15-day furlough to marry Judson Butler's daughter. Buck commented that "he had better stay single than get plural." He instructed Sister Jo to make him a waistcoat out of his old uniform, to send him his small blanket and Tom his overcoat. The good news was that that Tom had been baptized by Parson Willis in the Holston River the day before they came back to Virginia.[7]

Upon Charles Terrell's return to camp in Petersburg, he wrote that he hoped they would remain there for the winter. He was concerned about affairs on the farm and told his wife to go ahead and advertise for a cow. He said that she should do as she pleased about the corn although he really thought she would have enough to last out the winter.[8] On neither this trip nor the one back in November, did Charles mention seeing his brothers. There must have been times when they were no more than a few miles apart. Brother Joe Terrell probably remained with General Forrest's cavalry north of Chattanooga. The acquaintances on the train may have been fellows in the Caroline Grays of the 30th Virginia Infantry.

While the 15th Regiment was back in Petersburg, Joseph Thomas and the wounded Andrew McDowell, the recruiting officer at Hanover Court House, were sent on a 20-day detail in Hanover to bring back absentees. When they visited a home just south of Ashland, a "woman" in a "long-eared slat bonnet" came into the room and told them that her brother was not there. After the war they learned that the "woman" was the absentee they were seeking. Upon his return to camp, Private Thomas learned that his regiment had started back to Tennessee.[9]

In mid-October General Jones began to feel more threatened and requested the return of Corse's brigade. General Gabriel Wharton marched troops from Staunton and Winchester, through Orange and Warm Springs to Jonesborough (Tennessee), and Abingdon. Jones reported that they had been marching for three months and "the men were badly clad; scarcely one third of them were shod." The general said, "Corse's brigade was but little better provided for, and was without transportation. Every effort was made to procure clothing, shoes and transportation" before the troops were moved into Tennessee. He said that the enemy had come within five or six miles of Abingdon, but fell back after "destroying the railroad and other depredations."[10]

On November 7, the cavalry under General W.E. Jones captured 700 to 800 Federal cavalry and a "field battery of 4 pieces, 60 wagons, and about 1,000 horses and mules" at Rogersville, (30-40 miles west of Blountsville). Soon after that General Jones had to go to West Virginia where his line was threatened in the Kanawha Valley. Before he could return General Longstreet moved eastward from Knoxville and was given control of the troops in that part of Tennessee. Corse's brigade was put under the command of General Robert Ransom.[11]

Jo Terrell received a letter from her husband at Blountsville congratulating her on the birth of their daughter Emma. He was still concerned about the fattening of the hogs and he said that if she thought she could make a crop next year to go ahead and try, providing she found someone to help her. Charles told of a fight in which they captured 904 men, five pieces of artillery; and all the enemy's baggage and equipment. Plans were to send his letter in the next day or two by whomever would be taking the prisoners to Richmond.[12]

When the artillery arrived in North Georgia, Longstreet had already been victorious at Chickamauga three or four days before. Colonel Alexander left them in camp and went to consult with the general and learn the terrain. His diary shows little action during October:

> Oct. 5, Monday Shelled Chattanooga
> Oct. 10 to 12 Reconnaissance to Bridge
> Oct. 30, Friday Occupied Lookout Mountain & shelled everything daily until Nov. 4th.[13]

In November General Bragg sent Longstreet, with McLaws' and Jenkins' divisions, northeastward to confront Burnside and his Ninth Corps at Knoxville. The artillery did not join them until November 15. The rail service along the 140 miles had been slow, the train stopping to secure fence rails for fuel and warmth. Provisions were scarce. The colonel shot quail and rabbits for the officers' mess. The Ashland Battery had four 20-pounder Parrott rifles. During the fighting at Campbell's Station on November 16, one of Woolfolk's rifles burst open.[14]

The Confederate siege of Knoxville was unsuccessful. The artillery was often moving at night. There were high winds and intense cold. Many of the men were without shoes or tents for shelter. They crossed the Holston River at Cobb's Ford, set up their winter quarters on December 23 at Greenville, and built their huts on the southwest slopes of the hills.[15]

The 15th Virginia Infantry, like the artillery, was constantly on the move between Bristol, Blountsville, and Knoxville, never in one place longer than a week. Joseph Thomas has written that they forded the Holston River with the water up to their armpits. In early December they went to help Longstreet in the siege of Knoxville. He said that there was snow on the ground and ice in the river. Their shoes gave out and they marched barefoot on frozen ground. Food was scarce and they were often on half rations. Until their winter quarters were started in mid-December, the men slept in their fly tents. Thomas said that they left Bristol on boxcars about the first of February for Petersburg, where they transferred for Goldsboro, North Carolina.[16]

****

Back in Virginia the Hanover Dragoons were giving out of mounts. Jimmie Gray feared that his mare would not hold out until he could get her home. He urged his father to send him "Fleet Foot" by Tom Sheppard. Also he urged his brother Pomp to be brave and come with him. There were constant crossings at the fords north and east of Culpeper during the month of October. Stuart and his cavalrymen were attempting to get around behind General Meade. On October 17, they were joined by the infantry. Colonel John R. Chambliss took his men after the Federal cavalry along the Orange and Alexandria Railroad and soon they participated in what came to be called the "Buckland Races." Chambliss in his report gave Sergeant Henry C. Winston, of western Henrico, credit for being among those "who have on all occasions acted with marked gallantry."[17]

The local artilleries – Morris, Courtland, and Richmond Howitzers – were with General Lee at Bristoe Station during the operations in October. The general found that the enemy had destroyed so much of the railroads that he feared to be too far from his supplies. Nor did he wish to attack Meade in his entrenchments at Washington and Alexandria. He wrote President Davis that he was not prepared to invest these places at that time. So Lee turned to the Rappahannock River.[18]

Meade crossed the Rapidan River, which his aide Theodore Lyman called the "Rapid Ann", on November 26 initiating the Mine Run Campaign. Lyman, wrote that on December 2 at 2 a.m. they were glad to "roll themselves in our blankets in the same camp we had the night of the 26th." This ended what he called the "Great Seven-days' Flank," a failure due, he said, "to Slowness and want of Detail."[19] The ground was frozen and it was time for both sides to go into winter quarters.

However, General Lee had other plans for his cavalry. Fitz Lee received orders on December 11 to go into the Valley in search of W.W. Averell's raiders. The Henrico Dragoons marched through Charlottesville to cross through the Blue Ridge Mountains at Brown's Gap. They marched through a sleet storm, over frozen ground to Buckhannon, and terminated their search at Fincastle. On the way back they picked up, in a couple of counties in West Virginia, some cattle, sheep and other food for the Confederate army. They crossed back over "snow covered mountains on New Year's Eve." The weather was bitter cold and many had frozen fingers and toes.[20]

Jimmie Gray wrote to his sister on January 18 saying that he "was not frost bitten as you heard but two or three of the boys are slightly frosted." At that time, he said, "We are snugly fixed in our tents with chimneys to them and I think we can winter very well provided we can get something to eat." He had heard that the "soldiers around Richmond hadn't had any meat for ten days." He hoped it was not true.[21]

With the opening of 1864, General Lee had decided to try to take back New Berne, North Carolina, which had been lost to Burnside in 1862. Fort Anderson was just across the Neuse River. General Pickett with gunboats, infantry, and cavalry set out on an expedition from Kinston on January 29 to capture New Berne. After some skirmishing, this attempt was abandoned on February 3. Upon arriving in Petersburg from Tennessee, the 15th Virginia Infantry joined this expedition and was dispatched to Kinston, North Carolina, where it was assigned to the capture of Fort Anderson. The men marched through "miserable swampy country, over rivers, creeks, branches, and frog ponds, a distance of fifty-three miles, in twenty-seven consecutive hours."[22]

Buck Francis wrote home from a camp near Goldsboro on February 8 that the fort was found too strong for them and they did not attack. He said that they had been moving all the time in the last twelve days with hardly any time to wash their face and hands. By Buck's estimate they had all together marched 380 miles and ridden on "the cars" for an additional 530 miles. Half the company was barefooted. Charles Terrell, without shoes, was left on the last leg of the journey in

Kinston to be transported the rest of the way. Although the expedition was not successful, 200 prisoners had been taken, one gun boat with four guns, three pieces of artillery, a good deal of clothing and blankets, and best of all a sutler's shop.[23]

Five weeks later the Ashland Grays were again camped near Kinston, having marched southwest to Lexington, North Carolina, supposedly to quell an unrest in that locality. Tom Francis had found that the people were kind and friendly, the young ladies pretty.

He said that he hoped to go back there after the war to get a wife. Tom had apparently been home and brought Buck some writing paper from Jo but left a needle case made for him at their Aunt Mary Hendrick's house. Charles Terrell's record shows that he was granted a special furlough on February 29. On March 10 there was great concern in camp. The Francis brothers had heard that the Yankees had been in their home neighborhood and they wondered at the damage done.[24]

There was sadness in Dr. Terrell's household, certainly shared by the family and neighborhood, when word was received of the death at Point Lookout prison of the doctor's brother, Mahlon Terrell on February 1. Frances Cross, Finch's wife, recorded her step-brother's death in his mother's (Louisa Thornley Terrell) Bible, but gave no cause of death. Was it from a neglected injury, scurvy, or constant diarrhea due to an inadequate diet? How did the doctor and his wife Agnes explain to young Chapman and Julia that their beloved "Uncle Maly" would not be coming home?[25]

A government inspector in November 1863 had found the sick at Point Lookout Prison "in a filthy condition" with no stoves in their tents. A local gazette reported the men being "all in rags." Of the 8,384 prisoners at Point Lookout in January, 534 were sick. A recorded 587 prisoners were released during that month. The chances are that Mahlon's body was buried three times: first along the beach of the bay, second after the beach had eroded along Tanner Creek, and third in 1910 at Scotland on Maryland Route 5 where the Federal monuments have been erected.[26]

****

Increasingly the Henrico County Court had become aware of the needs of the people. They had the sheriff "make a list of all indigent soldiers and sailors enlisted from the County in the Confederate service or State service who had been or might be disabled or honorably discharged, and of their families,...and of the widows and minor children of such as might have died or might thereafter die in the service." They appropriated money for relief of the poor and set aside the second floor of the courthouse for storage of supplies and food, sent shoes and socks for soldiers from the county who might be in need and purchased salt for distribution. The county showed concern for the many refugees that had come into the county, the occupation of so much of the land, and the loss of slaves so the farmers could no longer produce. A special list was to be made up of those who had suffered outage due to the presence of the enemy and those who had been especially considerate to the soldiers.[27]

Charles Philips was overseer of the poor for the fourth district. The 1850 census had shown twenty Blacks, ten of them sixty years of age or over, in what was apparently the poor house of the district, overseen by Albert and Judith Michaels. The smallpox hospital was in the Fairfield area. The governor had ordered slave owners to send one or more slaves to work on the fortifications and other means of defense. On the list for Henrico were: Mrs. Frances Hopkins; Dr. John M. Sheppard, – three slaves; Dr. A.J. Terrell; John N. Powell – two slaves; C.G. Paleski – two slaves; and Abner Hilliard – two slaves.[28]

Some of the cases that came before the Henrico grand jury in March 1864 had to do with free persons of color. Betsy Smith was being held in the jail for failure to register. She was hired out to the county jailer until her jail fees of not less than ten cents a day could be paid. At that time they amounted to seventy-five dollars and fifty cents. Tom Charles was accused of stealing a side of beef worth $350.00 and belonging to Sampson Levy and Charles Rohr. A criminal court of Oyer and Terminal was opened. Evidence was heard followed by argument of counsel. He was found guilty and, in lieu of confinement in the penitentiary, was punished "by sale into absolute slavery."[29]

In 1864 Henry Holland wished to open a road from his place to Brook Turnpike. Anderson King petitioned the county to change the public road from "Half Sink" to Bowe's Bridge and Dr. Thomas Wooldridge wanted to build a road from his mill in Hanover to the Ryall's Mill Road in Henrico. The court instructed that any inconvenience to John Thomas' yard, garden or orchard be looked into should such a road from the mill be built.[30]

Chapter 15

KILPATRICK AND DAHLGREN'S RAID – 1864

It was late in January 1864, when Colonel Thomas E. Rose and a selected few officers in Libby Prison tunneled, using only their hands and a knife, the fifty feet from the east basement to a nearby building. They loaded the dirt into a spittoon. Using a rope, they pulled the spittoon into a windowless room the prisoners called "Rat Hell." This room, where unruly prisoners were often confined, could be entered by removing a stove in the first floor room and slipping down the chimney. One hundred and nine men escaped through the tunnel on the night of February 9. Some of the men made their way through the icy Chickahominy Swamp, their clothes freezing to them "as stiff as sheet-iron." They were hidden for a week in the homes of loyalists on the Hanover side. Fifty-one reached Federal lines.[1]

Miss Elizabeth Van Lew had darkened her windows and had her room ready that night, but was elsewhere. She wrote in her diary that she spent a few days trying to secure the dismissal of her brother who had been conscripted into the Confederate army. On February 15 she visited her friends near Howard's Grove where four of the escapees were being secluded. They had been led there by a Mrs. Greer and were secluded in her "humble house" by a Mrs. Rice. Elizabeth recorded, "Two of these gentlemen were quite sick and looked very feeble. Mrs. Rice herself was not in good health."[2]

One of the prisoners in Richmond was a 32-year old sergeant from the 6th Michigan Cavalry named Jacob Osburn. He, along with 433 others in his unit, had been captured by General Imboden's men at Charles Town on October 18, 1863. Eight days later, Washington Nelson, of the Hanover Artillery, was also captured by the Federals just a few miles away. The prisoners of the Confederates were marched, footsore in their cavalry boots, to Staunton and put on "cars" to pass through Hanover and Henrico to prison in Richmond.[3]

Cryptic letters passed between General Benjamin Butler and Miss Van Lew, addressed affectionately to "My Dear Aunt" from "your nephew." Butler did not wait to carry out her plans but staged his own unsuccessful raid from Williamsburg by way of Bottom's Bridge in lower Henrico.[4]

It had been a rainy, wet 1863-64 fall and winter along the Rapidan. Colonel Lyman recorded that John Minor Botts visited General George Meade in his camp and invited the general to dine with him. Lyman described Botts as a "tough and unterrified" character who told that the rebels had treated him badly, burnt the fences on his farm near Brandy Station, shot his cattle and took all his corn and provisions, and finally arrested him and took him as far as Culpeper, but there concluded he was a hot potato and set him free.[5]

Lyman, General Meade's adjutant, wrote to his wife that she must not come to join them with her "small hoops" because the roads were so bad, varying from mud "from fetlock to knees, then holes, runs, ditches and rocks." He said that the land had been camped on, fought over, until now it was just stumps and an occasional headboard where a soldier had been buried where he fell. There had been a review of the 2nd Corps on February 23 with Colonel Judson Kilpatrick leading the cavalry in the usual manner of "Gypsy and Don Cossack" (?), followed by the artillery and the infantry. It appeared that a raid was in the making because President Lincoln called for Kilpatrick. On February 28, the 3rd Corps and General Custer with his cavalry moved to Culpeper. That night Kilpatrick and his cavalry headed toward Richmond. General Meade heard at 2 a.m. that he was in Spotsylvania. Lyman wrote that was the last they heard from him.[6] The adjutant made no mention of Dahlgren's accompanying Kilpatrick.

With President Lincoln's approval General Kilpatrick and Colonel Ulric Dahlgren left the Rapidan on February 28 with 4,000 cavalrymen and six guns. The night was moonlit with a little ground fog, but the weather soon changed to snow, sleet and rain. Kilpatrick, age 27, and Dahlgren, age 21, were a study in contrast. Theodore Lyman, on observing Kilpatrick at the review a few days before this at Stevensburg, said of him that he "is hard to look at without laughing." He had been dressed that day "in a rakish manner, [and was] below medium height, small of body, with reddish-sandy hair, gingery sidewhiskers, and a hawklike face."[7]

Dahlgren, from his picture was a tall, handsome young man with sandy hair and trimmed chin whiskers. He was the son of Rear Admiral John A. Dahlgren, commander of the U.S. fleet at Charleston. Ulric had lost his right leg just below the knee soon after Gettysburg. After several months of recuperation and having been fitted with an artificial leg, he had been promoted to colonel and could ride with his crutch strapped beside him.[8]

They proceeded to Spotsylvania Court House and then divided. Dahlgren and his cavalry went by way of Frederick's Hall to cut telegraph lines and destroy the Virginia Central R.R. They wished to prevent Lee from sending infantry to support General Hampton and his 1,500 cavalrymen in the area. The plan was for Dahlgren and his men to go through Goochland, cross the James River, destroy the Richmond & Danville and Richmond & Petersburg railroads, and then to release the prisoners on Belle Isle. Some of Kilpatrick's men were to destroy the R.F. & P. Railroad at or near Guinea Station, join his main force at Carmel Church, and then proceed to Richmond by way of Hanover Junction. Rations had been issued for only three days: hard bread, sugar, coffee, salt but no meat. The *New York Herald* was projecting that this raid was to destroy artillery (at Frederick's Hall), the Virginia Central and the R. F. & P. railroads. The Richmond *Dispatch* was already setting its type to correctly deny that Lee and the Second Corps artillery had been captured and to say, "This raid is no doubt intended to disrupt communications between Lee's army and Richmond, but it is hoped that, like Stoneman's raid last spring, it may prove a failure.[9]

Carter Anderson was the conductor on the Virginia Central train the day that Kilpatrick approached Anderson's Ford, on the North Anna River, about two miles from Beaverdam depot. He said that the troopers struck the railroad at Terrell's Crossing and camped for the night on Colonel Edmund Fontaine's farm, "Colley Swamp." They took the "sleds and horses, but did not tear up and destroy track." Anderson recounted that Dr. Charles Terrell and G.N. Thompson, called Galley, both local residents and members of the Hanover Dragoons, were home on furlough and had planned to go hunting that day across Anderson's Ford in Caroline County. At the ford, Galley dropped the reins so his horse could drink and was talking over his shoulder to the doctor when a cavalryman across the river called for his surrender. Thompson was taken along by his own home. Seeing a neighbor, he called out, "Tate, tell Lucy Ann [his wife] the damn Yankee have me, but I will be home to dinner tomorrow." He was true to his word. By digging himself out of a tobacco house that night, he made it home the next day for dinner.[10]

The doctor was far enough behind to escape capture. He rode to Beaverdam to give the warning and then to his home to send their meat by ox cart to a safe hiding place in the woods. With the sound of Anderson's train coming from Richmond, Dr. Terrell rushed to the tracks to give the alarm that invaders were between them and Beaverdam. Anderson told a hair-raising account of their race backwards to Hanover Junction with what they took to be Federal cavalry. The passengers hunched down between the seats and the black brakeman hung down on a step of a car on the opposite side from expected bullets. They had to take on water at Noel. Upon reaching Hanover Junction, Anderson was told to take the train on the R. F. & P. tracks and report to Richmond, "dead-heading" all passengers with tickets for west of Hewlett's. Dr. Terrell was brandishing a pistol on his way home near Beaverdam when he met a man in a Federal uniform. He was about to fire when the soldier threw up his hands and called out, "Friend!" It turned out that he was a member of the Maryland Line as were the cavalrymen on the stampeding horses who had raced the retreating train.[11]

In November, Colonel Bradley Johnson and his Maryland Line had been assigned the duty of protecting the six bridges over the North and South Anna and Little rivers. They were instructed to destroy all the boats on the Pamunkey River as far as New Kent County and to alert General Lee of any movement of the enemy from that direction. Johnson set up a camp he called "Saint Mary's" at Hanover Junction.[12]

The skies darkened. Snow and sleet began to fall as Kilpatrick and his men neared Beaverdam Station. Soon the night was alight from twenty burning buildings, including the new freight house, telegraph office, passenger depot, water tower, and outbuildings. The telegraph operator was captured before he could send a message. However, word had already reached Richmond that they were on their way. Two Confederate spies, Hugh Scott and Dan Topping, after relieving two of the Federals of their horses, slipped into the line of march and out again. Another scout had watched earlier in the night, before the skies darkened, as the cavalry rode by in the moonlight. Wade Hampton alerted Colonel Johnson and told him that he would join him at Hanover Junction.[13]

Dr. L.B. Anderson, of Hewlett and captain of the North Anna Home Guard, got word that the Federal soldiers were at Beaverdam. He collected his men and, slipping through the woods avoiding all roads, was watching when the raiders stopped for a short while for food and coffee. As soon as the Federals were back in their saddles, Dr. Anderson entered a nearby house and wrote a dispatch to Richmond. Rain, snow, and sleet continued to fall and the riders' frozen clothes crackled as they rode along. Kilpatrick feared that the rivers would rise. Only the South Anna remained to be crossed. He had planned to cross Ground Squirrel Bridge, but the guide took them closer to Ashland and they crossed the river three miles above the town. A number of pickets were captured, and they told Kilpatrick that 2,000 Confederate infantry and six guns were nearby guarding a railroad bridge. He dispatched 450 of his men of the 6th New York Cavalry to cover the movements of his column. It was then daylight, March 1, and they had been on the move since 2 a.m. Liz Davis recorded in her notes on the war that the Yankees were at her place on March 1.[14] It may have been the 6th New York.

When Colonel Johnson was notified that the Federals were approaching, he already had dispatched many of his men to scout the region and had only sixty men left back at camp and two guns from the Baltimore Light Artillery. His men came upon Kilpatrick's pickets at Beaverdam and heckled them in the rear through Taylorsville and Ashland to Yellow Tavern. There they set up a false picket line in Federal uniforms and intercepted Kilpatrick's communication from Dahlgren. The Richmond *Dispatch* later reported that Kilpatrick had been on Brook Turnpike near Yellow Tavern. It said that his first stop was on Mrs.Hillyard's farm (a little southwest of the tavern). From there they moved forward to Mrs. Taylor's farm.[15]

Colonel Walter H. Stevens was in command of the Richmond defenses. He got word of the approaching enemy on Monday,

February 29. He moved his artillery to three strategic points and doubled his pickets at the main road intersections. When he rode out Tuesday morning, he heard artillery firing in the direction of Ashland. Back at his office, he received word that the raiders were confronting his pickets along Brook Turnpike. According to Virgil Jones in his book *Eight Hours Before Richmond,* there were remaining under Stevens' command in the city only "500 men and six pieces of artillery."[16]

The trainman, Carter Anderson, told of Mrs. Chisholm's reaction at Hanover Tavern during the time of Kilpatrick's presence in the area. Fearing the uncertainty of Clive Chisholm's responses, she hid him under two featherbeds and hung her grandson's nightshirt in front of the bar, saying. "If they be Union, we are Union, if they be southern, so then are we." The first to appear was General Wade Hampton and his cavalrymen. The lady boarders were peering around the proprietress at the handsome officer when the general asked where all the men folk were. Mrs. Chisholm replied that all who were any account were in service and the remaining were down at the depot. Hampton said that he was looking for the Yankees and needed to know the roads in the area.[17]

About a dozen men were huddled around a stove in Barney Briell's store at the depot when the general called out, "Hallo!" Seeing the yard filled with cavalrymen, someone shouted, "Kilpatrick's men!" Almost all the men dove for a hiding place, behind the counter, in a ditch, or in a culvert. It was so funny that one man said that he could only sit there laughing. A soldier gently opened the door and walked in saying, "General Hampton is out here and he wants to know about the road to Richmond." Mr. Briell rushed out to the mounted general but got so confused in his explanations that he finally sent a redheaded boy for "Colonel" Andrew Wingfield to come and give proper directions.[18]

Hampton's cavalry took the road that would have led to Brook Turnpike. But when his men got to Booker Hazelgrove's store at the intersection of the Richmond road and the one to Atlee Station, they learned that Kilpatrick had turned southeast toward the station. About midnight, they could see through the snow and sleet the reflection of the Federal campfires in the woods east of Atlee. The troopers were fifty yards away from the sleeping men when the Carolina sharpshooters opened fire into their midst causing a stampede and the capture of 150 men, 200 horses and equipment – "saddles, bridles, blankets, pocketbooks, etc." John Jones, the Richmond clerk, wrote in his diary that General Hampton sent in seventy-seven prisoners, one of whom was a colonel and more horses were coming in each day.[19]

Dr. Thomas E. Williams, a surgeon in the 2nd North Carolina Cavalry was called upon to treat the wounded prisoners and ordered to take them back to Hazelgrove's store where they could be more conveniently cared for until removal to a Richmond hospital in the morning. The doctor had gotten the fires going at the store and was awaiting the arrival of the ambulances when he heard the sound of approaching cavalry. This time it was Dahlgren and his men who were looking for Kilpatrick. The doctor explained that he was caring for wounded Federals. The courteous Dahlgren allowed him to keep his horse and to pillage the nearby house for stimulants for the suffering men. The next morning neighbors searched the campsite for valuables left behind. One lady found a purse with many greenbacks. She was able to trade them for $1,000 in Confederate money and to purchase land for her and her husband's home after the war. She was heard to comment, "It's an ill wind that blows nobody good."[20]

Custis Lee, the general-in chief's son, had been drilling five battalions, one each from the armory, the arsenal, Tredegar Ironworks, the Navy, and government workers. The Virginia

Armory housed the munitions from Harpers's Ferry. By afternoon the tocsin in the Capitol Square was sounding the alarm. In the basement at Libby Prison stood a six foot high mound of dirt covering enough explosives to blow the prison "sky high" should the raiders come nearby.[21]

The Stewart girls were at school on the morning of March 1. They heard the frantic ringing of the alarm bells and rushed outside to see old men, boys, and hospital patients march out to defend the city. The story goes that the men put their hats and coats on sticks like scarecrows and rigged up logs and wagon wheels to resemble cannon. With a yell, they fired what guns they had. In the swirling fog, the enemy pickets were convinced that the defenders had more men and guns than they were using and, fearing a trap, they fell back.[22]

In Marian Stewart Peterkin's account: "The quiet of the winter was broken by a cavalry force of about two thousand five hundred men passing through on the first of March 1864." She went on to say that the Federals got as far as the second fortifications. They were repulsed by eighty artillery men firing from Young's field, assisted by 250 to 300 townspeople. The fighting went on from noon to 3 p.m., some of the shells passing over Emmanuel Church. The Federals who were not engaged camped on Brook Hill and helped themselves to forage and horses throughout the neighborhood. Reverend Walker and his son were caught between the lines but were not held long. The invaders left by way of the Meadow Bridges. Others (Dahlgren's men) came through that night. They left by way of "Half Sink" on the Telegraph Road, hence over the Chickahominy River.[23]

John Jones wrote in his diary Dr. Powell's account of the soldiers at "Melrose" during the raid. The doctor and his wife had been called to Petersburg where Blanche was visiting and had apparently fallen ill. The slaves saw the soldiers approaching and one of the women picked up the silver and took it to her house. They told the invaders that there were no spoons in the house, that the master had his watch with him, and kept his money in the bank. The house was searched, drawers and presses opened. Nothing was found except some milk which was eagerly drunk. The soldiers could not induce the slaves to go with them. Two horses and eight mules were left on the farm and at least one cow, which Dr. Powell sold with her calf for $2, 500 in May.[24]

Dahlgren, after causing destruction in Goochland County, had been unable to cross the flooded James River. He sent a sergeant and five men to tell Kilpatrick that he would attack Richmond at dusk. The young colonel proceeded along muddy roads with the sleet still falling. The chances were that the stump of his leg was "burning and chaffing against the wooden limb." On the Three-Chopt Road near the intersection of the Westham Plank Road and the Benjamin Green home, Dahlgren first came upon the "carbine factory boys" and then the city clerks led by Custis Lee. There was nothing to do but to charge right though them, taking prisoners. The Federals heard the firing from Kilpatrick, but when it died down they thought it had failed.[25]

Darkness fell and renewed firing convinced Dahlgren that the Confederates had been reinforced. He gave the order to retire and, finding his way around the road blocks, skirted to the north of the city. Captain John F.B. Mitchell, bringing up the rear guard in the newly fallen snow, became separated from Dahlgren. They were fired upon and could see what they thought to be campfires as they approached Hungary Station. It was a miserable night. On toward morning, Mitchell and his men crossed the Chickahominy at the Meadow Bridges and joined up with Kilpatrick near Tunstall's Station on the Richmond and York River Railroad.[26]

The 9th Virginia Cavalry had been assigned picket duty from the Mattaponi River to the Piankitank River (east of Richmond). Many men were home on furlough so only about one hundred and fifty men were on duty. They marched over frozen ground between Hanover Junction, Taylorsville, Ashland, and Hanover Court House. General Hampton sent them word that Kilpatrick's men had turned toward Tunstall. There they found the half-extinguished campfires and met up with a picket from Colonel Bradley Johnson's command. Soon a courier brought Colonel R.L.T. Beale, in charge of the 9th Cavalry, a message that some of his men had ambushed Colonel Dahlgren and his men (at Mantapike in King and Queen County) and that Dahlgren had been killed. The young colonel and his small group had pushed to the north, crossed the Pamunkey at Hanovertown and the Mattaponi at Aylett. They had been heckled through King and Queen County by the county home guard and a portion of the cavalry from King William County under Lieutenant James Pollard. Ulric Dahlgren was killed, his body rifled of his wooden leg, a finger bearing a ring, and the papers he was carrying. He was buried without a coffin the next day in the country.[27]

The lieutenant reported that the next day they captured about one hundred and fifty men and officers, about forty slaves, more horses than there were men, and the silver goblets, pitchers, and cups which were tied to the saddles. Orders came from General Fitz Lee that Dahlgren's body be brought to Richmond for identification. Pollard said that the body was taken up, put in a newly made coffin, and sent along with the papers the thirteen year-old William Littlepage had found on the body. The papers were instructions that the Belle Island prisoners be released, and "once in the city it be destroyed, and Jeff Davis and Cabinet killed."[28]

Elizabeth Van Lew made the longest entry in her journal on the Dahlgren affair. She appears to have instigated the raid by her letters in cipher to General Butler, starting in January 1864, by reporting on the troop strength around Richmond and that the prisoners would be moved from Belle Isle to Georgia. She recorded that the colonel had been buried "in a slashy mud hole about two feet deep in the fork of two roads." A few days later, she said, he was disinterred and brought to Richmond and lay in a boxcar on the York River Railroad. He was secretly buried by the Richmond authorities on the edge of Oakwood Cemetery among other Union prisoners.[29]

Miss Van Lew must have been present at the removal of the body "on the cold, dark, rainy night of April 5th." It was put into a wagon and carried to the farm of a Mr. R., outside the city. The next day the young colonel's remains were placed in a metal casket. She described his appearance in detail – attired in a coarse shirt, dark trousers, a cotton sock on the only remaining foot, wrapped in a blue military blanket – and the lack of a little finger where his ring had been cut off. Elizabeth cut locks of his hair to send to his father. They proceeded out the Brook Turnpike with the coffin concealed under a load of young peach trees. At the picket station, the driver chatted with the guard but his cargo was not searched. At Yellow Tavern, the wagon was turned on a country road to go about ten miles to a farm (said to have been that of a James Orrock, near Hungary Station) for burial under one of the peach trees.[30]

To her brother, a midshipman on Admiral Semmes's ship the *Alabama*, on March 4, 1864, Mrs. President Davis wrote telling of the Dahlgren raiders and their instructions to burn the city and kill the leaders. She said that she and her sister Maggie had no horses or carriage to flee with their baggage. She had put on all the clothes she could: "seven petticoats, 3 chemises, 2 pair of stockings on my legs and six pair buckled round my legs by my garter." Maggie had on "quite as much with the addition of two dresses and her cloth coat." They were weighed down so that they could not possibly have run. She expected the raiders, although already forty miles away, to return to make another attempt.[31]

General Henry E. Davies, of the Federal 3rd Cavalry Division commanding detachments from New York, Maine, and Indiana, reported that they were the ones who had tried to capture the rebel train that backed away from them. They had burned the building at Beaverdam, and skirmished with about twenty-five dismounted men before camping about six miles farther on the road to Ground Squirrel Bridge. He said that three hours later they crossed the South Anna at daybreak, destroyed the railroad bridge, crossed the R.F. & P. Railroad two miles below Ashland and destroyed the telegraph wires.[32]

When Davies and his men met artillerymen at Brook Bridge, they found the ground "too soft and muddy, and intersected with wide and deep ditches," not suitable for maneuver of cavalry. Davies reported that they left the area by way of the Meadow Bridges to camp near Mechanicsville. Soon they made connection with Captain Mitchell and his detachment and then with some of Butler's men on the Williamsburg Road. From April 11-14, they were being shipped from Yorktown to Alexandria.[33]

On March 5, Colonel Theodore Lyman wrote to his wife, Mimi, saying, "I fancy that Kill [Kilpatrick's nickname] has dished himself. It is painful to think of those poor prisoners hearing the sound of guns and hoping a rescue was at hand! Now all that cavalry must be carried back in steamers like a parcel of old women going to market." There were questions concerning the authenticity of the papers found on Dahlgren's body: his note book, instructions to Sergeant Mitchell, and the message to the troops stating that President Davis and his officials be slain. Mitchell testified that he was given his instructions, but it was never verified that the message was given to the troops. General Meade wrote to his wife that "Kilpatrick's reputation" and the evidence produced make it unlikely that the papers were forged.[34]

The correspondence continued between Miss Van Lew and Benjamin Butler. She expressed her outrage at the way the Confederates had treated the body and the absurdity of the documents reported to have been found on Dahlgren's body. After the war his body was moved to Washington and then to lie in state at Independence Hall in Philadelphia. The controversy over the papers lasted well into the next century. They were passed around until now only a photographic copy remains in the National Archives.[35]

Chapter 16

THE ROAD TO YELLOW TAVERN –MAY 1864

Stuart had been conferring with General Lee on May 9 when word came of Sheridan's movement toward Richmond. Fitz Lee's Division was immediately dispatched in his pursuit. Stuart and a few of his officers started at 3 p.m. His aide, Theodore Garnett, wrote that the general was in a sinister mood, not humming his usual songs - "Her Bright Smile Haunts Me Still," or "Ever of Thee I'm Fondly Dreaming." The 19 year-old bugler from Waynesboro, George Freed, riding just behind Stuart, remarked, "General, I believe you are happy in a fight?'' Jeb's reply was, "You are mistaken, Freed. I don't love bullets any more than you do. It is my duty to go where they are sometimes, but I don't expect to survive this war."[1]

A major of the 5th Michigan Cavalry has described Sheridan:

> There was nothing about Sheridan's appearance at first glance to mark him as the principal figure in the scene except for the fact that he rode in the front one might have mistaken one of the other officers for the chief. But close inspection easily singled him out. He was well mounted and sat his horse like a real cavalryman. Though short in statue he did not appear so on horseback. His stirrups were high up, the shortness being of leg and not of trunk. He wore a peculiar style of hat not like that of any other officer. He was square of shoulder and there was plenty of room for the display of a major general's buttons on his broad chest. His face was strong with a firm jaw, a keen eye, and extraordinary firmness in every lineament. In his manner there was a alertness, evinced rather in look than in movement. Nothing escaped his eye, which was brilliant and searching and at the same time emitted flashes of kindly good nature. When riding along or past his troopers, he had a way of casting

> quick, comprehensive glances to the right and left in all directions.[2]

General Theodore F. Rodenbough has written that Sheridan's men were well chosen. Of his division commanders and other commanders, he said: D. McM. Gregg had the confidence of the entire corps; Wilson was quick and impetuous; Custer was like a meteoric saber; Irvin Gregg was steadfast; Merritt had the old guard manner and Devin that of an old war horse; Davies was gallant; Chapman was student-like; and McIntosh seemed to be the last of a fighting race. Custer had his blond locks cut short for his February wedding. A remark had been made that it was hoped that Custer would not share the fate of Sampson.[3]

The story goes that on the day before the raid Sheridan and General Meade had words over the proper use of the cavalry at Spotsylvania. Disgruntled Meade went to Grant with Sheridan's words that he "could whip Stuart if Meade would only let him." Grant's comment was, "Well, he generally knows what he is talking about. Let him start right out and do it." Rodenbough said that they spent little time in preparation, stripping the command of unserviceable wagons, animals, and tents. They took the ammunition train, only two ambulances to a division, three days' rations, a few mules, and each man a half day's forage on his saddle. They started from Hamilton's Crossing and scouted around the outer edge of the Confederate pickets and took the Telegraph Road to Chilesburg and toward Richmond. Within a couple of hours they were passing Massaponax Church.[4]

Williams Wickham and his cavalry joined in the pursuit. They made contact with the 6th Ohio, serving as the rear guard, at Jarrald's Mill. There the Confederates took some prisoners. The Federals turned toward Beaverdam and their rear guard was strengthened by the 1st New Jersey Cavalry. After a brief skirmish the Confederates withdrew, only to harass Sheridan's rearguard again at Mitchell's store above Chilesburg. Wickham was coming through Chilesburg at 5 p.m. when the first of Sheridan's men arrived at Beaverdam and began burning the supplies there. By that time Wickham had been joined by Stuart, Fitz Lee, and two more brigades. The Federals encamped that night at Andersen's crossing of the North Anna. Stuart's men remained in their saddles all night.[5]

Bradley Johnson had gone on a scout to Yorktown, leaving Ridgely Brown in charge of his encampment at Hanover Junction when word came that Sheridan was raiding behind Lee's lines and had already destroyed rail lines and stores of provisions above Hanover Court House. The gleam of Sheridan's campfires could be seen from their camp at the junction. Colonel Brown set out westward toward Beaverdam with about 150 cavalrymen. As they neared the station, they could hear the Federals laughing and shouting while they set fire to the railroad cars. Upon Bradley Johnson's arrival thirty minutes later with 80 or 90 dismounted men, the arsonists had disappeared up the road and pickets posted. The area was lit by the still burning cars and supplies. Prisoners were taken. Captain Schwartz and Lieutenant Pue, of the Maryland men, were wounded and taken to the home of a Mr. Redd, five miles away, where they were carefully cared for. The skirmishing continued between the mounted and dismounted men until daylight revealed that it was not a raiding party but Sheridan's advance. Word had come from Stuart that they must "harass the enemy as long as possible as he was in pursuit."[6]

Colonel Bob Randolph led the 4th Virginia Cavalry through the smoke of burning woods and fences toward Beaverdam. They crossed the North Anna at what Theodore Garnett called "a very bad ford," and near the station, they came upon "a body of the enemy standing in the road to dispute their approach." Charging into them, the Confederates were able to retake twenty prisoners who had been taken in the fighting in the Wilderness. In the skirmishing Albert Blake, of the Hanover Troop, was wounded in the thigh and three days later he was admitted to the Chimborazo Hospital.[7]

The Philadelphia Inquirer carried Sheridan's report that on May 10 he had turned the enemy's right and had gotten into their rear, causing great excitement among the citizens. Sheridan said that his cavalry had taken back 500 prisoners including two colonels, had been successful in destroying eight to ten miles of the Orange (Virginia Central) railroad, two locomotives, three trains, and a large amount of supplies. He added that they had not encountered a sufficient number of the enemy to stop them but expected to fight them below the South Anna River.[8]

A member of the 1st Maine Cavalry remembered the entanglement with Brown's men as a veritable "hornet's nest." So many of his fellows were killed by the Confederate sharpshooters that a metal chest was confiscated from a nearby house, its partitions knocked out, and the corpses placed in it for burial. The owner protested the use of his chest, but got quiet when a Federal brandishing a revolver threatened to include his body with the already deceased.[9]

We have the recollections of one of the prisoners being marched to Richmond. He said that the local people along the way had been heard to remark that they looked just like their men. He said that he could not help but hope that some of the pretty girls along the way would not despise them. A rumbling of trains was heard and whistles sounded for the guards to hurry them up. One train contained rations and the other medical supplies for Lee's army. While the Federals destroyed the trains, local Blacks handed out the sugar from the damaged barrels to the famished prisoners and tried to scoop up the gushing whiskey. The prisoners were told to stay nearby and to pick up any arms or take what mounts they could less they be taken prisoner again. Major J.H. Kidd, riding with Custer, spoke of the capture of commissary supplies, saying that they destroyed everything that they could not carry, "every trooper having his horse loaded to the limit with such supplies as he thought he could use."[10]

In the early morning of May 9 residents near Davenport's Bridge may have been aware of the presence of some of Sheridan's men in the area, seeking to cross the North Anna. Had the neighbors heard that General Wickham and his men were pushing the Federals hard and trying to encircle them? Sheridan already had some of his men around Beaverdam wrecking havoc. He wished to consolidate all of them there where there was forage. Then he would proceed along the Negrofoot Road, cross the South Anna at Ground Squirrel Bridge, burn the bridge and take the Mountain Road to meet Stuart at Yellow Tavern.[11]

One of the Federal cavalrymen remembered how very hot it was for an hour or so that day. The bridge was being repaired from earlier damage and a local black man showed them a ford that the Confederates had been using. Confederate scouts found another ford upstream. Soon the 2nd and 3rd Virginia cavalries created a "general melee, sabers and pistols being used freely." The Virginians claimed that they scattered Captain Abraham Arnold's 5th Cavalry in all directions. However, the route was kept open to Little River, where Sheridan's rear guard crossed and the bridge was dismantled just ahead of the Confederates. The Federals used the Negrofoot Road to Ground Squirrel Bridge, burned the bridge then proceeded along Mountain Road.[12]

In Richmond heavy firing had been heard from south of town for several days. The militia, city clerks, and the city battalion had been called out until there were no longer any local defenders within the city. Mrs. Judith McGuire heard that raiders had cut the Virginia Central Railroad, had burnt cars with supplies for Lee's army, and had damaged public and private property. The telegraph lines had been cut and there had been no word from General Lee except by private telegrams from Guinea Station. Mrs. McGuire wondered how the city could be so calm. Her son, who worked for the war department, came in with news that had come by courier that 7,000 raiders were within 17 miles from Richmond and headed toward the city. She said that women in her neighborhood dressed and went out on their porches and into the streets. When word came at 2 a.m. that Stuart was in pursuit, the women went back into their houses and back to bed.[13]

Leaving Wickham in Sheridan's rear on May 9, Stuart, Lomax, and Gordon took their men to the west toward Davenport's Bridge and crossed the North Anna the next morning. At that point Stuart slipped off to Beaverdam to visit his wife and children who were staying with Colonel Edmund Fontaine's family. Miss Fontaine said that the general did not dismount, but ate some fresh cooked asparagus brought to him from the kitchen, dropping some of the gravy on a poodle dog he held in his arms.[14]

Upon returning from his visit with Flora, Stuart again divided his forces, leaving Gordon to follow Sheridan along the Negrofoot road by old Trinity Church, while he and Fitz Lee took the road leading to Hanover Junction. Theodore Garnett said that they halted at Fork Church, turned the horses to graze on Major Price's clover. ("Coolwater" was the home of Captain Thomas Price of the Revolution). General Stuart stretched himself out "at full length on his back in the fresh rich clover and with his hat over his face was shading his eyes from the glare of the setting sun." Stuart turned to Garnett, lying at his side, and said, "I know where you want to be ... Well go on and join me in the morning wherever you can find me." The young man needed no further urging. Soon he was with his father, mother, and the family at a mere seven miles distant. He stabled and fed his horse, quieted the family's fears that the enemy might be passing along that road, and fell asleep in his own bed.[15]

Stuart found the road to Richmond blocked by felled trees. He had to take a parallel road to Hanover Junction and Taylorsville. Riding with Stuart and Fitz Lee were Lomax's and Wickham's men, and Stuart's adjutant Henry McClellan, first cousin of the union general. Henry was a native of Philadelphia who had studied for the ministry. At the opening of the war, he was a private tutor in Cumberland County, Virginia. Sympathetic with the Southern cause, he joined the 3rd Virginia Cavalry and was made Stuart's adjutant at the death of Channing Price in 1863. It was a few hours after dark when Stuart reached Hanover Junction. Stuart wished to continue on, but Fitz Lee's men were too tired. A bivouac was ordered until 1 a.m. McClellan was ordered to see that Lee's men were on the move at the appointed hour. Stuart stretched out for a few hours of rest with his head upon his saddle. Reid Venable was beside him. Colonel Bradley Johnson arrived to get Stuart's assurance that the guns he had borrowed from him would be returned. The general was sleeping so soundly that Venable and McClellan did not awaken him.[16]

The horsemen had left Hanover Junction when Garnett got there. He trailed them to Ashland, arriving a few moments after some of Sheridan's men, who were still tending the burning cord wood and rail cars, were taken prisoner. A Southerner was making sport of them, suggesting that they too would be thrown into the flames. Stuart sent his aide off immediately to determine the exact location of the enemy. Near a cloud of dust some neighbors revealed that some of the

Federals had been down the road to Dilly's Mill. Garnett later wrote: "The dust disappeared westward and I turned to ride in the direction of the Mountain Road where I heard distinctly the sound of the guns at Yellow Tavern, showing that the enemy had showed up just where we were expecting them." [17]

****

On May 10th the Federals had crossed the South Anna at Ground Squirrel Bridge and there they burned the bridge and Sheridan sent a contingent off to Ashland. The brigade was just eating breakfast at Ground Squirrel Bridge when firing was heard from the nearby woods. One man from Maine recalled, "There was a scramble for their horses and the men scarcely got mounted before the enemy appeared in three columns but a few yards away. . .Charging down upon them like so many demons. "Gordon's North Carolinians had found a ford downstream."[18]

On May 11 Sheridan's men proceeded along Mountain Road with the instructions to take only what they required, one man from Vermont recorded that their requirements "extended to hams, butter, chickens, flour, meal, (and) anything of edible nature they could lay their hands on; and by long experience. They knew where to look for such articles when they struck a rich old planter's premises." Hostility flashed from the eyes and denouncement from the mouths of the old men and women they passed. However, when a man from Massachusetts, feeling sick, stopped at a farmhouse, the lady answering his knock at the door said, "I can't give you a square meal, but I reckon I can give you a snack and some blackberry vinegar."[19]

Goodall's was a tavern on the stagecoach (Mountain) road to Gordonsville. General Gregg's men encamped around the old hotel, but Carolinians flanked the building. Horsemen from Maine were pushed into the New Yorkers, resulting in a "bewildered mass." One Federal said that: "for a few moments it was everyman for himself and the rebels take the hindermost." Sheridan went on to destroy the Allen Station, and sent a contingent to destroy the rails toward Hungary Station. A young rebel soldier was spotted up a tree. The sullen boy claimed that he was just home visiting his family. An officer from Michigan recorded: "The air was mild, the country charming, and we thought it was a holiday-time we were having as we rode easily along."[20]

What about the women, children, and everyday travelers along the road to Yellow Tavern? There were 12,000 men in the three divisions, each division having two batteries of horse artillery. The van had left the Ground Squirrel Bridge at 5 a.m. and probably passed into Henrico County at 8 a.m., in time for the clatter to arouse the late sleeping travelers at the 23 room Chickahominy Tavern. The late H. Douglas Pitts has identified some of the homes they passed along the way. Within the first mile, they came to the lane into "Meadow Farm" the home of Dr. John M. Sheppard, his wife Virginia, son Hamilton, and daughters Helen and Libby. There on the hillside south of the house some local militia contended against men of the Michigan cavalry. General George Custer and his staff rested on the front porch while 11 year-old Libby defied their presence by sitting on the bottom step. A slave betrayed a haunch of meat in an upstairs closet, its door obscured by a wardrobe.[21]

The contingent under General Davies, who had been sent to Ashland at 3 a.m. to destroy the track, a locomotive and its cars, joined the raiders at Allen's Crossing over the R.F. & P. Railroad. This was the home of Susan Allen, whom John Cussons, the venturesome scout for General Evander Law, would marry in Richmond on May 19, 1864, a week after his exchange from Fort Delaware. Cussons had been taken prisoner at Gettysburg. Being still a subject of Queen Victoria, he was under no compulsion to remain with the Confederate army. Instead he found his way back to the beautiful widow.[22]

There certainly must have been a clatter as Sheridan's forces passed "Walkerton," the home of Mrs. Fannie Hopkins about a half mile from the railroad. She lived with her daughters, Josephine, 36, Delia, 41, and 51 year-old Mary Hopkins. Fannie's son, Captain George Hopkins of the Henrico Dragoons, had been on disability because of poor eyesight. His record shows that he had gone back into service and was reported present on April 29. The record also shows that he was taken prisoner at Yellow Tavern. Perhaps George was taken there at his home because the 10th Virginia Cavalry was not used in the fighting.[23]

There was a frame house on the right, possibly the home of James G. Francis and later that of the Litchfields, used as hospital as was "Walkerton." There was a Harris home at the intersection of the Mountain Road and the Ashland Road where a member of the 5th Virginia Cavalry went to have his hand treated and a Powell home at the intersection of the Mountain Road and the Telegraph Road also used as a hospital. With fighting anticipated between the Mountain and Telegraph roads, a Confederate scout was sent to the Cross home to alert them. Catherine Cross sent her daughters, Lucy Ann and Bettie, to the adjoining Gray farm. There from a hillside, they and Jimmie Gray's sister Betty Gray, would watch the fighting around "Half Sink," a Sheppard home.[24]

Chapter 17
STUART AT TURNER'S RUN – MAY 1864

One of Sheridan's cavalrymen wrote that they arrived in the area around 9 a.m. They moved along a level stretch of the Mountain Road. The trees (locust?) were in full bloom. In the open fields, the corn was three inches high. He felt that nature looked too beautiful "to be devastated by war." Just as they came to a junction of two roads (probably the Mountain Road and what came to be called the Ashland or Greenwood Road), they ran into skirmishers from the 6th Virginia Cavalry.[1]

General Alfred Gibbs ordered his Reserve Brigade into battle formation. He was soon joined by Custer on his left and Devin on his right. Since Wesley Merritt's was the only division to arrive, Sheridan did not stage a full scale attack. It seemed some of Wickham's cavalrymen were beginning to form on a ridge to the north and Lomax's pickets were taking an "adjacent stand of woods."[2]

When we look at the scenario for Stuart's last battle, we can see on the old maps the narrow winding Telegraph Road. It wound its way north from its juncture with Brook Turnpike near Yellow Tavern and Turner's Tavern. The road ran along a diminutive stream which soon entered Turner's Run and flowed eastward into the Chickahominy. Local farms, some with acreage in cultivation, others in woodland, had converged at the road, hence the many fences and gates mentioned in the military reports. Turner's Run, with its penchant for making ditches and gullies, flowed through Cross, Mosby, Green, and Taliaferro farms from the west and Sheppard, King, and Powell land to the east. Much of the former Owen land, whose mansion house had been about where present U.S. #1 and #295 intersect, had been bought up by Richard Cross and the various branches of the Sheppard family. The northernmost Sheppard farm on the Telegraph Road and bordering on the

Chickahominy was called "Half Sink". Its very name attests to the fact that the area was not all flat but slightly rolling.[3]

Subsequent subdivision of the area in the 20th century makes it difficult to picture the locale of the morning battle on May 11. It appears to have run southeast from New York Avenue, through Pennsylvania, and Maryland avenues, along Telegraph Road and U.S. #1 to Scott Road or Athens Avenue. Biltmore Baptist Church sits high on New York Avenue before the land drops down to the ravines cut by Turner's Run. Even today there is some scattered woodland. Before # 295 cut through the area, a definite rise could be seen from the northern branch of Turner's Run (2 ½ blocks north of New York Avenue) to present Francis Road and Virginia Center Parkway. Some remains of breastworks may be seen in the woods along Francis Road to the east. The morning battle appears to have been fought along the southern branch of Turner's Run, the afternoon battle along the northern branch.

General Lomax had with him the 6th, 5th, and 15th cavalries. He placed them along the Telegraph Road from the small stream near New York Avenue to the main body of Turner's Run (now at #295). Colonel Henry Pate was in charge of the 5th Virginia Cavalry. He had been acquitted of the charges against him when they were stationed at Hanover Court House and, by order of General R.E. Lee, "resumed his sword." Pate assumed command of the 5th Cavalry upon Tom Rosser's promotion and transfer. Breathed's Battery lay to the northeast. Wickham's regiments, the 4th, 3rd, 2nd, and 1st cavalries, came into position along the slightly higher grounds on what is now Francis Road. There were woods that partially concealed Wickham's men.[4]

General Fitz Lee supervised Wickham's troopers and General Stuart those under General Lomax. Lomax's men bore the brunt of the fighting that morning. Stuart was already there, but Wickham, coming from the fighting in Ashland, was yet to arrive. Theodore Garnett, moving to the sound of the fighting, found his way back to Stuart. He passed Colonel Bob Randolph leading Wickham's men. Garnett said that the colonel, "usually so bright and cheerful," that morning was "gloomy, depressed and apparently dispirited." The aide reported to Stuart that Wickham was still far behind. Colonel Pate was placed in charge of Lomax's line. There were open fields to his front and then dense woods. Mounted men were placed as lookout to the west and sharpshooters in the gully where the fields met the woods. A friend of Pate's recorded that the skirmish line received the enemy "with a warm fire and such a precision of aim that Sheridan's first line gave way… Pate's men raised a yell and started in pursuit, but were recalled by the commanding officer."[5]

It was at this point that Garnett brought Pate word from Stuart "to hold that position at all hazards," Garnett said that he believed Pate saw it as a "veritable death sentence." The men of the 5th Cavalry pressed around their colonel in the road, leaving them exposed from the field to the west. "It was a death trap and they knew it," Garnett said. The first line was broken as Sheridan's men charged toward Breathed's guns. Pate had to assume his second position, in a deep cut to the east of the Telegraph Road. Stuart and the colonel had not spoken to each other for months. But earlier in the day the general grasped Pate's hand and said, "How long can you hold this position?" Pate replied, "Until I die, General." Again they clasped hands. Stuart was heard to remark, "Pate is a hero!" For, as the general watched though binoculars, he saw the colonel fall.[6]

Captain J.H. Kidd, of the 5th Michigan Cavalry under George Custer, wrote that they were dismounted but backed by the mounted men of the 7th Michigan and the 1st Vermont. "Between the ridge and the edge of the woods where our line was halted was a big field not less four hundred yards across, sloping down from their position to ours." To attack, the Union men had to cross that field and move up the slope. This subjected them to crossfire from Lomax's artillery along a road (Telegraph) that ran at right angles to them. Kidd said that as soon as they left the woods, "Confederate artillery opened with shell and shrapnel; the carbineers and sharpshooters joined with zest in the fray and the man who thinks they did not make that part of the neighborhood around Yellow Tavern an uncomfortably hot place, was not there at the time."[7]

Private Leiper Robinson, a King William boy in the 9th Virginia Cavalry, fighting that day with the King and Queen County men of the 5th Cavalry, recorded in his memoirs, "Colonel Pate … was shot dead … while standing on the high ditch bank, waving his hat and calling to his men to stand fast." Robinson recounted:

> Where I was stationed, in a deep ditch, there was a plank fence on the bank just above our heads, and behind us, on the other side of the road, was another deep ditch, and on that field, just plowed, which extended some three-quarters of a mile to a declivity bordering on the Chickahominy… I could hear the minie balls pattering against the planks like hailstones … Our horses had been taken back over the Chickahominy by a bridge bridge above us, but as the enemy now held the road, had to ford the stream to reach them. To add to the disaster, a tremendous thunder storm with heavy rain came on and our wagon train had gotten in a panic.

Thirty of the King and Queen Cavalry had come into the fight. After the battle only ten were left.[8]

A teenaged orderly in the regimental commissary, Jimmy Moore, rode through the storm of bullets to take Colonel Pate's body to a house on Dr. Sheppard's farm ("Half Sink"?) There he and Otho Pate (the colonel's brother and his adjutant) had just time enough to lay the body on the floor and pin a note of identification before the enemy came riding into the yard. During a lull in the fighting, a grieving Lomax told Theodore Garnett that Pate's body was in a small house nearby. Stuart's aide dismounted and entered to pay his respects. He saw that Colonel Pate had been shot "full in the forehead." When the fighting had ceased he was buried in the yard but four days later moved to Hollywood Cemetery.[9]

General Stuart on the afternoon of May 11 was fighting along side with the men who loved him best, his old regiment the 1st Virginia Cavalry. He had been their first colonel and, according to William B. Poindexter, a native of Henrico later in the Rockbridge Dragoons, in drilling them well "had endeared himself to his men, and the men endeared themselves to him." The most poignant accounts of his wounding have come from the rank and file of men in Company E, the Valley Rangers and Company K, made up of men from the Maryland Line. Corporal James Oliver, age 23, from Charles County, Maryland, saw Stuart about five o'clock in the afternoon come riding alone out of the woods and whistling. Oliver said that the general stationed the dismounted men of Company K along the edge of the woods and along a "deep cut in the road as it descends from the higher grounds to the valley of the Chickahominy." The Federals soon came charging along the road toward "Half Sink", Oliver said, and "we filled the cut with dead horses and men in less time than it takes to talk about it."[10]

This was probably where the Telegraph Road crossed or forded Turner's Run. Ancient rains, wagons, carts, and stagecoach wheels had deepened the cut over the years. The Federals were making an attempt to drive a wedge between Lomax to the east and Wickham to the west and then to drive them to "Half Sink" in their rear. General George Custer's account of the fighting that afternoon told that the Confederates were "strongly posted on a bluff in the rear of a slim skirt of woods, their battery being concealed from our view by the woods … The edge of the woods nearest my front was held by the enemy's dismounted men." Custer said that he dismounted his 5th and 6th Michigan and used them to divert attention while he formed his 1st Michigan in a squadron to charge the enemy's battery on its flank. He was able to drive the Confederates about a quarter of a mile beyond the position of their guns. His men had to open five fences and cross a bridge just wide enough for three abreast.[11]

Upon crossing a deep ravine, the Confederates reformed and checked the advance of the 1st Michigan. Then Custer ordered in the mounted 7th Michigan, led by Major W.J. Granger. Soon the major fell mortally wounded by shots to his head and heart. He had led his men into the muzzle of their guns, but the 7th Michigan was forced to retire. Two guns had been captured and a number of prisoners taken. An unidentified Confederate courier said that Stuart was "sitting on his horse, close behind a line of dismounted men." Using his revolver, he shot over the head of his troops, encouraging by saying, "Steady, men, steady. Give it to them." Soon he reeled in his saddle, having been shot in the midsection, and his hat fell off. The general said to his courier, "Go and tell Lee (Fitz) and Dr. Fontaine to come." Upon receiving the message, Fitz Lee, riding a light gray, "went like an arrow down the line."[12]

Captain Gus Dorsey, also from Maryland, picked up the narrative. He told Henry McClellan that he was stationed on the Telegraph Road with 80 men when the enemy charged past and met with the mounted men of the 1st Cavalry and were driven back. It was at this point that one of the retreating Federals turned back and shot the general. Some say that he was shot by one that was fighting dismounted, Private John A. Huff of the 5th Michigan, others (Henry McClellan for one) by one of the men who had been unhorsed.[13]

Captain Theodore Rodenbough, 2nd United States Cavalry, Alfred Gibbs's reserve brigade of Wesley Merritt's First Division, wrote after the war that a dispatch from Stuart to Bragg had been intercepted, revealing the enemy's weakness. "Under the circumstances," the captain wrote, "The Confederates are entitled to the greatest credit for the pertinacity and pluck displayed." Finally (that afternoon) when part of Wilson's division joined Merritt on the left, the advancing line "broke the enemy's grip and the fight was won." Rodenbough said that it was at this point Stuart received his mortal wound. The captain continued, "Deep in the hearts of all true cavalrymen, North and South, will ever burn a sentiment of admiration mingled with regret for this knightly soldier and generous man. Sheridan had succeeded in his purpose, but he had found a foeman worthy of his steel."[14]

Tom Waters, from the District of Columbia and a private in Company K, had been taken prisoner at Gettysburg but, escaping from Point Lookout, was back with his regiment. He was in the woods and on the extreme left when they were driven back. Just then Stuart appeared. Waters wrote, "I took off my hat to cheer him and I discovered that he was wounded." Stuart at this time may have been on a horse belonging to one of his couriers, Ben Weller, a member of the 1st Cavalry who had been wounded a few days before at Todd's Tavern. Elliott "Fish" Fishburne had also been wounded at Todd's Tavern on May 7 but had returned to duty. He described Stuart's wounding, "The ball entered into the left side of his body through the top of his breaches pocket – passing through the kidney & body & out above and behind the right hip.[15] The gold sash which the general was wearing at the time is now at the Virginia Historical Society.

Colonel Goldsborough, although he was still in a Federal prison after being captured at Gettysburg, in his account of the Maryland Line at Yellow Tavern, has written that Captain Dorsey witnessed the wounding, rushed to the general's assistance, "took him from his horse and placed him against a tree. General Stuart then expressed the belief that he was mortally wounded and could be of no further use, and then ordered Dorsey to go back to his command. But this Dorsey declined to do until he saw him safely off the field. Calling to Private Wheatley, they placed him upon a horse and led it to a place of safety, when an ambulance was procured, and [the general] supported in the arms of Wheatley the ambulance was driven off."[16]

Betty R. Cross, who with sister Lucy Ann and brothers, had inherited land from their father's estate which stretched to the Telegraph Road, said that it was a holly tree on the line between her land and that of the Mosby family where Stuart was taken to rest before they could get him around the Federal lines and into Richmond. There must have been debris scattered all over the Cross farm. At least two swords, one with a broken blade, were picked up. One was later found at the bottom of the trunk owned by the slave Buck Owen at the time of his death. Someone in the family came to possess an Eli Whitney revolver with a shaped barrel like the one carried by Jeb Stuart when he was shot. The United States government ordered the 1860 model six-shooter and distributed it to volunteer units throughout the war. Also some of the Union officers purchased the same model for their use.[17]

Living on a farm on the battlefield of Yellow Tavern was a second cousin of the partisan ranger, John Singleton Mosby. Both went by the name of John S. Mosby although this one was John Spotswood Mosby. There was a strong resemblance between the two. John Spotswood Mosby was older by sixteen years and had a wife and children: Margaret, Robert Calvin, and John W. They called their home "Yellow Tavern Plantation." The story has been handed down through the generations that they watched the battle in their front yard (field), saw a soldier fall, and knew it must have been Jeb Stuart because there was a plume in his hat. Less than two months later, a Richmond newspaper carried the story that John W. Mosby and another boy found an unexploded shell on the battlefield. They tried to open it, whereby the shell exploded killing both the lads.[18]

Mary Powell wrote to their son Junius, who was with the signal corps in South Carolina, that the fighting had come very close to "Melrose." She, his father, and Blanche had set out for Richmond. On approaching the turnpike, they were told that the Yankees were coming down Mountain Road and had reached Peter's shop. They returned home, had the horses and carriages put up and Dr. Powell went to ascertain the cause of the dust along the (Telegraph) road between the Taliaferros and the Kings ("Level Green"). He found that it was Stuart's cavalry under Generals Wickham and Lomax. They were coming down to intercept the Federals at Yellow Tavern. This they might have done, Mrs. Powell thought, if their cavalry had gone a mile further down the turnpike. "Instead they "fixed their lines along the road by Waldrop's old place, in King's field and up nearly to Taliaferro's."[19]

Mother Powell said that the Yankees flanked our men and drove them back nearly to "Half Sink," taking two batteries of the Maryland Line. There was one battery disabled near Mr. King's bars (barns?). All day the Confederate couriers had to take the circuitous route through the Powell farm, Captain Paleske's ("Solitaire") and J.B. Crenshaw's. She said that Stuart rallied a portion of his command and fought desperately hand to hand but received a mortal wound from which he died 28 hours later.[20]

"Half Sink" was up the Telegraph Road from "Melrose", with its entrance perhaps at the bend where Stuart was placed in the ambulance. Maps of the time showed a Mrs. Sheppard living there. The earlier 1853 map showed the home of Dr. Sheppard bordering the river, also a road that ran parallel to the river from which there were two bridges across the Chickahominy (Winston's and Bowis' bridges?). Across the river on the Hanover side, the Sliding Hill Road led to the Ashcake Road to Atlee Station, and was possibly the route the ambulance took bearing Stuart into Richmond.[21]

Colonel Goldsborough said that two guns of the Baltimore Light Artillery and Captain Griffin had been captured and several of his men but not until they "inflicted fearful destruction in the ranks of the Michigan cavalry." Sergeant Poindexter said that they had just finished mounting and were expecting Stuart to arrive at any second when Fitz Lee appeared and announced that the general had been wounded and the artillery captured. The men shed tears at the news and Fitz Lee had tears in his eyes. Twenty year-old Corporal Robert Bryaly, of Company B in the 5th Cavalry, wrote they had a severe fight at "Half Sink" bridges in which they lost Stuart, Colonel Pate, and their Captain G.N. Hammond. He himself was wounded in the thigh, died in a Richmond hospital on May 16, and was buried in Hollywood.[22]

Vivian Minor Fleming, of the engineers, was intimately associated with the Fontaines. He was passing their home on the day that Stuart was shot and was asked to take the message to Mrs. Jeb Stuart that her husband had been seriously wounded and to see that she and the Fountaine ladies got on the train to Richmond. Fleming said that he "went as the crow flies not observing fences, ditches or creeks." Mrs. Stuart was upstairs giving one of the children a bath. Dr. Fontaine, president of the Virginia Central Railroad, had one of the old engines turned around and advised them to go by way of the R.F. & P. tracks from Hanover Junction into Richmond. Fleming got the ladies, the children, and a minister on the train and then he rode his horse behind them. When they arrived at Ashland, the tracks between there and Richmond had been destroyed, so they had to take an ambulance and drive through the afternoon storm. The bridge over the Chickahominy was out but some cavalry pickets found them a ford downstream. They reached Richmond at 8 p.m. on the 12th. The general was already dead.[23]

The *Daily Dispatch* from Richmond on Friday morning, May 13, spoke of General Stuart's death the previous evening having resulted from a wound sustained "during the fight at "Half Sink" on Wednesday afternoon." It erroneously gave the place of his death as the residence of Dr. Burwell instead of Dr. Charles Brewer, Stuart's brother-in-law. The marker on the house on West Grace bore the general's declaration: "I must save the women of Richmond."[24] The house is no longer standing.

Judith McGuire did not get to the funeral. She wrote in her diary a description given her by a close friend. There was no military escort as the procession wound its way through the rain to St. James Church and the only military salute was the roar of distant guns. The flowers with the casket were delicate white ones forming a sword, white roses forming a cross, and a wreath of bay leaves, symbolizing the heavenly crown. Pastor Peterkin led the services at the church and the Reverend Dr. Minnigerode led the committal at Hollywood Cemetery.[25]

John Esten Cooke wrote:

> On a summer morning a solitary man was seen beside the grave of Stuart, in Hollywood Cemetery near Richmond. The dew was on the grass, the birds sang overhead, the green hillock at the man's feet was all that remained of the daring leader of the Southern cavalry who, after all his toils, his battles, and the shocks of desperate encounters, had come here to rest in peace. Beside this unmarked grave the solitary mourner remained long, pondering and remembering. Finally he plucked a wild flower, dropped it upon the grave, and with tears in his eyes, left the place.

This lonely mourner at the grave of Stuart was the ranger, John Singleton Mosby.[26]

Sally “Aunt Sally” Anderson:
courtesy Tom Scott

“Brook Hill” – Stewart home in Henrico County:
courtesy Ora Lee Pitts

Bettie Richard Cross

Cross home in Henrico County

Frances Greer Cross

Joseph Finch Cross

John Cussons

Nathaniel "Nat" Cross and Betty Gray Cross:
courtesy Mark Cross

Mary "Liz" Francis Davis and family

First Baptist Church in Ashland

Emmanuel Episcopal Church in Henrico County

John Thomas "Tom" Francis, Lucy Ann Francis, Bettie R. Cross, and Fannie C. Cross

Margaret Mosby Isbell:
courtesy Martha Lupton

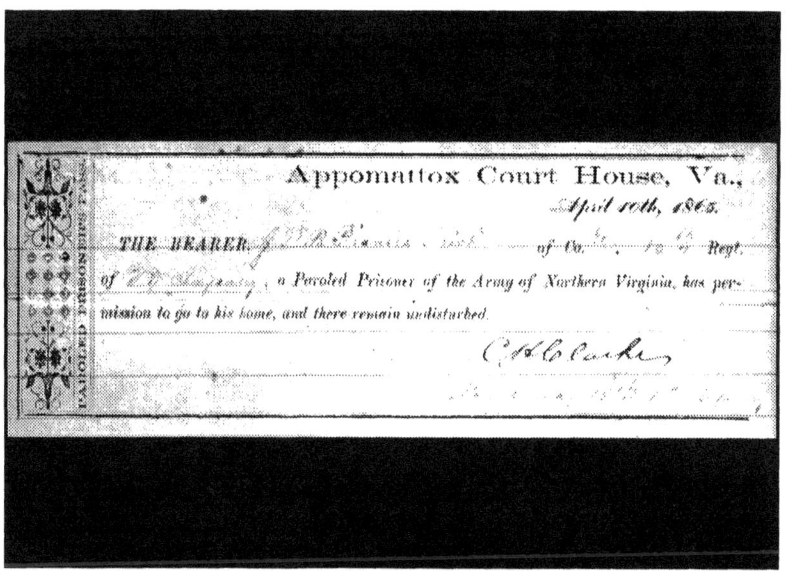

PAROLED PRISONER'S PASS.

Appomattox Court House, Va.,

April 10th, 1865.

THE BEARER, [illegible] of Co. [illegible] Regt. of [illegible], a Paroled Prisoner of the Army of Northern Virginia, has permission to go to his home, and there remain undisturbed.

[illegible]

Tom Francis' parole from Appomattox

J.E.B. Stuart monument in Henrico County

Martha "Mat" Francis Jenkins

1861

REUNION

15th Reg't Va.
Infantry

Ashland, Va.

1909

Last reunion attended by Tom Francis

George Edmond Massie: courtesy Jayne Massie

"Meadow Farm," Sheppard home in Henrico County

"Melrose," Powell home in Henrico County

William "Buck" Owen: courtesy Betty G. Faber

Francis sawmill crew

Dr. John M. Sheppard: courtesy Meadow Farm Museum

Mary "Libbie" Sheppard: courtesy Meadow Farm Museum

Virginia Young Sheppard: courtesy Meadow Farm Museum

Slash Christian Church in Hanover County

Emeline "Jo" Francis Terrell and Charles Terrell:
courtesy Leland Terrell

"Stuckley Hall," Dr. Terrell home in Henrico County:
courtesy of Henrico County

Winn's Baptist Church in Hanover County

Flags used on Stuart's Monument in 1930s

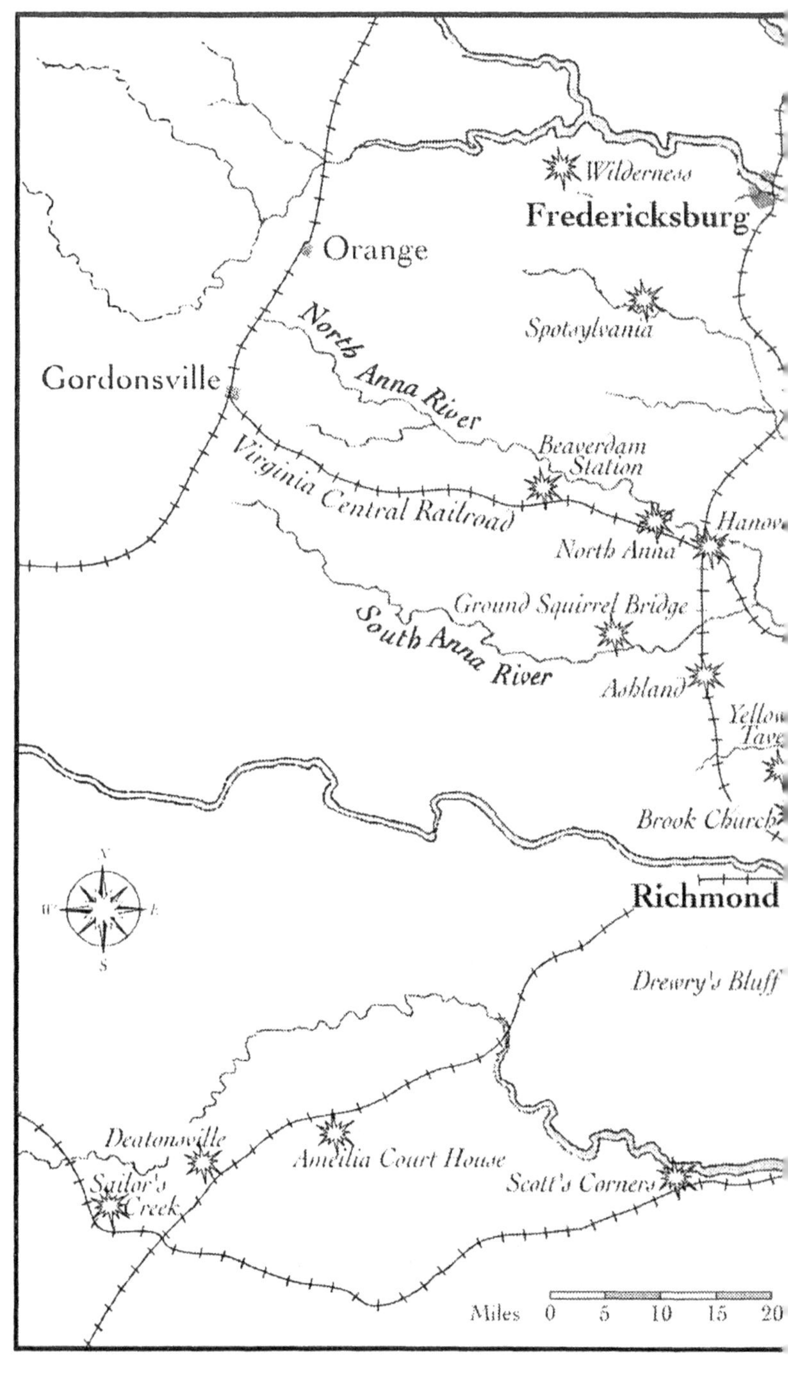
Wilderness
Fredericksburg
Orange
Spotsylvania
North Anna River
Gordonsville
Beaverdam Station
Virginia Central Railroad
North Anna
Ground Squirrel Bridge
South Anna River
Ashland
Brook Church
Richmond
Drewry's Bluff
Deatonsville
Sailor's Creek
Amelia Court House
Scott's Corners
Miles 0 5 10 15 20

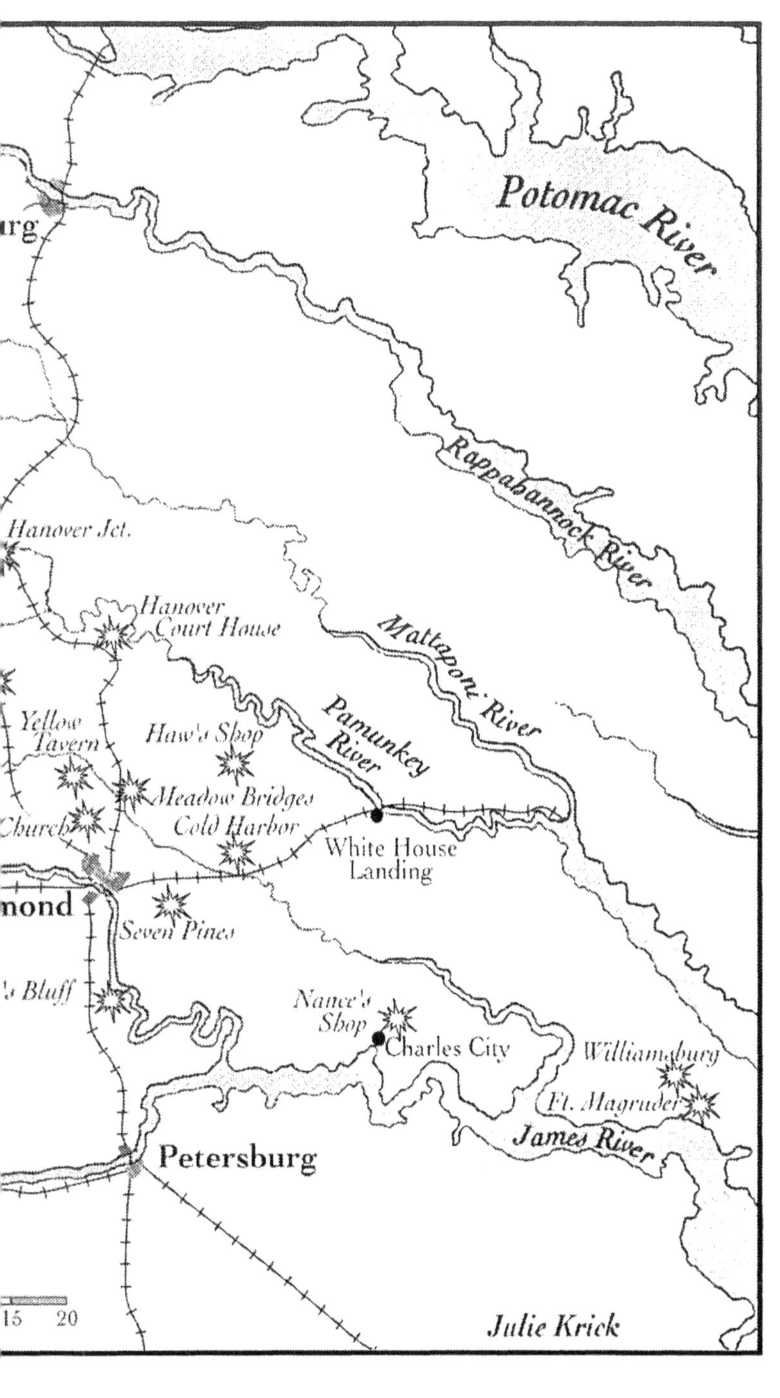

rg
Potomac River
Rappahannock River
Hanover Jct.
Hanover
Court House
Mattaponi River
Pamunkey
River
Yellow
Tavern
Haw's Shop
Meadow Bridges
Cold Harbor
Church
White House
Landing
nond
Seven Pines
's Bluff
Nance's
Shop
Charles City
Williamsburg
Ft. Magruder
James River
Petersburg
15
20
Julie Krick

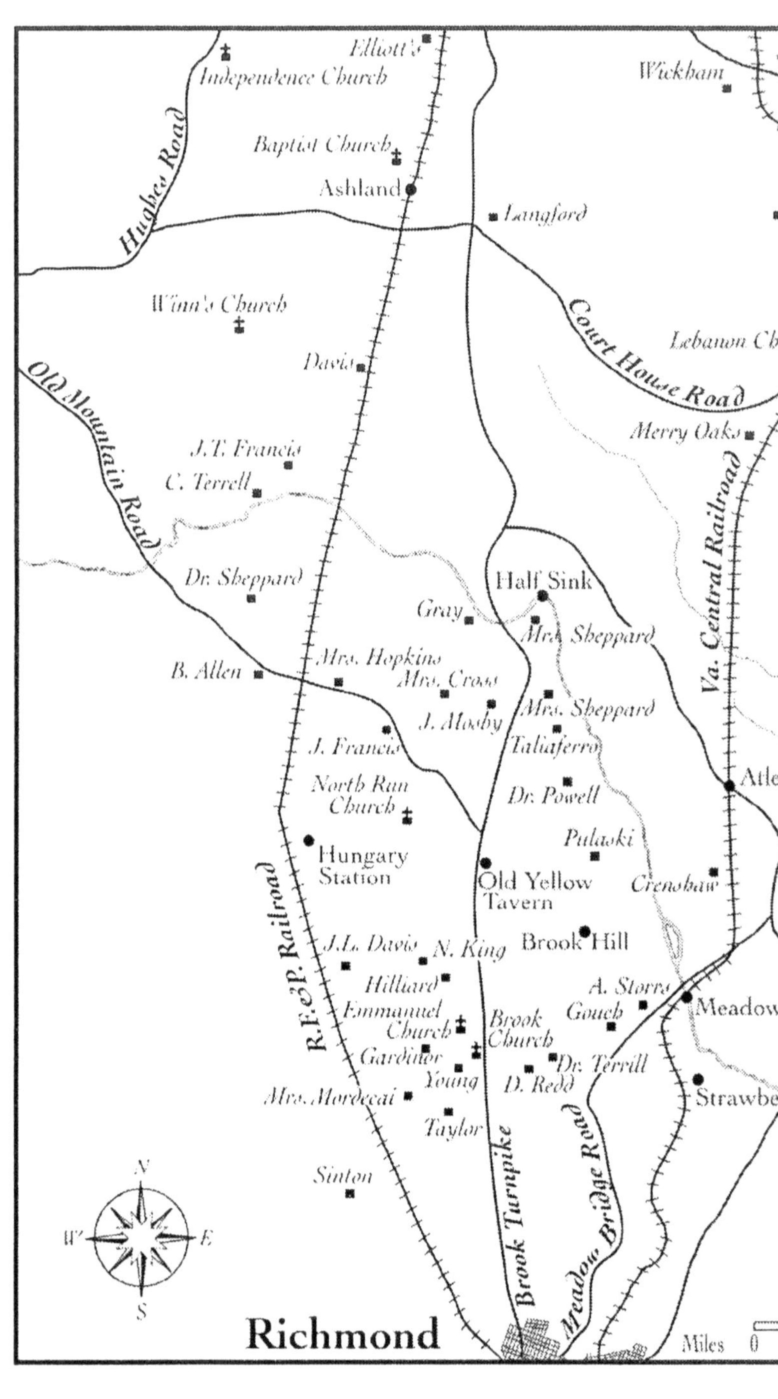
Elliott's
Independence Church
Wickham
Hughes Road
Baptist Church
Ashland
Langford
Winn's Church
Court House Road
Lebanon Ch
Davis
Old Mountain Road
Merry Oaks
J.T. Francis
C. Terrell
Va. Central Railroad
Dr. Sheppard
Half Sink
Gray
Mrs. Sheppard
B. Allen
Mrs. Hopkins
Mrs. Cross
J. Mosby
Mrs. Sheppard
Taliaferro
J. Francis
North Run Church
Dr. Powell
Pulaski
Hungary Station
Old Yellow Tavern
Crenshaw
R.F.&P. Railroad
J.L. Davis
N. King
Brook Hill
Hilliard
A. Storrs
Emmanuel Church
Brook Church
Gouch
Gardiner
Dr. Terrill
Young
D. Redd
Mrs. Mordecai
Taylor
Sinton
Brook Turnpike
Meadow Bridge Road
N
W
E
S
Richmond
Miles
0

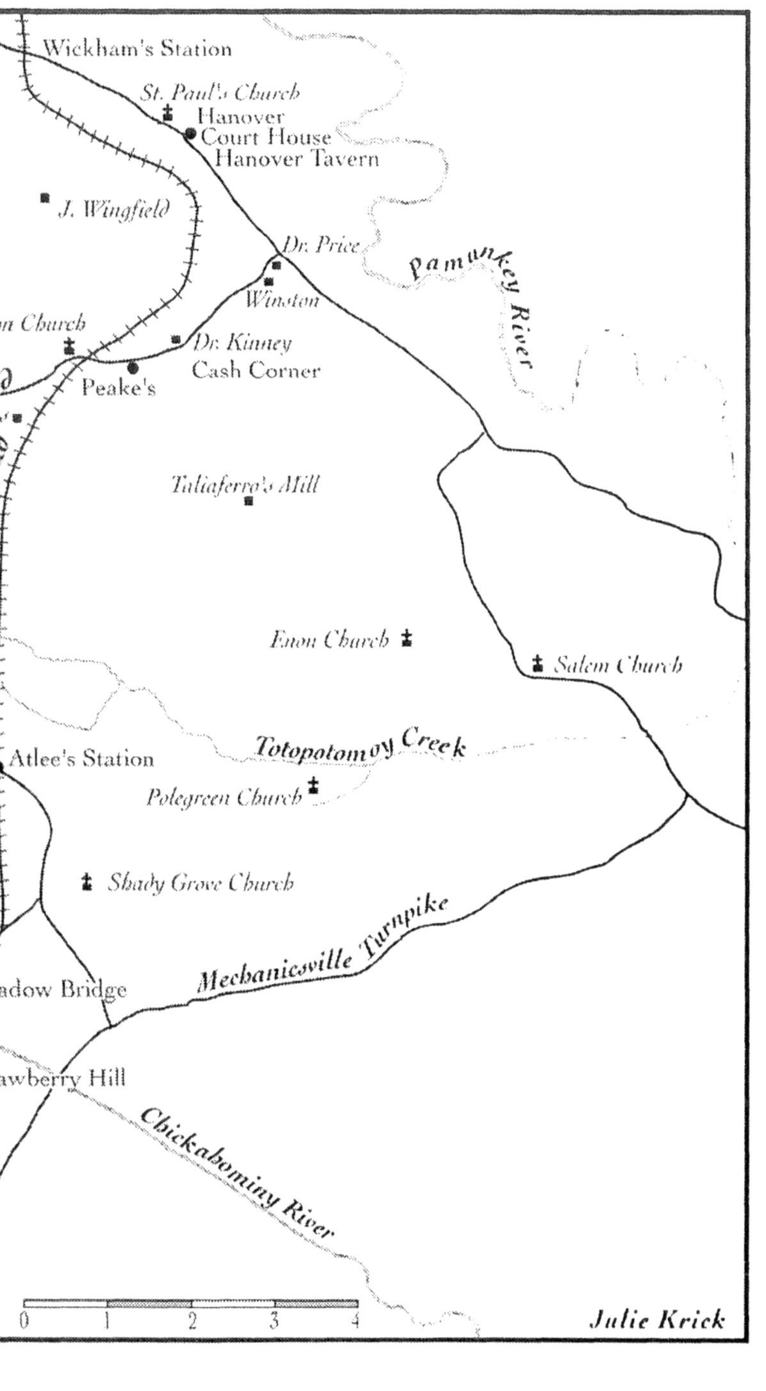
Wickham's Station
St. Paul's Church
Hanover
Court House
Hanover Tavern
J. Wingfield
Dr. Price
Pamunkey River
Winston
Dr. Kinney
Cash Corner
Peake's
Taliaferro's Mill
Enon Church
Salem Church
Totopotomoy Creek
Atlee's Station
Polegreen Church
Shady Grove Church
Mechanicsville Turnpike
Chickahominy River
0
1
2
3
4
Julie Krick

Chapter 18

MEADOW BRIDGES - MAY 1864

The honeysuckle and dogwood were blooming in the woods behind Rosewood, the Mordecai home southwest of Yellow Tavern. Emma Mordecai had moved from Richmond just after the Jewish Passover to be with her brother's widow, Rosina Young Mordecai, called Rose, and niece Augusta, caller Gusta. Emma wrote in her diary that with the tinkling of the cowbells and the twittering of the birds, it was hard for her to realize that the war was raging just fifty miles away. A cow pen had been built behind the kitchen just in time. Thieves came the following night. Finding the cows no longer at the barn, they stole the Negro Cy's two hens.[1]

Rosina and her seamstress were busy making adjustments to Gusta's dresses for summer. Emma and niece Caroline sadly sorted through a trunk of Aunt Caroline's former possessions. Their thoughts must have been on the fighting in the Wilderness where the Mordecai boys were with the 2nd Richmond Howitzers. The word came on May 7 that the Howitzer's old commander, Lieutenant Colonel J. Thompson Brown, had been killed, shot in the forehead while helping set up a battery on the edge of some woods.[2]

The following day was Sunday and Gusta walked along the turnpike to Sunday School at Emmanuel Church. Her mother later rode to church. Emma walked out by the ice-house and up by the pond, finding the woods "indescribably lovely." News came that another Yankee gunboat had been destroyed on the river. The tocsin sounded calling out the militia. The Reverend Mr. Walker came to call but would not stay for their supper of tea, muffins, clabber, and sweet milk.[3]

On May 10, they were concerned about the 40,000 Union troops reported to be south of the James River. John Young, Rose's brother, came from "Westbrook" with word that another raid was on the way and that they had best hide their valuables. The women put their treasures in their pockets, had the meat taken down in the smokehouse and put under the hen house. Plans were made for the servants, Cy and John, to hide the horse and mule in the west woods. Emma wrote in her diary, "We are aware that at any moment the Philistines might be upon us, but we went on quietly with our occupations." Blue lupines were blooming in the woods.[4]

May 11 was a beautiful morning. Emma went out to help Lizzie, Mary, and Georgianna work the strawberries. John Young sent a message that the Yankees were within three miles of his place. Cannon and musket firing could be heard all morning. That afternoon Emma and Georgianna walked over to "Westbrook" and found the women packing some things in case they had to leave the house. They paid only a short visit before returning by way of the breastworks, the creek, and the mill. The sound of brisk firing could be heard again beginning at 4 p.m., slackened for a while during a severe thunderstorm, and then continued until dark. It didn't seem to be far off. Emma wrote, "I sat knitting in the dark till 9, when I went to bed, after committing our household to the care of the All Powerful & felt no fear."[5]

The John Stewart family at "Brook Hill" and the Walker family at the Emmanuel rectory on Wilmer Avenue could hear the fighting. At "Brook Hill" that day there were possibly Mr. Stewart, his wife Amanda, five daughters - Amanda, Isabel, Marion, Hope and Annie - and servants both slave and free. The butler, John Young, hid the family silver in two clothes baskets and in his excitement forgot where he had put them. One basket was found in 1923 when a chimney flue was repaired. The other has yet to be found. Fifteen year-old Marion watched from an upstairs window. She said, "Sixty of our men contended with a regiment of Yankees for every inch of ground to our gate."[6]

The rectory was on slightly elevated land and from it the Reverend Mr. Cornelius Walker could see the cavalrymen approaching the outer fortifications. He sent his wife and their children to the attic to be out of the range of the bullets. From the roof of the house, the minister watched the picket fight in the direction of Walton's shop. Marion Stewart saw a Union soldier shot in their walkway and his body carried off toward the toll house. A picket line was posted around the house. Late that afternoon the minister unknowingly passed through the line on his way over to "Brook Hill" to say prayers with the Stewarts. He said that he hurried home at dusk to put out the lights. The fighting ceased with the darkness and the Union forces rested and treated their wounded in the one half mile stretch between the abandoned Yellow Tavern and "Brook Hill" It is thought that under cover of darkness they buried one officer and twenty-five men in unmarked graves in the Emmanuel cemetery.[7]

Colonel Thomas Devin's men of the 6th and the 7th Pennsylvania cavalries were situated at "Belmont" the Warren home north of Brook Run. It is a two story brick home now used as a club house. Jeanette Warren, sister of the rector, said that all of their meat and fowls plus many little things were stolen. Moreover, she added, her father-in-law, an elderly non-combatant, was taken off to Fort Monroe where he was released and compelled to walk home. Many other non-combatants were made to walk to City Point and then retained at the fortress for several months.[8]

The raiders on May 12 swung to the south and southeast between the outer and intermediate fortifications. They pivoted at Brook Church on to the Military Road (Azalea Avenue) and emerged on to the Meadowbridge Road before reaching the Meadow Bridges. In their wake were the homes of the Redds ("Buena Vista"), the Ladds, the Grants

("Montrose"), the Terrells ("Stuckley Hall"), the Gooches, the Storrs family, the Davenports ("Strawberry Hill"), the Nashes ("Picquenoque") and probably many smaller farms.[9]

Although Fitz Lee with Lomax and Wickham had retreated north to cross the Chickahominy at "Half Sink" into Hanover County, Gordon was still pushing Sheridan. There were no viable roads to the west for the raiders to join Butler around Richmond, which forced Sheridan to face Fitz Lee at the Meadow Bridges where the Confederates would soon be entrenched in the abandoned 1862 earthworks. Two causeways crossed the now much flooded marsh land at the Chickahominy. Both bridges, for the Virginia Central Railroad and one for road traffic, had been damaged.[10]

About 2½ miles east of Yellow Tavern, as the crow flies, Brook Run empties into the Chickahominy. This is a swampy area necessitating, along with the bridge trestle for the Virginia Central Railroad, numerous small bridges. The road here from Richmond to Mechanicsville was alternately called the Richmond Henrico Turnpike and the Road to the Meadow Bridges. The area could be reached by Ashcake Road through Hanover County to Atlee, by the old Wilkerson Road in Henrico County - between Yellow Tavern and Brook Bridge, or the Military Road, later called Azalea, which lay just north of the city between its outer defenses and the intermediate defenses along Laburnum Avenue.

The Yankee commander started his men out at 11 p.m., having been encouraged about dark when one of his men intercepted a courier from Braxton Bragg to Stuart with a message saying there were no troops to spare in Richmond. The turnpike was wider than the other roads he had been traveling for several days. It passed over an arched bridge spanning Brook Run. The rain seemed to fall harder with each flash of lightning and roar of thunder. The retreating Confederates had planted torpedoes with trip-wires along the road. After loosing several men and horses, the Federals made twenty-five prisoners crawl on their hands and knees to discover the location of the mines. The Military Road was reached at 1 a. m. and a halt was called until daylight.[11]

In the storm and darkness, some of the artillery with Colonel McIntosh turned west as directed by a man in a blue coat. It seems that as they moved along past "Westbrook" to the pond on the Mordecai farm they were being greeted by cannon fire from nearby fortifications. The traitor was shot and they retraced their steps back to the Military Road.[12]

The folks at "Rosewood" awoke to the sound of cannon and musketry coming from the east toward Mechanicsville. The Negro George, having spent the night at "Westbrook" came in with word that a number of Yankees had spent the night there and the turnpike was full of them. Thunderstorms began again at 8 a.m. Emma Mordecai wrote, "Picket firing heard very near through the woods. Heaven's artillery has answered peal for peal of ours." Some Confederates came in to get out of the rain and were of the opinion that every man in Richmond was under arms, the enemy was surrounded, and Fitz Lee was driving them. Confederate pickets had retreated to the inner fortifications, making the Mordecai home within the lines. Augusta and Dan Gardiner had spent the night in town because the R.F. & P. trains were not running.[13]

The Reverend Mr. Walker at the rectory had a restless night. He awoke to the sound of small arms fire at 1 a.m., which continued until 3 a.m. The cannons began to resound at daybreak. The family could hear a great deal of musketry in the woods between the rectory gate and the Military Road. By noon, the rector had decided that it was best to get his wife and children into the cellar. There would be fighting on three fronts that day. Fitz Lee had come down the Chickahominy and arrived at the Meadow Bridges at sun up. The swampy land was flooded by the heavy rain. The Confederates encamped on the Hanover side of the river at Mrs. Crenshaw's farm.[14]

The Richmond Daily Dispatch on May 13 told of an attack the day before by the City Battalion at Brook Church at 9 a.m. It also told of fighting near "Strawberry Hill" on Mr. H.P. Taylor's farm, where an unnamed infantry battalion drove the enemy into a dense body of woods. General Gregg was trying to hold off General Gordon until the Federals could escape from the area by way of the Meadow Bridges.[15]

The story is told that on the day after Stuart was wounded there was fighting in the woods near Brook Church. The Federals were making a stand while a needed bridge could be prepared. Some Confederate infantrymen (perhaps the Department Battalion that had joined Gordon's Carolinians) were pushing them when a voice rang out, "Where is my boy? I am looking for my boy!" In his broadcloth coat, tall hat, clerical collar and cravat, with his deep voice, the man was recognized as a well known elderly Methodist minister. "Go back; go back!" the southerners called out. "No, no; I can go anywhere my boy has to go, the Lord is here. I want to see my boy, and I will see him!" About that time the order of "Forward!" rang out, the old man, his long hair streaming, beaver hat in one hand, big stick in the other, called out, "Come on boys!" He led them into the depths of the woods. It has been said that no one who saw him that day will ever forget the parson who led the charge at Brook Church.[16]

The fighting along the Military Road was about a quarter of a mile from the Old Brook Church. "Buena Vista" was built of brick with basement walls three feet thick. When fighting was going on in the area, the family would descent to the cellar. Crawford Redd, a boy in knee pants at the time, said that a loyal Negro would take the horses to the woods. Once the Yankees found one horse that the Negro said wasn't worth stealing. The Redds did not fare as badly as some of their neighbors. Dr. Terrell and the Grants had lost horses earlier in the year when the Terrell home was ransacked. Two of the Ladd brothers were serving with 25th Virginia Battalion.[17]

General David Gregg posted his men facing west on the Military Road and Colonel Irvin Gregg his men on the north side, with General Henry Davies to the south. A small stream meandered to the south for about a quarter mile near the Burton home. There General Gregg built some shallow breastworks and posted a battery on a little hill. General Gordon turned his North Carolinians on to the Military Road and faced Gregg with two regiments dismounted and the third ready to charge the battery. He sent word to Richmond that he needed more troops and guns.[18]

A hospital was set up in the three story Gooch house on the left side of the Military Road. Colonel Charles E. Phelps, of the 7th Maryland, a Union man who had just been freed from capture, has written that he walked down the lane to the Gooch house. There he found the surgeons laboring over the wounded and the floor slippery with blood. Some of the prisoners approached, cautiously carrying the round black mines. To Mrs. Gooch's query as to what would be done with them, a doctor quipped that they would probably be put in her cellar, but she need not fear because her house had lightning rods. There came another loud clap of thunder and the house shook. When the doctor and Phelps picked themselves up off the floor, Mrs. Gooch and her elderly mother were nowhere to be seen. They had fled to an interior room and were seen no more. The dark clouds hung low over the battlefield while the rain came down in torrents and forked lighting split the sky.[19]

A wounded man was taken to the rectory at 2 p.m. Shell

fragments and spent bullets were picked up in the yard. A mere lad of 14 years, John Barry Purcell served as a temporary courier for the Confederates. That night he had slept under a tree by the Meadowbridge Road and was awakened in the morning by the firing of the great Columbiad in the Intermediate Defense Line. He saw Confederate Archibald Gracie deploy his men in front of the fortifications. They cast aside their blankets, crossed an empty field, and entered a body of woods. Purcell was sent on horseback with a message for the general. He overtook him on the Meadowbridge Road where the road rises slightly and falls down to a creek. The boy delivered the dispatch but stayed with the Confederates while they pushed the Federals down over the creek and up another hill to the intersection with the Military Road. From this vantage point on horseback, he could see the skirmishing in Mrs. Gooch's yard about 200 yards away.[20]

Braxton Bragg, President Davis's military advisor, sent General Eppa Hunton and his Virginians - including the 56th Virginia Infantry with its Hanover men, the 25th City Battalion, and two guns to assist Gordon to the west. To the Immediate Defense line to the east at Ladies Mile Road, he sent General Gracie with his Alabamians, the 19th Virginia Battalion Heavy Artillery and the 6th Virginia Local Defense Troops (known as "The Tredegar Battalion") under Major Anderson. Gordon found the greenhorns, with only one gun, to be of little help and diverted his attention to his cavalry. He was shot in the arm and died six days later. At "Strawberry Hill," the home of the Davenports, General Wilson was trying to hold off the Confederates until Custer and his men could repair the Meadow Bridges. It seems that McIntosh was again facing fortification guns and Gracie was bringing his men against him. Both Wilson and Colonel Chapman dismounted their men and extended their line into the woods. Lieutenant Charles Fitzhugh, discouraged, had begun to pull his guns back when Sheridan reminded him that they were only facing city clerks.[21]

From his vantage point the Purcell boy could see the Federals crossing the railroad tracks. He saw someone ride up and give a message to General Gracie, who soon thereafter discontinued his pressure on General Wilson. Later the boy learned that it was word from General Bragg saying that it appeared that Sheridan was leaving and he recommended no further action upon the Federals. The hope had been that Gracie and his men could crush Sheridan in a vise while Fitz Lee held at the bridges. Gordon's requested artillery had arrived at 9 a.m., the second battery proving to be more effective than the first. Eppa Hunton and his men arrived at 10 a.m. with the City Battalion following them up the Brook Pike. They never seemed to get fully coordinated with Gordon's cavalrymen. Moving to the east along the Military Road, Gracie handled his men and the Tredegar fellows very well. He was slightly wounded and his horse was struck three times.[22]

General George Custer and his Michigan men had moved in the rear of Sheridan's command. Custer reported that he left the battlefield (Yellow Tavern) about midnight and was put in the advance toward the Meadow Bridges. At the Chickahominy they used the railroad bridge to jump from tie to tie and took position in the swampy bogs. Their riflemen waded into the flooded lowlands with only their heads showing above the water. They kept Fitz Lee's men at bay while Merritt's pioneers used every scrap of wood available to repair the flooring of the road bridge. A member of the 2nd Virginia Cavalry, serving with General Wickham, remarked that they had not recognized the men in the murky swamp, saying, "Those damned rascals played the turtle on us."[23]

By 4 p.m. the bridge flooring was completed and Colonel Alfred Gibbs began crossing his Reserve Brigade in the midst of another heavy downpour of rain. Riding four abreast the horsemen traveled along the 12-foot roadway for about a mile, bounded on both sides by the flooded land. Their riflemen fired down through the Confederate entrenchments and into their rifle pits, causing Lee's men to retreat to secondary earthworks. Some riflemen were shooting from behind bushes and trees. The Richmond Sentinel on May 21 said that the 2nd Virginia Cavalry had counterattacked but it had failed. Colonel Robert Randolph, of the 4th Virginia Cavalry, had called for "one more volley before we leave," when he received a mortal shot through his brain.[24]

By May 13, General Sheridan sent word to General Grant of his success in destroying supply lines at Beaverdam and Ashland, and that he had proceeded to Yellow Tavern, where they captured two of the enemy's artillery before pushing them back across the north fork of the Chickahominy. He had captured the first line of fortifications and camped for the night on the bluffs overlooking the Virginia Central Railroad and the Mechanicsville Road. The Meadow Bridge had been found to be partially destroyed and a battery of Confederate artillery defending the crossing. He claimed that it might have been possible to have taken Richmond; however, his men had existed for six days on the rations that they had brought to last them three days. Their mounts had been living off of grass almost ever since they started out. He said, "The country passed through by my command is entirely destitute; there is nothing for man or animals."[25]

It had taken three hours under the heavy artillery fire for the Federals to repair the bridge. Generals David Gregg and James Wilson confronted the defenders who came out of the second line of fortifications. There was a large body of dismounted cavalry (Hampton's) and the fighting was severe. Gregg and Wilson collected the wounded, leaving the most crucially wounded in the surrounding farmhouses to be cared for there.

Then, according to Sheridan, they recrossed the Chickahominy River and camped for the night of May 12 at Walnut Grove (Church) and Gaines's Mill. As they proceeded to move toward General Butler and his forces, they must have found themselves so well surrounded that their communication from Bottom's Bridge at 11 p.m. had to go by way of Jamestown Island.[26]

The Daily Dispatch from Richmond on May 17 spoke of the speculation in the city on the size and intent of the expedition. Incoming prisoners said that there were three divisions. However, the editorial comment was, "If the force had been a very strong one it would have never allowed Stuart's cavalry to dog it all the way from Ashland, attacking whenever it chose and gaining advantages without having turned upon it and given battle"[27]

Fitz Lee reported on May 13, "The enemy's cavalry has retreated this morning in the direction of Tunstall's and Dispatch Station [New Kent] after a spirited effort to capture Richmond." He quoted General Bragg as saying that "the Confederates' vigorous fight on May 11 (Yellow Tavern) had enabled him to draw troops from Drewry's Bluff to repel the assault on Richmond the next day." He told of the deaths of Stuart, Pate, Randolph, the wounding of Gordon and many others, leaving many companies without a commissioned officer and squadrons commanded by second lieutenants.[28]

The companies of the 5th Virginia Cavalry had been devastated, especially those who had been dismounted. Their colonel was dead, their surgeon - Samuel Meredith - mortally wounded, and their adjutant Otho Pate slightly wounded. Captains of Companies C, E, and G were dead. Lieutenants of Companies B, C, D, F, I, and K were wounded and/or taken prisoner. Lieutenant Fontaine Boston who had been exchanged barely seven weeks before this, was sent with others to Fort Monroe and then back to Point Lookout. Three of the privates who were captured had just joined the troop on April 1 and another had been conscripted in February. Their roster shows a loss of at least sixty captured at the Meadow Bridges.[29]

General Eppa Hunton had his brigade at Chaffin's farm or Chaffin's Bluff, on the north side of the James below Richmond. They used the log cabins that General Wise had previously used for his troops. The Hunton family consisted of the general, his wife Lucy, and their eight year-old son Eppa Junior. The mother taught the boy reading, writing, and spelling while the father attempted to teach him mathematics. However, the boy's attention was on military life and drilling, not arithmetic, so one day he had to have a whipping. The general had dubbed him a captain on his staff, confusing the boy when he could draw no pay. Eppa Junior was even more chagrined when the commandant in the fortifications promoted him to a major and gave him a star but referred to him as a "militia Major " whereby the youngster wished that he had never seen the star.[30]

Each time the Union cavalrymen threatened Richmond in the early months of 1864, the 56th Infantry, as part of Hunton's Brigade, marched from Chaffin's Bluff to meet them. On the first occasion (Kilpatrick and Dahlgren) they found that other Confederates had turned the enemy back. On the second occasion Mrs. Hunton and the boy were staying with a relative in the city. Some ladies in the city sent Eppa Junior and a young Negro boy to the general with a basket of provisions. No one knew where the father was and already the boys were too close to the front. Reluctantly they gave the hamper to an officer to be delivered.[31]

On May 12, the 56th Virginia Infantry formed a line across Brook Turnpike and was ready to charge when they received word that the enemy was gone. General Braxton Bragg, fearing that Sheridan would slip by them into Richmond, sent Hunton word to return to the fortifications. The general said that he had heard from some of his prisoners that they were at the point of shooting their horses and surrendering. Upon the regiment's return to the bluff, General Hunton sent his adjutant down the river each day to reconnoiter General Butler's movements. Soon it was determined that Grant might try to flank Lee and get into Richmond and that Hunton and his men should join Lee. Lucy and the boy went to stay in Lynchburg where the general's army pay could not provide them enough food without additional rations from the army supply. One day she had only a soup bone on the stove. She left the kitchen, instructing her son not to touch the pot, but he decided to stir it and spilled all the contents on the floor, Lucy was left with no food for herself and a little bread and molasses for their son.[32]

General Merritt had taken Algernon Storrs from "Hunslett Hall," his home near the Meadow Bridges, to direct him to Mechanicsville. Pursued by Fitz Lee, Merritt felt perhaps that he had been tricked, but a local man assured him that was the only way and Storrs was released. When the Reverend Mr. Walker heard that the enemy had crossed the Meadow Bridges, he sent his son Willie into the woods to bring back the cow. He closed his diary with, "Thus ends the most exciting day thus far of the war. Thanks to a Merciful Father and Savior we are all spared."[33]

At "Rosewood," Emma Mordecai wrote that the sound of firing had subsided at 2 p.m., on the 12th. When the storm had passed, she and Rose walked to the "Westbrook" lane. The pickets told them that the firing had been on the other side of Mr. Stuart's place. One of the men was riding a Yankee horse which he had found still saddled but rider-less. The man also had a Federal gun which he said would fire seven times without reloading. Their neighbor, Mrs. Taylor, sent a servant over to say that she had been ordered to leave her house because the "fight would be resumed in the field at the top of the hill." Rose sent back word that she had heard nothing of the sort and would not leave unless she was forced to do so, but Mrs. Taylor was welcome to spend the night with them. The ladies at "Westbrook" stayed dressed all night for fear they might be "overrun by Yankees."[34]

Mr. Linton (from the railroad crossing?) came with the news that the Yankees had been driven off and were across the Chickahominy with Fitz Lee still in pursuit. Ambulances had been carrying the wounded into Richmond all day. Some servants had carried wounded to the schoolhouse and neighboring homes along the turnpike. He also brought news of Stuart's death and Gordon's wounding. That night some pickets came to "Rosewood" to ask if they could have shelter in the barn from the rain that begun falling hard again. Rose gave them some wheat coffee and hoecakes for their supper. Emma closed her journal for the day saying, "So ends this stormy, harassing, exciting day."[35]

On May 14, Emma and Rose filled bottles and jugs with sweet milk and buttermilk and drove the carriage up the turnpike to see if they could be of assistance to the wounded that had been left in the neighboring homes, only to find that they had been moved to the hospitals in town. Then they went to survey the battlefield. There they saw shattered trees and deep ruts but no other evidence of a great battle. Other women and girls were searching in the woods for any plunder they could find. On their way to pick up Gusta at her school, they saw that everything looked like war. Soldiers in the barracks were lying on the ground wrapped in their blankets; women, young girls, and servants were serving the men refreshments. Few people were on the streets. The post office, stores, and most of the markets were closed. The Mordecais left the milk and biscuits they were carrying at the officers' hospital.[36]

In her letter to their son Junius with the Signal Corps in South Carolina, Mrs. Powell wrote of the effect of the presence of the Union troops in their neighborhood. She said that Mrs. Gooch's house was left in shambles with not enough food remaining for one meal and all the men and boys gone except old Patrick. Two of the Negroes from "Melrose," Charles and Davy, had gone with the soldiers, but Davy returned a few days later. Nat King had lost two Negroes and the Delaplanes two, plus two mules and all their corn and poultry. Dr. Terrell's house was "riddled with balls."[37]

During the damp and rainy weather, Dr. Powell and the servant Susan had been suffering from rheumatism. Blanche was at home. The father sent Junius fifty dollars on at least two occasions and may make a request for his promotion. On the farm, the corn had come and it appeared it would be a good fruit year. Mother Powell admonished their son not to be uneasy about the family, saying that they can "get along as well as anyone else." She stressed that he not be depressed for, "All's well that ends well . . . God bless you my son."[38]

Philip Sheridan conferred with General Butler at the Charles Friend house in Chesterfield. He brought news of Grant's success in the Wilderness before they left for Yellow Tavern. Butler concluded that Grant would be in Richmond in seven days and Sheridan should wait for him south of the James. However, Sheridan only promised to clear the river bank of torpedoes.[39]

Chapter 19
DREWRY'S BLUFF – MAY 1864

When the spring of 1864 opened up, some of the men in the Hanover Troop were still in search of fresh mounts. Horatius Anderson was taken captive in Hanover County in March and Ashbury Brock was wounded, perhaps when forty of them rode with John Mosby around Grant before he moved to Fredericksburg and the Wilderness. This may have also been the time when Thomas Dunn was wounded near Warrenton. David Timberlake had been made captain of the troop in October 1863. Colonel Robert Lee (Bob) Randolph, formerly captain of the Black Horse Troop, was in charge of the 4th Virginia Cavalry when they moved to support Lee at Spotsylvania Courthouse. Bernard Pollard of "Williamsville" and Reuben Nuckols, who had transferred to Stuart's Horse Artillery, were killed in action at the courthouse.[1]

During the fighting at Yellow Tavern and the Meadow Bridges, most of the local artillery units were supporting General Lee in the Wilderness and near Spotsylvania Court House and serving under General Ewell in the Second Army Corps. Reorganization of the artillery came about as they emerged from their winter quarters. In April the Hanover Artillery was still camping in Orange County. Elihu Parrish wrote to his wife Emma saying that he hoped that she was well but he was so hoarse that he could barely talk. He had been on detail getting timber to make wagons. He expressed his love for her and their children, little Bob and Emma, and sent his love to Anna, Ella, and (big) Bob. He was not far from home, but he felt so far away from them![2]

Hilary Jones, of both the Hanover and Morris Artilleries, had been elevated to full colonel and made chief of artillery in the Department of North Carolina. Major Wilfred Cutshaw was put in charge of the former Jones Battalion, which included their neighbors with the Courtney Artillery and the Second

Richmond Howitzers. He was a kindly, much respected man who would settle in Richmond after the war and become the city chief engineer. The Courtney Artillery participated in the battle at Spotsylvania Court House on May 12 with disastrous results. In the "Bloody Angle," twenty-three men of the battery were taken prisoner, including their lieutenant in charge, Benjamin Maxwell. Two were killed, including Richard Vaughan, and two wounded. Sergeant Giles Courtney, although also wounded, was the only officer left with the battery. The prisoners from Hanover and Henrico were: Benjamin Bennett, Damascus Harlowe, James and Thomas Tyler. The latter two may have been sons of the Widow Tyler who had six other boys in service and petitioned the Secretary of War Randolph for the release of her son Joseph after the fighting around Richmond in 1862.[3]

The Richmond Howitzers had moved out of their camp near Frederick's Hall to Orange, bringing with them newly enlisted Creed Davis of Hanover. They did not participate in the fighting in the Wilderness, but were near the line of battle. The Second Company went into position along General Robert Rodes' line on May 10 one mile west of Spotsylvania Courthouse. The 3rd Company Richmond Howitzers were at Spotsylvania under Benjamin Smith of Richmond. He had been wounded at Charles Town in 1862, taken captive, had his left foot amputated, but was back with his men after being exchanged.[4]

On May 10 at Spotsylvania, Captain Smith of the 3rd Howitzers had his men about a mile west of the courthouse. He positioned his battery within 250 yards of the 2nd Howitzers, to their left. One by one their guns were lost. When a gun was being moved back into position after its recoil, Major David Watson was mortally wounded and died a few days later. Captain Smith's brother, Edward, was also mortally wounded. His funeral was at 2nd Presbyterian in Richmond on

May 19. It was the worst day for the 3rd Company since the beginning of the war. Three men were killed, two mortally wounded, and nine others wounded. Captain Smith and twenty-three of his artillerymen were captured and 25 battery horses. Richard Chamberlayne, William Courtney, Edward Crump, Charles Fourquerean, all of Henrico, were sent to Fort Delaware. Sergeant William "Buck" White's family lived in Hanover County near Polegreen Church. His howitzers were supplied horses from the captured batteries. It was reported that he and his men manned their guns with distinction at Spotsylvania on May 14.[5]

The news of the fighting filtered down to Yellow Tavern. Mrs. Stewart had Marion write to the Mordecais on some Yankee paper she had found in their camp near the barracks. She wished to know if they had any news of their boys. The Stewarts and Mordecais were not only neighbors but fellow parishioners at Emmanuel Church. Some of the Mordecais in Richmond converted from Judaism to Christianity and it contributed to controversy in the family through generations. Emma Mordecai's brothers George and Augustus, husband of Rosina Young (an Episcopalian) both converted. Emma gave it serious consideration during her engagement to a young man in Raleigh. Afterwards, during a period of despondency, she decided to remain with her heritage. She would attend synagogue when in Richmond and have her own private devotions at Rosewood. Occasionally she would attend Emmanuel with Rosina.[6]

Rose and Emma had just returned from Emmanuel on Sunday, May 15, when they heard Lizzie shriek out, "Mas Georgey's come!" They all rushed to the door and saw John Young and George in the buggy. George came limping in but said that he was only wounded slightly in the thigh. He had been wounded on May 10 in Spotsylvania. Some five-cent pieces in his pocket had deflected the minie ball so that it did not damage the bone. Quiet settled over "Rosewood." George slept in with his mother. In the days to come, they would visit his mother's cousin, Lawrence Young, in the Seabrook Hospital. Emma, distressed at Rose's account of the soldiers "more prostrate & helpless than infants, and the urgent need there at the hospital," began taking their supply of milk and other things to the hospital, making Lawrence's cot the center of distribution. Lawrence's father and sister had been to see him, but his mother was too upset by his injury to leave her home. The stories George Mordecai must have told while recuperating at home: the death of their beloved Colonel John Thompson Brown from a sniper bullet through his forehead, their march through the Wilderness by way of Shady Grove Church, his own wounding and the disaster experienced by the 3rd Company. Mr. Linton brought him the "cheering news" in the Richmond *Examiner* of Beauregard's success south of the river on May 16.[7]

****

There had been uncertainty in the Confederate command concerning the direction Burnside would take when he came east from Tennessee. Would he go to assist Grant in Virginia to approach Richmond overland or to the assistance of Federal forces in North Carolina at Weldon? Grant conferred with Butler at Fort Monroe during the first weekend in May 1864. He told him to take City Point and, sticking close to the south side of the James, dig entrenchments and strive to push the Confederates toward the Richmond defenses. Should he be able to do that the Army of the Potomac would join him to act as one unit. Beauregard was in charge of the area of North Carolina and Southside Virginia. When Burnside went toward Grant, Beauregard headed toward Petersburg, where an ailing Pickett was in charge. Butler left only a few men at City Point, moved his forces by water to Bermuda Hundred, and began to push up the turnpike and the railroad toward the outer fortifications. By May 14 Beauregard's command had been extended to include Drewry's Bluff and he was combining his Carolina and Virginia troops to defend Richmond. General Beauregard came up from Petersburg, skirting to the left to avoid Butler's troops. He arrived in the rain on May 14 at the Drewry Mansion inside the fortifications, and was met with the news of the fighting in Spotsylvania. Later in the day President Davis came to confer with him. Beauregard felt that Lee should draw south for a junction with him to defend Richmond. Davis did not agree.[8]

Joseph Thomas, of the 15th Regiment, remembered that they had marched (from New Berne) to Raleigh and then went by boxcar to Petersburg and found that Butler was threatening that area. Buck Francis was not with them having taken sick on the march from New Berne. He was kept in the hospital at Raleigh for three days and then sent to rejoin the regiment by way of Danville. On the day he left Danville, his fellows were involved in the fighting at Drewry's Bluff. Thomas said that their fortifications extended from the bluff, on the James, to west of the Richmond and Petersburg Railroad. The Confederates had a hot picket fight (on May 14) that drove them (the Federals) behind their line of works, with some killed and wounded. Thomas said that the next day being Sunday they remained quiet behind their works.[9]

Twelve men from Hanover in the Patrick Henry Rifles were wounded at or near Drewry's Bluff, most of them from the action on the skirmish line near Halfway House on May 14, led by Major Charles H. Clark and Sergeant Lucius Clark of Hanover who were also wounded. Four of these men died of their wounds. The cousins Richardson and William Haw from Studley in the Hanover Grays were also wounded. Two days later George Edmond Massie, son of Peter and Eleanor Jackson Massie of "Iron Hill" west of Ashland, would be left for dead on the battlefield. Some Richmond ladies found him, took him to their home and nursed him back to health.[10]

LaSalle Pickett, who had married General George Pickett at Petersburg only a year before this, remembered May 16 as being a beautiful sunny morning, while at the Drewry farm south of the James only a few miles away it was so foggy that approaching soldiers could be seen only from the waist down. Pickett was sick and General Robert Hoke was commanding Corse's as well as three other brigades. Corse's brigade faced the Federal General Quincy Gillmore's men of the 81st and 96th New York regiments, and the 39th Illinois. The dense ground fog swirled between them. One Confederate soldier said that he "drew his hat closer over his eyes, looked once more at his accouterments, and waited with bated breath the order to clear our works and charge the enemy."[11]

Beauregard ordered the whole line to charge across an open field. The 15th Virginia was on the right of the brigade, and just west of the railroad. The men moved ahead against the enemy's works, Thomas said, "for about three hundred yards with shot and shell pouring into us." Corse feared for his right side which was largely unprotected. General Thomas Clingman's North Carolinians "advanced with spirit, but the effort was sadly lacking in coordination" and failed to connect with friendly forces in the center. General Hoke said of Clingman's regiments and Corse's Brigade, "They went forward in good style, and drove the enemy from their front, but owing to the superior numbers and strong entrenchments they were not able to drive them entirely from their positions … They were small commands, but did their duty well. …The losses of these commands were necessarily heavy, owing to a front attack." The 15th had about 95 killed or wounded. Butler had been pushed back to Bermuda Hundred where he was under the cover of his gunboats. Corse's men stayed there watching them until sent back to Richmond May 19-20.[12]

The regimental adjutant of the 15th, James August, whom Tom and Buck Francis often spoke of in their letters, was so seriously wounded that he had to spend the remainder of the war as a conscript officer. In the Ashland Grays, four from Hanover had been killed: Joseph James, William Daniel, John Woodson, and Richard Green – one of Lucy Ann Cross's admirers. Seventeen other men in the regiment from Hanover and five from Henrico were wounded and eleven from the two counties had been either killed or mortally wounded.[13]

Joseph Thomas said that they had charged "the enemy's works across an open field on May 16 for three hundred yards with shot and shell pouring into us." Both Charles Terrell and Tom Francis were among the wounded who were sent to the General Hospital # 9 in Richmond. It appears that Tom had a gunshot wound in his hand and Charles was wounded in his thigh. Jo Terrell was at their camp at the time of their wounding and tried to get her husband on the train to Richmond, but it would not stop for him. Tom was transferred the next day to Chimborazo Hospital # 1. Then he was furloughed for sixty days. Charles Terrell was transferred to St. Francis de Sales Hospital on Brook Road (the present location of the Children's Hospital). He was a large man and he died on May 25 of nervous shock from the amputation of his leg at the thigh. It is not presently known where he was buried.[14]

General Beauregard reported his success to General Bragg in Richmond on June 10 saying that General Robert Hoke had become "hotly engaged and handled his command with judgment and energy… An afternoon storm and then darkness prevented further advance." Beauregard said that night, May 16, the enemy "retired to the fortified line … leaving in our hands some 1,400 prisoners, 5 pieces of artillery, and 5 stand of colors." Joseph Thomas said that the next day they followed the enemy some distance into Chesterfield County, where they stayed until the 21st. That day they were ordered to Richmond and camped for the night in the Capitol Square. On Sunday, May 22, they were put on the R.F. & P. Railroad at 8th and Broad Street to join Lee in Caroline County where they would watch out for Grant's movement of cavalry and infantry.[15]

Some of Corse's men were used to guard the railroad at Chesterfield Station (Ruther Glen in Hanover County), others at Hanover Junction. By May 25 the brigade had been rejoined and they moved to Atlee Station on the Central Railroad in Hanover. Eppa Hunton and his men were back with Pickett's Division and along side of Corse's men. Buck Francis wrote to Lucy Ann Cross that he had found only seven men left in his company after the fighting at Drewry's Bluff. By July it would be up to twenty-two.[16]

****

The Powells of "Melrose" had been aware of the skirmishing near Chester Station and the battle at Drewry's Bluff and that Breckinridge was holding Sigel in the Valley. In her letter to Julius Mrs. Powell expressed concern about his brother Johnnie at VMI from whom she had not received a letter since the fighting at New Market in which forty-seven cadets had been wounded and seven (or eight) killed. Marshall Vass, a neighbor's son, wrote to his mother that Johnnie Powell and the Reverend Mr. Walker's son Charlie were unhurt. The local papers reported that the corps had "behaved splendidly;" and that they might be sent to serve as regular army in the defense of Richmond. In that case, Dr. Powell planned to try to get his boy transferred to a branch of service other than the infantry.[17]

Johnnie Powell must have had quite a tale to tell his family how on May 15 at New Market the boys surged across and up out of a gulch ahead of the veterans to capture a six-gun battery. General John D. Imboden wrote after the war, "A wild yell went up when a cadet mounted a caisson and waved the institute flag in triumph over it." Their Professor Ship had taken the 225 strong corps of 16-18 year-old students to assist Breckinridge's infantry, cavalry, and artillery to hold the Shenandoah Valley at the little village of New Market. The militia of Rockingham and Augusta counties had also been called out. The Valley was Lee's "bread basket" which Grant would strike again and again, this time with Franz Sigel. New Market straddled the Valley pike, with the north fork of the Shenandoah to the west and Massanutten Mountain to the east. There is a small gap in the mountain where supplies could be transported over a mud pike to Luray and points eastward. The Confederates were successful this time and Breckinridge was sent to assist Lee. By June 1, Sigel was replaced by David Hunter who pushed Imboden out of New Market.[18]

****

J.H. Kidd, who rode with Custer, has written that they took a three day rest on the James River, May 14-17, before marching through Charles City County to destroy Bottom's Bridge over the Chickahominy River on May 19. From there they came back to Hanover Court House by way of Newcastle, Hanovertown, and the Price's ("Dundee"), with no opposition until they reached the courthouse.[19]

A bugler showed some of them a way across the fields to the back of the station. They helped themselves to the commissary supplies and destroyed the tracks and two trestles while their advance guard confronted the Confederates. That day "the brigade bivouacked on a large plantation where [there] was a colonial house of generous proportions. It fronted on a spacious lawn, which sloped to the highway and was fringed with handsome old spruce and Austrian pines." Kidd went on to say that the house had large porches on the back and front, a center hall with large rooms on either side. Back of the house was a spacious garden. Custer paid his respects to the ladies and assured them protection. He left them with his regards to his "friend Rosser." (This would have been "Courtland," the home of Betty Winston where she and Tom Rosser were married.) The next day, May 21, they found that they could not cross the South Anna because Lee's infantry, cavalry, and artillery had already come up from Richmond. They had to cross over the newly repaired Pamunkey River Bridge at the White House and go through King William County to join Meade at the North Anna.[20]

The fighting at the center of the Yellow Tavern area had passed out to the fringes. While Grant shifted to the left from Spotsylvania Court House, Lee took the interior lines to the North Anna. He kept the cavalry busy on his flanks. Both Rooney Lee and J. Lucius Davis had been released from prison in early spring, but Davis did not return to his troops until July. Members of the 10th Cavalry (Henrico Dragoons) were directed by Generals Rooney Lee and John Chambliss. It appears that the dragoons remained on the left flank. The last letter from Jimmie Gray was written on May 1 from Picket Post Robertson. He said that the Yankees had broken through their lines and "dashed into Madison Court House and captured the mail." They were doing very well, getting eight pounds of corn a day (for the horses) but did not know how long that would last. There were no letters from Nat Cross during this time.[21]

On May 21, Lee learned that General Hancock was already at Milford Station. He started Ewell and the Second Corps to Hanover Junction, just three miles past the North Anna. The juncture was important to Lee throughout the war. There the Virginia Central from points west met the R.F. & P. Railroad, running north and south, with supplies from the Valley. The Confederate forces fell back from Spotsylvania to cross the North Anna River. Porter Alexander took his artillery along the Telegraph Road to their winter camp grounds of 1862. He rode to the Wortham home and found them greatly disturbed for fear they would soon be within Federal lines. They were sure that they would lose their chickens, livestock, and fences but were determined to try to save their house. On Sunday, May 22, the artillery was parked near the home of Parson Fox, whom Colonel Alexander had come to know when he stayed with the Worthams. That afternoon the colonel was sitting in a basement window when the house was struck by a shell. He was not hurt but a courier standing nearby was killed.[22]

The 4th and 10th cavalries containing the Hanover and Henrico Dragoons had constant skirmishes with Grant's men as they moved down the Telegraph Road and were engaged near Mudd Tavern. They tangled on May 22 with Colonel Joshua Chamberlain's Pennsylvania, Michigan, New York, and Maine infantrymen on Littleton Flippo's Farm (west of Bowling Green). Chambliss had assembled his three regiments, their ambulances, wagons, and guns in Flippo's field when he saw Chamberlain approach from the north. Immediately Chambliss set two of his guns near the house, sent the 9th and 10th regiments into the woods to fend off the approaching infantry and had the 13th Regiment escort the remaining guns to safety. Once his equipment was out of range, Chambliss fired his two remaining guns and "a wide gap was made in the column, and a good many of the enemy ran in confusion." Rooney Lee led the regiments off along familiar byways. That afternoon they crossed the North Anna and camped near Hanover Junction.[23]

Grant thought that Lee was retreating and followed him. Lee was setting a trap of an inverted V-shaped salient designed by his trusted engineer, Martin Smith. Its apex rested on the river at Ox Ford. Lee's left stretched to Little River and his right to Hanover Junction. Grant divided his armies only to find Generals Anderson, Breckinridge, and Hill within the salient. Generals Ewell, Rodes, Fields, Gordon, and Early were to Grant's left toward Hanover Junction, with Mahone and

Kershaw lined to his right and Heth, Pickett, and A.P. Hill waiting in reserve near Little River. Grant had walked right into the trap and could not communicate with the two flanks of his forces without going back across the North Anna. Lee had been sick for days and could not spring the trap. Longstreet had been wounded at the Wilderness. Hill had just returned from sick leave. Lee did not feel he could trust Anderson, Ewell, or Early to direct that large an operation. They were able to hold the salient until Grant moved back across the North Anna.[24]

There are very few accounts of life in northern Hanover during the North Anna Campaign. Theodore Lyman, an aide to General Meade, told of arriving at the river during a violent thunderstorm. "The lightning fell so near that it really hissed, which was disagreeable, as there was an ammunition train close by." He goes on to describe the North Anna as a pretty stream with banks so steep that he wondered how they ever got the trains down. Along the road were many dead horses, shot by Sheridan and his men because they were so broken down from their trek to Richmond and back by way of Fortress Monroe. The countryside had been stripped of food. At a poor house near Chesterfield Station, he saw little children crying and their mother who said the cavalry had taken everything and left them to starve. "So the soft-hearted General [Meade], who thought of his own small children, gave them his lunch, and five dollars also."[25]

We can follow the movement of the Richmond Howitzers on May 27-28 by the account of William Meade Dame of Danville, who had joined the 1st Company at Brandy Station and had been wounded at Spotsylvania. Apparently he remained with his unit as it marched to the North Anna. He said that they moved back and forth on Major Doswell's farm, but were subject only one day to sharp infantry fire. Then they took an all night march through the slashes of Hanover. They had to wade through water up to one foot deep from the recent heavy rains. Their gun wheels would mire in the mud and have to be pried up so they could move on.[26]

Creed Davis, of the 2nd Howitzers, described their passage that night through the slashes on the Ashcake Road, near his ancestral home. It was midnight and the rain was coming down in torrents until it stood six to eight inches deep in flat areas. He stumbled along, half asleep with his hand on the mouth of a cannon to keep himself from falling. "Not a sound was to be heard save the splashing of the water by the horses, and of the battery, as it was dragged along wearily by those animals who had neither rest or food for a great while – probably forty eight hours." They saw along the road, in the impenetrable darkness, not a light from a solitary house, nor heard a chicken crow or a dog bark. No one spoke. There was an occasional snorting of a tired horse. To Creed, it felt like "the shadow of the Valley of death." He would not have known where he was had not his Uncle Shelton Ragland, also of the 2nd Howitzers, called it later to his attention.[27]

Chapter 20
HAW'S SHOP - MAY 1864

Grant and his forces crossed the North Anna over bridges and pontoons, burning the bridges and leaving some pontoons until all had crossed. They, too, found the roads muddy and traveling difficult. Grant made his headquarters the night of May 27 at Mangohick Church in King William County. The next morning Sheridan crossed his cavalrymen over the Pamunkey at Hanovertown on pontoon bridges. During the day two elements of his armies crossed and the next day two more corps crossed on two pontoons upstream at Mrs. Nelson's, six miles from Hanover Court House.[1]

Now that Stuart was gone, General Lee sometimes used Colonel Bradley Johnson and his Maryland troopers as his eyes and ears. He sent for Johnson and his lieutenant colonel Ridgley Brown, to determine the direction Grant was moving and from whence his supplies would be coming. They passed around Grant and determined that he was moving through Bowling Green, drawing his supplies from Tappahannock and that Sheridan was moving his cavalry through King William County. Johnson was highly complimented for this report. On May 27, he was told to report with his men to Fitz Lee at Hanover Court House.[2]

On May 27, as soon as Capt. Van Brocklin of the New York Engineers got the first pontoons in the water at Hanovertown, Custer began crossing his cavalry over the Pamunkey River into Hanover County. To the west along River Road, they were met by the 5th North Carolina Cavalry, now led by Colonel John A. Baker, the very ones who had fought against Gregg at Brook Church. The 1st and 5th Michigan cavalries pushed the Carolinians pass the Newton home, "Summer Hill," to Mrs. Hundley's fields opposite Nelson's Crossing. Custer set up headquarters at Dr. Brockenbrough's house "Westwood" and sent some of his troopers south along a road to Haw's Shop at Studley.[3]

Lomax, in charge of the cavalry stationed at Hanover Court House, dispatched Bradley Johnson and his men around their flank to assist Colonel John A. Baker and his North Carolinians who had been watching the crossing near Hanovertown. Johnson went about a mile along a side road, but before he could deploy his men on level ground, he met Baker's pickets "retiring in good order, followed by the enemy." The fighting was fierce for twenty minutes and most devastating when they passed through a gate on Pollard's farm. The Marylanders lost 50-60 men, killed, wounded, or taken prisoner. The colonel lost his sword and had his horse killed from under him. His lieutenant-colonel had severe slashes to his head.[4]

Fitz Lee reported to his uncle that Federals had called off their pursuit about noon. It was still undetermined whether Grant would be moving through Haw's Shop or Hanover Court House. That night the New York engineers checked the crossing at Mrs. Nelson's. The next morning within an hour they had erected a canvas pontoon bridge there using the surplus pontoons left over from the bridges at Hanovertown. Bradley Johnson was on the hillside overlooking the river at 2 a.m. May 29. He reported to Fitz Lee that Grant had been crossing two of his corps during the day. The colonel was unable to ascertain the safety of those in the house, (possibly Mrs. Nelson and her daughters, Kate and Letitia), because there was a security guard posted at the door. The Nelson boy had gone to be with Wickham in the 4th Virginia Cavalry.[5]

Generals Grant, Meade, and Hancock made their headquarters at "Williamsville," a large brick house between Nelson's Bridge and Studley. This was the home of Dr G. William Pollard, his wife Mary Todd, three or four sons and two daughters. At the beginning of the war, one daughter, Ellen, was about 20 years old and young Harry was six. Mary Pollard had died of tuberculosis six months after McClellan's men came through "Williamsville." She was buried in the family cemetery. It was Harry who later wrote of their experiences - the raiding parties, the presence of McClellan's men, Custer's men fighting on their farm, and Grant, Meade, and Hancock pitching their tents in front of the house and eating in their dining room. The family retreated to the upstairs and the Negroes moved into the basement, bringing their household goods. Even one man brought a hog which one day came up the stairs.[6]

The body of their eldest son, Bernard killed at Spotsylvania, was never recovered. The younger boys piled up stones at the entrance to the yard to protect the family. The four-year old carried a brick bat saying he would "kill that Yankee who stole his hen if he ever found him," but he never did. The brothers watched Custer line up 500 men for battle and were fascinated with his appearance, gold braided suit, long yellow hair and mustache, and blue eyes. They saw the wounded stripped of their clothes before they were tended to, the blood gushing out from the back and front of those who had been shot through their bodies. Dr. Pollard brought into the house a Southern soldier who had been left for dead on the field. Ellen and an elderly Negro nursed him night and day for three months. When he went back in service, he asked Sister Fannie to marry him. Young Harry said the she had not "lifted a hand" for his care.[7]

On one occasion, a raiding party knocked at the front door while four Confederates went out the back door. Ellen answered the door and replied that she would die before telling where the men had gone. Later when one of the same Yankees returned and accused her at pistol point of not recognizing him, she replied that she knew no one in the Yankee army. In May 1864, when George Pollard saw that breastworks would cut through the burying ground, he asked the Yankees to respect his wife's grave. General Hancock said that he would be glad to comply with his wishes and the earthen works were diverted around the sacred ground.[8]

While Grant slipped away from the North Anna through King William County to cross back into Hanover County Lee's forces, including the artillery, took a shorter route to Totopotomoy Creek, southeast of Hanover Court House. Colonel Alexander camped with his artillery the night of May 27 at "Half Sink," near where Stuart had been mortally wounded two weeks before that. The colonel took the road through Atlee to join Lee on the left flank as he set his line toward Cold Harbor. Pickett's Division joined Hill's men on May 27 on their march south. They moved to Ashland and camped the first night between Hughes Crossroads and "Half Sink." The next night they could be found between Hundley's Corner and Walnut Grove Church.[9]

With Lee headed toward the Totopotornoy were the Corps under Generals Anderson, A.P. Hill, and Jubal Early. The commannding general dispatched his cavalry from Atlee Station at 8 a.m on May 28 to Haw's Shop. Wade Hampton took his column of about 4,500 men past the old Shelton home, "Rural Plains." Besides his South Carolinians and his Georgians, Hampton had with him Generals Wickham and Tom Rosser with their Virginians, and Rooney Lee with Chambliss's brigade. They formed a line from the marshes of Crump's Creek, where their artillery was planted, and, southward across Atlee Station Road and in the direction of Totopotomy Creek, where Breckinridge could buttress them on Lee's flank.[10]

Sheridan sent his men under Generals Alfred Torbert and David Gregg, starting at Crump's Creek and Dr. William Brockenbrough's farm, pass Haw's Shop and Salem Church to meet the Confederates on the level fields of John Haw's farm. Custer had with him his Michigan men and General Henry Davies had men from Pennsylvania, New York, New Jersey, and Ohio. The Federals were backed by artillery from Maine and Massachusetts. They fought both mounted and dismounted, leaving their mounts with horse-holders and giving at times the impression that they were infantry. The slaughter was great around Enon Church and in the woods that bounded the narrow farm roads. General Gregg took over "Oak Grove" for a hospital while Mr. and Mrs. Haw and their daughter retreated to the cellar.[11]

During the fighting around Haw's Shop, Chapman Tyler of Gary's brigade served as a guide to Fitz Lee. He was sitting on his horse near the general when a nearby shell exploded, a fragment striking Tyler on his head. This took place only a short distance from his childhood home. A few days later he was dead. Private St. George Brooke, a member of Wickham's brigade, was wounded in the thigh during the initial charge. A Federal placed the wounded boy in a fence corner with a rail to protect him from the charging horses' hooves. When the Yankees moved their wounded to Salem Church, the Haw family requested that young Brooke be left in their house. That night a surgeon returned to remove the bullet and the next day the doctor came back four miles from the front to put a wire splint on the Confederate's leg and a chaplain from Maine brought St. George some lemons.[12]

According to Joseph Haw, conditions had been quite traumatic around the Haw home. The line of battle was only one-half mille away. The Federals set up horse artillery in the yard, drawing the Confederate fire and destroying the surrounding oak trees. Five horses were killed in the yard, two nearby, and forty on their farm. The family's outside kitchen was used as a hospital until the chimney was struck, a shell rolled under the operating table, and the medical services were moved to

Salem Church, the Haw shop, and the community school. Shells went through the smokehouse and a storage house while the grandmother and a sister huddled in a shallow basement.[13]

Cavalry men under Captain Thomas Pinckney of Charleston had come up from South Carolina and camped below Emmanuel Church. When they reached Richmond, they had been promised carbines that would shoot four or five times without being reloaded, to replace their long muzzle loaded Enfield rifles. When Wade Hampton ordered them into Hanover, they had not received their cavalry rifles. During the fighting, Captain Pinckney noticed a Confederate artillery person standing beside him who was handling a gun very skillfully. On closer observation he saw under the artillery cap the smooth face and the plaited tresses of a woman. "Madam, what are you doing here in this guise?" he asked. "Just what you are," she answered. Both were taken prisoner that day and he never heard what became of her. The story is told of a Confederate female prisoner who gave birth to a child at Point Lookout.[14] (Could this have been the same woman?)

When the fighting subsided, the Federals buried their dead close to Enon Church, carving their names on boards from the church as temporary markers until they could be removed to a national cemetery. They buried the Confederates in shallow graves until the neighbors could move twenty-six bodies to the churchyard. Many South Carolinians were never found. One family came by and was able to identify a loved one whose foot was sticking out the ground and whose name was written on his underwear. Generals Rosser and Hampton came through on June 3 and the Haw family sent the letters that they had written for the Carolinians to their families.[15]

The losses on both sides were about the same. Sheridan considered it a "hard contested engagement" and Custer reported that his loss "was greater than in any other engagement of the campaign." The inexperienced Hampton made some misjudgments, especially that of withdrawing when Rooney Lee thought that they were facing infantry. Rosser told one of the Haw brothers after the war that their position was strong at that point and it could have been held. The green South Carolinians had proved themselves, although the 4th regiment had lost 127 out of its 300 men. Captain Pinckney was captured and had to give up the prized sword which his grandfather, a signer of the Declaration of Independence, had carried in the American Revolution.[16]

The Union armies headed toward Totopotomoy Creek and Cold Harbor. Grant used his cavalry under James Wilson to protect his rear. Some were stationed at Crump's Creek, others took up position a couple of miles west on River Road. Wilson made his headquarters at Dr. Price's house. Colonel McIntosh parked his guns in Bickerton Winston's yard, "Signal Hill," on the road to Cash's Corner. A hospital was established for wounded cavalrymen. Soon their scouts ran into Confederate pickets on the River Road. Wilson was ordered to take Hanover Court House, and to destroy the railroad there and at the South Anna. Chambliss with his 9th, 10th (Henrico Troop) and 13th cavalries, Colonel Gilbert Wright with Georgia and Mississippi men, General Pierce Young with Colonel John Baker's North Carolinians and Captain William McGregor's Horse Artillery tried to stand in Wilson's way, The Union troops were too strong for them and the Confederates fell back toward Ashland.[17]

Warren's headquarters was said to have been temporally in a house at Cash's Corner (between Peakes and Hanover Court House). In that area Colonel Richard Beale of the 9th Virginia Cavalry said that the depredations were similar to those caused by Sheridan in the Valley. It appeared that they "had not been committed by irresponsible stragglers and vagabond camp followers, but under the eyes of commanding officers." He saw some homes inhabited by women and small children where no food was left except "poultry not yet feathered." The cavalrymen gave the children what food was in their haversacks and the next morning left the company's bacon with the mothers. They were able to extinguish the flames in one house which had been set afire to hide the fact that all the furniture had been broken up.[18]

Two Ohio men have described the terrain as they approached Mechumps Creek, below Hanover Court House, "Before us was a narrow belt of timber on the extreme verge of a steep bluff, and at the foot of the bluff a narrow meadow, cut up with deep ditches full of running water, and girdled by a thick, matted growth of brush, briars, and blackberry bushes - and on the opposite side of the meadow the bluffs of Hanover, on which were stationed two brigades of rebels with four pieces of artillery." Those who crossed the road found themselves fired on by the artillery and also dismounted North Carolinians shooting from behind "fence-rail breastworks." They dropped to the ground and laid flat between the corn rows while the shots rattled against the dead cornstalks. Colonel Beale heard McGregor call out, "Pour it in, boys!", but the Union men had too much momentum and the defenders could not hold. It began to get too dark for the Federals to pursue them. The Union Colonel John McIntosh and his men had been joined by those under George Chapman. They spent the night on the courthouse grounds.[19]

Federal General Wilson set out the next morning, June 1, to destroy the railroad bridges, leaving some men in regiments from Vermont, Indiana, New Jersey, and New York behind. They followed in the wake of Rooney Lee, with Chambliss, the 10th Virginia Cavalry, and the Carolinians who had evacuated the courthouse region the previous night. The men were divided into two groups - those with McIntosh following the Ashland Road and those with Chapman the River Road. Along the latter road, they soon ran into Bradley Johnson and his Maryland men and the Baltimore Light Artillery. The colonel did not feel he could handle such a large force and sent to Rooney Lee on the Ashland Road for help.[20]

Young Lee sent Johnson word that he could not spare any men because he was already involved with Mclntosh, but for Johnson to do what he could about the bridges. This miffed Johnson and he was even more embittered when, upon returning from a ride west to check roads for retreat near Ellett's Crossing, he found that his trusted lieutenant colonel, Ridgely Brown, had received a mortal wound through his neck. Johnson was demoralized and refused the help of the regiment led by Rooney's aide, Captain Theodore Garnett when it did arrive, saying "Colonel Brown has just been killed. I cannot stop the enemy here." Johnson retreated southward down the R.F. & P. tracks toward Ashland, leaving the way open for Chapman to take Ellettt's Crossing, destroy the trestle, the superstructure and many small bridges in the area.[21]

A Virginian, reporting to the Richmond Sentinel, said that Ridgely Brown had come from Montgomery County, Maryland, on June 1, 1861, and exactly three years later had been killed. "Of the many brave and noble men who have fought the invaders of Southern soil, and have died in defense of Southern homes and Southern rights, none deserve a higher tribute of praise, or a larger measure of thanks from the Southern people than Colonel Brown." He was credited with contributing much to the "success in thwarting Kilpatrick and Dahlgren in their designs against Richmond."[22]

Tom Rosser was able to take some of the pressure off Rooney Lee and followed the Federals into Ashland, interrupting their supply train, taking prisoners, spare horses, and provisions.

Yet before Tom's men reached the turnpike the Federals had burnt the water tower, two hand cars, and the blacksmith's shop. The story is told in Ashland that many of the troopers were in the hotel when the Confederates got into town. When Rosser' s men came in the back door, McIntosh's men were going out the front windows and doors, leaving thirteen of their men dead in the street in front of the hotel.[23]

Wade Hampton, a few miles away at Atlee Station, heard of the melee. He, General Pierce Young with the North Carolinians, along with Rooney Lee's brigade – including the Henrico Dragoons, blocked McIntosh on the Telegraph and the other roads below Ashland leading toward Richmond. It was a hot day and, as had been the case lately, they fought dismounted, beginning around noon and lasting until dark. One of Lee's men wrote that it was "the hardest day's work I ever did! We had to double-quick a great deal and marched altogether several miles." When relieved by some Vermont men, McIntosh retreated up the tracks to join Chapman at Ellett's Crossing. It had been a battle that Wilson had not meant to fight, loosing almost 200 men and his opponents about the same number. The bridges had been destroyed, but the Confederates rebuilt them in a few days. Hampton had proved he could improvise and came close to destroying part of the Union force. And now, thanks to Tom Rosser, his men had 300 to 500 fresh horses.[24]

DeWitt Gallaher, a courier for Rosser, told in his diary of an attempt by General Custer to capture Rosser at Hanover Court House. They had been friends since their days together at West Point. During the spring and winter of 1864, when Rosser and his men were in the area, the general would often spend the night at his wife's home, "Courtland." One day a Negro alerted Custer that Rosser would be there that night. The Yankee took a few men and and drove in the Confederate pickets. A faithful servant slipped into Rosser's bedroom, awoke him, and then saddled his horse, allowing Tom, still half clad to escape. Custer left a note with Bettie Rosser saying: "Dear Tom – Hearing you were 'at home' I called to see you and sorry not to find you there." It was signed "Custer." The next day Custer came back with a larger force. Rosser had returned briefly, but knowing his friend would be back, he left the note: "Dear Custer – Hearing that you were at my house I called to show more hospitality and sorry you had left!" and signed it "Rosser."[25]

Letcher's Battery of Henrico men, had been a mile north of Ashland when word came that the enemy was in the area. Their guns were ordered into position under cover of tree limbs and branches. Lieutenant John Tyler was in charge of the battery at that time. When within a half hour no enemy had appeared, the lieutenant took two guns in search of the Federals. They did not see them as they passed through Ashland but posted a picket at the railroad, at the turnpike, and at Kilby's Station (Elmont). The men were rewarded for their diligence with delectables from the quartermaster's store.[26]

From May 21 - 23, the 2nd and 3rd Richmond Howitzers were moved to protect Hanover Junction. Then on May 27, they were sent to Atlee Station. On June 1, the batteries were placed a few hundred yards from Pole Green Church. Before the day was out, Sergeant William White, of the 3rd Howitzer, had seen the church of his forebears set on fire and burned by the activity of his own men.[27]

There are no Terrell-Francis letters for this period or during the fighting at Cold Harbor. Joseph Thomas of their company mentions in his memoirs only that they went up to Caroline to meet Grant. Then they fell back across the South Anna River and marched to the lower part of Hanover (Cold Harbor). He said "Grant made a desperate effort to break through our lines but failed with a heavy loss."[28]

Pickett's Division was stationed a little left of center of Lee's line at Cold Harbor. The Federal attempt to break through the lines had been made on June 1. The next day was hot and dusty and both sides did little more than work on their trenches. It began to rain and continued through the night. On June 3, Grant attempted to break through the center. Companies of the 15th Virginia Infantry were used out front as skirmishers. Captain Campbell Lawson, formerly of the 2nd Howitzers but now of Company H, sustained an injury that resulted in the loss of his leg. William Goodman, of the Patrick Henry Rifles, was also wounded. Two days later near Cold Harbor Thaddeus Jones, of the Henrico Guards, sustained injury.[29]

The 56th Infantry Regiment with its Hanover men had been sent to Hanover Court House to meet Lee's army on May 23. There was a battle on Edward Kelley's family's farm during the fighting around Cold Harbor. The enemy made the house into a temporary hospital. Blood from the amputations ran out the front door, across the porch, and down the steps. All the family linens were ripped up for bandages. The barn siding was torn off for coffins to bury hundreds of soldiers in the yard.[30]

General Evander Law, wounded on June 3, no longer had with him his trusted scout, John Cussons, who had settled at Allen's Station with his new bride. There had been controversy between Law and Longstreet for a number of months. The Alabama general had been arrested, cleared by the Secretary of War, and returned to his command, but on his recovery he was made a major general in the cavalry under Wade Hampton.[31]

Surely there was grieving in Ashland and Milford when Captain Clarence Woolfolk had been killed on June 3 at Cold

Harbor. His brother Pichegru had been taken prisoner just two days before that while he was home with the family. Pichegru, captain of the Ashland Artillery, was sent to Fort Delaware and was not released until August. The Morris Artillery under the direction of Major R.C.M. Page was used in Early's line near Bethesda Church and beyond the Old Church Road on June 3. They participated in an intense enfilade fire in the defense of Rodes' division until 7 p.m. Neither the 4th nor the 10th Virginia Cavalries appear to have been used.[32]

The 2nd Howitzers were heavily engaged on June 3 south of the Old Church Road. They were again in action on June 7 and then moved the following day to a grove of trees on the William Gaines farm. George Mordecai was still recuperating at "Rosewood" and anxious to get back with his company. They could hear the heavy cannonading and rapid firing. George rode out toward the action on June 3. When he returned shortly with his brother Willie the womenfolk were alarmed, but Willie was a quartermaster sergeant and had come to get clover from their neighbor, Mr. Grant. He reported that the fighting which they had heard was very severe and they "gave the Yankee a good whipping."[33]

There was much joy at "Rosewood" that night. Gusta had not been able to get to school and there was her darling brother at home. She wished that she could go back with him, at least to be one of his wagoners and take orders from him. They feasted on "delightful fried chicken, onions, boiled and fried, asparagus, cold ham, rice, fresh butter & a dessert of a fine large dish of strawberries & cream." Emma was certain it would have cost at least five dollars in town. George Mordecai rode back with his brother the next day. It was a beautiful sunny day. Emma and Gusta took a long walk and picked wild flowers. When George returned, he brought news that their other brother, John, had been in the fighting all day but was all right. George had seen a train of ambulances a half a mile long going for the wounded and also many wagons taking the wounded into the city.[34]

For many days they would see men going by with horses that had been either injured or their riders killed or disabled. They were being taken to a horse recruiting station on the river. Willie was home many nights while getting provender from the neighbor-hood. The trains were not running and Gusta was unable to get back home from school. George took his aunt to town in a rickety wagon pulled by a soldier's skittish horse. She was concerned about someone she called Morton who was not getting the proper care at the St. Francis de Sales Hospital on Bacon Quarter Branch. Emma was also worried about a cousin's servant, Moses Morrill, who was reluctant to go out of his home for fear of being taken up in the impressments of Negroes.[35]

Chapter 21

TO THE VALLEY – SUMMER AND FALL 1864

William Robertson, in his book on the Bermuda Hundred campaign, has concluded that Grant had expected to join Butler on the James by May 15. Such was not to be the case. Beauregard had brought his troops in from North Carolina. Not only had he held Drewry's Bluff and the south side of the James, but he had sent some troops to help Lee at Cold Harbor. By June 15, what Beauregard had feared was happening. Grant was crossing the James on pontoon boats and threatening lightly held Petersburg. The Confederate general got Robert Hokes' North Carolinians and Bushrod Johnson's Tennessee men there just in time to hold the city. To do so he had to abandon the lines at Drewry's Bluff. Soon Pickett's Virginians, having followed Grant over the James, crossed over on pontoons at Drewry's Bluff. They were able to retake the works and remain there during the ensuing months while Petersburg was being assaulted.[1]

General Hunton recorded that General Pickett was ordered to march on June 16 back to Drewry's Bluff and to arrive as soon as possible. Since the bluff was just across the river from Chaffin's farm, Hunton knew the area very well and was asked to lead the troops along the country byways and across the pontoon bridge. They marched a mile or two down the Richmond and Petersburg Turnpike to below the bluff, through an area that has been characterized as "tangled brush, undergrowth, briars and … highly wooded." Joseph Thomas of the 15th Regiment said that when they came upon the enemy they were used as skirmishers, firing from behind trees until their Captain Govers gave the command, "Let's charge them!" Also directing this charge was Captain James W. Waid of the Hanover Grays. They drove the enemy down past the breastworks which Beauregard had abandoned to go to Petersburg and Pickett's men again occupied the works. General Hunton said that Major Drewry, who lived in the area, witnessed the action and spoke often of their feat that day. Buck Francis, in his letter to Lucy Ann Cross, wrote that they retook the works with little loss. His hopes were "to drive old Grant from our soil never more to return and [we can] be restored to a speedy and honorable peace."[2]

Lucy Ann's neighbor, Jimmie Gray, lost his life in Charles City County when the 10th Virginia Cavalry was pushing Grant's men down the Chickahominy and over to the James, below Malvern Hill in Henrico. They had remained on the fringes during the fighting around Cold Harbor and did not go with Hampton in the pursuit of Sheridan to Trevillians in Louisa County. Along the James River they fought dismounted and had no earthen works for protection. Starting June 13, there were several skirmishes near Nance's Shop, in the area of Samaria or St. Mary's Church. On June 24, the 10th Cavalry was being led by Colonel R.L.T. Beale, along with his men in the 9th Virginia Cavalry and the 24th Virginia Cavalry, when Jimmie Gray was killed.[3]

Colonel Beale has recorded that the Federals had hastily set up a barricade of "logs, rails, and earth." The Confederates had to cross a field which was several hundred yards wide. This they did in an "orderly manner … at double quick time." Major William Clement of the 10th Virginia was commended on his leadership. The sprightly Lieutenant James Lucius Davis, Jr., Company E, mounted the barricade, called out. "Lookout boys, I will be first in the enemy's works." Just then he received a mortal wound in his face. "But the works were carried and the enemy's right turned."[4]

In this action the cocky Jimmie Gray must have received his mortal wound. One day in a somber mood he had expressed his dread of his body being returned home across his horse. Somehow a companion obtained a wagon, perhaps a rickety one. Bearing the boy's already blackened body, they appeared

in the lane to the Yellow Tavern home of the Gray family on the upper Chickahominy River. Was horse Fleetfoot pulling the wagon or the Yankee one he had written his aunt of capturing not long before this? The grieving Richard and Frances Gray with perhaps their daughter Betty, a younger brother Pomp, an older sister Pris and the beloved "Aunt Mat" from Keysville buried Jimmie in the Gray-Cross cemetery which overlooks where Stuart had been mortally wounded only a few weeks earlier.[5]

****

After Gettysburg, the Hanover artillerymen received few injuries. Pettus Ragland, an ambulance driver, died in a Richmond hospital of unknown injuries on July 15, 1863. Alpheus Nuckols received a slight back injury, no one seems to know where. Perhaps it happened at Spotsylvania, Cold Harbor, or around Richmond. It was recorded on June 23, 1864.[6]

****

On June 30, Emma and Rosina Mordecai set out to visit some of the neighbors across the turnpike and through the area of the fighting on May 12 at Brook Church. There was still much devastation – trees topped by cannon balls, fences broken down, and fields lying in waste. The soldier's horse pulling their carriage "behaved so vilely" that they stopped at Westbrook and sent back home for another. Mrs. Gooch told the dreadful tale of the use of her house as a hospital, with amputations on her mahogany table, irremovable blood stains on her well kept floors, and the wounded and dying being left in the house. In addition to taking all her meat, chickens and eggs, Sheridan's men had ransacked her daughter's trunk for all her jewelry.[7]

It was a hot and dry summer. Rosina found enough blackberries to make a cobbler. Willie Mordecai often stopped by when he continued to collect the neighbors' tithes of oats to feed the army's horses. They heard of the capture of prisoners, artillery, wagons and horses from Wilson's cavalry, even chests "full, no doubt of stolen spoons, &c." Surprisingly they heard no celebration from the Yankee gunboats on the river on July 4. Refugees with their wagons from Petersburg were pouring into Richmond. Emma wondered how those from Fredericksburg, Norfolk and now Petersburg would be fed and lodged, "to say nothing of many exiles from Maryland."[8]

****

The year 1864 was full of ups and downs for Colonel Davis and his family. They had lost their son Lewellyn Catesby Davis to camp fever in South Carolina in July 1863 at the age of 19 years. Now James Lucius Davis, Jr. died in a hospital at Nance's Shop after being wounded in the neck. A cousin Lewellyn C. Davis was killed in the same fighting. The colonel had been exchanged from Point Lookout in March of that year, but his record does not show him present for duty until July. Their youngest son, Bathurst, had joined the Dragoons in 1862 at the age of 17 years, but he had resigned to attend VMI for two years. Now in July 1864 he reenlisted while they were in Dinwiddie County.[9]

DeWitt Gallaher shows in his diary that the men under Tom Rosser were constantly on the move during the summer of 1864, passing through Yellow Tavern and Ashland. He said that on June 8 they marched from Ashland in pursuit of Sheridan into Louisa County. Within a few days they caught up with him on the railroad at Trevillians. By July they were back in the Richmond area, crossing over the James on three pontoon bridges. They were in Charles City County, at Chaffin's Bluff. Below Petersburg Gallaher spent a lonely 19th birthday night on guard duty. He had taken a bath the day before, his first in a week. The birthday dinner consisted of "cold water, cornbread and fat bacon." A friend came in from a furlough before the night was over and shared a snack with him. Over the next couple of days, he was able to forage for some peaches, buy a canteen of sorghum, and finally eat a "wartime dinner" at a Mrs. Brick's when he visited a sick friend there.[10]

Rose and Emma Mordecai kept busy in June visiting at the hospitals, Seabrook and St. Francis de Sales, Camp Winder, and with other sick friends in Richmond. Some were improving, other not doing well at all. Word came from Mr. Stewart at "Brook Hill" that it was not going well for the Confederates in the Valley of Virginia. General William E. "Grumble" Jones had been defeated and the Yankees were entering Staunton. General David Hunter was wreaking havoc in the countryside.[11]

Grant was launching a three-pronged attack against Lee's forces: his around Richmond and Petersburg, Butler's movement up the James River; and Hunter's thrust up the Valley toward Lexington, Lynchburg, and the James River-Kanawha Canal. General John Breckinridge had brought his small force to help Lee at Cold Harbor. Now he was sent back to the Valley. On the day that Breckinridge marched from Mechanicsville Sheridan started out to hook up with Hunter. Fitz Lee and Hampton were sent with their men to try to stop the Federal cavalrymen. They met up with them in Louisa at the Battle of Trevillians. Although a copy of the order has not been found, it appears that General Lee told General Jubal Early on June 12 to take what remained now of Stonewall Jackson's 2nd Corps - Generals Robert Rodes, John Gordon, Dodson Ramseur, and Armistead Long with his twenty-four guns to stop Hunter.[12]

General Early left Gaines' Mill on June 13 at 3 a.m. His corps went through Mechanicsville, crossed the Chickahominy at the Meadow Bridges and on to the Brook Turnpike (possibly along the Military Road). From Yellow Tavern, they went up the Plank Road (the present Greenwood Road) to Goodall's Tavern (just west of Ashland). There they crossed to the Mountain Road to camp that night near Auburn Mills on the South Anna River with their headquarters at Chewning's, a half mile from the mill. The next morning was cool, but the day became warm and the roads dusty. They crossed the South Anna and turned back onto the Mountain Road at St. Peter's Church. Jed Hotchkiss had been working on the maps of Hanover County before they left. He made corrections to the Louisa map as they went along and he said that the wagons were traveling along parallel roads.[13] Certainly neighbors for miles around Yellow Tavern must have heard the tramping and seen the dust from the passage through the area with such a massive force of men, guns, and wagons.

The Mordecai brothers were much disgusted about their inactive status with the local defense while the rest of their corps had gone with Early to the Valley. John would walk home from Chaffin's Bluff. George reported to a surgeon only to find that his wound was not yet healed enough for him to go back to his company. Their mother tried to lift their spirits with a good dinner and a blackberry dumpling. On July 8 a rumor was picked up in town that Early's, Imboden's, and Breckinridge's corps would go to Point Lookout in an attempt to liberate 35,000 Confederate prisoners.[14]

Colonel Bradley Johnson was promoted to brigadier general in June at the death of William E. "Grumble" Jones in his stand against Hunter at Piedmont. Johnson was given command of his cavalry brigade. General Lee had been considering an attempt to free the prisoners since January. When Early crossed the Potomac in early July, Lee sent Johnson word to have his command at Point Lookout on July 12 to release the prisoners. General Early had already ordered Johnson to destroy all the railroads north of Baltimore. Johnson replied that it was a distance of 400 miles and that his 1000 horses could not make it by July 12. He started out at daybreak on July 9, covered Early's flank during the Battle of Monocracy, and burned the Northern Central Railroad into Harrisburg. Johnson sent Colonel Harry Gilmor to burn the railroad bridges into Philadelphia and to release the prisoners so they could join Early in Washington. However, when it was learned that Grant had dispatched two army corps to Washington, Early ordered Johnson to rejoin him in Virginia, leaving the prisoners in Federal hands.[15]

On Sunday, August 7, DeWitt Gallaher was passing through Richmond in a cloud of dust that only a brigade of horses could make when he saw Miss Laura Kent, whom he had known in Waynesboro. She insisted that he come in. Tying his horse in front of her house on Franklin Street, he entered a parlor which was filled with "well dressed officers in flashy uniforms and shining boots." He said that they were "evidently swivel-chair officers around Richmond." Laura fixed his lunch, but he was able to eat very little, embarrassed to be a dusty private sitting at a marble table set with silver and china. However, he asked if she could fix a lunch for a "sick comrade?" He bid her goodbye to overtake his command. Soon, he said, "I threw my reins on the neck of my horse and the 'sick comrade' ate and enjoyed that lunch." Joining his fellows at Yellow Tavern, they went on to camp that night in Ashland and marched to within two miles of Beaverdam Station the next day.[16]

Fitz Lee's command was on the way to assist Jubal Early in the Valley. It moved through Louisa, Orange, and Front Royal to Luray and Winchester. When they reached the Potomac on August 31, Gallaher's horse, Don, became lame with a disease called "greasy foot." This was common in the army and was caused by hard marches over muddy ground. Dewitt had ridden him in all their activities since Spotsylvania. The private stayed with Rosser until the end of the year. For Williams Wickham and the Hanover Troop, under the Atlee native Captain David Timberlake, the days of facing Sheridan were far from over. They strove to drive the Federal cavalry from the fertile Valley. No sooner had they crossed the south and North forks of the Shenandoah River than, on August 16, they met their opponents of the fighting at Yellow Tavern, Wesley Merritt and his cavalrymen. The activity, with the help of W.T. Wofford's Georgia infantry, was on the banks of Crooked Run and down the Valley Turnpike toward Winchester. The countryside was often alight with the barns, mills, grain and hayracks set ablaze by the Federals to destroy the commodities upon which Lee's army depended for subsistence.[17]

Mrs. L.P. Lewis, living in Monroe County (now West Virginia) wrote to Emma Mordecai in September that they had had no mail since the Yankee raid on Dublin Depot, a prominent supply point, in May, nor had they been left with much writing material. She sent her letters by "chance" and those were hurried ones to her children. She spoke of "that compendium of human villainy, Genl. Hunter." At the last minute they had been given a guard so that the furniture was not broken nor the beds destroyed. They had been left a few bed sheets and tablecloths, some pillowcases and three blankets and could take meals after a fashion using the necessities of life picked up in the yard, meadow, and fields – five tablespoons and six teaspoons. All keepsakes, jewelry, pictures (except those on the wall) and medicine were gone. Bottles were broken up and cooking utensils confiscated.[18]

Mrs. Lewis said that they were not despondent. She was sustained by the sympathy of her friends and the affection of her children. The little ones had not complained nor asked for bread. She wrote that they were fat and healthy, living like birds off of the apples, fruit, and the onion stalks dropped by the soldiers. The elderly had gone back to work and remained cheerful. Mrs. Lewis concluded that the enemy could not take away God's sunshine, the sweet air, or the love of friends.[19]

General R.H. Anderson had been left to guard Front Royal and the Luray Valley. In the weeks that lay ahead, Wickham and his men would be ranging along the Shenandoah River and Opequon Creek south of Winchester, from Milford, through Strasburg, Waynesborough and Tom's Brook to their final encounter before winter set in at Rude's Hill, near Mt. Jackson on November 22. They were meeting again and again their old opponents under George Custer, James Wilson, Tom Devin, and Albert Gibbs.[20]

The Hanover troopers would fight under a succession of leaders. General Wickham had been elected to the Confederate Legislature that spring. The time was fast approaching when he must leave his men to serve in Richmond. On September 19, at Cedarville and Winchester, Fitz Lee showed "great courage and energy in attempting to save the field," but "in the midst of terrible artillery fire his horse Nellie was shot and he received a wound in the thigh which disabled him for several months." The command of the division then fell to Williams Wickham. Colonel Tom Munford, a Richmond native of the 2nd Cavalry Regiment who had served ably since First Manassas, assumed command of the brigade. Munford had his men fight dismounted as they supported the artillery along Abram's Creek, near Winchester. On the 20th, Jubal Early sent those under General Wickham to "Millford Pass to hold Luray Alley." There they fought on September 22, Wickham's men detaining the enemy until Early could move his men up the Valley to New Market. Jed Hotchkiss, Early's topographer, was very lavish in his praise of them.[21]

The Confederates moved to Waynesborough and Rockfish Gap. There as reported by General Early, "The enemy was engaged in destroying the railroad bridge and the tunnel." Wickham drove the wrecking parties from Waynesborough. In the fighting on the 28th, the 4th Cavalry was directed by Lieutenant Colonel William Woodbridge, a Chesterfield native who had lost a leg after having been wounded at Spotsylvania. Two days later, perhaps as the cavalrymen searched out the location of Sheridan's pickets, William Priddy, of "Medley Grove" in Hanover, was wounded in the face and paralyzed in his left arm. On October 12, he died in a Charlottesville hospital.[22]

Sheridan and his men were on the move down the Valley and continued to burn as they went. Tom Rosser arrived from Richmond on October 3 with reinforcements. Then Wickham felt free to leave for his duties in the legislature. Rosser took over the division and, with the help of William Payne who was temporarily commanding Lomax's men of the 5th, 6th, and 15th Cavalries, they kept at the heels of Sheridan's rear guard.[23]

Hotchkiss wrote in his journal that October 8 was cold and windy, with both hail and snow. That night Rosser's men encamped at Tom's Brook (near Strasburg). The next day, Sunday, at first light "Boots and Saddles" was sounded. The 4th Virginia skirmished along the banks and Payne's men formed behind them. Dismounted Federals were firing from the opposite bank when suddenly the enemy charged across the stream, causing panic and retreat. Although Munford's sharpshooters (1st, 2nd, 3rd, and 4th Cavalries) were rallied, allowing the line to reform, upon the appearance of mounted Federals the Confederates fell back into the woods. A two-hour battle ensued. One participant wrote that it was mainly with sabers. Many of Early's cavalrymen had no sabers and they escaped with only their rifles and the clothes on their back. They were depressed, cold, and hungry. Captain David

Timberlake, of the Hanover Troop, had been wounded in the back.[24]

The Howitzers were engaged on September 3 near Berryville and camped at Winchester. George Mordecai went to Richmond to make final arrangement to return to his unit. He had to be careful not to be taken up by the draft. Many men were being impressed for the army or local service. He left for the Valley on October 12 after the family had received two letters from John. This brother was depressed with the conditions in the Valley and at Richmond. Early's initial success on October 19 at Cedar Creek was turned into a rout that afternoon when Sheridan returned unexpectedly. The 2nd Howitzers were the last to leave the field and then not until the enemy was within 300 yards of their guns. The artillery was lost, including the 2nd Company's four Napoleons. Their company lost thirty-two horses, two men wounded, and twelve captured or missing.[25]

Creed Davis, whose family lived in the Slashes just below Ashland, had joined the 2nd Howitzers just after they came out of winter quarters in 1864 when Lieutenant Lorraine Jones was made captain. They were not yet part of Cutshaw's Battalion when they were sent from Cold Harbor to aid General Early in the Valley. Creed Davis fought along with them at Cedar Creek when Early lost his artillery. Reported missing or captured at that time were: John James, of Hanover, and Hugh Hutcheson of Henrico, who had joined the 2nd Howitzers at about the same time as Creed Davis.[26]

We do not have Emma Mordecai's comments concerning the disasters experienced by the 2nd Howitzers in the Valley after October 12. John had written that their "trust in the Divine Power ... has brought us out of many critical periods." During the closing six months of the war could Emma, with her feminine ingenuity, see that this "Divine Power" was removing the timbers that supported the Southern cause, first in the loss of their guns at Cedar Creek and later of their officers as they came up against the superior numbers of Grant and Sheridan?. We will never know. When Emma went to copy her journal after the war, she found that the insects and mice had destroyed the pages from mid October to early April and she had to fill in the details of the war from letters that she had saved.[27]

Private DeWitt Gallaher stayed with Tom Rosser in the Valley until the end of the year. At Christmas on Mother Gallaher's invitation, General Rosser went to "Courtland" at Hanover Court House and brought his wife Betty and little daughter Sallie to stay at the Gallaher home in Waynesborough.[28]

Chapter 22

BELOW RICHMOND – FALL AND WINTER - 1864

While the local artillery and Hanover Rangers faced Sheridan in the Valley and toward Washington, the infantry suffered in the trenches and the Henrico Dragoons tried to ward off Grant along the James.

The line of defense, according to Joseph Thomas of the Hanover Grays, extended from the Chickahominy to the James, and from the James to the Appomattox River. From the Appomattox the line went around Petersburg. Thomas wrote that they were on the front called the Howlett Line. His brigade was located 500 to 600 yards from the James River. The Howlett House was between them and the enemy but it was so badly shelled that it was torn down. Also the Ware Bottom Church was below them. The enemy sharp-shooters fired from the church until a detail was sent to burn it down. At some places their breastworks were only fifty yards away. Sentinels were posted but little firing was done. He and his fellows remained there until January 1865. Buck Francis wrote that their places in the trenches were only two feet apart. They would raise their blankets for some shade. There was plenty good water to drink and their rations consisted of good corn dodgers, bacon, peas, coffee and sugar. The Hanover Grays remained there until the end of the year.[1]

Buck Francis was the only one of his family on the Howlett Line for several months. Tom was on medical leave, probably dividing his time between brother James, wife Sally and their children; Sister Liz, husband John J. Davis and daughter Mollie; Sister Mat and her husband Dumps; and Sister Jo, her boys, and baby girl. Liz Davis, in her memo on her troubles during the war, wrote on November 19, "Tom goes back in service. Buck has been home on furlough and goes with him." While Tom was on leave, her son, little Charlie, had died of croup on August 31 and just one month later they lost their last son, John Minor, to colic.[2]

Jo Terrell, still in deep grief over the loss of her husband, in September wrote a kind affectionate letter to her brother Buck telling of her concern for him. She told him that she had changed the name of her soon to be one year-old daughter to Emma Charles. Her boys, Jim and Wash, had just had their fifth and seventh birthdays. Buck in reply wrote to her:

> Give me up into the hands of the lord and ask him to take care of me, and all of us and let his will be done not ours and let us submit ourselves to his holy will. While everything looks dark and gloomy around us God is not idle. His mighty hand is at work. He is watching us he knows our movements, and the suffering which we have to under go. And if we pray to him in earnest he will give ear to our cries to bless us he will soon rool [sic] away those dark clouds that now hang over us and the bright sun of peace will soon spread its butiful [sic] light over us once more.

Buck had been detailed as a cook and said that he must make up his bread before dark. Sister Martha's letter had come with Jo's letter. He closed his letter with "your brother until death."[3]

Five weeks later, Buck Francis wrote another letter to Jo Terrell to be delivered by Sergeant (William) Woodson along with a coat which he had picked up in camp for Jo to make a vest out of it for him. He also asked for Sister-in-law Sallie to send him the flannel shirt he left at her house and for Dumps (Mat's husband) to send the cap. When Woodson returned he brought the vest and some of Jo's pies and wine. Buck shared the pies with some of the men and "it came near making them run mad." The wine was not strong enough to make him drunk and he gave a little to the other cook, Jimmie Collins of Hanover. The two of them were cooking for forty-four men at that time. Buck promised to ask Captain Govers about her husband Charles' back pay. She must tell Tom to stay at home as long as possible. Buck had to bid her good morning so he could carry the rations to the company.[4]

Private Luther Swank, of Company B, 15th Infantry, was a hospital steward at Chester in the summer and fall of 1864. Apparently this was the barracks for the Invalid Battalion. In his letters to his sister, Katie, he spoke of going into town with Lieutenant Benjamin Bates, who was the commandant for the soldiers' home in Richmond. In July at the 6th Street market, they could buy beef at $3.50 per pound, cymblins at $2.00 a dozen, one-half peck of tomatoes at $2.00, a quart of butterbeans at $4.00, a pound of butter for $5.00, and a pound of flour for $1.25. By October, sweet potatoes sold for $40.00 a bushel, Irish potatoes for $6.00 per bushel, molasses at $80.00 a galloon, a small head of cabbage for $2.00, butter for $11.00 a pound, and flour $400 per barrel. His individual fare was rice, beef soup, beef loaf, bread and sweet potatoes.[5]

Private Swank was one of four brothers with a young sister he called Katie. The family had moved from Richmond for the remainder of the war, leaving behind their dog, Louisa, who, according to their former neighbor, had visited their deserted house the day after the family left but would not go back again. Luther hoped that they would soon be satisfied with exchanging its "gaieties for the sober dog-trot of a life in the wilderness." Brother Bud was with General Early and Bradley Johnson in the Shenandoah Valley and Brother William with the artillery on the Weldon Railroad. They had another brother Walter, who does not appear to have been in service and who owned a slave, Henry Williams, supposedly working at Tredegar Ironworks. When Luther tried to visit him there, he had been reported sick and could not be located. Their father had not been well and Luther sent him word to follow the doctor's injunctions.[6]

Luther Swank wrote to Katie in July to tell of the recapture of the breastworks below Drewry's Bluff. The Division had advanced into the enemy pits on the previous day. They had taken sixty-one prisoners while losing about forty men. He did not believe that William's battery was involved. The 30th regiment's band had preformed in the Capital Square. In his October letter, he told that their regimental surgeon, Dr Henry Ghent, was on leave in Alabama and would probably be married before he got back. Luther had been building a brick chimney and fireplace in his tent and was sad because he had broken his "looking glass" for he had been "cultivating a fine pair of whiskers a-la-militaire." Their brother Bud had been also turning one out and was apparently already "quite a bluebeard." He closed the letter "with a fond farewell to my Little Sister Subscribing myself always her affectionate Brother, Luther."[7]

****

After Nance's Shop, the Henrico Dragoons crossed the James River on pontoon boats, passed the suburbs of Petersburg, and went down the Weldon Railroad to occupy the crossroads at Sappony Church. There they used rails to construct breastworks and, fighting dismounted, they held off the assaults of Wilson's cavalry plus sixteen pieces of artillery until a captain of the Petersburg Artillery brought up two Napoleons. The next day they followed the enemy to Reams' Station and captured some of the troopers. They were helped by Chambliss' Brigade.[8]

Before Chambliss halted his men they had been joined by Fitz Lee's Division. Fitz Lee reported to his uncle that they had seized eleven guns and all of Wilson's ambulances and wagons, enabling them to replenish their needs. Colonel R.L.T. Beale of the 9th Cavalry remembered that "all our men not previously supplied were now furnished with good McClellan saddles and Colt revolvers." The Henrico Dragoons scouted behind the enemy lines to the James while the brigade camped at Hatcher's Run and Gravelly Run in Dinwiddie County.[9]

It was from the Darbytown Road in Henrico that Lucy Ann Cross had a letter from her brother Nat on July 20 saying that they had come back over a few days before that. The 9th Cavalry had a skirmish and lost some men but the 10th Cavalry was not involved. His horse was nearly well but there was little or no grazing there. They were drawing only five pounds of grain a day. Many Yanks and Rebs were there when they got there but they had gone back (across the James) and he expected they would too. He sent his respects to enquiring friends and especially to Miss Bettie Shepherd. Lucy Ann did not hear again from her brother until September 23 and they were back in Dinwiddie County. He did not tell her that they had been back across the river and had camped at White's Tavern on the Charles City Road, nor did he tell her of the mortal wounding and death of General Chambliss on August 16.[10]

The fighting had been in a swampy area. Colonel Beale of the 9th Cavalry described it as a terrible day when "not a drop of water could be had; the heat was intense, and the wood was dense and tangled." They moved through an area of woods and briers directed by Rooney Lee and Colonel Lucius Davis. The colonel had them fall back into a better position while Rooney's and Martin Gary's men advanced into the jungle. General Chambliss went ahead to reconnoiter but his horse came back with out him and Colonel Davis took over his command. The day was muggy, but they had kept pushing until the Federals left their barricades, having lost heavily in killed and wounded.[11]

Robert Priddy with the Henrico Dragoons had been wounded in his left thigh and sent to a Richmond hospital. From the hospital he was furloughed to Lunenburg County and he spent most of the year there near Keysville. It appears that he might have been a cousin of Jimmie Gray, as well as Henry and Catesby Priddy of the Yellow Tavern area. In Aunt Mat's last letter to Jimmie from Keysville she had asked about Catesby and Henry.[12]

The 10th went back across the James on August 19. They guarded the right flank of the Confederate infantry south of Petersburg along the Petersburg-Weldon Railroad near Reams' Station. Major Robert Caskie, a Richmond tobacco merchant had commanded the regiment for nearly a year, raising it "to a high state of efficiency" when J. Lucius Davis recommended his promotion to the colonelcy. Caskie was wounded in the leg near Reams' Station on August 23.[13]

General Hampton said of Colonel Davis that he "played his part well" in commanding the brigade. He had taken his men to Malone's Crossing on August 25. There the mounted 9th Cavalry charged the enemy barricades while the dismounted 10th Cavalry advanced into the woods in their front, "capturing the enemy picket line and taking about fifty prisoners." The fighting had continued all day with the breastworks being entered and more prisoners taken. Benjamin Perkins of Henrico was wounded in the right hand and sent to a Richmond hospital.[14]

Nat Cross told Lucy Ann in his September 23 letter that they were camping in a pretty place and getting a pound of beef, a third of a pound of bacon, and a pound of flour a day. He did not tell her that his mess mate, Lieutenant McDowell, had gone with General Hampton on the "Beefsteak Raid" near Coggins Point on the James where they seized over 2,800 head of cattle and took more than 300 prisoners. Nat said that the lieutenant was eating with him and they were drawing three rations a day. He saw little chance of getting home because his horse was not "poor enough to bring a detail." Nat wrote that she must send him the pair of pants she was making because he would need them soon.[15]

Lucius Davis took leave of absence on October 17 and the control of the brigade rested on Colonel Beale of the 9th Cavalry. During Davis' absence the Dragoons participated in the Battle of Peebles Farm on the Vaughan and Squirrel roads and at Burgess's Mill on the Boydton Plank Road where it crossed Hatcher's Run. The 10th Cavalry was on picket duty when they were attacked by Union men. They again fought dismounted and "drove the enemy from several positions." James Thornton of Henrico was captured at Dinwiddie Court House and sent to Point Lookout Prison where he remained until the war was over. Sergeant David Watford's mare was killed and he was compensated $3,000.00. Captain George Hopkins, still a prisoner at Fort Delaware, was sent with the "Immortal 600" to Hilton Head during the siege of Charleston. Lieutenant McDowell had been commanding the Henrico Dragoons since September and was elected their captain on November 12.[16]

****

Back at "Rosewood" word came that Wilmington, North Carolina was being threatened and two Confederate blockade runners had been captured. Many men who had been exempt from service were being called up in the draft. Green tea was selling for $75.00 a pound. Emma Mordecai wrote, "Still, people are undismayed & I trust in God, and am hopeful and cheerful." Rose was busy preserving peaches and the apples were being put away for the winter when it was discovered that they were being stolen from the trees. Yankee soldiers were below Rocketts and the alarm bells had been ringing.[17]

Emma Mordecai returned on October 5 from Richmond, where she had been participating in the observance of Rosh Hashanah. She wrote of both General Lee's attempt to recapture Ft. Harrison and the enemy's attempt to take Ft. Gilmer. Both attempts had been unsuccessful. A friend, Edward Meyers, had ridden down to the fortifications and he told Emma that the trenches were full of dead and wounded Negroes. One battle had taken place on Mr. James Taylor's farm. Surgeons were busy amputating in his house while he was "making syrup, as if nothing unusual was going on."[18]

Emma had also seen a Mrs. Dewitt in Richmond whose brother, John Fontaine of Hanover, had been killed near Petersburg. Her comment was, "This war is taking from our country all its noblest, and best young men, and there is scarcely a house in which there is not one dead." Also there was word that Mr. Harrison and his eldest son, William, had been taken prisoners at Craigton, below Richmond, where they had emigrated from Charles City County. Mrs. Harrison, the daughter of a neighbor, had visited "Rosewood" with six children –"large and small" – just a few weeks ago, telling of the "abominable treatment she received from the Yankees."[19]

John Boursiquot Fontaine of Beaverdam, formerly a member of the 4th Virginia Cavalry and Jeb Stuart's medical director, had been made chief medical director of the cavalry of the Army of Northern Virginia under Wade Hampton in August 1864. He was with the general on October 1, 1864, southwest of Petersburg in the area of Arthur's Swamp. The roads were a quagmire due to recent storms. A surprise attempt to outflank the enemy had succeeded only in driving two regiments eastward back across "the boggy ground to join their main body east of the swamp."[20]

General John Dunovant, who with his 5th South Carolina Cavalry, had fought along side General Wickham and the Hanover Dragoons at Haw's Shop and sustained a hand injury, was now with Hampton below Petersburg. Dunovant was of the opinion that their next action should be a frontal attack, beginning at 4 p.m. Barely ten minutes into the fight, a courier brought Hampton word that Dunovant had been mortally wounded. Dr. Fontaine, with an aide, galloped to be of assistance. Passing a battery engagement, he was struck by a fragment from an enemy shell which glanced his chin and passed into his throat.[21]

Five days after the battle, Elizabeth Price Fontaine of "Dundee" received a letter from Major George Freaner telling of her husband's last hours. Freaner, a native Marylander who had also been on Stuart's staff, had witnessed the event. He said that John had not fallen from his horse, but unable to speak, was lifted down and carried on a litter to a house about a quarter of a mile behind the lines. There he was examined by a Doctor Gilliam who determined that there was internal bleeding and there would be no hope for recovery.[22]

Twice Fontaine spoke softly, saying possibly that he would die soon. He whispered, "What would become of my poor wife?" He was unable to swallow a stimulant, and soon fainted from another hemorrhage. Elizabeth was told, "After intense suffering, he became suddenly quiet and in a few moments passed calmly away." His body was immediately placed in an ambulance, taken to a doctor's quarters, dressed and started on its way to Richmond and Beavedam. Maria and Edmund Fontaine, Sr., buried him alongside four other of their eleven children in the cemetery at "Beaverdam." John was only twenty-four, a newly wed of eighteen months. In November

1862 he had become Fitz Lee's brigade surgeon and was the first to administer to Stuart's wound at Yellow Tavern. His brother, Edmund, had been a casualty at First Manassas in 1861. John's tombstone is inscribed:

> He had been spared through the dangers of many
> a skirmish when he rode in the ranks with Stuart
> and Hampton and at last was mortally wounded
> while rendering professional aid to a dying general.

It has been said of John Fontaine, "Caring for more than six thousand men as well as their horses, his death could be directly attributed to his intense devotion to duty and his desire to fulfill his Hippocratic oath."[23]

****

Lucy Ann's cousin, James H. Cross, did not return to service from his wound at Spotsylvania until September 4. The Morris Artillery had been used against Yankee ships during his absence. They were still active in the 2nd Army and considered to be part of Cutshaw's Battalion, but they were still calling themselves Page's men. The 2nd Richmond Howitzers were also in Cutshaw's Battalion when they fought against Sheridan in the Valley. Their captain, Lorraine Jones, was wounded in the head, Hugh Hutcheson, of Henrico, was taken prisoner and sent to Point Lookout and John W. James was missing. General William Pendleton reorganized his artillery in November, saying that they lacked almost everything – men, horses, guns, and all kind of supplies. Some men were used in the defense of Richmond while others remained camped near New Market.[24]

Bettie Shepherd's letter to Lucy Ann on November 10 from Chesterfield County gives us a picture of the life and concerns of the young women at that time. She was with her sister and perhaps her sister's husband in the home of a Charles Whitlock. He was building a house and it appears that Mr.

Whitlock was also is in the process of buying forage for the army. A camp was only a couple of miles away. These may have been men of the Henrico Dragoons because she mentions the handsome soldiers coming by to see her - Mr. Alley and Mr. Perkins, possibly her neighbors in the Dragoons - 25 year-old Mosby Alley and 28 year-old blond, blue eyed Benjamin Perkins. She expected "Dr. Mc" (Was this Nat Cross's friend, James McDowell, who commanded the company?).[25]

Bettie said that she had been reading *East Lynne* and plaiting straw to make hats. She thought that the house there would be a pretty little one when finished, off the road and in the woods and near a railroad. There were no churches nearby which she could attend and she wanted to know if Lucy Ann had been to hear "Bro. Johnson" (at Winn's). She said that Lucy must try to get to see Nannie (Mrs. Mosby?) while she (Bettie) was away. She should "tell Peter (a slave?) to be a good boy & not to eat dirt."[26]

General Porter Alexander wrote of the terrible Thanksgiving for his six hundred artillerymen north of the Appomattox. They had "182 pounds of meat, a quantity of moldy bread, and four or five bushels of turnips and potatoes." Whereas the Federal cavalry hospital at City Point had served "turkey and chicken, cheese, bread and butter, cranberry sauce, tomatoes, celery, apples, peaches, pies, and cakes."[27]

After Tom Francis returned from his medical furlough, it appears that romance had blossomed between him and Lucy Ann Cross while he was home on leave. In his first letter to her he addressed her as "Dear Friend" and later as "Dear Cousin," as Buck always did, and signed them "Your Friend Tom" or "Your Cousin Tom." Buck wrote to Lucy Ann that he believed Tom had fallen in love with someone up there. Since coming back, Buck said that Tom was "as pert as a cricket."[28]

Buck wrote to Lucy Ann on November 30 saying that her brother Finch had joined their company and he "seems to get along quite well but he says that as soon Capt. Govers comes back he is going to try to get a transfer to the 1st Texas Regt." Joseph Finch Cross may have meant the Texas Rangers, a Richmond company organized in 1861 which became Company K of the 10th Virginia Cavalry. His record shows that he was issued clothing in the cavalry in December 1864. Buck wrote to Lucy Ann from Fort Gilmer in January 1865 saying that he was glad Finch had "gotten home before he was taken sick as he would have a hard time of it here."[29]

James Cross wrote to Lucy Ann on December 7 from Fishersville, saying that they were on their way to winter quarters. They were running out of food. He was ashamed to go to anyone's house because his britches were so badly torn and he couldn't get any more. He said that if he had his way concerning the quartermasters he would "turn all of them out." He hoped to get a furlough for Christmas. In the meantime he sent his regards to: Miss Sarah, Mat, Tinny, Betty Gray, and Bettie Shepherd. He had heard that Sarah has been riding like a man and he thought that she "had better stay at home the next time."[30]

Tom Francis, in his letter of December 8, spoke of wishing to spend Christmas with Bettie Shepherd in Chesterfield. Lucy must try to find out if she would still be there. He would very much like to be with some young ladies at Christmas. He had heard that they might be in a fight soon. His Christmas letter showed that he was very low in spirit although there were some ladies in camp singing. He spent half of his time on picket duty. Half the company was "on the block" (AWOL), he said, and it made it hard on the rest of them. He hoped that she had enjoyed herself at Christmas and closed the letter with the words, "I claim you a Christmas gift."[31]

Christmas was not a joyous time with the artillerymen. James H. Cross wrote that it was the worst Christmas of his life. He wrote to Lucy that he had seen but one lady since Christmas came in and she was so cross-eyed that he could not tell when she was looking at him. She had invited him over and said she was a good dancer, but he doubted that she was any better at it than he and it wouldn't be much fun. James had not heard from his sweetheart and he said perhaps she has "kicked" him. Lucy Ann must try to set him up with Miss Sarah back home. He hoped her mother has gotten well and sent his love to Bettie Shepherd and Samuella Bowles. James wondered what she has heard from her brother Nat and his brother Joe because he had not heard from them since they left Petersburg. The army had finally come up with a new pair of pants for him, but he said they were too small and he had sent home for another pair.[32]

The Henrico County Court was concerned not only for the indigent Blacks but also for those in the local companies who did not have the necessary shoes, socks, and winter clothing and also about the needs of their families left behind. By mid-summer the court had started plans to set up a supply depot in the two upper rooms of the courthouse "for the relief of the indigent soldiers and sailors of the State of Virginia who had been or might be disabled in the military service and the widows and minor children of soldiers and sailors who had died or might thereafter die in said service, and the indigent families of those then in service."[33]

Earlier in the war slaves had been requisitioned by the county to work on the fortifications. In the latter years they were needed to fill the county quotas for work in the salt mines in the western part of the state. The court records show one to three slaves were requested from many farms including those run by women – Ann Christian and Lavinia Shepherd, the elderly James G. Francis on the Mountain Road and C.J. Paleski, Dr. Powell's neighbor. The slaves were to be either purchased by the county or the owners reimbursed if they escaped or were carried off by the enemy. Local farmers complained that since the enemy raids through the county there were much fewer slaves and horses to work the fields.[34]

Outrages had been experienced by both citizens of the county and its "refugee sojourners" due to the presence of the enemy. The court felt it important that a record be kept not only of those who aided and encouraged the enemy but also "any instances of heroism, devotion and courage exhibited by any persons in resisting these outrages, and any cases of marked liberality to soldiers and their families." The Governor of Virginia was notified by the Henrico County Court in November 1864 that "many persons supposed to be soldiers and wearing the Confederate uniform have recently frequented the suburbs of the city of Richmond in considerable numbers in the night time, committing depredations, and frightening the peaceable citizens of said suburbs." Because the war has drained off so many of their men, they did not have enough remaining "to organize a proper patrol." The governor was asked to take "such steps as may be proper to check and repress the above irregularities."[35]

Chapter 23

FORT FISHER AND FALL OF PETERSBURG – 1865

Buck Francis wrote to Lucy Ann Cross on November 30, 1864 rejoicing that they had not been sent to Georgia or Wilmington. He was still cooking for his company and they had been ordered to cook up rations for several days for a quick move. Could it have been that Buck expected that the regiment would be sent to support General Robert F. Hoke and his Carolinians in their efforts to keep the port of Wilmington open for the blockade runners? It would not have been the first time that Corse's Virginians had fought along side of them.[1]

General William T. Sherman had occupied Atlanta on September 2, and wished to join Grant at Richmond, nearly 1,000 miles away. He was on his march to the Atlantic and his first objective was to establish a base at Savannah, Georgia, 300 miles away. This, the general wrote, he "accomplished from November 12 to December 21." Actually they had arrived at the seaport on December 16, but they did not gain possession until five days later. He said that he followed the Duke of Wellington's concept that "an army moves upon its belly, not upon its legs" and felt that "no army dependent on wagons can operate more than a hundred miles" before the driver and horses began to consume all the food needed by the fighting men at the front. His men began to forage on the supplies the Confederates had gathered near the railroads for their own use.[2]

Wilmington, North Carolina, was on the Cape Fear River, whose entrance was guarded by Fort Fisher. The city had become "the primary entrepot of foreign trade with the Confederacy." As other larger ports were sealed off by the Union fleet, it became a haven for commerce raiders. Over thirty vessels were taken by the CSS Tallahassee during a fortnight in August. Grant, busy at Petersburg, nevertheless sent 6,500 troops from the Army of the James in December to cooperate with the navy in the first siege of Fort Fisher. This one, under the direction of Generals Benjamin Butler, Godfrey Weitzel, and David Porter on December 25, was unsuccessful. Here they had found two brigades of Hoke's Division and others were on the way.[3]

General Robert E. Lee sent word to Colonel William Lamb, commander of Fort Fisher, that the fort "must be held, or he could not subsist his army." On the night of January 12, an even greater Federal armada began to return with transports carrying 8,500 troops. The District Commander, General W.H.C. Whiting and his staff walked up from Battery Buchanan, at the peak of the cape. The general said, "Lamb, my boy, I have come to share your fate." After the first siege, Lamb had requested more ammunition, but had received none. Now, with some companies of "light and heavy artillery, North Carolina troops, and some 50 sailors and marines of the Confederate navy" arriving, Lamb had 1500 men in all, including the sick and wounded, but little ammunition. Colonel Lamb continued to send messages to General Braxton Bragg, even after he himself was wounded in the hip, but there was no reply. The ammunition gave out and he was not able to hold the fort. Whiting blamed Braxton Bragg, who was actually in charge, for giving up the fort. The general, who had volunteered his services, was taken prisoner and died at Fort Columbus in the New York Harbor on March 10, 1865.[4]

Junius Powell had been in the Signal Corps since late 1862. He was now a sergeant on the ship "Flag" or "Stag" and wrote to his father from St. Georgia, Bermuda on January 1, 1865, telling of their treacherous trip from Wilmington, North Carolina. It seems that they had no trouble with the blockade because most of the ships were participating in the siege of Fort Fisher. He was glad to see that the Confederate guns from the fort were proving effective.[5]

They had left the city on Christmas Eve and experienced no excitement on Christmas Day except for two accelerations to top speed to evade a cruiser lying off the Gulf Stream, thereby taking them 60 or 70 miles off course. A heavy storm sprung up during the night and intensified the next day, causing many to be seasick. When the time came for the sighting of land, they realized that they were lost somewhere in the Atlantic Ocean with only two days supply of coal remaining, few provisions, and little water on hand. The sergeant wrote that there was "some talk of our being reduced to the necessity of turning cannibals." After six days and six nights and "another fearful gale", they came safely into harbor at St. Georgia. Another Confederate ship, the "Talisman," which left Wilmington just behind them, had sunk and its men pulled out of the sea by a Yankee merchant ship also in a sinking condition. The sailors ashore reported that nearly all the ships which had come into port in the last several days had been damaged.[6]

Junius wrote that, should the enemy be successful in closing the port of Wilmington, he may go to Galveston, Texas, or Havana. He surmised, "There is no denying the fact that things are looking rather blue for now, but I hope we will come out O.K. yet." He wrote that Confederate bonds were worth very little but that "cotton will go up rapidly on the strength of the late news – wish I had 1000 bales out (to sell)." He closed his letter with, "You know that I am safe. If you should not be able to hear from me again don't be unhappy." The next letter that the Powells received from their elder son was dated February 10, 1865, and was from Point Lookout Prison. He had been captured off the coast of Smithville, North Carolina on January 19, and taken first to Fort Monroe and was not released from prison until May 29.[7]

****

Nat Cross's letter to his sister written on January 1 shows that the 10th Cavalry was in Greeneville County, south of Petersburg. He said that they had plenty of beef and coffee, although her brother Finch had complained that he was not getting enough to eat. Their coffee and sugar had been put in a house that Nat had built, to keep it from getting wet when it rained. Lucy Ann must send him his pants, jacket, and some grain for his horse Bones. There would be a detail in a few days to select horses that needed to be replaced but he did not expect his to make the list so he could get to go home for another. He was sure that all the ladies back home enjoyed their Christmas with all the blockade runners. There was only one from his company - a married man.[8]

The Francis letters in January and February 1865 were written from Fort Gilmer, on the north side of the James near Chaffin's Bluff. Corse's Brigade had moved back across on January 4. Some of the men lived in the fort, others in the breastworks, which were cold and muddy – not like the log houses that they had left south of the river. Tom received a Christmas present from Lucy Ann. He wrote to her that he had nothing to send in return. She would have to accept him as a New Year's gift. He envied those who "ran the block" and were home for Christmas, but he would not like to spend time in the division guardhouse. They were only six miles from Richmond. He said that perhaps he might go into Richmond one night. Apparently he did go. Buck mentioned that Tom may have seen her brother Finch who was sick in Richmond.[9]

According to Joseph Thomas, food was quite scarce at Fort Gilmer, consisting primarily of hard crackers and fat salt pork, which they ate raw and enjoyed. The peas would be full of bugs which could be skimmed off after they were boiled. They had rice and sometimes flour or meal, never sifted. Each biscuit would have two to four worms in it. There was seldom coffee. A substitute was made from wheat or corn, drunk without sugar. Buck Francis wrote that they were getting pretty much the same rations that they had had for the last twelve months with the exception of meal in the place of flour and potatoes in the place of sugar and coffee. He told Lucy Ann, "Old Jef is all right as long as he can raise corn dodgers and salt pork and a few rebs to eat it … You lady managers must make good crops for to support the Reb Soldiers." Both he and Tom wrote of the bad weather and the mud, with Buck saying, "Hogs can stand a good deal and we are living a hog's life." Buck closed on a saucy note, "Give my respects to Cousin C [Lucy Ann's mother]. Tell Bet [Lucy Ann's sister] that she did not send me her respects so I will not send her mine."[10]

Tom had been hoping desperately for a pass to go home. He wanted to see Lucy Ann as badly as he wanted to see his sisters but the captain had kept his request in his pocket. There had been talk of their being sent to Georgia and that half the regiment might refuse to leave Virginia. By February 20, they were back in their old camp near Chester. Brother-in-law, Dumps Jenkins had been left behind in the old camp to guard the luggage. Tom's request for a leave had gotten as far as Longstreet and then disapproved. He took it with a bit of levity saying that maybe "Longstreet heard of what one lady said about my being too short to mary (sic) he thought that it would be best to put it off a while to let me grow some more …[then] he will give me a pass."[11]

Years later the following penciled verse, headed "Henrico Co. February the 27th 1865," was found among Lucy Ann's keepsakes:

To a Friend:

May all thy future footsteps press
The paths of peace and happiness
May all thy chosen friends prove true
And cheer thee all life journey through

Tis vain to wish thee lasting bliss
In such a fickle world as this
But may the sand of fortune blow
Gently around thy path below

May virtue, truth and lofty worth
Be thy attendant while on earth
And when at last thou comes to die
Oh may thou have a rest on high
From a Friend
To J.T. Francis[12]

****

The 2nd Richmond Howitzers were brought back to the Petersburg area in February 1865 and settled in at Fort Clifton on the Appomattox River. Half the company alternated with the other half on picket duty with no more danger than an occasional harassment or misadventure. John Pryor of Hanover was killed one night as he lay asleep on the second floor of the guard house. A fellow soldier came in off duty, threw his rifle into a corner, causing it to discharge. The shot went through the ceiling and into Pryor's heart. Sheridan again threatened General Early in March and the Howitzers were sent, armed with muskets, back to the Valley. When the threat did not materialize, they went on to High Bridge and then back to Fort Clifton.[13]

After the fighting in the Wilderness and Cold Harbor, Grant was continuing his circuitous clockwise route around Petersburg in order to come up below Richmond. The Confederate defenses consisted of a quadrant about Petersburg. Grant made his headquarters at City Point. Wade Hampton and his cavalry faced any threat along the Weldon-Petersburg Railroad while the infantry tried to hold back Grant's Second Army as it swung to the northwest and to make connection with General Sheridan. General Gordon's attempt to retake Fort Stedman from the interior lines was unsuccessful.

Lucy Ann's letter from Tom Francis in January told of the shelling of Fort Harrison. He said that he preferred a quiet life and there is much talk of peace. Buck's letter written at about the same time spoke of the fight with the ironclads, known as the Battle of Trent's Reach, "which amounted to nothing but the loss of the little Drewry and five kill (sic) on the Virginia no good done." Buck had lost hope that the war would be over by June. Lucy Ann's letter from her brother Nat in March spoke of looking for deserters along the Nottoway and Roanoke rivers and told of the return to the regiment of Malor Redd, supposedly as a result of old bob's (Lee's amnesty) proclamation."[14]

General Porter Alexander with the artillery was not easily discouraged. He wrote to his wife Betty that he still expected "to live to make old bones." While inspecting the lines near Howlett House he was kicked by a shying horse and suffered one or more broken ribs. He was allowed a five week furlough to go to Georgia to see the again pregnant Betty. Sherman was already in the Carolinas and Alexander had to take a roundabout way, but even so encountered a train and a hotel full of refugees.[15]

When Tom Francis wrote to their sister Jo from Chester on March 4, he expected to go on guard for the division. Then he would have more privileges such as going into Richmond with the prisoners. He would like news from James' wife Sallie since she hasn't written to him. This is Tom's last extant letter to his sister. He closed with, "Your brother until Death."[16]

Three days later, after a divisional review, two of Pickett's brigades marched to Manchester. Then two days later General

Corse led his men over muddy roads and through incipient darkness to arrive at the camp in Manchester at 3 a.m. They then continued on March 12 in early morning marches across Mayo Bridge, on up Main and Broad streets to Brook Turnpike and the outer defenses. March 13 found them on the Military Road to the defenses between the Meadow Bridges and Mechanicsville, only to return north along Brook Turnpike toward Ashland on March 14 to serve along with the 17th Virginia as skirmishers for Pickett's Division against Sheridan and his men.[17]

At this point Tom Francis appears to have slipped off to visit Lucy Ann Cross. In his next letter to her, he spoke of the hard time he had catching up with his company at Slash Church. But, he said, he would do it again if it meant seeing a pretty lady and eating a good meal. They had pushed toward Ashland only to find that Sheridan had already left. The division returned to near Peake's Station on the Virginia Central Railroad. There they rested, distributed rations, and then moved on to Hanover Court House.[18]

Private Joseph Thomas had gotten a 15-day furlough starting on March 3. He spent much of his time dodging Sheridan's men around his father's home in Hanover. He hid in the woods with three other men, Mr. John Snead, a Mr. Terrell, and Mr. John J. Davis and spent the nights at his father's house. One day Mr. Davis, Tom Francis' brother-in-law, said that his place was full of Yankees and their artillery. Later in the day they heard firing on the Telegraph Road. Mr. Snead said that if he was going to be killed, he would rather it be at his home. He waded across the creek and left them. Later the other two left also. Thomas slipped back home and joined his regiment the next day at Hanover Court House. Then he learned that it was his own fellows who followed Sheridan into King William the previous day. The next day they marched to Highland Springs and were through Petersburg by March 26.[19]

The 15th Regiment camped along Swift Creek on March 28, but they were called out the next day to support their neighbors in the Henrico Dragoons against Sheridan's cavalry-men who were threatening Lee's encirclement of Petersburg. The troopers marched to the Southside Railroad and boarded the cars for Sutherland Station, south of the Appomattox River. There they jumped off and got some sleep until aroused at 2 a.m. when they were directed along the White Oak Road to Five Forks. There was heavy skirmishing that day as they drove the Federals southward toward Dinwiddie Court House. When it was determined that the Federal Cavalry would be supported by a superior number of infantry, the Confederates were ordered back to Five Forks.[20]

The Richmond Howitzers were not in on the fighting at Dinwiddie Court House when Sheridan encircled Lee's right flank in order to cut it off from the Southside Railroad and Richmond. Affairs went very well, but then the leadership began to slacken. Thinking their men were well positioned on April 1, Pickett and Fitz Lee joined Rosser that afternoon at a shad roast. This left Rooney Lee's cavalry, Montgomery Corse's infantry, and Willie Pegram's artillery to stand against Sheridan and portions of Warren's Fifth Army Corps. Pegram was mortally wounded at the beginning of the fighting.[21]

Young Private Josiah Moore, of Company B, has recorded that the 15th Infantry was spread out as skirmishers in front of Corse's Brigade and that they held until the third attack when they found that the enemy had come through a weak point and was in their rear. Most of Moore's company was taken prisoner. Thirty-four from the regiment were either wounded or taken prisoner, including Major J.F. Clarke from Henrico. Edwin Haw, from Studley, was wounded and also his brother

William of the Hanover Grays. George Edmond Massie, of the Hanover and the Patrick Henry Rifles, was made a prisoner along with William Talley, John Woodson, and John Watkins. They were among those marched by City Point on their way to Point Lookout Prison in Maryland. Others made it back to the Southside Railroad, Petersburg, or Hatcher's Run before being captured.[22]

Fitz Lee, now that Wade Hampton had gone to South Carolina, realized that General Warren's Federals were threatening the Confederate right and had thrown up breast-works and placed Rooney Lee's men to connect with other cavalry coming from Petersburg. Even with desperate fighting on the afternoon of April 1, Rooney's men were out-numbered and forced to retreat beyond Hatcher's Run. They, including the 10th Cavalry and Corse's men with the 15th Virginia Infantry, kept the afternoon from becoming a complete rout. During the weekend, General A.P. Hill was killed. Sheridan broke through the Petersburg lines and Richmond was evacuated. Men of the 15th Infantry were captured in and around Petersburg, Fort Gregg, Hatcher's Run, and the Southside Railroad.[23]

Dr. Douglas S. Freeman has put together in his biography of R.E. Lee the various accounts of the death of A.P. Hill. On the morning of April 2 Lee was feeling unwell and was still in bed at 4 a.m. when Longstreet and Hill came to confer with him at his headquarters west of Petersburg. Suddenly Colonel Charles Venable brought word that the Federals were coming down Cox's Road toward Petersburg. The Confederate line had been broken. Hill ran to his horse and Lee called out to Venable "to caution Hill not to expose himself." Lee dressed and rode out in the growing light to where he could observe approaching troops. They wore blue.[24]

After Venable had separated himself from them, Hill and his courier, Sergeant G.W. Tucker, encountered two Federals. Hill's call for their surrender was answered with rifle fire and the general toppled from his horse. Tucker returned to General Lee on Hill's dapple-gray horse. Tears came to Lee's eyes as he surmised the worst. Lee sent Hill's adjutant, Colonel William H. Palmer, and Tucker off to break the news to Mrs. Hill as gently as possible and to get her and the children across the Appomattox. The pregnant widow was singing as they rode up. Seeing someone else on the dapple-gray, she too knew that her husband was dead. Lee gave over the charge of Hill's troops to Longstreet.[25]

Joseph Thomas was experiencing chills during his regiment's involvement in the Battle of Five Forks and the evacuation of Petersburg. Sometimes he rode in an ambulance and other times he was left beside the road with only the shelter of a small tent to protect him from the cold and wet, hardly able to walk 100 yards without lying down to rest. At a hospital set up for the wounded from Five Forks, a doctor gave him some little black pills. The next morning when they began to retreat from Petersburg Joseph asked for a ride in the ambulance, but there was no room for him. Joe Cross, of Hanover, rode by with Coleman Taylor. They saw him lying beside the road, talked to him but never expected to see him alive again. The private did catch up with his regiment near Amelia Court House and continued to ride in the wagon train until the battle at Saylor's Creek.[26]

Lee was moving his Army of Northern Virginia along the north and south sides of the Appomattox River toward a meeting with President Davis and his cabinet in Danville. He directed his supply wagons to meet him at Amelia Court House and from there he hoped to reach the railroad at Burkeville. Such was not to be the case. There were no provisions for man or beast awaiting them at the courthouse.

Already Sheridan's cavalry was bearing up on them from the south, with Grant's and Meade's infantry and artillery not far behind.

Chapter 24

RICHMOND TO AMELIA - APRIL 1865

It seemed quiet in Richmond on the night of March 31, yet Captain William Parker of the Confederate Navy's training vessel noticed members of the home guard making their way out toward Brook Turnpike. Members of the guard could see a red glow and hear muffled gunfire across the James, but they were not alarmed. Joseph R. Haw, of Studley, was serving as a clerk in the Confederate Ordnance Department. He wrote in the *ConfederateVeteran* in 1926 that he had gone on Sunday morning, April 2, to the Presbyterian Church where the Reverend Moses Hoge announced that the lines had been broken at Petersburg. Outside on the Capitol grounds a man was consigning some Confederate bonds to a fire he had built. Haw said that he was among the few in the Ordnance Department who were ordered to go by rail to Danville. They managed to get on a freight car that was stuffed with bullet molds, pig iron, and the household effects of some fleeing officer. The sick and wounded evacuees had draped themselves on top of the freight car. It was late when the wheels of the train began to rumble toward Danville.[1]

With the abandonment of Richmond, the artillery crossed Mayo Bridge on April 3. General Porter Alexander was stationed at the entrance to the bridge. He said that every building in the city seemed to be lit up and the people swarmed the streets. No one was near the depot except one old lady helping herself to blankets. Porter procured for himself a felt for his saddle and a new bridle. When the last battery had crossed, the flames were already licking through the floor boards. From high ground in Manchester, the general looked back on the city for which they had fought long and hard. He later wrote:

> It was a sad, a terrible solemn sight. I don't know any moment in the whole war [that] impressed me more deeply with all its stern realities than this. The whole

> river front seemed to be in flames, amid which occasional heavy explosions were heard, & black smoke spreading & hanging over the city seemed to be full of dreadful portents. I rode on with a distinctively heavy heart & a peculiar sort of feeling of orphanage.[2]

Emma Mordecai wrote to a friend in North Carolina on April 5 telling how surprised they were with the evacuation of Richmond. Word was brought from town by a newly paroled lieutenant who had come to visit her niece Caroline. Since it was a Sunday all the servants were away and the carriage was broken down. The two young people walked back into the city leaving "three helpless & unprotected females" shaking in their limbs and their hearts seeming to stand still. Neither Rose nor Gusta slept that night and Emma only intermittently. They could hear the trains on the nearby R.F. & P. and the more distant Danville Railroad. Just before light, a loud explosion shook the house. Emma groped her way downstairs to lie terrified and trembling in bed with Gusta and her mother. They hoped that Caroline had made her way back to Carolina and they made plans to send Gusta to stay with a friend in Richmond.[3]

That morning they sent word to Mr. Gordon to return the barrel of flour they had left at his store and for him to try to get their box of valuable old silver plate at a bank in the city. With Gusta and her mother's clothes packed in a trunk, Emma and the young girl set out for town in a mule cart driven by the slave George. They could hear incessant sounds of cannon fire and bursting shells and could even see smoke and flames. Knowing that the tobacco and defensive works would probably be burned, they were not unduly alarmed. Refugees on the Military Road who were fleeing the city with their possessions told them "you are going to a bad place." The enemy was expected but had not yet arrived.[4]

At Camp Lee, the white tents filled the day before with paroled prisoners were now empty. They heard that the enemy had come quietly into the city that morning, were now in the Capitol Square, and the looting had begun. George was anxious to get into town for some of the food. Reluctantly Emma left the contents of the wagon with a family by the name of Luck and returned by foot to "Rosewood." They met a young Negro woman headed into town who asked, "Missis, you gwine away from dem nasty Yankees?" Emma replied, "We are going home … Where are you going?" The reply was, "I'm gwine to town to hunt up my young mistice [sic] – I'll risk my life to git her."[5]

Back home the aunt packed her clothes and left them standing in the hall with the keys in the locks so they would not be broken open. She and Rose hid the boys clothes in the beds and then settled down to read the book of *Psalms* and took up their knitting. Emma was amazed at Rose's composure the next morning when she got up and went to set a hen. On Tuesday, word came of the destruction along Cary, Main, and Franklin streets. The enemy soldiers had helped put out the fires. Negro Dragoons came to the Mordecai's door demanding a saddle for the horse they had just appropriated from Cyrus in the field. Finding it useless to refuse them, the house servant, Mary, was sent to fetch it. Emma set out to get redress from the provost marshal for the soldiers taking their only horse, leaving Rose to pray until her return.[6]

She took the Negro girls with her. On her way a very polite Irish officer offered to let Emma ride his horse. Upon her refusal, he rode for a ways along beside her. The inhabitants of Screamers Ville (near Lombardy) were rejoicing. Some Negroes along the way were drunk, others polite and some insolent. The provost marshal was too busy to be of help. She was told that she needed a pass. Broad Street was covered with shattered plate glass. It and the Capitol Square were filthy. The sutlers had moved into town and all kinds of goods were being sold on the streets that had not been available for many moons. General Godfrey Weitzel was living in the White House of the Confederacy and Mrs. Davis's white housekeeper was keeping house for him. When Emma heard that Lincoln was entering town, she decided it was time for her to leave. At the pump on Ninth Street, she found a slightly tipsy George, their cart and mule. They retrieved their trunks at the Lucks' house and were soon relieved to get back home.[7]

Throughout the week, Emma said, "Every step, every sound filled them with terror." Ruffians came to the house demanding arms, searched the smoke house and the dairy. They entered the house and took trinkets and keepsakes from the closets and drawers. Mr. Young lost his law library, eight handsome rugs, and his service of china. Now his servants were leaving him. When Emma went over to "Westbrook," she was surprised at how calm Frances Young was. Little Fanny wept inconsolably at the loss of her playmates, Martha and Caroline, when their father Cyrus sent for them.[8]

Cyrus had stopped working the fields, saying that he had heard it read from the courthouse steps that everything belonged to the Yankees now and they were "gwine to divide it 'mong the coloured people." George came back for the mule and cart and carried off all the corn in the barn. Rose asked Mary if she was glad to be free, who replied that she had just as "leave to be slave as not." Little Mary and Georgiana left one morning taking their bedding with them. They had always slept beside their mistress who had promised at their mother's deathbed that she would always care for them.[9]

Frances Ann Doswell witnessed the fall of the capital from the heart of the city. She had grown up near Peaks at "Mt. Pleasant," the daughter of Mary Oliver and James Sutton. Her father had died the previous year. Frances Ann and her three small children appear to have lived in rooms at the American Hotel while her husband, Major Thomas W. Doswell, served as provost marshal of Richmond. They had moved into town from their home at "Bullfield" near Hanover Junction. Mother Doswell, upon her return home after the fighting there, saw so many dead bodies that she had a stroke and died two days later. Other members of the Doswell and Sutton families were living near the Capitol Square and Frances Ann and the little ones were able to move in with a sister-in-law.[10]

Frances Doswell kept a diary from April 3-26, telling of her distress when her husband left for Danville with the government officials, of her fright at the explosions and the smoke that came billowing up from Main Street. The porch where she was standing caught fire and she lost all her furniture when the hotel burned. She saw the looting, Negro soldiers marching in the streets, and she did not undress for two nights. No one was allowed on the streets after 8 p.m. Her brother talked to the guard stationed on Fifth Street who sent her word to let him know if she was disturbed.[11]

Mrs. Doswell wrote that she with other ladies heard the guns honoring President Lincoln's arrival and from their window saw the president, his son, and four officers in an "ambulance drawn by four splendid horses, then came a carriage with four more officers and then about thirty men on horseback ... He was gallanted to the President's house where he now resides." On April 5 they watched the ambulances and wagons drawn by six mules and the Negro soldiers mounted on splendid horses on their way to Camp Lee. Frances Ann wrote that the pickets "ride as fast as their horses could run and how often do I wish our men were in pursuit."[12]

Katherine M. Jones in her book *Ladies of Richmond* included stories of some ladies who had come to Richmond from

Hanover County. One of them was Thomasia Christian Winston from Hanover Junction. She was raised by her uncle Major Thomas Doswell. Her daughter wrote that her mother, who was widowed at the age of 23 years, always kept a room available for a needy private soldier. They witnessed the departure of President Davis and his cabinet just prior to the fall of the city and the bridge being burned behind them. Soon their house was on fire and they moved uptown to the home of their uncle Phil Paul Winston. The little girl had in a bag over her shoulder two dresses and a straw hat she had just bought for $60.00. She had a little dog, Frank, under her arm. Soon after they returned home two of Major Doswell's servants (Blacks) came to them. One said, "Miss Thomasia, I expect to have more money than you have now, in silver and gold, so we wish to give you each 25 cents to start up life with."[13]

With the fall of Petersburg and Richmond, the local defenders of Richmond in the Armory Battalion, Arsenal Battalion, Naval Battalion, and Departmental Regiment were disbanded. Custis Lee took with him the heavy artillery from the Richmond, James, and Howlett line defenses. He traveled with General William Mahone to cross the Appomattox River. Colonels Frank Huger and Porter Alexander had with them the Ashland and Parker artilleries in the 1st Corps. The Courtney, Morris, and 2nd Richmond Howitzers were with Cutshaw's artillery in the 2nd Army Corps and the 3rd Richmond Howitzers were with Hardaway's Battalion in the 2nd Corps. The Purcell and Letcher artilleries had seen much action around Petersburg and remained with the 3rd Corps now under Longstreet.[14]

The 4th Virginia Cavalry was in Fitz Lee's Division. The 5th Virginia Cavalry had been reorganized with the 15th Cavalry into the Fitz Lee-Rosser Division. The 10th Virginia and the 9th Virginia cavalries were serving in the Chambliss-Beale Brigade in W.H.F. (Rooney) Lee's Division. The 15th

Virginia Infantry continued under Corse and Pickett and the 56th Virginia Infantry was under Hunton and Pickett in the 1st Army Corps with Longstreet.[15]

Dr D. S. Freeman, in his biography of Lee, shows that there were three bridges over the Appomattox: Bevill's Bridge, where Longstreet and Gordon were to cross; Goode's Bridge where General William Mahone and the men from the Howlett Line were to cross; and Genito Bridge where he had planned for General R.S. Ewell with forces from the Richmond area and the wagon trains to cross. Lee and Longstreet stopped for supper at "Clover Hill" plantation, the home of Judge James Smith, the owner of the coal mines at Winterpock which supplied the fuel for Tredegar iron works. Smith's daughter Kate was especially kind to them. One of her brothers was buried in the garden, another was in the retreat. Kate cut up the meat for Longstreet whose arm was still weak from his wound in the Wilderness. There Lee learned the condition of the bridges and that it would take longer to bring the weary hungry men together. Longstreet and Gordon were rerouted to Goode's Bridge. The water at Genito was too low for pontoons and Ewell was sent word to cross wherever he could. The remnants of Pickett's men from Five Forks had arrived at Exeter Mills and found no bridge there and the river too high to ford. They were sent word to join Anderson and Longstreet.[16]

The family of Mary Teresa and John A. Scott lived near Amelia Court House, perhaps at Scott's Shop where General Gordon said that he halted. John Scott's mother was Mary Goode and he was born on the Chesterfield side of the Appomattox, but was living in Powhatan County when the war stated. He had joined the Powhatan Artillery for one year in July 1861, leaving Mary behind to raise their four children: George Emmett, (age 7); Virginia (age 5); Arthur (age 3); and Samuel (age 1). Mary Teresa's portrait shows her with sad blue eyes. And well she might be sad. John served his year and then was discharged for being over 35. He was home long enough to get Mary pregnant with their fifth child, Rosa Lee, before re-enlisting as a 3rd sergeant. He was wounded at Gettysburg and taken prisoner on the way back at Waterloo Bridge, held at Fort Delaware and Point Lookout, and released in February, 1865.[17]

It is not known whether John Scott stopped by home on his way to Appomattox. However, by this time the women in his family were thoroughly disillusioned with army activities be they either northern or southern. In 1867, the sixth child, Eberland, was born to Mary and John A. Scott. He had curly hair and twinkling blue eyes, looking not at all like his somber mother. By 1870, she was dead. The following ditty was passed down through the family for generations, originating with either Grandmother Mary Goode Scott or Mother Mary Southall Scott. Perhaps Mary Scott and her family lived in the area canvassed for food:

> Longstreet come along with his critical company
> Struck a streak right cross my tater patch
> Knocked down my lye gum
> I paid two dollars and a half for in 'Lanta
> Nasty stinking dog![18]

R.M. Doswell, possibly of the Hanover Doswells, wrote for the *Confederate Veteran* in 1915 that he was near Amelia when Federal cavalry approached a portion of the wagon train guarded by Confederate Negro men. He watched in admiration when the first charge was turned back. On the second charge a number of the black soldiers were taken prisoner. Doswell galloped away before he drew the attention of the enemy soldiers.[19]

Dr. William Stauffer, of the Richmond Civil War Roundtable, has written of the misfortune of the Confederates finding no food awaiting them at Amelia Court House and of their frustration while they scoured the countryside for food and provender. "It was as if fate were decreeing that everything should go awry, thus to enable the enemy to make up in time for the slight advantage that Lee's hurried evacuation had given him over his pursuers. There was food for the guns at Amelia — so much of it in fact, that a vast store had to be blown up since it could not be carried along - but the stomachs of the soldiers were, for the most part, empty as the march was resumed." More and more weak, hungry, and disspirited men gave up the will to go on and slipped into the surrounding woods.[20]

The 2nd Howitzers had been evacuated from Fort Clifton on the Appomattox to cover the retreat. They were told to spike their guns and leave them behind. Not enough horses had returned from their pasturing at home to pull the equipment. Some men were given muskets and a few cartridges and caps to carry in their pockets. Their rations at Amelia were two ears of corn per man which they parched with oil in their skillets and ate on the march. They with Cutshaw's battalion were the last to leave the Amelia Court House. Twenty men under Lt. Henry S. Jones of Hanover were left behind to slow the enemy's advance. Jones was mortally wounded and others were killed or captured. Cutshaw's battalion moved on and was subject to severe artillery fire. The guns of the 3rd Howitzers came streaking from the rear to their rescue and the enemy slipped oft into the woods.[21]

Chapter 25

SAILOR'S CREEK TO APPOMATTOX – APRIL 1865

Lee set out with his armies from Amelia Court House on the wet and gloomy morning of April 5. The infantry trains went to the right to be protected by Martin Gary's brigade. It was soon learned that Federal cavalry had met the wagons before they reached Painesville, burned them, and taken the Negro teamsters and 320 soldiers as prisoners. With a cavalry shield in the front, Lee traveled with Longstreet in the van, followed by Wilcox and Heth's divisions, then Anderson's and Ewell's corps with Gordon's division in the rear. Lee did not actually leave until 1 p.m. and had changed his plans, not to go by way of Jetersville, but by Amelia Springs and Deatonville. They passed the old spa and Lee spent the night at Richard Anderson's home "Selma."[1]

The next day half of the army had crossed one branch of Sailor's Creek when a gap opened up in the line near Harper's Plantation allowing Sheridan to slip through between Mahone and Anderson. Ewell's command was left with no protection. Lee wondered why Anderson had not come up. From a high knob he could see Federal wagons. He rode a little ways northward toward the Appomattox River and then saw that "streaming out of the bottom and the ridge to them were teamsters without their wagons, soldiers without their guns, and shattered regiments without their officers, a routed wreck!" The general grabbed a battle flag, held it high while some of the fleeing soldiers rallied around him, and then passed it on to Malone to form the line. He learned that Anderson and Ewell had to fight back to back. Wise managed to slip away and Gordon saved some of the wagons. He had gotten them across the creek and to High Bridge. Lee had lost 6,000 to 7,000 men in one day.[2]

General Eppa Hunton had united his command with Pickett at Sailor's Creek. He related to his son that the fighting was fierce. When the Union infantry appeared on their rear, they were pressed hard. Hunton, General Corse, and four other generals – Richard Ewell, Custis Lee, Seth Barton, and Dudley DuBose – were captured. Hunton said that he surrendered to one of General George Custer's staff officers. Seeing that he was sick, Custer put him on a captured Confederate horse and sent over his personal physician and later furnished a hair mattress for his comfort.[3]

The 15th Virginia Infantry had been losing men wounded and/or taken prisoner since around Petersburg. Company E's Captain John Govers and Captain John Vannerson of the Henrico Guard were captured at Dinwiddie. Nicholas Jennings and three others in the Henrico Guard had either been killed or wounded. James Jones of the Patrick Henry Rifles had been wounded. Now at Sailor's Creek their leaders, General Montgomery Corse and Lieutenant Colonel Emmett Morrison, were taken as prisoners.[4]

Joseph Thomas and his companions, Polk Glazebrook and William Truel, moving with Ewell and the wagon train, had fled the wagons before Sheridan burned them. They managed to cross High Bridge over the Southside Railroad before it too was mostly burned. The regiment roster shows the following men captured at Harper's Farm or Plantation there at Sayler's Creek: Gideon Morris, James Brown, Henry Sherrer, and P.H. Wright from the Henrico Grays; David Bourne, John Cone, John Cottrell and Luther Duvall from the Patrick Henry Rifles; and William Short and George Talley from the Hanover Grays.[5]

At Farmville eighteen men from the 15th Regiment were taken as prisoners. Some were already wounded and taken from the hospital. Four of these men were from Hanover: John Gibson, Junius Timberlake, William Norment from the Hanover Grays and Sergeant William K. Woodson from the Ashland Grays.

While their fellows were being captured, Joseph Thomas, Polk Glazebrook, and William Truel were still going along the road. They built a fire to cook some peas. Polk still had his rifle and upon seeing a pig along side the road, shot it. He and William took it into the bushes to skin while Joseph stood watch. That night they begged some meal and found a black woman to cook it for them. The next morning they stuffed the meat into their haversacks and continued on.[6]

****

The cavalry continued to try to screen the retreating lines from Sheridan's attacks. Colonel Reuben Boston had been put in charge of a brigade in Rosser's Division after the consolidation of the 5th and 15th cavalries and the wounding of General William H. Payne at Five Forks. While leading a charge near High Bridge, Boston was shot through the cheek. As he fell from his horse, a private attempted to help him from the field, but an officer called out, "You cannot do him any good; go on fighting." With that the soldier took the pistol from the colonel's grasp and, using it, helped in the arrest of prisoners. Brevet General Theodore Read, of the U.S. Volunteers, was killed in the same fighting. Both bodies were placed under the same tree in a Mrs. Watson's yard. Each was wrapped in a blanket and buried in separate graves. Colonel Boston's body was later moved to Red Hill Cemetery in Fluvanna.[7]

****

At Sailor's Creek on April 6, the Richmond Howitzers were fighting under Major Cutshaw when he was wounded in the leg and captured. His leg was amputated that night. Lieutenant Henry Jones of Hanover was mortally wounded and three privates were killed or wounded. Creed Davis, of the Hanover Davis family, his uncle John Ragland, the wounded James McKinney of Hanover, and William "Springy" Winston of Henrico, were among the fourteen from the battalion who were captured at that time and sent to Newport News. Second Lieutenant Wallace McRae of Henrico then led the men in defense of their wagon train while the Federal skirmishers fired on the unarmed drivers. He conducted them across the creek and onto the High Bridge over the railroad and on toward Farmville, where they obtained a little bacon.[8]

Creed Davis said in his diary that he had been captured with the wagon train and that there was a desperate fight that evening in which many of his company were wounded, including his uncle, Shelton Ragland. He estimated that there were approximately 8,000 prisoners. They had not had their rations and were marched under heavy guard that night to Black and Whites (Blackstone). The next morning they were tossed out corn on the husk from a corn crib just as if they were hogs. They tumbled "pell-mell over each other" to get it and were "so weak and feeble from being starved out" they could hardly stand. The men had only their filthy clothes on their backs. Creed held desperately to his blanket.[9]

Over the next four days, the prisoners were marched in the rain over mucky, much traveled roads. Creed recorded that they had not half enough food or sleep or any cooking utensils or wood for fires. The nights were chilly. Upon arrival at City Point on the James, their line stretched out for a mile and they slept in a deluge of rain. The steamer *Maryland* lay just off shore and at midnight the prisoners were loaded on board. With the day word came that Lee had surrendered. Their prison at Newport News was a new one without any fences. On April 15, "A tent was issued to every six men, a better tent [Davis said] than we have ever seen in the Confederate army." So far the officers had been kind to the prisoners, but trouble and humiliation would come from the black guards.[10]

****

Men who had not been supplied with arms at Amelia Court House picked up abandoned muskets and cartridges along the way, placing the latter in their pockets with parched corn. They each had been issued two ears of corn, originally intended for the horses. When they got a chance, they cooked the corn on the coals of a small fire, mixed it with salt and stored it in their pockets to chew along the road. Carlton McCartney said that it made their jaws and gums ache and their teeth so sore it was almost unbearable.[11]

Lieutenant McRae continued to lead them on improvised infantry details. When the forces became too strong for them, he instructed the men, "Don't let them see you running, boys!" Dragging their old muskets behind them, they loaded as they slowly retreated. When all were reloaded, they would halt and return the fire.[12]

General Porter Alexander, head of the artillery, wrote of their march to Farmville, splashing and floundering in a sea of mud, stopping in the darkness and floundering on again. There were with them ambulances, cavalry, and hungry men on foot with their blankets and ammunition. Alexander had the job of firing the bridges as they left Farmville. They received a three-day supply of light rations, but there was little or no time to cook it.[13]

When they passed through the village of Appomattox Court House, the men supplied themselves with four rounds of ammunition from the boxes which had been dropped along their lines, so now their britches were filled to the brim. Should a little flour come to hand, they spread out their oilcloths, mixed flour and water and cooked the pones on boards broken from limbers and held near the fire. Cutshaw's men camped for the night in some woods near Appomattox Courthouse. A lieutenant could not understand why some wagons and guns were parked so carelessly in a field the next day. He was told there had been surrender. "I don't believe it, sir!" replied the furious officer. "You mustn't talk so, sir! You will demoralize my men!" Seeing the Federal cavalrymen walking around with no apparent concern for the Army of Northern Virginia, he concluded, "Well, boys, it must be so, but it is a very strange behavior. Let's move on and see about it." Lieutenant McRae, Carlton McCarthy, the Mordecai brothers, and twenty-four others from the 2nd Howitzers received their parole at Appomattox.[14]

Ham Chamberlayne had been released from prison and again made temporary captain, this time of Greenlee Davidson's old command, Letcher's Battery. However, one listing shows him with his own battery in Major William Owen's battalion, which fought alongside Lindsay Walker's men and were with them at the surrender. The Letcher and Crenshaw batteries struggled along with their weakened men and horses through Amelia Court House and Lynchburg, sometimes having to double the horses to keep the guns moving. Six miles west of Appomattox, they disbanded and disabled their guns. The only Richmond men of Crenshaw's battery shown as paroled were some who had escaped capture.[15]

Colonel Bob Caskie of the 10th Virginia Cavalry Regiment had been in a Richmond Hospital in March. Now on the flight from Richmond he had led his men to Amelia Court House, serving as a rear guard for the army. They were in a fight there on April 4 and 5. They drove the cavalry from the wagon train at Jetersville, engaged the enemy at Sailor's Creek, defeated both infantry and cavalry at High Bridge, and helped capture the Union cavalry general, Irvin Gregg and his staff. One sergeant wrote that their flag was in perfect condition at Petersburg, but by the time they reached Appomattox Court House it "was a bullet ridden rag." The colonel told his men of Lee's surrender. He did not know how to advise them but felt that those who owned their own horses perhaps should leave with them. Caskie and his staff surrendered as did Nat Cross and George Hopkins of Henrico, who is shown as back commanding the regiment. Nat Cross's mess mate was still on sick furlough. Some of the 10th Virginia Cavalry rode off toward Lynchburg with Lieutenant Colonel William Clement to join Joseph Johnston with his army in North Carolina.[16]

Rooney Lee was with his father at Appomattox. Fitz Lee led many of the cavalry away with the determination not to surrender. Benjamin Doswell had been made a prisoner at Farmville and also Frank Blunt three days prior to that. Now at Appomattox, Thomas Ellett, W.T. Huffman, Richard Talley, Luther Vaughan, and Thomas Dunn, from the Hanover Troop, surrendered with their leaders.[17]

By General Lee's reckoning, there were on the afternoon of April 7 only "7,892 organized infantry with arms, with an average of 75 rounds of ammunition per man, the artillery [had been] reduced to 63 pieces with 93 rounds of ammunition. ... This comprised all the supplies of ordnance that could be relied upon in the State of Virginia."[18] It has been said that many of the rifleman had stuck their arms with bayonets into the ground and had gone off looking for food.

The infantry trio from Hanover, Joseph Thomas, Polk Glazebrook, and William Truel, finished off their pig the day of the surrender. Thomas wrote in his memoir that some cavalry men came by and told them that Lee had surrendered at Appomattox and that they were making their way to North Carolina.[19]

Dr. Freeman has written that Pickett had about 800 men there, but only sixty of them still had their muskets. Their roster shows that thirty-seven in the 15th Virginia Infantry at the surrender were from Henrico or Hanover, including Tom and Buck Francis from the Yellow Tavern area and Richardson

Haw from Haw's Shop. Like Tom seven of them had been wounded within the last year. Second Lieutenant Beverly Bumpass had just been released from a nine-month stay in a Federal prison. The total surrendering from the regiment was fifty-nine men and ten officers. They were led by Major Charles Clarke from Richmond.[20]

Tom Rosser's last wound had been near High Bridge on April 6, but he still assisted in the capture of General Gregg and the rescue of a wagon train near Farmville. On the last fatal morning, April 9, a little after daybreak he led a charge against the Federal cavalry and managed to escape with his command. In spite of his injured arm, he slipped away before the signing at Appomattox and made his way to Danville where the Confederate government had assembled. Rosser was reorganizing the scattered troops of the Army of Northern Virginia under the direction of the secretary of war and Virginia Governor "Extra" Billy Smith, but was made a prisoner about the time Johnston surrendered.[21]

A printing press was set up in an adjoining room in the McLean house to process the paroles the next day. Grant asked Lee if 25,000 rations would feed his men. The Confederate general's reply was that would be adequate. This appears to have included those who came in during the night. The paroles were printed on check size paper and distributed on Tuesday, April 11. The blank spaces had been filled in with the date, prisoner's name, company, regiment, and signed by their commanding captain. Early in the morning they broke camp, slung their blanket and oilcloth over their shoulder, collected their canteen, put a few trifles in their haversack and ate what scraps of food they had left. Once they showed their parole to the picket, in small groups they were on their way.[22]

Joseph Thomas and his two friends were still somewhere on the James when they heard of the surrender. They turned their feet toward home, first crossing on a ferry over the river at Bent Creek and traveling the next day through pouring rain into Nelson County. Families along the way were very kind to them, giving them good breakfasts, suppers, and places to sleep. They passed through Fluvanna and Goochland counties, reaching Hanover County at a Captain Dabney's near Rockville on Friday, April 14th. They crossed the South Anna (perhaps at Terrell's Mill). The trio ate their last breakfast with a Mr. and Mrs. Bryce. At home Joseph found only his father and sister. His mother had died two years before while he was in Suffolk. All the slaves and the horses were gone.[23]

At "Rosewood" on April 9, they could hear firing all night. They later learned that it was in celebration of the news of Lee's surrender at Appomattox. Rose Mordecai sat on the floor in front of the fireplace and wept. Emma Mordecai wrote in her diary:

> Gusta was dissolved in tears, and felt as if every ray of joy had departed from her young life…felt terrified as to what the consequences might be, -- That the earth might open & swallow us all up, was the only wish I could form. Gradually we felt that all was in the hands of God, that he had willed this in His unerring wisdom, and that we must submit ourselves to Him – that in thus doing we were not humbled before our foes but before God… Other nations had been through similar and worst afflictions -- we must bear our turn. The day was a dark, dreary, rainy day, in accordance with our feelings."[24]

Chapter 26

PRISON LIFE AND DEATH

The process of exchange of prisoners had been worked out in 1862 and consisted of a quota system with a private as a unit, a non-commissioned officer as two units, on up to twenty to sixty units for a general. The cartel stipulated: "All prisoners of war are to be discharged on parole in ten days after their capture." However, exchanges ceased for periods of time starting in 1863.[1]

Some of the Henrico-Hanover men of the Morris Artillery had been taken prisoner at Waterloo, Pennsylvania, in 1863 while they escorted Lee's wagon trains back from Gettysburg. They were still in prison in 1865 at Fort Delaware and would not be home before late May or June. Others would not be coming home having died of their injuries or sickness. William Chapman, who had entered the artillery when an 18 year-old student at Hanover Academy, had died of measles. He was the eldest son of Mildred and Archie Chapman. Marcellus Lowry had died of inflammation of the lungs, leaving a widow, Mary, and two children. William Yarbrough and the former Mary Gentry had five children. James Eddleton was the eldest of five sons of Allen and Frances. Privates Lowry, Yarbrough, and Eddleton were buried at Finn's Point in New Jersey, across the Delaware Bay from Fort Delaware. Henry Coleman died of undetermined causes on May 5, 1865. There is no record of what happened to William Browning. His mother Polly, a widow, had already lost her younger son John at Gettysburg.[2]

William Thacker, also taken at Waterloo, was more fortunate. He would be coming home to wife Sarah. Also coming home from Ft. Delaware would be Richard H. Cross, son of Nancy Cross. Mother Cross had welcomed home his brother James in September after his injuries sustained at the Bloody Angle on May 12 when Richard had been taken prisoner and sent with fellow artillerymen to Fort Delaware by way of Belle Plain. Ann Perkins and her five children would be greeting their father Edward in June. Captain Pichegru Woolfolk, of the Ashland Artillery, had been at Fort Delaware for two and a half months in 1864, but was released. H.R. "Robin" Berkeley, a private under Woolfolk, was taken prisoner near the end of the war but not released from Fort Delaware until June.[3]

Fort Delaware was a fortification in the Delaware River opposite Delaware City. It was located on Pea Patch Island, a shoal on which local tradition claims a ship wrecked and the peas sprouted, silted over and formed an island. The fort there was built on thousands of piles. It combined with batteries on the New Jersey side to dominate the entrance to the Delaware River and the approach to Wilmington and Philadelphia. A dike around the island kept out the river at high tide. A water boat was sent up the creek for fresh water but seldom reached that point. Barracks were built all over the island. The influx of prisoners after Gettysburg took the population to 12,000 men and it never fell below 6,000 until the last days of release at the end of the war. About 2,700 men, prisoners and guards, died and were buried on the Jersey shore.[4]

The barracks at the prison were 20 feet by 500 feet, each housing 500 men on berths stacked three deep. There were twenty on the island, each with a large dining hall, kitchen, bakery and washing shed. Toward the end of the war the prisoners' fare consisted of two light meals a day. Dinner at 3 p.m. was three bites of meat and a pint tin cup of bean soup. Robin Berkeley said that from his narrow window he could see the Delaware shore, Delaware City, the river up to New Castle, the hospital, the death house, and the piles of waiting coffins. Each morning the dead were taken to be buried.[5]

Officers captured at the battle of Yellow Tavern were among the "Immortal Six Hundred" who in August 1864 were sent from Fort Delaware to Morris Island off of Fort Sumter. Charleston, South Carolina, was still in Confederate hands. They were held on the island in retaliation for the Union prisoners in line of fire in the city. There the guns from Federal batteries fired over them into the city. The guns from Fort Sumter retaliated. Those from Yellow Tavern were two captains of the 6th Virginia Cavalry, a captain and four lieutenants of the 5th Virginia Cavalry, a captain of the 1st North Carolina Cavalry and one of the Baltimore Artillery. Captain Henry Clay Dickinson had been captured at the Meadow Bridges and Captain George Hopkins of Henrico and the 10th Cavalry had been captured May 13. Also among the 600 was 23 year-old Captain George Washington "Wash" Nelson of the Hanover Artillery, taken captive on October 26, 1863, while having dinner with a friend at Millwood, near Winchester.[6]

Captain J. Ogden Murray of the 7th Virginia Cavalry who had been captured in 1863, Captain J.J. Dunkle, of the 25th Virginia Infantry, and Lieutenant Peter B. Akers, of the 11th Virginia Infantry were among the 600 officers and recorded their experiences. They said that they had been called out from the officers' barracks at Fort Delaware in August 1863 and loaded on the steamship *Crescent City* and headed south. They thought they might be exchanged and endured the poor ventilation, the dim light, and the strong odor of tar and grease. All were seasick and their quarters reeked of vomit and waste. After eighteen days they were landed on Morris Island and told there would be no exchange.[7]

The writers said that the atmosphere at Morris Island on some mornings was pleasant, but the hot southern sun would soon make the sand almost unbearable to their bare feet. The sand would hold the heat until midnight. They were kept in a 3-

acre pen surrounded by a 12-foot high parapet over which the sentinels walked day and night. Inside there was a rope thirty feet from the wall, a literal dead line which if anyone approached it they would be shot. The prisoners' rations were: "Breakfast, four rotten hard tack crackers; dinner, one half pint of sandy soup; supper, all the wind one could inhale." Drinking water was obtained by digging holes in the sand. Their medicine was dispensed by a "red-headed cow doctor." It consisted of one opium pill or a dose of Jamaica ginger, no matter the complaint.[8]

In December 1864 the prisoners were loaded on to gunboats and carried down the coast to either Hilton Head Island or Fort Pulaski, off shore from Savannah. At Hilton Head they were put in log barracks, but the cold wind off the Atlantic blew through the cracks and no fires were allowed inside. They had little clothing. Some had no shoes and few had blankets. Their rations consisted of ten ounces of corn meal and a half pint of onion and cucumber pickle. Fours ounces of meal and four ounces of potatoes per diem were added to their diet in December.[9]

At Fort Pulaski the battered walls were cold and damp and the men slept on rough plank bunks in the casement with no blankets or heat except for an occasional lump of coal in a camp kettle. Each division was allowed twelve sticks of pine wood a day and a stove at noon to do their cooking. Hunger drove them to eating rats, cats, and dogs. One colonel's wife had a pet cat which she begged them to spare. They honored her request, but it was especially hard on Christmas day when there were four inches of snow on the ground. They swapped memories of home and wondered if their comrades back in camp had anything other than their army rations.[10]

Captain Hopkins was among the thirty-one sick prisoners who were exchanged from Fort Pulaski in December 1864 due to the largess of Colonel Philip Brown, commanding the fort. A letter to Colonel Brown appeared in the Charleston *Daily Courier* on December 7 from seven of those exchanged expressing their gratitude for his care of them with "the courtesy of a gallant soldier and Christian gentleman." Brown was reprimanded for allowing those in his charge to compliment him and he was reminded that he had been notified repeatedly not to exchange them or give them full rations.[11]

The ensuing treatment of those remaining at the fort was graphically described by Captain Wash Nelson in letters to his wife Mollie and Henry Clay Dickinson in his diary. They wrote of worms in the crackers, of days when they were given no food and other days when they had only cornmeal and a sour pickle. They had scurvy which caused putrid flesh and hard knots that contracted their limbs. Some died from starvation. They received few letters or packages from home and when packages did arrive, possibly from friends in northern states; their guards opened the boxes and substituted old clothes for the new ones.[12]

Hopes of exchange had abounded in March 1865 when the prisoners at Fort Pulaski were loaded on a two mast square rigged schooner the *Ashland* and taken to Hilton Head where they and the other prisoners were put on the larger *Illinois*. Exchange was expected when they lay off shore at City Point for several days. Instead they were taken back to Fort Delaware where they were among friends and could at least receive mail from home. To the returnees, those who had remained at Fort Delaware looked fat and well dressed. Captain Nelson said that a low necked flannel shirt was his only undergarment. He wore red flannel drawers in lieu of breeches. An old once white overcoat served as coat, shirt, and vest, and a scarf covered his head. He was very thin and lame in his left leg from scurvy. Twenty-three of the 600 had died since they were shipped south. Soon those returning settled back into the life at the prison. There were "law schools," "medical schools," and "divinity schools," and the roles of "prison gamblers, barbers, tailors, laundrymen, workers in rubber, and a minstrel troop, which gave performances in the mess hall of the prison when the commandant gave the permission."[13]

****

With Sheridan snipping at their heels from Petersburg, Five Forks, Amelia Court House, and Saylers Creek, men of the 15th Virginia Infantry were taken prisoner and sent off primarily to Point Lookout (62 men) and there they remained until June 1865. Lieutenant Colonel Emmett Morrison remained at Johnson's Island Prison along with Lt. William Parsley of Hanover and Company A – The Henrico Guards. The captain of the Ashland Grays remained at Fort Delaware. Among those of the 15th Regiment at Point Lookout were eighteen men from Hanover and nine from Henrico. James Butler, John Conner, N.C. Dickerson, John Gibson, George Kelley, Edward Leadbetter, Cornelius Mantlo, Sgt. George Massie, Benjamin McKenzie, John Richardson, William Short, Charles and William Talley, Philip Thacker, William Thompson, Jehu Tiller, Joseph and William H. Woodson were from Hanover. J.F. Clarke, Luther Duval, William Gates, Sgt. James Hendricks, Daniel Jordan, Frederick Jude, Jervance Robinson, Charles Walker, and John Whitlock were from Henrico. Four other men from the area were in prison. John Gary, William Talley, Andrew Hazelgrove, all of Hanover, were at Hart's Island a small prison in the New York harbor. Sgt. Lucius Meredith, of Hanover, was at Newport News. Hazelgrove died on May 23 of consumption and was buried in the Brooklyn National Cemetery there in New York.[14]

William Talley, of the Hanover Grays, had transferred in from the Richmond City Battalion in January 1865, apparently to be near his youngest brother Charles, who had joined the regiment in August 1864. The family had lost two sons at Sharpsburg. William was captured at Five Forks, Charles at High Bridge, and both held at Point Lookout. Neither would be released until June.[15]

The prison at Point Lookout Maryland was on a low, sandy spit of land located where the Potomac River empties into the Chesapeake Bay. It was marshy, indented with coves, and exposed to the heat of the summer and the freezing winds of winter. A lighthouse had been there and a resort hotel with cottages. It had been taken over by the Federal government for a hospital but later converted to a prison for Confederates. During October 1863 some of each shipment of prisoners was already suffering from small pox. The prisoners slept in conical shaped "Sibley" tents with a 15 inch hole in the top, twelve men to a tent. There was a plank fence around the tents and nothing green in sight. A prisoner wrote that many were afflicted with an eye condition, probably caused by the glare from the water, the white tents, and the board fence. They would become blind when the sun went down and have to be led around until the next morning light. Some days a little vinegar was poured over their bread to try to prevent scurvy. A medical inspection found the sick in the hospital tents "in a filthy condition" with no stoves to keep them warm. The wells were shallow and diarrhea was prevalent. A local gazette described the prisoners being "all in rags." Their treatment worsened when troops, including black regiments who had no combat experience, were brought to guard them. The prison population of 11,000 in March 1865 rose to 20,000 by the end of April.[16]

Mr. John B. Ladd, a neighbor to Marion Stewart at "Brook Hill" and later a member of the vestry at Emmanuel Church, had joined the 25th Infantry (the City Battalion) in 1864 to serve with his brother Thomas. They were stationed at Dutch

Gap on July 14 on outpost picket duty when the Federals attacked. One of their fellows was killed and the next morning when the sun came up, John and thirteen others found themselves in enemy hands. Somehow or other Thomas Ladd had escaped and found his way into Richmond to join back with the army. As John Ladd said fourteen of them were taken as prisoners to Point Lookout and held there for a month where the food was terrible. At roll call in the morning they were given a hunk of bread, some meat around noon, usually fat pork, and later "a plate of slim soup," which was sometimes so bad that "they would soon vomit it up. The only drinking water they had must have been polluted for it smelt like rotten eggs."[17]

From Pt. Lookout, Private Ladd was transferred to the prison at Elmira, New York, where he remained until after the war. There the food was better, consisting of bread with meat in the morning and bread and soup in the afternoon. Yet he said that he remained hungry all the time. The only clothing they were furnished was one pair of thin cotton pants. The winter was so cold that parts of one prisoner's feet were amputated three times. The prisoners did not know until June 21, 1865 that Lee had surrendered and, if they took the oath of allegiance, they could go home. After the war he read statistics stating that 1,000 of the 10,000 men at Elmira had died there.[18]

Elmira, New York, was the hometown and burial place of Mark Twain. After the war this island prison on the Chemung River became a pioneer in modern penological methods. However, all accounts of war years paint a much grimmer picture. For the prisoners there conditions were always bad, partly on account of insufficient shelter and partly because of a feud between the commandant and the surgeon. The prison, opened in May 1864, was located on ground lower than the river and a lagoon of stagnant water contributed to much sickness. There too the prisoners lived in tents until barracks could be built. Federal artillery stood guard over them. Faced with the prospect of either death from disease or shells, some men chose to tunnel their way to freedom.[19]

About 50 men of the 5th Virginia Cavalry from the battle at Yellow Tavern were sent first to Point Lookout and then to Elmira. Many were fortunate to be exchanged. Alexander Merchant, Joseph Meyers, and M.R. Woodson, all of Hanover, were exchanged. John Blake, of Mechanicsville, died at Fort Monroe after being exchanged. Joseph Chandler, taken prisoner at Beaverdam on May 9, was exchanged. Two others, after exchanged were taken again at Five Forks and returned to Elmira. By the time of the surrender at Appomattox six had died and four had been sent to Fort Delaware. Fourteen remained at Elmira. It was the later part of May or June before they were released. By that time two more had died and one of the four at Fort Delaware. N.N. and W.W. Atkins returned to Hanover. Private Joseph Waldrop, of Henrico who had been taken prisoner at Winchester on September 19, 1864, had spent almost two months at Elmira before being exchanged.[20]

Samuel Mills was held prisoner in March 1865 at the White House in New Kent and Francis Taylor was captured at the South Anna in March 1865 and sent to Point Lookout. In April 1865 Patrick O'Brien was cut off from his forage wagons in Dinwiddie and taken prisoner.[21]

A private of the 14th Virginia Cavalry asked Rooney Lee where his command was located. Rooney replied, "They are gone." At first thought it might be interpreted that he meant they had gone with Fitz Lee to join with Johnston in North Carolina. The roster for the 10th Virginia Cavalry shows that about eleven took their parole in North Carolina, but many of them were residents of North Carolina, none from Henrico or

Hanover. Yet the record of Johns Scott of Spotsylvania states that he surrendered with Johnson's army in North Carolina. Actually about thirty-five had been taken prisoner while they were screening the march from Petersburg, many at Ford's Depot. Some few were held at Fort Delaware, Hart's Island, and Johnson's Island on the Sandusky Bay in Lake Erie, although it housed predominately officers. Some on Johnson's Island had been there since Brandy Station, Gettysburg, and Spotsylvania. Marion Stewart said of her neighbor, Captain Frank (Francis) Chamberlayne of the 4th Virginia Cavalry, that his daughter died while he was in prison and he did not know it until he returned home.[22]

Creed Davis wrote of the tedium of the day to day existence in the prison camp at Newport News. On April 19 he wrote in his diary that he was still sick He said, "Most of the prisoners are prostrated with dysentery and other bowel complaints – thought to be the results of the bad water … obtained from barrels sunk in the low places of the surfaces of the ground inside the prison inclosure." On May 8 he wrote, "At this moment I would rather be one of the rotting carcasses on one of the battlefields around Richmond than the incarnate prison wretch I am today." That night he said that a severe thunder storm and hurricane hit the camp and blew down their tents and scattered everything around. Another storm came in from the sea and struck a nearby tent, killing one man and wounding two or three others. Creed thought his time had come but said that he "was spared to grind more hard tack and eat more rotten codfish."[23]

Davis fared better after his bed mate, Calvin Cocke, sold his watch and they could buy some loaf bread. Even so he said that he looked yellow like a pumpkin. Cocke and George P. Hughes were successful on their fourth attempt to dig their way through the soft sand under the fence on June 1. Creed refused to go with them for fear that his being barefoot would hold them back as they traversed the woods and swamps on the way to Richmond. He had received his first letter on May 18 and then on June 6 he received one from his sister Ella with a dollar bill enclosed from his mother. On June 10 came a letter from Hughes, using an alias, which told of his safe return home. A welcome relief came to Creed Davis on June 12 when he was detailed for office duty at headquarters to fill out paroles. He was out of the hot sun but already his feet were encrusted over from its rays. In his slack time he made a list of all who had died in that prison.[24]

James McKinney, of Hanover, was released on June 15, and William Winston, called "Springy Dick," of Henrico released on July 1. Creed took his oath on June 24. A group of them were put on a boat for Norfolk where they were registered on June 29, given their transportation papers and loaded on to the steamer *Thomas Colyer* to arrive in Richmond that evening. Creed said that they felt "as light as corks." He had served for twelve months in a battalion for home defense, twelve months in active service, and languished in prison after the war for three months. Creed Davis arrived home on July 1.[25]

With the close of the hostilities, the Howitzers who had been among the twenty-five artillerymen captured along with Captain Ben Smith at Spotsylvania were still languishing at Fort Delaware. They were: Richard Chamberlayne, William Courtney, Edward Crump, Sergeant Thomas Quarles of Henrico and Henry Jones, Samuel Liggan, and Edlow Morris of Hanover. Some of these were released on May 29. Others did not take their oath until June 14. Captain Smith had been exchanged in January or February, 1865. He had returned to service and was commanding Hardaway's Artillery Battalion at Appomattox.[26]

General Hunton, after his capture at Sailer's Creek, wrote of his trip by City Point northward to prison. On passing through

Petersburg, they heard of Lee's surrender. They were put on a boat bound for Washington where Hunton was allowed to buy medicine with some money received from the mother of one of General Corse's staff officers who had escaped capture. On the Jersey ferry they learned of Lincoln's assassination. At Boston they were put on a boat and taken out to Fort Warren in the harbor.[27]

The guns at Fort Delaware were seldom fired even for practice, but on April 4 the prisoners heard a 100 gun salute honoring the fall of Richmond. On April 9 a 200 gun salute announced the surrender at Appomattox. There was rejoicing among the Union men and much fraternization with their prisoners. The mood changed on Easter Sunday as the guns started rumbling, "chanting a slow and measured requiem over Abraham Lincoln." Prisoners were cautioned to show no sign of rejoicing or they would be shot. The mail was stopped, rations cut, and sutler's shops closed. The war was over but it was June before many of the prisoners took the oath of allegiance to the United States and were released. By June 27, the remaining 1,000 at the fort were released by order of General Grant.[28]

Lonnie Speer has written about the conditions at the military prisons during the Civil War. He has concluded that the most held at any one time at Fort Delaware was 12,000, of whom 52 escaped and 2,460 died. At Point Lookout the maximum held was 22,000 of whom 50 escaped and 3,584 died. At Johnson's Island the numbers were 3,256, 12, and 235; while at Elmira they were 9,441, 17, and 2,933. Conditions were no better at the Confederate prison at Andersonville, GA, where there were 32,899 maximum with 329 escapees and 12,919 deaths or on Belle Island where 300+ died among the 10,000 held. Speer concluded. "For those who did survive, their time in those hellholes no doubt remained the most harrowing experience they would ever live, and relive, to the end of their days."[29]

Private James Huffman, of the 10th Virginia Infantry, taken prisoner May 1864 in Spotsylvania, told of the harrowing transfer over two days and a night by ship from Point Lookout prison to Elmira. He said that they were herded on like livestock and "so crowded we did not have room to stretch out to sleep, but sat upright and snoozed a little." He also remembered that in the extreme cold that winter "some of the men froze their feet while standing on the snow and ice at roll call."[30]

Local news media and officials both at Elmira Prison Camp and in Washington claimed it was a model camp where the inmates were well housed, fed, and cared for. Yet in little over a year's time 24.3% died during its 369 days of existence. There was an ill-fated attempt by the Confederacy to ship and sell its cotton to supply them with blankets, clothing, and food held in warehouses in Baltimore and nearby. Was it in retaliation for the deaths in the Confederate prison in Andersonville, Georgia? We will never know. The village of Elmira sat in a thriving agricultural community which had been untouched by ravaging armies.[31]

Dying at a rate of eight a day, the prisoners were buried in Elmira's Woodlawn Cemetery. A stone has been erected by some local high school students in memory of the gravedigger from Virginia. It reads, "Confederate soldiers were buried here with kindness and respect by John W. Jones, a runaway slave. They have remained in these hallowed grounds … by family choice because of the honorable way in which they were laid to rest by a caring man."[32]

Chapter 27

HOME TO YELLOW TAVERN - 1865 - 1889

Private Berkeley took his Oath at Fort Delaware on June 27. He recorded that he was put on a boat to Baltimore, from whence a city steamer took him past Pt. Lookout, Fort Monroe, and Newport News to Richmond. Upon arriving in Richmond they were met by Federal cavalry and escorted to Chimborazo for a meal and a place to sleep. By that date the Virginia Central Railroad was running to Staunton and its president, Colonel Edmund Fontaine, had ordered that all returning Confederates be allowed to ride free.[1]

Robin Berkeley recorded in his diary that when he got to his home on the "White House" farm near Fork Church, "Everything was so quiet, still, and peaceful. I looked around several times expecting to see a Yankee guard spring up out of the bushes." The first person to see him was the Negro Frank, then his father who was plowing corn in front of the house. Soon the entire family "crowded around," giving him a "most hearty and loving welcome." The war was finally over for him.[2]

Frances Doswell of "Bullfield" anxiously awaited in Richmond the return of her husband, Major Thomas Doswell, who had gone south with President Davis and his cabinet. She wrote in her diary of her fear that she could not raise their three small children alone if he were to be gone an extended length of time. She watched some New York Infantry march into the city and saw them establish discipline by arresting the unruly Negroes and putting them to clean up the Capitol Square. She recorded that General Lee came home on Saturday, April 14. She and some other ladies tried to get a glimpse of him. A crowd was standing around, but the general went into his house before they got down there. On Sunday night came word of Lincoln's death. Frances said that on Monday "the papers were all in mourning for him." The next

Sunday her minister preaching on the text "No Man is Sure of Life," spoke of Lincoln's death, and "condemned the murderer in the strongest of terms."[3]

Mrs. Doswell got news on April 24 that her husband was not on his way home, but two days later her brother, Phil Sutton, told her that the major would be home either that day or the next. Major Thomas Doswell's parole was dated April 24 and was signed by H.W. Ryder, major and provost marshal of the 5th Army Corps. Now the Doswells could return to Hanover Junction.[4]

Junius L. Powell was released from Point Lookout on May 29. We can easily imagine the rejoicing at "Melrose" when Father and Mother Powell, Brother Johnnie, Sister Blanche and possibly some of the faithful house servants welcomed home their beloved Junius. Of the forty-two Blacks, only two left during the war and one of those had returned. Mrs. Powell estimated that, as a result of the emancipation, they had lost $17,000 of their investment; a figure she declared was on the low side.[5]

Twenty-seven Henrico-Hanover men in Ashland-Hanover Artillery had been paroled at Appomattox, six having been with the unit since May 1861: Luther Duke, Charles Ragland, Samuel Sims, James Southard, William Terry, and Nicholas Terrell. It had become a battery of brothers with Captain Pichegru Woolfolk and his brother, Lieutenant Edmund Woolfolk, in the leadership. John and Billy Terrell had joined their brother Nicholas, William Simms with his brother Samuel, John Hancock his brother Rufus, and Alex Jackson with his brother Thomas. The Jackson fellows' parents were Elizabeth and John. Mother Woolfolk welcomed home her sons Pichegru and Edmund, but her joy was short lived. The captain was killed in the Capitol disaster of 1870.[6]

Father Joseph Zachery Terrell and Jo Terrell, still grieving for their spouses, welcomed home Nicholas and John Terrell. Brother Billy may have already gotten home on disability. Soon to greet them were the sisters Mary (Mollie) Goodwin Terrell, Barbara Johnson, Ann Yeamans, Martha (Tommie) Snead, and their Aunt Ann and Uncle Joe Carr and their families. They could be seeing soon old Great-aunt Mary Henley Thompson Terrell, whose husband David had served in the Virginia militia during the War of 1812.[7]

There is no family account telling of the return home of Nat Cross to Mother Catherine, Sisters Lucy Ann and Betty Richard. He probably soon visited Brother Finch, Frances, and their frail little Fannie. Did he often visit the nearby grave of Jimmie Gray?[8]

Neither is there a first hand account of the return of the Francis brothers, Tom and Buck, to their ancestral home, except that they walked from Appomattox subsisting on parched corn. Their brother Jim, his wife Sarah, and their three children were living there. Certainly the brothers and dear friend Nat Cross would often talk of experiences in the war, but the later generation would not listen, saying that war was so terrible that they did not want to hear about it. Tom and Buck would visit with Sister Liz, her husband, John J. Davis and girls, Sister Mat, her husband Dumps Jenkins and their girls. Perhaps Jo Terrell brought Johnny, Jimmie, and little sister Emma Charles to see their Uncle Buck and Uncle Tom soon.[9]

Fences were down at "Rosewood," horses and chickens gone, and the cattle wandered about aimlessly over the fields and into the woods. The Negro George left one night, taking the cart, and all the produce it would carry. Rosina Mordecai made pies and cakes whenever she could get the ingredients. An old faithful house servant would take baked goods in baskets into town to sell to the soldiers. It was weeks before they heard from the boys, not knowing whether they were alive or dead. John, George and William came straggling in one by one, foot sore, ragged, and half starved. William had appropriated a mule, which was so poor that it had to be led with frequent stops so it could graze. When he got to a ferry he found two officers haggling with the ferryman over transporting them across with the payment in Confederate dollars. William Mordecai produced a small bag of coffee which was accepted as toll for all three of them.[10]

Emma Mordecai wrote that William arrived home one morning soon after they had finished breakfast. He looked well but was worn, depressed, and quiet. A couple of days later, wanting time to think things through, "he walked through the woods to the head of the pond, a place usually wrapped in beauty and solitude." A swarm of Yankee soldiers were having a swimming party. His daughter later wrote in the family account, "His sense of humor came to his rescue, for he said, as he walked back he was amused at the irony of it!"[11]

Soldiers and stragglers continued to pass through the neighborhood, breaking into houses and taking what they could carry. At "Brook Hill" they promised Mr. Stewart that they would not go upstairs and molest Mrs. Stewart and family if he would give them some whiskey. This he did, exposing the location of his supply. The soldiers tied him up and became drunk, were more unruly and threatening Mrs. Stewart if she did not unlock her jewelry box. Then someone called out that they had found the silver. She had told the soldiers that all the money, jewelry, and silver were in the bank. But this was the communion silver for Emmanuel Church which for convenience had been kept at "Brook Hill." Mrs. Lizzie Drever, the Scotch housekeeper, slipped among the staggering men and by slight of hand retrieved all but one of the pieces from their sacks. Mary Stewart saw two officers outside and called out, "For God's sake come in and stop these desperadoes!"[12]

John Stewart despaired for the safety of his family at "Brook Hill." The next month he took then by boat to New York. He avoided the overland route to keep from taking the "Iron Clad Oath" of allegiance to the United States. His daughter wrote that they arrived in New York and sailed that very night on *The Cuba,* of the Cunard Line, for Europe, not to return until the fall of the next year.[13]

Young Margaret Mosby answered a knock on the door one night at their home at Yellow Tavern. There were two soldiers demanding to see her father. She replied that he had not been well and had already gone to bed. However, they took him from his bed and carried him off to a prison in Alexandria. He was held until he could convince his captors that he was not the ranger John Singleton Mosby. Not long afterwards Margaret received a letter from one of the soldiers apologizing for his action and asking if he could call on her. The irate young lady destroyed the letter and said in later years that she did not even remember his name.[14]

Margaret Mosby on March 29, 1869, married William Isbell. William was a farmer and Margaret a horticulturist with some carpentry and veterinary skills. They lived at "Oakhill Tavern" and on his grandfather's farm, both on Studley Road in Hanover County. She was a pioneer in developing hybrid seed and worked for Burpee Seed Company. Her family says, "She would hand pollinate her plants and put tiny cloth sacks over the heads of the blooms to catch the experimental hybrid seeds." They are both buried at Salem Presbyterian Church at Studley, the current name for Haw's Shop.[15]

In Richmond, General Marsena Patrick served as the head Provost Marshal for the Army of the Potomac. When he was stationed at Culpeper in 1863, John Minor Botts had invited Patrick and three other generals to dine. He penned in his diary, "Of course I did not go and would not, under any ordinary circumstances." General Patrick was stationed with General Grant at City Point on the day that Richmond was evacuated and visited Elizabeth Van Lew at her home a few days thereafter. The general served as Marshal in Richmond until June. He had visited and conferred with General Lee before he was removed from the capital city.[16]

The editor of Patrick's diary stated, "It was General Grant, who had shown little evidence of personal animosity toward Southerners, who suggested Patrick's removal from the post of Provost Marshal of Richmond because of Patrick's well known kindness of heart might interfere with the proper government of the city." General Patrick and John Minor Botts were on the same boat bound for Geneva, New York, on June 12, 1865. Both men avoided each other.[17]

****

Nat Cross got home with his horse in time to get a crop in for the 1865 growing season. He had the help of the Negro Buck Owen, who had been with the family since they were both small boys. Mother Cross gave Buck some land to build a house on and he stayed on with the family as a hired hand. Nat married Betty Gray, Jimmie's sister, in early 1867. Their first child was a girl, Mattie, who barely lived a year. Tom Francis came home to marry Lucy Ann Cross, Nat's sister and apparently farmed Lucy's part of the Cross estate, that of her unmarried sister Bet and also that of her deceased sister Mary Jane Davis.[18]

Finch Cross, his wife and little Fannie moved to Baltimore where he could work as a bricklayer. Certainly there would have been enough bricklaying to be done in the rebuilding of Richmond but perhaps not enough money to pay good wages.

Tom Francis' children were admonished in later years, "Don't say anything against the poor because after the war everyone was poor!" Apparently Tom was studying bricklaying when the war broke out. Finch in a letter to his mother in 1870 admonished Tom to stick with his success that year in farming and not go back to his old trade. By this time Tom and Lucy had 2 year-old Walter. Finch wrote that Fannie would like to see "the little man." He himself was out of work and wondered what bricklayers were being paid in Richmond. He said that he might go west.[19]

The lure of the west had already drawn family members. Frances Cross had lived out there during her marriage to Eddie Crew. Charles Terrell was in 1862 contemplating moving after the war because he did not feel that his Virginia acreage would sustain his family and he had apparently bought land in Kentucky. After the war Jo Terrell tried to collect rent on the Kentucky land and ended up selling the land in Hinkleville for $900. Times were so tight that Jo paid Dr. Sheppard by knitting some socks for him.[20]

Buck Francis came home to farm his land "Rebel Hill" and apparently lived with Jim and Sally until he could get his house built. He married Fannie Terrell, daughter of Timothy and Harriet Anderson. They had a son which Buck named John Samuel for his father and the brother he had buried at Sharpsburg. Their joy was short lived when Fannie died in 1867. Little Sammie went to live with his grandparents, Timothy and Harriett Terrell. Buck married twice more, eventually having ten children. Brother Jim and Sarah's family grew to four: Mary Jane, William James, Ann Thompson, and Wirt S.[21]

Mother Cross died of typhoid fever in 1877. By this time Tom Francis had built his and Lucy Ann's house on her portion of the land and had also bought her late sister Mary Jane Davis's part of the estate and would continue to buy other small parcels. Sister Bet came to live with them and Tom Francis farmed her land too. The family grew to be four sons and three daughters and Tom supplemented his profit from farming by sawmilling and building houses.[22]

The Powells continued to live at "Melrose" at least until 1873. Blanche was married in November 1867 at the age of 17 years to Captain John William Drewry, who was twelve years her senior. Mother Powell was nineteen years younger than Blanche's father. Unfortunately Captain Drewry died 5½ years later of pneumonia there at "Melrose" and is buried with the family at Emmanuel Church. Junius Powell studied medicine and was connected with the Surgeon General's office during the Spanish American War. He did not marry until he was 39 years old and had one child, a daughter. John J.A. Powell married a widow and they had three sons and three daughters. Dr. Powell was Henrico County's first superintendent of schools. He died at his Richmond residence on Grace Street in 1874. Mother Powell survived him by about eleven years.[23]

William Mordecai took up the farming at "Rosewood" and struggled to bring order to the chaos. He married in 1875 Helen Norwood, the daughter of the first minister at Emmanuel, and had six children. William served as a vestryman at Emmanuel and as a supervisor of Henrico County. George Mordecai went down to North Carolina in October to operate one of his Uncle George Washington Mordecai's plantations. This undertaking lasted for eighteen months and then he and a cousin left to take up land in California to manage for their uncle. There were dry years when other Southerners went back home. George Mordecai married, purchased land of his own, eventually served as a state assemblyman, and died on his ranch there in California.[24]

John Mordecai resumed his education and studied law with his Uncle John Young. He was a quiet, well liked fellow. In 1873 when the young lawyer was only 33 years old, he got distraught over a poem which appeared in the Richmond *Enquirer*, possibly referring to a local belle. The argument that ensued ended in a duel in which John was mortally wounded and the other man left crippled for life. Mother Rosina Mordecai lived on at "Rosewood" until her death at the age of 88 years.[25]

George Edmond Massie, of the Patrick Henry Rifles, had been reluctant to take his oath of allegiance at Point Lookout until his father convinced him that he was needed back on the farm. The Massies had invested money in Confederate bonds. Soon they lost their home, "Iron Hill," and then leased a place called "Edgewood." George moved there with his parents and two maiden aunts. They were very active in St. Peter's Methodist Church, to which Father Massie contributed some land. Five children were born to George and his first wife, Mary Catherine Jackson, his first cousin. The youngest child, Peter, died at the age of five, two years after his mother had died of tuberculosis.[26]

Times were hard. Mollie Goodwin Terrell wrote to Jo Terrell on April 26, 1866, of the long dreary winter. Her father had not been well and Aunt Nancy (Mrs. Joe Carr Terrell) had been in bed all winter. Mr. Snead (?) had committed suicide, troubled about the hard times. Mollie said that in her imagination she could "often see him see him hanging, bereft of hope, friendless and alone, launching his soul unbidden into the unseen world, then the little ones left without protection." She spoke of her brother Billie and his wife living with them, of Brother Nick and family leaving for Kentucky, including the "sweet little red headed daughter." She was most sad that her sister Barbara was "leaving her best and most faithful friends." Mollie married F.L. Weathers in 1867 and died the following year.[27]

Life moved on with its joys and sorrows. Barbara Johnson, Charles Terrell's sister apparently did not stay away long. In July 1877, she wrote Jo Terrell describing her Brother Billie's wife, Etha's, death. They had had six children in nine years. Etha asked Barbara to write to all her friends saying that she had gone to be with her two little angels and hoped all would meet her in heaven. She left behind Virginia, 9, Juliette, 6, Martha, 5, and the baby, William Jr., 6 months. Her death went the hardest on young Virgie, who cried herself to sleep that night and the next day screamed for them not to put her mother in the ground.[28]

The ordinance for public schools had been passed. Jo Terrell eventually sent all her children to stay with Cousin Timothy and attend school in Beaverdam. Mollie G. Terrell had started the boys out well, loving them and bribing them to learn their letters. Jo treasured the letters which they wrote to her, to each other, she to them, and Cousin Mollie's letter to her telling how well they were doing. A Mr. Duke had thirty scholars and all the families were pleased with him and hoped he would be back the next year. He would whip the boys one day and promise to whip the girls the next day.[29]

Jo cautioned her sons to be good boys and her daughter not to get a whipping. She was kind, loving, and playful as she teased them about their flirtations. Jo told about her work with the oats and the garden. Emma Charlie wrote, "Our hog had seven pretty little pigs 9 weeks ago and our other one had 4 Tuesday Uncle Buck has 10 Uncle James has 10 so we are suplie (sic) with little pigs," She wrote about someone setting Mr. Waldrop's barn on fire, burning all his corn, Cousin Clay's fodder, and barring the door so that "it burned Mr.Waldrops horse smack up."[30]

Sadly Jo Terrell wrote to one of her sons that she went to Richmond the day before to buy the black (material) that his Aunt Sallie would be wearing. If the boy had not gotten her previous letter, she wanted him to know that his Uncle Jim Francis had died two weeks ago, on Friday soon after he left home. She wrote him that the culvert in that road had been fixed so anytime he could get someone to bring his trunk down they could come that way. It would be a sad Christmas. James Thompson Francis was forty-nine years old. He had been home from the war only twelve and one half years.[31]

George Washington Nelson married his Mollie in October 1865. Jobs were not available in Hanover. They first settled with her parents in Shepherdstown, West Virginia. Wash, who while at Ft. Pulaski had conducted Episcopal services for his fellow prisoners, decided to study for the ministry and later obtained a church in Warrenton. He and Mollie lost several children at an early age. His friend, Captain Dickinson, became mayor of Charleston, West Virginia.[32]

Hamilton Sheppard of "Meadow Farm" had dreams of serving with the Second Richmond Howitzers. He wrote to his mother while serving as a guard at Libby Prison that all the other boys who wanted to go had been transferred to that unit. He was not sure that she wanted him to go so would wait until April. This was probably during the last year of the war when Hamilton was only seventeen years old and there is no record that he ever served with the Howitzers or family record of what became of him.[33]

****

The Virginia General Assembly of 1865 began the stabilizing of the communities by legalizing the status of the Black marriages. But the next year they failed to give them full suffrage. The Assembly also rejected the Fourteenth

Amendment to the United States Constitution. At this point the United States Congress made Virginia a military district and the Reconstruction Acts of March 1867 "admitted freed blacks to suffrage, excluded many former Confederates from voting, and required a test oath for all office holders." The military and the Freedmen Bureau watched carefully while 1,228 whites, and 1,879 black people registered to vote for candidates to the Constitution Convention of 1867-68 that came to be known as the Underwood Constitution. Henrico was allowed one delegate of its own and shared another delegate with Hanover County. That shared delegate was a former slave of Hanover, Burwell Toler, who was instrumental in organizing a number of black churches throughout the countryside.[34]

On May 2, 1867, some Blacks, who had been worshiping peacefully with the white members at North Run Baptist Church on Hungary Road, decided that they wanted a church of their own. The Henrico Court records show that the trustees of Mount Olive African Church of Baptist purchased 1.7 acres from Mary Crenshaw. The land is just off Mountain Road, not far from its beginning at the Telegraph Road. They cleared the heavily wooded lot and built a brush arbor to shelter their gatherings. Later a log cabin and a frame building were built. The Reverend Toler was their first pastor, assisted by Timothy Harris, M.R. Toler, and the Reverend John Jasper. Supportive prayer meetings were held in the homes of Sisters Hardenia Booker, Rose Tinsley, and May Ann Tilman. Early pastors were the Reverends Timothy Harris and M.R. Toler. Their history says, "Under the leadership of Reverend Toler, associate ministers included Reverend Richard Wells and Reverend John Jasper, who preached many lasting sermons under the trees. The Reverend John Jasper, the pastor of Sixth Mount Zion in Richmond, was known for his rhetorical skills and his "Sun Do Move" sermon. Starting in 1878, that sermon was preached 253 times to white and black audiences alike from Richmond to Philadelphia.[35]

The neighborhood Blacks organized another church farther up Mountain Road in 1882 and called it St. Peter Baptist Church. They built their church on a plot of land given by Mr. John Clacker and their first pastor was the Reverend Timothy Harris.[36]

The history of Taylorsville Baptist Church shows that at one time there were 150 black members and only 100 white ones. About 1868, thirty-two Blacks withdrew from Taylorsville Baptist to meet on the farm of Dr. Frank Taylor, a white land owner who lived about five miles away. The Reverend Burwell Toler was their first pastor and they named their church Jerusalem Baptist. They moved to about a half mile from Hanover Junction. but when the trains came by their horses would run. It was 1879 before the congregation had its own building.[37]

Winn's Baptist Church when the Francis family attended it was made up of white and black members, both slave and free. Forty families were shown as being slave holders. In 1854 there were 148 "colored" and 133 white people. Two Blacks were chosen as deacons to supervise their fellow Blacks; otherwise they could neither hold office nor vote. After the war when all the Blacks had left, the church would often not have a quorum of ten to twelve members to conduct business.[38]

Creed Davis in 1889 returned to the Slashes of Hanover. He had not been in the neighborhood for eight or nine years and wrote, "I was appalled at the desolation and ruin that I beheld, and for the first time in many years I sat upon my horse and wept as I rode through the once familiar haunts of my boyhood, now almost unrecognizable." He felt that the decline had begun with the building of the railroad (R.F. & P.) that denuded the woodland, diverted trading from the local markets, followed by the "invasion and vandalism of the Federal Army," and the departure of the young men for the Confederate army and the slaves after the emancipation. All this had left the land "worn out by long and poor cultivation; with its fences gone and roads overgrown and ditches filled, with the water courses undrained – mere quagmires; with its mills in a state of ruin." But, he wrote that he saw "a redeeming feature in this impoverished land … It is the sprightly and beautiful little village of Ashland that nestles in the very heart of the slashes. It always reminded me of a nest in a brush full of partridge eggs, looking so white, clean and cozy and homelike withall."[39]

We might say that the "eggs" hatched in 1868 when Randolph Macon College purchased the Ashland Hotel and the 14 acre Mineral Well Company and moved to Ashland from Boykin, Virginia. The student body of sixty-seven that fall grew to 100 the next session. At first the students lived in the frame cottages, with no heat, running water, or bathrooms. The college used the larger resort buildings for a chapel, lecture rooms, and society rooms. Washington Franklin Hall replaced the hotel and was the first brick building in town. Later were built the Pace Lecture Hall, the Duncan Memorial Church to replace the old ballroom chapel which burned in 1879, the Science Hall built in 1891, and frame buildings replaced the resort cottages. One half the students boarded in town and a new Ashland Hotel was built in 1873-75.[40]

The war was over. The people of Yellow Tavern could work their fields. They could take their produce by wagon into Richmond or ship it by the rails of the two railroads which were being repaired. Eventually there would be employment in the city now rising from its ashes. They would educate their children in their own county's emerging public schools and could send their youth for classical instruction at Randolph Macon College in Ashland or to Richmond College or Westhampton College in western Henrico County. Virginia Union University would be the end result of northern teachers coming down to educate the Blacks in the area.

EPILOGUE

What has become of Yellow Tavern? Neither fighters nor defenders would recognize the area in the 21st century. Only those born into the hands of one of its country doctors or black midwives, who has walked its dusty roads and jumped its briery branched streams during the 20th century can feel the emotional tug and see it as a definite entity. I am one of those, though educated in Richmond and employed in West Virginia. When I came to settle in King William County and was asked if I was from Yellow Tavern, I felt I should respond in the affirmative. Tom Francis was my grandfather and my dad worked the family farm. Jeb Stuart was wounded on the edge of the farm which extended to the Telegraph Road where his first monument was erected.

Grandfather Tom took his 10 year-old son Wilton, my father, to the dedication ceremonies in 1888 led by Governor Fitzhugh Lee. When the bass drum sounded a loud "BOOM," Dad remembered that he "took off" across the former battlefield. Grandmother Lucy Ann, the beloved "Aunt San" to Nat Cross's children, died in 1908. Grandfather lived until 1911, attended with men of Corse's Brigade the reunion of the U.C.V. at the unveiling of Lee's statue in Richmond in 1890, saw the laying of the cornerstone for the President Davis monument in Richmond, and was at the reunion of the 15th Regiment in 1903 and 1905 in Richmond, and the 15th Regiment reunion in Ashland in 1909. In later years, our dad had the job of decorating the Stuart's monument for Memorial Day. I had the joy of helping him. We wrapped the shaft in a large Confederate flag and placed small ones on the iron fence.

Our home was a mile and a half from Solomon's Store, a large two story frame building at the junction of what had been the old Brook Turnpike and the Telegraph Road, barely one eighth a mile north of the old Yellow Tavern site. In the 1930s a kindly old man, Mr. Jim Mallory with a bushy white moustache, ran the store and sold cheese cut from a big round block, also peppermint and horehound candy sticks. I have been told that Mr. Mallory went down and started the fire in the Yellow Tavern School and generally kept an eye out for the children until the truck came to take them to school.[1] Nearby were a blacksmith shop and a service station operated by members of the Epps family, where one could buy five gallons of gasoline for a dollar. A two storied Powell house nearby which was used as a hospital during the battle is no longer standing.[2] On the Telegraph Road still stands a simple two story house built by Tom Francis for the King family.

Fortunately, in spite of the spread of suburban Richmond, a traveler today can see the stately spired brick Emmanuel Church on Brook Road. For years it was covered with stucco painted gray and approached through the lyche gate on the old toll road. Amidst its trees, it would be barely noticed except when its throaty bell tolled for a funeral. Now it stands as a sentinel overlooking the nearby breastworks of Richmond's outer defense line. Across the road is "Brook Hill" on its park like grounds. The open space at St. Joseph's Villa, about a mile and a half north on U.S. # 1 (Brook Road) from Azalea Avenue (the old Military Road), can serve as a visual nucleus for Yellow Tavern. Here lay "Brookside" plantation where Gabriel had learned to read and write and planned his insurrection.[3] Across the highway were the tavern and Yellow Tavern Public School built by Tom Francis after his return home from the war.

****

Tom Francis had little chance at an education but his educational heritage began with his father's bequests, written in his will in 1843, that his widow should educate their children so that each child received at least three years "tuishon" (sic). Should she die or remarry, enough of his personal estate was to be sold to "board and educate" the children before any division be made of his property.[4]

Tom sent his children to a Mr. Anderson, who is said to have attended Harvard, and to have been a friend of Edgar Allan Poe. The children said he had the largest dictionary they ever saw! His small home, in the midst of the battlefield, still had bullet holes. Later the neighborhood children, including my dad and mother, the former Minnie Scott who lived at "Melrose," went to Yellow Tavern School. Tom's oldest son, Walter, married Sarah Sutton, a teacher at the school. With the turn of the century most of the schools in Henrico County were one or two rooms, but at some of them advanced subjects were taught. One of these was Yellow Tavern School where Minnie Scott studied Latin and Algebra.

Miss Virginia Randolph, a Richmond native who was a daughter of a slave, had already opened a one room school on Mountain Road for black children. She had studied at the Baker School in Richmond and the Colored Normal School and started teaching when she was sixteen. She rode the train to the Glen Allen crossing and walked the several miles to the school. She said, "I believe in educating the hands, the eyes, the feet and the soul." Along with the academic skills, she combined cooking, sewing, woodworking, and gardening. Mr. Jackson Davis, the superintendent of schools, a white man, was so impressed with her work that he secured a grant from the Anna T. Jeanes fund started by a Quaker lady in Philadelphia who was interested in education for the Blacks in the South. Miss Randolph was made a Supervising Industrial Teacher in 1908 and oversaw all the industrial instruction in the county's schools for Blacks. Her idea spread throughout the South and came to be known as the "Henrico Plan." The training center, the only black high school in the county, burned in 1929, and was replaced by a nine classroom building. At her funeral, in 1958, she was commended for her leadership toward a better life for girls and boys, women and men "which she almost alone in her time, foresaw for them." Her school is now a National Historic Landmark and can be utilized by all children with learning disabilities.[5]

It is fitting that Major James Dooley, who had made his fortune with the railroads after the war, was one of the main contributors to the Richmond Sisters of Catholic Charity which built an orphanage for girls at the St. Joseph's Villa. It has now become a training center for disadvantaged children. Dooley and philanthropist Lewis Ginter, a New Yorker who served with the Confederate army and came back to Richmond to make his fortune in tobacco and other investments, did much for the physical and educational development of the area to the south called Ginter Park. He divided it off into lots, built a community center, encouraged Union Theological Seminary (Presbyterian) to move to the area, bought the Young's estate, "Westbrook" and built a psychiatric hospital there. His niece, Grace Arents, started the area's first public library at the community center. The bequest of her very lovely "Bloemendaal" house and gardens is being developed into the fabulous Lewis Ginter Botanical Gardens. Ginter purchased ten acres beside Brook Run and built the Lakeside Wheel Club. It became the Lakeside Golf Course. Residents in the city rode the newly installed Richmond electric trolley lines from the developing Barton Heights and Ginter Park areas. The lines went to the lakeside park and also to the park in the Westhampton end of Henrico County. "Rosedale," on Hermitage Road across from the A.P. Hill monument, became the first Deep Run Hunt Club, later the Hermitage Airport, and is now the location of Imperial Plaza Retirement Home.[6]

Marion Stewart Peterkin had said that the turnpike was their only road into Richmond. "It had deep ruts in it which made hard pulling for the horses and quite uncomfortable at times for those in any vehicle... The only thing that was ever done to repair the road was to dump red clay on it, which in wet weather, particularly, made a terrible slush." While tolls were still being collected, neighbors would often pull vehicles out of muddy by-passes on the Military Road. The Richmond and Chesapeake Bay Railway Company, financed by the Jay Gould family of New York, built tracks in 1907 from Broad Street to Ashland, through the Yellow Tavern area, bringing electricity and opening the area to residential development.[7]

The trolley ran out from Laurel and Broad streets along Brook Road, past "Laburnum," the home of the Bryans, "Westbrook," behind Emmanuel Church and through Lakeside and "Belmont," now a country Club. It went behind "Hollyfield" (St. Joseph's Villa), by the lady slippers and mountain laurel growing along the old Federal trenches, and by Mt. Olive Church. The streetcar would emerge on Mountain Road at a stop called Yellow Tavern, where lay double tracks so the southbound car could pass. From there it ran through land where the battle had raged and came to be developed into Biltmore, Longdale, and Greenwood subdivisions. From Greenwood, near the Francis and Cross farms, the track went to cross Cedar Lane and on to Ashland. If it had only been put through earlier, Grandfather Tom could have used that trolley to visit his sisters and reach Winn's Church. He remained faithful, walking the four miles to the church on some special occasions. Eventually he joined North Run Baptist Church on Hungary Road, but insisted that a church (Biltmore) should be built nearer by. Later his son John was one of the builders of Biltmore Church. The John Francis house still stands on Old Francis Road.

To get an internal feel for the area, one would need to visit the churches in Henrico, starting with Emmanuel Church, followed by a black church on Hungary Road. Emmanuel continued to reach out to the community after the war. Its rector supervised for a few years the oldest black Episcopal church in Richmond, St. Philips. He ministered to the Blacks living around Emmanuel. The congregation established the Church of the Epiphany in Barton Heights on Hanes Avenue (now on Hermitage Road). The minister also conducted teaching and preaching missions, one being in an elementary school at "Half Sink."[8]

Hungary Road Baptist Church occupies the building formerly used by North Run Baptist, which is now located farther west on Lydell Drive. The churches of the neighborhood cooperate at Easter Sunrise services and at Thanksgiving. Many had their beginnings as Union, Free Churches, or Meeting Houses used by all denominations. Other churches had their organization encouraged by teachers or instructors in nearby schools or institutions.

The Methodists of the area, served by circuit riders, met with other denominations at the old North Run Union Church on Hungary Road beginning in 1840. They constructed a brush arbor and built their own frame Greenwood Methodist Church in 1874 on a one acre of land donated by Joshua Taylor, a former mayor of Richmond. It was attended by the King, Gray, Barnes, and Ryall families.[9]

There has been continued cooperation between the neighbors in the area. In June 1923, Greenwood Methodist sponsored, with the participation of community churches, two weeks of revival services under a large tent next to their newly built parsonage on Virginia Road. One night there was a violent storm which collapsed the tent, greatly frightening and slightly injuring some of the people, who were taken to a nearby home. However the tent was restored for services the next night. It was reported that 2,000 people attended the meetings and over 150 presented their names for membership in the various churches.[10]

The first Greenwood Church had two wings added for the Sunday School and a steeple with a bell. The bell would vibrate the old building and was seldom rung except when fire had gotten out of control in the nearby woods. In 1926 they built a brick church about a half mile down the road on land donated by Mr. and Mrs. E.T. Long, the developers of the subdivision, and next to Longdale School.[11] When Biltmore Baptist Church was organized in 1929 by members from North Run Church, they met in Longdale School and Greenwood Church later presented the new church with a pulpit Bible. The school burned in 1933 and while it was being rebuilt some students had classes in Biltmore Church on New York Avenue. The Reverend W. Roy Carner, former pastor of North Run Church, served Biltmore and Glen Allen Churches until he left to be a chaplain in World War II.

The congregation at Greenwood assisted in the operation of a union Sunday School at Taylor's Crossing from 1915 to1925, meeting first in the individual homes. Then a building was erected on Old Washington Highway Classes were taught on Sunday afternoons by members of Greenwood Church with Mr. Alexander Wyatt as superintendent. Sermons were delivered by theological students and visiting ministers. Baptists in the neighborhood had built their own church at Taylor's Crossing in 1915 on land donated by Dr. J.H. Winfrey. Dr. W.H. Lawson of Glen Allen Baptist served as chairman of the planning committee. It was called Hunton Baptist Church and now has a beautiful sanctuary and Sunday School rooms.[12]

Glen Allen Baptist, also a very beautiful brick church, began in 1867. They built a brush arbor near the railroad station on land belonging to the Allen family. In cold weather the members met in Mrs. Allen's house. The Hopkins family of "Walkerton" gave some land on their estate and John Cussons cut timber for a building free of charge. The first building, having only three windows and one door, was 24x36 feet. The small frame church also had a steeple with a bell. This church was built in a gothic style and would rattle and echo with the passage of the trains. The current building was dedicated in 1961.[13]

****

For our church tour of Hanover churches, we can start with Winn's Church, the one attended by the Francis family and some of the Cross family. After the war, Nat Cross migrated, perhaps because of Betty Gray, to Greenwood and then to Emmanuel. Winn's Church continues to build and rebuild until this day. Dr. J.R.Garlick was the pastor from 1892 to 1906. The building used during the war was probably torn down about 1909.[14]

Ground Squirrel Christian Church used the small brick church at the South Anna River during the war but it was partially destroyed by a storm in 1897. Its third building on the same site was declared unsafe and was replaced by a brick building in 1969. It goes by the name of Cavalry Christian Church. Independence Christian Church on Falling Creek was first a Meeting House used by all denominations. It was taken over by the Disciples of Christ in 1889 after other congregations had moved out and built their own places of worship.[15]

Gwathmey Baptist, on the railroad south of Ashland, was begun in 1892 by a school superintendent, Dr. J.R. Garlick, and Dr. H.L. Quarles, an instructor at The Hanover Female Institute located just across the road. Cavalry Episcopal Mission for Blacks at Hanover Court House was fostered by the chaplain at the Hanover School for Boys. Miss Louisa Webb, an English governess at "Courtland," encouraged the further development of St. Paul's Episcopal Church after it moved to Hanover Court House.[16]

Dr. John A. Kern and his students at Randolph Macon College were operating a union chapel on Cedar Lane in 1891 when a member of the group, Mrs. Addie Stover Crawford, the daughter of a Methodist minister, secured land for a church building. She was allowed to name it Kenwood for her home, and it became part of the Ashland Charge with preaching once a month on a Sunday afternoons. It went off the circuit in the 1920s and on its own with many of its student ministers going on to become prominent in the Methodist Conference.[17]

Other Methodist churches like Greenwood were served by circuit ministers: Forest Grove, Mt. Herman, Shady Grove, and Enon at Studley, built on land given by Mr. John Haw, a member of Salem Presbyterian Church. Salem is one of three churches in the county started by the Reverend Samuel Davies. It first met at Hanovertown but was soon moved to Haw's Shop.[18]

During the Civil War the Baptists were the only ones in Ashland who had their own building and it was used as a hospital. Now they have a large building to the west and the old one is used for a cultural arts center. All other congregations met in the Masonic building on England Street and even the Methodists held services there until their move to the Randolph Macon campus for the Duncan Memorial Church. The St. Ann's Catholic Church building was the gift of a Richmond patroness, Mrs. Ann Pizzini, and was served by priests from Richmond and Fredericksburg. Their lovely little building has been bought by Randolph Macon College and the congregation meets elsewhere in Ashland. Members of St. James the Less (Episcopal) were largely from the St. James Church in Richmond.[19]

****

The streetcar from Richmond to Ashland ran every hour and, by its whistle in the quiet neighborhoods, the families hardly needed to set their clocks to know when it was time to get up, leave for school, work or church services. A parish school was run at Emmanuel Church, an elementary school operated at the beginning of Chamberlayne Avenue, and a new school, Ginter Park Elementary, opened in 1915 on the edge of town. Some of the local children would ride the Richmond-Ashland streetcars to attend these schools.

The Ashland Carline was called a "jolly trolley," with the camaraderie of students, professors, card playing business men, stenographers, and shoppers. The story has been told that whenever Rosewell Page, a brother of the author Thomas Nelson Page, rode across the Chickahominy on a return into Ashland, he would stand, raise both arms, and cry out, "We are in Hanover County, God bless her!"[20]

Men cut a right a way for the Richmond-Washington Highway in the early 1920s, using scoops pulled by tasseled horses to level the ground. The farmers in Hanover and Henrico needed no longer to drive their two-wheeled carts along the winding Telegraph Road or the potholed Brook Road to get their produce to the 6th Street Market in Richmond. That highway became U.S. Route #1 and was widened to three lanes and then four lanes. Fewer people would drive by Stuart's monument on the Telegraph Road.

Tom Francis and his beloved Lucy Ann rest in the family cemetery along with the bodies of Nat Cross, his wife Bettie Gray Cross, and children of the two families lost in infancy. The cemetery overlooks U.S. # 295 that encircles Richmond and the Yellow Tavern battlefield, near its interchange with Interstate #95. The highway passes over the site where Tom built the four room house where Lucy Ann cooked all their meals on the hearth. Major H.B. McClelland came by their home in the 1890s with the book he had written on his experiences with Jeb Stuart. The adjutant wanted to give a copy to whoever owned that house. Nat Cross replied that he was the present owner and the gift is now the proud possession of one of his great-grandsons. For a number of years the family had the impression that Stuart spent his last night in that house, but it has since been proven not to have been the case. Perhaps the aide had set up their headquarters there before the general was wounded. The Cross house burned in 1941.

The road through the battlefield is now called Old Francis Road or Francis Road. Nearby the site of the Cross house is the historical marker denoting General Williams C. Wickham's defensive line. Across the U.S. #1 highway on the edge of what was Mosby-Cross land are the remains of the Confederate entrenchments. Many houses have filled up the farm land and Virginia Center Commons has spread out its commercial development. The name Jeb Stuart Parkway shows that the area might be of historical significance.

There is a barroom called Yellow Tavern at an elaborate conference center nearby built on the site of "Ethelwood," the Sheppard home which burned in 1912 and was replaced by a similar model. The frame "Half Sink" house, with bullet holes across its front from the battle, still stood into the early twentieth century. It had a wide entrance hall with two rooms down and three up. Now even its solitary chimney has disappeared.[21]

The area is called Glen Allen, Virginia. In the early twentieth century, my dad would walk or ride on horseback to "Walkerton," perhaps weekly, to get the mail for our family and the neighboring Cross and Terrell families. Then the mail came to be delivered over two rural routes from a very small station at Allen's Crossing on the R.F. & P. Railroad at

Mountain Road. Captain John Cussons, after marrying the widow Susan Allen during the war, had dreamed of making the area a resort, serving travelers from all up and down the east coast.

Mrs. E. Guy Hopkins, who lived at nearby "Walkerton," has described Cussons' undertaking as an over 100 room hotel, six stories high with porches gracing three floors. There were stairways rising on either side of the entrance and an auditorium with a stage for theatrical performances. She said, "Master painters were employed to decorate the main rooms with murals depicting a full range of outdoor scenes from the tropics to snow covered mountains." The grounds covered a thousand acres with lakes, woods, rose hedges, and parks. "Peacocks strutted on the lawns." In the woods, she said there were "rabbits, turkeys, partridges, squirrels and deer." It was called "Forest Lodge" and was supported by the captain's International Label Printing Establishment (Cussons and May). The neighbors called him "Captain Cussons." He was active in veterans' organizations and published his own book, *A Glance at Current* History, in 1899. The lodge was popular for picnics and parties but never attracted "the number of out-of-state patrons to make it a financial success." After the captain's death in 1912, it was sold a number of times, made into apartments, and the structure was gradually taken down and the land sold for subdivisions.[22] Today all that remains of the captain's dream is the small turret located on Mountain Road at the Old Washington Highway.

Miss Maude Trevett was one of the teachers at the elementary school at Glen Allen. Teachers for the high school would be met on the 8:30 a.m. train from Richmond. Some of the Litchfield family rode the train into town to work at Cussons and May. Others took the train to go into town to do their shopping or go on their honeymoon. Mr. Victor Litchfield was overseer of the poor about 1900. A Mr. Allen ran a store and a Masonic lodge was built at Glen Allen.[23]

The R.F. & P. ran two accommodation trains into Richmond, one leaving Ashland at 7:30 a.m. to return at 7 p.m., the other at 11 a.m. to return at 5 p.m. The first train was for the commuters, the second for the shoppers. Ladies from Ashland could do their shopping for several hours and designate that their packages from certain stores be sent to Elba Station, near Harrison and West Broad streets, where their purchases would be put on the baggage car and dropped off in the late afternoon in Ashland.[24]

"Walkerton," used as a hospital during the Civil War, and "Meadow Farm," on the Mountain Road, both now owned by Henrico County, are each in a beautiful state of preservation. "Meadow Farm" has a museum and grounds used to depict the way of life during the Civil War area and later. Adjoining the farm is a state-of-the art nursing facility bequeathed by descendants of the Sheppard family. Just across Route #33 the Springfield Road leads to Francistown Road. There Tom Francis set up his sawmill business. So many Blacks worked for him and settled in the area that it came to be called Francistown. A new Glen Allen post office, serving over 20 rural routes, is located at the Innsbrook Corporate Center. This business area is so spacious and elegant that John Cussons would have been proud.

The northern and eastern side of Yellow Tavern was opened up in the 1930s by Virginia State Route #2 and U.S. Route 301. They pass from points north through Bowling Green and Hanover Court House to form a more ready access to downtown Richmond. There has been shipment and passenger service along the Central Railroad of which General Wickham had become the president. The story is told that one day the train neglected to stop at Wickham's Crossing to pick up his son, Senator Henry Wickham from "Hickory Hill," and it had to back up a number of miles to get him.

Farmers took their produce across the Meadow Bridges and along the Richmond-Henrico Turnpike to the old 17th Street Market. The battleground has become the Strawberry Hill race track and the Virginia State Fairgrounds. Pine Camp, a facility for tuberculosis patients, was built along the Military Road where Major Ginter had cut down the trees. The land given by Mr. John Stewart for a cemetery for free Blacks is across the road. "Stuckley Hall," Dr. Terrell's home, is still standing. At Forest Lawn Cemetery many of the 20th century members of the Francis, Terrell, and Cross families are buried, also a great number of the residents of Yellow Tavern area, including Dr. Joseph Winfrey who faithfully birthed many of the neighborhood babies.

Dr. Winfrey was often assisted by Sally Sheppard Anderson. "Aunt Sally" was at my birth and that of my sisters. She and her husband Sandy are buried in the Anderson Cemetery for Blacks, between Connecticut and New York avenues. The land was given by the white Anderson family for the price of one dollar. Possibly Mandy Anderson, a midwife for another local doctor, was buried there as well as Chloe Banks, who lived along Mountain Road and cared for destitute black children. Other revered Blacks were of the Harris, Valentine, Booker, and Kenny families. The cemetery is in a wooded area, but a mid morning sun shines brightly on the tombstone for "Buck" Owen who served faithfully the Cross and Francis families and that of Howard Johnson who worked for the Terrell family after the war.

NOTES TO INTRODUCTION

1. Virginius Dabney, *Richmond, the Story of a City* (New York: Doubleday, 1976), 6-9.
2. Ibid.
3. Ibid.
4. Jeffrey Marshall O'Dell, *Inventory of Early Achitectecture and Historic Sites* (County of Henrico, VA, 1978), 34-39; Robert Bolling Lancaster, *A Sketch of the Early History of Hanover County Virginia* (Richmond, VA: Whittet & Shepperson, 1979), 34-39; Margaret T. Peters, *Guidebook to Virginia Historical Markers* (Charlottesville, VA: University Press of Virginia, 1986), 19, 22 & 103.
5. *Old Homes of Hanover County Virginia* (Hanover, VA: Hanover County Historical Society, 1983), 84.

Notes to Chapter 1

1. Samuel Mordecai, *Richmond in By-gone Days.* 1860 ed. Richmond: Dietz Press, 1946), 71-72.
2. Louis H. Manarin, *History of Henrico County.* Charlottesville, VA: University Press of Virginia, 1989), 192-94; Acts of the Virginia General Assembly, 1812-13: 60-64; Acts of the Virginia General Assembly, 1818-19: 127-28.
3. Manarin, *Henrico County,* 167.
4. *Richmond Times Dispatch*, 3 March 1889.
5. Douglas R. Egerton, *Gabriel's Rebellion* (Chapel Hill, NC: University of North Carolina Press, 1993), 19-29.
6. Ibid., 31-32; James Sidbury, *Ploughshares into Swords* (Cambridge: Cambridge University, 1997), 55-57.
7. Egerton, *Gabriel,* 58-63.
8. Ibid., 64.
9. Ibid., 70-72.
10. Ibid., 75-76.
11. Ibid., 81-87.
12. Ibid., 85-110.
13. Ibid., 148-49.
14. Ibid., 22.
15. Sidbury, *Ploughshares,* 175-76.
16. *Henrico Deed Book*, 3 & 5; Egerton, *Gabriel,* 84-92.
17. Sidbury, *Ploughshares,* 107-09; Egerton, *Gabriel,* 70-71.
18. Meadow Farm Museum; Sidbury, *Ploughshares,* 115; Egerton, *Gabriel,* 149.
19. Jeffrey Marshall O'Dell, *Inventory of Early Architecture and Historic Sites,* County of Henrico, VA, 1976, 25.
20. Manarin, *Henrico*, 191-95.
21. Oliver W. Holmes, *Stagecoach East* (Washington: Smithsonian Institution Press, 1983) 84; 40-42; 140; William E. Griffin, Jr. *One Hundred Fifty Years of History along the Richmond, Fredericksburg, and*

Potomac Railroad (Richmond: R.F. & P. Railroad, 1984) 1.

Notes to Chapter 2

1. Reuben Alley, *History of the University of Richmond, 1830-1937* Charlottesville, VA: University Press of Virginia, 1977.) 180-89.
2. Stephen E. Row, *Emmanuel Church – Brook Hill.* (Richmond, 1988), 2, 4.
3. Dianne A. Jones, "Slash Christian Church, Disciples of Christ," MS.
4. *Herald Progress – Hanover County, 1721-1971* sec.4, 19.
5. Ibid., 17.
6. Winn's Baptist Church Records at the Virginia Baptist Historical Society (Richmond).
7. *Herald Progress,* sec. 5, 6, 15.
8. Ibid., sec.4, 20.
9. Ibid., 12.
10. James Keily, *Smith's Henrico County Virginia*, (Robert Smith, Richmond, VA: 1853), map; United States Census, 1850, Henrico County, Virginia.
11. *Smith's map.*
12. United States Census, 1850, Hanover County, Virginia.
13. Ibid.; Census Henrico.
14. *Smith's map;* O'Dell, Jeffrey M., *Inventory of Early Architecture and Historic Sites* (County of Henrico, Virginia, 1976), 169.
15. O'Dell, *Inventory,* 184.
16. Griffin,William E. Jr. *Richmond Fredericksburg Railroad, (*Lynchburg, VA: TLC Publishing, 1994), 2.
17. Ibid.; *Acts of the Virginia General Assembly,* 1833: 127.
18. Griffin, *R.F. & P.*, 3.
19. Ibid., 5.
20. Ibid.
21. Charles W. Turner, *Chessie's Road,* (Richmond, Garrett & Massie, 1953), 1, 3, 23.

22. Ibid., 34-35.
23. Egerton, *Gabriel*, 88, 89; Marion Stewart Peterkin, "History of Emmanuel Church," ed. Kathleen B. Francis (Glen Allen, Virginia, 1986), 1; O'Dell, Inventory, 26.
24. Peterkin, "Emmanuel," 3 – John Stewart to Rev. Richard H. Wilmer, July 27, 1858, from Richmond.
25. Ibid., 22, 29; Roe, *Emmanuel,* 64.
26. Peterkin, "Emmanuel," 5.

Notes to Chapter 3

1. Henrico County, Virginia, *Deed Book,* I.
2. Charles C. Jones, *A Catechism for Families and Sabbath Schools,* (Philadelphia, PA: Board of Publications, 1852); family memorabilia.
3. Henrico County, Virginia, Ended File, 1860, Cross versus Cross.
4. Ibid.
5. Ibid.
6. Henrico County Archives, "Dr. John M. Sheppard's Medical Journal."
7. Family memorabilia.
8. Meadow Farm Museum, Glen Allen, Virginia.
9. Ibid.
10. William Ronald Cocke, III, *Hanover Country Chancery Wills and Notes,* (Baltimore, MD: Genealogical Publishing Co., 1978), 56, 57.
11. Hanover County, Ended File 1860, Francis versus Davis, 1860.
12. Family memorabilia.
13. Blanche Norment Powell, "Journal," January 12-February 12, 1862, ms. Privately owned; O'Dell, *Inventory,* 160.
14. Powell, "Journal," October 4, 1862 – February 27, 1863.
15. "The Mordecais of Rosewood." *Henrico County Historical Society Magazine,* 12: 33-46.
16. Emma Mordecai, "Diary", May 1864 – May 30, 1865, (Southern Historical Collection, University of North Carolina Library, Chapel Hill), MS copy of 1896.
17. Joseph R. Haw, "The Battle of Haw's Shop, Va." *Confederate Veteran* 33 (October 1825): 340, 341, 373-76.
18. Ibid.

19. Katherine Turner Cross, *The Crosses along Falling Creek, Hanover County, Virginia,* (Ashland,, VA: Virginia, privately published, 1972), 45.
20. James M. McPherson, *Battle Cry of Freedom,* (New York: Oxford University Press, 1988), 179.
21. Emeline J. Terrell from Mary H. Terrell (her grandmother?), August 8, 1857. Terrell – Francis letters.

Notes to Chapter 4

1. Burke Davis, *Jeb Stuart the Last Cavalier*, (New York: Rinehart, 1957), 3-5; Dabney, *Richmond,*156.
2. Lee A. Wallace, Jr., *The Richmond Howitzers*, (Lynchburg, VA: H.E. Howard, 1993), 5.
3. Family memorabilia.
4. Dabney, *Richmond,* 157; Wallace, *Richmond Howitzers,* 5.
5. Lee A. Wallace, Jr., *Guide to Virginia Military Organizations, 1861-1865,* (Lynchburg, VA: H.E. Howard, 1964) 234, 258 & 259.
6. Louis H. Manarin, *15th Virginia Infantry,* (Lynchburg, VA: H.E. Howard, 1990), 3-5.
7. Emeline J. Terrell, Hanover, from Martha W. Terrell, May 1860.
8. Charles Terrell, Chickahominy P.O., Hanover from Mary G. Terrell, July 3, 1860.
9. Ellen Mordecai from Emma Mordecai, March 26, 1861, at Richmond.
10. Ellen Mordecai from Emma Mordecai, April 21, 1821, at Richmond; Emily Bingham, *Mordecai, an Early American Family,* (NY: Hill and Wang, n.d.), 245-253.
11. Ibid.
12. Manarin, *15th Virginia Infantry,* 3, 4 & roster.
13. Emeline J. Terrell, Hanover, from Charles R. Francis, May 8, 1861.
14. J. Staunton Moore, *1861-1911 An Address Delivered at the 50th Re-union of the Fifteenth Regiment at Williamsburg, Virginia, May 24, 1911,* (n.p.:n.d), 4, 5 & 11.
15. Manarin, *15th Virginia Infantry,* 4.
16. Henry Robinson Berkeley, *Four Years in the Confederate Artillery,* (Chapel Hill, NC: University of North Carolina, 1961), xv.
17. Wallace, *Richmond Howitzers*, 4, 46-48 & roster.
18. Ibid.

Notes to Chapter 5

1. U.S. Henrico Census, 1850.
   Robert J. Driver, *10th Virginia Cavalry*, (Lynchburg VA: H.E. Howard, 1992), 2 & 3.
2. Mark H. Cross, "Old Soldier Fades Away," 1996, MS.
3. Wallace, *Guide*, 36; Louis H. Manarin, *Richmond Volunteers*, (Richmond, VA: Westover Press, 1966), 124-25.
4. Douglas Southall Freeman, *R.E. Lee*, (New York: Charles Scribner's Sons, 1934), 1:541, 547 map, & 579.
5. Ibid., 579; Manarin, *Volunteers*, 125.
6. Freeman, 1:573; Manarin, *Volunteers*, 125-6.
7. Clifford Dowdey, *The Wartime Papers of R.E. Lee*, (New York: Bramhall House, 1961), 80 & 81,
8. Cross, "Old Soldier," Manarin, *Volunteers*, 126.
9. Kenneth L. Stiles, *4th Virginia* Cavalry, (Lynchburg, VA: H.E. Howard, 1985), roster.
10. Joan E. Cashon, "Landscape and Memory in Anti-bellum Virginia." *VMHB* 102 (October 1994): 493-96; Michael Trotti, "Freedmen and Enslaved Soil," *VMHB* 104 (October 1996): 458-465; Census Hanover; *Old Homes of Hanover*. 85 & 104.
11. Stiles, *4th Virginia Cavalry*, roster; Census Hanover.
12. Stiles, *4th Virginia Cavalry*, 6 & roster.
13. Robert J. Trout, *They Followed the Plume*, (Mechanicsburg, PA: Stackpole, 1993), 119 &122.
14. Stiles, *4th Cavalry*, 6-8.
15. Frederick S. Daniel, *Richmond Howitzers in the War* (Richmond: Butternut Press, 1891), Howitzers, 17-18.
16. Ibid., 29-32.
17. Powell, "Journal," January 15 & 25, 1862.
18. Cross, *Falling Creek*, 47-79; rosters of *Morris Artillery* & *10th Cavalry*.

19. Gregory J. Macaluso, *Morris, Orange and King William Artillery*, (Lynchburg, VA: H.E. Howard, 1991), 1 & roster.
20. Ibid., 3-8.
21. Bailey, *Henrico Home Front*, xxi – xxii.
22. Ibid., 238-240, 50, 13, 189 & xxiii; Henrico Census.
23. Ibid., 5 & 126.
24. Ibid., 99-199, 133 & 134.
25. Ibid., 83-84 & 92.
26. Ibid., 28, 40 & 44.

Notes to Chapter 6

1. Powell, "Journal," January – February 1862.
2. Ibid.
3. Ibid.
4. Ibid.
5. Ibid.
6. Ibid.
7. Manarin, *Richmond* Volunteers, *263-67.*
8. Ibid.; Salllie Brock Putnam, *Richmond During the War* (New York: G.W. Carleton, 1867), 76.
9. Putnam, *Richmond During the War*, 97.
10. Ibid., 98.
11. Emeline J. Terrell from Charles Terrill, February 16, at Camp Deas, Warwick County.
12. William A. Young, *56th Virginia Infantry,* (Lynchburg, VA: H.E. Howard, 1990), 29 & roster.
13. Ibid.,15-26.
14. McPherson, *Battle Cry,* 238; Young, *56th Infantry,* 26-27.
15. Young, *56th Infantry,* 28-29.
16. Ibid., 30-32.
17. Ibid., 33, 35 & 38: McPherson, *Battle Cry,* 401-402.
18. Emeline J. Terrell at "Clifton," from M.G. Terrell, January 26, 1862, at "Locust Row."
19. Emeline J. Terrell from M.G. Terrell, March 5, 1862, at "Oak Level."
20. Emeline J. Terrell from Charles Terrell, February 12 & 16, 1862, at Camp Deas.
21. Emeline J. Terrell from Charles H. Francis and Eli Samuel Francis, February 16 & 17; March 28, 1862, at Camp Deas.
22. Emeline J. Terrell from Charles Terrell, Charles H. Francis, John T. Francis & Eli Samuel Francis, March 14, 17, 19, 27 & 28, 1862.

23. Emeline J. Terrell from Charles Terrell, March 14, 1862, at Camp August & from Charles H. Francis, March 19, 1862, at Camp Lebanon.
24. Georgie Terrell from Mahlon Terrell, March 15, 1862, near Yorktown.
25. Ibid., March 27, 1862.
26. Rowena Reed, *Combined Operations in the Civil War* (Annapolis, MD: Naval Institute, 1978), 37-43; Ambrose Burnside, "The Burnside Expedition," *Battles and Leaders,* (Secausus, NJ: Castle), 1:660-69.
27. Warren Lee Goss, "Yorktown and Williamsburg," *Battles and Leaders*, 2:189.
28. Ronald F. Bailey, *Forward to Richmond* (Alexandria, VA: Time Life Books, 1983), 94.
29. Emeline J. Terrell from John T. Francis, March 27, 1862 at Camp Lebanon; James T. Francis & wife from possibly John T. Francis, March 28, 1862, at Camp Lebanon; James T. Francis and wife from Chas. R. Francis, from Camp Lebanon, Warwick County.
30. Marilyn B. Koleszar, *Ashland, Bedford, and Taylor Artilleries,* (Lynchburg, VA: H.E. Howard, 1994), 2, 20, 41 & roster; Stewart Sifakis, *Compendium of Confederate Armies, Virginia*, (New York: Facts on File, 1992), 20, 41, 47 & 74.
31. Emeline J. Terrell from Charles Terrell, January 26, 1862, at Camp Deas & from Charles R. Francis, March 19, 1862; Emeline J. Terrell from Charles Terrell, April 20 & May 1, 1862, at Camp August.

Notes to Chapter 7

1. Manarin, *Volunteers,* 126 & roster.
2. Peterkin, "Emmanuel," 9.
3. Ibid., 25.
4. Manarin, *Volunteers,* 73-74.
5. Putnam, *Richmond*, 101.
6. John Minor Botts, *The Great Rebellion*, (New York: Harper, 1866), 279-280.
7. Ibid.
8. Stiles, *4th Virginia Cavalry*; 10 & roster.
9. Ibid.
10. Ibid.
11. Ibid.; Driver, *10th Virginia Cavalry* , 19; Manarin, *Volunteers*, 126.
12. Thomas, "Memoirs," 4.
13. Emeline J. Terrell from Charles Terrell, May 22, 1862.
14. John M. Gabbert, *Military Operations in Hanover County, Virginia, 1861-1865* (Roanoke, VA: Gurtner Graphics, 1989), 14-20.
15. Ibid.; Jed Hotchkiss, *Confederate Military History, Virginia*, (Blue & Grey Press); 686.
16. "Miss Page's Wedding," anon. poem, Richmond, 1853, courtesy Mrs. William B. Newton, "Summer Hill," *Hanover County Historical Society*, 9, (November 1973).
17. Census Hanover; Judith W. McGuire, *Diary of a Southern Refugee* (Richmond, VA: J.W. Randolph, 1889); 137-38.
18. Gabbert, *Military Operations*, 14-19.
19. Ibid.
20. Emeline J. Terrell from Charles H. Francis, June 5, 1862, at a camp near Richmond.
21. Richmond *Dispatch*, April 29, 1862.
22. *Old Homes of Hanover*, 73 & 76.
23. Ibid., 76 & 38.

24. Ibid., 63-64 & Manarin, *15th Virginia Infantry* & Stiles, *4th Virginia Cavalry,* rosters.
25. Ibid., 26.
26. Ibid., 48 & 76.
27. Joseph Kyle, "The Most Unhappy Contest," *Hanover Tavern Foundation,* 4: 1 (Winter 1977).
28. Ibid.
29. Ibid.; Stiles, *4th Virginia Cavalry* rosters.
30. Peterkin, "Emmanuel," 9.

Notes to Chapter 8

1. Emeline J. Terrell from Charles H. Francis, June 5, 1862, near Richmond.
2. McClellan, *Stuart,* 53, 56 & map to first edition; Burke Davis, *Jeb Stuart* (New York: Rinehart, 1957), 112
3. Richard Wheeler, *Sword over Richmond* (NY: Harper, 1986), 268-270; Davis, *Jeb Stuart*, 112.
4. Joseph H. Haw, "Haw's Shop Community of Virginia." *Confederate Veteran*: 32:341.
5. Robert E.L. Krick, "Letters Cast New Light on Burial of Latane." *Hanover County Historical Society Bulletin*, (Summer 2001):64.
6. McClellan, *I Rode with Jeb Stuart*, 57-58.
7. Emeline J. Terrell from M.G. Terrell, June 20, 1862, at Locust Grove.
8. Walbrook D. Swank, *Train Running for the Confederacy 1861-1865*. (Charlottesville, VA: Papercraft, 1990), 24.
9. Peterkin, "Emmanuel," 10 & 20.
10. James I. Robertson, *Stonewall* Jackson (NY: Maxmillan, 1997), 460-61.
11. Nuckols family memorabilia – Roland, from Grandfather Nuckols, January 10, at Elmont, VA.
12. Swank, *Train Running*, 28
13. Ibid., 12-13.
14. Dowdey, *Wartime Papers*, 198-99.
15. Robertson, *Stonewall Jackson*, 468-473; Rosanne G. Shalf, *Ashland, Ashland* (Lawrenceville, VA: Brunswick, 1994), 62-65.
16. Driver, *10th Virginia Cavalry*, 21.
17. Richard L. Nicholas, *Powhatan, Salem, and Courtney Artillery* (Lynchburg, VA: H.E. Howard, 1997), 121-25.
18. Judith W. McGuire, *Diary of a Southern Refugee* (Richmond: J.W. Randolph, 1889), 121-25.

19. Nicholas, *Powhatan, Salem, Courtney* Artillery, rosters.
20. Marilyn B. Koleszar, *Ashland, Bedford, and Taylor Virginia Artillery,* (Lynchburg, VA: H.E. Howard, 1994), rosters.
21. Robert J. Driver, Jr. *5th Virginia Cavalry* (Lynchburg, VA: H.E. Howard, 1997), 22.
22. Ibid., 27 & roster.
23. Driver, *10th Virginia Cavalry*, 21-22.
24. Gregory J. Macaluso, *Morris, Orange, King William Artillery* (Lynchburg, VA: H.E. Howard, 1991), rosters.
25. Young, *56th Virginia Infantry,* 46-51 & roster.
26. Thomas, *Memoirs*, 5; Manarin, *15th Virginia Infantry,* 19-22.
27. Joseph R. Haw, "Haw's Shop Community," *Confederate* Veteran, 32: 341.
28. Peterkin, "Emmanuel," 21.
29. Elizabeth Van Lew, *A Yankee Spy in Richmond,* David D. Ryan, ed. (Mechanicsburg, PA: Stackpole, 1996), 42-48.
30. Ibid., 44.

Notes to Chapter 9

1. Cooke, *Wearing* of the Gray, 52 & 195.
2. Swank, *Train Running*, 21-23.
3. Angus J. Johnston, II, *Virginia Railroads in the Civil War* (Chapel Hill, NC: University of North Carolina, 1961), 77-78; *O.R.* 22, pt. 3:502.
4. Johnston, *Railroads*, 126-29.
5. Emeline J. Terrell from Charles Terrell, July 14 & 22, 1862; Charles Terrell from Emeline J. Terrell, August 10, 1862, at Clifton.
6. Mary E. Davis, "Some Troubles of the War," November 1864. Emeline J. Terrell from Charles Terrell, September 5; Emeline J. Terrell from Mollie Goodwin Terrell, September 8, 1862, at "Oak Level;" Emeline J. Terrell from Barbara Terrell, September 26, 1862, at "Locust Row."
7. Manarin, *15th Infantry*, 24-25.
8. Ronald H. Bailey, *The Bloodiest Day* (Alexandria, VA: Time Life Books, 1984), 69 & map.
9. Thomas, *Memoirs*, 6-7; Manarin, *15th Infantry*, 28 & roster.
10. Manarin, *15th Infantry*, 29-30 & roster; Emeline J. Terrell from Charles Terrell, October 6, at camp near Winchester.
11. Manarin, *15th Infantry*, roster.
12. Family memorabilia; Otelia F. Bodenstein from Samuel E. Pruett, November 24, 1965, at Hagertown, MD.
13. Koleszar, *Ashland Artillery*, 11-12.
14. Ibid., 12-13 & roster; Emeline J. Terrell from Barbara Terrell, September 26, 1862, at "Locust Row."
15. Edward Porter Alexander, *Fighting for the Confederacy* (Chapel Hill, NC: University of North Carolina, 1989), 161 & 190-92.
16. Powell, "Journal," October 4 – December 4, 1862; Emily White Fleming, "Vivian Minor Fleming,"

Hanover County Historical Society Bulletin 66 (Summer 2002): 5.

17. Ibid.
18. Driver, *10th Cavalry*, 23-25; McClelland, *Stuart*, 137-161 & map.
19. Ibid.
20. Robert J. Trout, *With Pen and Saber* (Mechanicsburg, PA: Stackpole, 1995), 106-08.
21. McClellan, *Stuart*, 160 & 163.
22. Stiles, *4th Cavalry*, 21 & roster.
23. Ibid., roster.
24. Martha J. Jenkins from John T. Francis, November 29, 1862, at camp near Fredericksburg.
25. Martha J. Jenkins from John T. Francis, December 17, 1862, at camp in the woods.
26. Carmichael, *Purcell Artillery*, 35-36 & roster.
27. Fleming, *"Vivian,"* 5-6.
28. Ibid.
29. Driver, *10th Cavalry*, 29; *B. & L.* 3:147.
30. Powell, "Journal," December 5-11, 1862.
31. Peterkin, "Emmanuel," 11.
32. Martha J. Jenkins from John T. Francis, November 29, 1862, at camp near Fredericksburg.
33. Mary E. Davis from Charles R. Francis, December 14, 1862, at Richmond.
34. Powell, "Journal," December, 1862 & January, 1863.
35. Emeline J. Terrell from John T. Francis, January 31, 1863, at camp near Guinea Station.

Notes to Chapter 10

1. Powell, "Journal," January 3 – February 27, 1863.
2. Ibid.
3. Ibid.
4. Ibid.
5. Emeline J. Terrell from John T. Francis, January 31, 1863, at camp near Guinea Station; Charles Terrell from Charles R. Francis, February 12, 1863, at camp of the 15th Regiment
6. Manarin, *15th Infantry*, 38.
7. Steven A. Cormier, *Siege of Suffolk* (Lynchburg, VA: H.E. Howard, 1989), 9; Lucy Ann Cross from Richard Green, March 2, 1863, in Hanover.
8. Emeline J. Terrell from Mollie G. Terrell, February 1, 1863, at "Locust Row".
9. Lucy Ann Cross from James H. Cross, March 16, 1863, at camp near Milford.
10. Emeline J. Terrell from Mollie G. Terrell, March 1 & 25, 1863, at "Locust Row."
11. Ibid.
12. Emeline J. Terrell from Charles R. Francis, March 15, 1863, near Petersburg & from Charles Terrell, March 27 & April 2, 1863, at Camp Ivor.
13. Emeline J. Terrell from Charles Terrell, April 7, 1863 & from Charles R. Francis, April 7, 1863, on the Blackwater River.
14. Emeline J. Terrell from J.C. Terrell, April 15, at "Oak Level;" Service records.
15. Hanover County Chancery Court. *Ended File*, no. 11 (1860) – Davis vs. Francis Administrator.
16. Ryan, *Cornbread*, 62, 141-42. Note: There was a Cross family connection with the Glazebrooke family of Hanover. However, there has been no mention in family circles that Larkin White Glazebrooke was ever claimed as one of their own kin. dfa

17. Ernest B. Furgurson, *Chancellorsville* (New York: Alfred A. Knopf, 1992), 62-64, 282.
18. Shalf, *Ashland*, 67-68.
19. McGuire, *Diary*, 209-214.
20. Gerry Van Der Heuvel, *Crowns of Thorns and Glory* (New York: Dutton, 1988), 162.
21. John B. Jones, *A Rebel War Clerk's Diary of the Confederate States* (Philadelphia, PA: J.B. Lippincott, 1866), 306-07.
22. Ibid., 309; Bailey, *Henrico*, 87n.
23. Peterkin, "Emmanuel," 11 &18.
24. Gabbert, *Military Operations*, 49-50.

Notes to Chapter 11

1. McGuire, *Diary*, 185; W.W. Goldsborough, *The Maryland Line, 1861-1865* (Gaithersburg, MD: Olde Soldier Books, 1987), 10 & 68.
2. Goldsborough, *Maryland Line,* 19-20.
3. Ibid., 122-23.
4. Ibid.
5. Robert J. Trout, *They Followed the Plume* (Mechanicsburg, PA: Stackpole, 1993), 123 & 223; *Hanover Tavern Foundation*, 4 (winter 1977).
6. Carmichael, *Purcell Artillery,* 170-71.
7. Ibid., 175-76.
8. Wallace, *Richmond Howitzers*, 82.
9. Driver, *10th Virginia Cavalry,* 32-34.
10. Ernest B. Furgurson, *Chancellorsville* (New York: Knopf, 1992), 283; Shalf, *Ashland,* 10.
11. McGuire, *Diary*, 211-14.
12. Emeline J. Terrell from Charles R. Francis, April 24, 1863, at camp of 15th Virginia Infantry.
13. Cormier, *Siege of Suffolk* Howard, 1989), 98 & 346n; Manarin, *15th Virginia Infantry*, 41; Thomas, *Memoir, 8;* Emeline J. Terrell from John T. Francis, May 1, 1863, at camp near Suffolk.
14. Douglas S. Freeman, *Lee's Lieutenants,* (New York: Scribners, 1943), 2:485-490.
15. Alfred Horatio Belo, *Memoirs* (Gaithersburg, MD: Old Soldiers Books, n.d.), 14-19 and notes & 39.
16. William C. Jordan, *Some events and Incidents during the Civil War* (Montgomery, AL: Paragon, 1909), 35, 36ff.
17. Emeline J. Terrell from Charles Terrell, May 8, 1863, at Petersburg.
18. Charles Terrell from Emeline J. Terrell, May 9, 1863, at "Clifton" (Hanover County?).
19. Emeline J. Terrell from Ann E. Terrell, May 17, 1863, at "Oak Level," Hanover County.

20. Emeline J. Terrell from Mollie Goodwin Terrell, May 25, 1863; Terrell memorabilia.
21. Terrell letters.
22. Alexander, *Fighting for the Confederacy*, 199.
23. Ibid., 201, 203 & 214-15.
24. Ibid., 221 & 583n; Michael Golay, *To Gettysburg and Beyond* (New York: Crown, 1994), 125-26, 135, 140 &142.
25. Peterkin, "Emmanuel," 20.

Notes to Chapter 12

1. Betty Gray from James W. Gray, May 31, 1863, camp at Culpeper Court House (in Terrell - Francis letters); Driver, *10th Virginia Cavalry*, roster.
2. Louis Manarin, *Richmond Volunteers* (Richmond. VA: Westwood. 1969), 126-27.
3. Fairfax Downey, *Clash of Cavalry, the Battle of Brandy Station* (New York: David McKay, 1959), 3-5.
4. Botts, *Great Rebellion,* 294.
5. Dabney, *Richmond*, 171.
6. Botts, *Great Rebellion,* 294 & 299.
7. Emory Thomas, *Bold Dragoon, the Life of J.E.B. Stuart* (New York: Harper, 1986), 220-21.
8. Ibid., 223-24.
9. Ibid.
10. Hotchkiss, *Virginia*, 686; Stiles, *4th Virginia Cavalry*, 28.
11. Robert E. Lee, *Wartime Papers of R.E. Lee* (New York: Bramhall House, 1961), 512.
12. Betty Gray from James W. Gray, June 10, 1863, camp near Culpeper.
13. Driver, *10th Virginia Cavalry*, roster.
14. Peterkin, "Emmanuel," 11 & 12.
15. Thomas, *Memoirs*" 9; Manarin, *15th Virginia Infantry*, 43-45.
16. *O. R.*, 27, pt. 2: 793-99.
17. H.B. Porter, "General Made Hostage," *Washington National Tribune*, June 21, 1897; William J. Shirley in *Grand Army Scout & Soldiers Mail,* January 19, 1884.
18. Captain Robert E. Lee, *Recollections and Letters of General Robert E. Lee* (NY: Doubleday, 1924), 97-100.
19. Stephen Tripp, "Fighting Them Over," *Washington National Tribune,* June 4, 1896.
20. Lee, *Wartime Papers,* 545 & 547; Lee, *Recollections and Letters,* 100.
21. *O.R.*, 27, pt. 2: 837-853; *Old Homes of Hanover*, 104.

Notes to Chapter 13

1. Edward J. Stackpole. *They Met at Gettysburg*, (New York: Crown, 1956), 101-111.
2. Ibid.
3. Carmichael, *Purcell Artillery*, 181-83.
4. Ibid., & roster.
5. Koleszar, *Ashland Light Artillery,* 23-24 & roster.
6. Carmichael, *Purcell Artillery,* 193 & roster; Sifakis, *Compendium*, 67-69, 77-78 & 81-83.
7. Nicholas, *Courtney Artillery*, 160ff & roster.
8. Wallace, *Richmond Howitzers*, 63-64.
9. Macaluso, *Morris Artillery*, roster.
10. Ibid.
11. Stackpole, *Gettysburg*, 264-67; Young, *56th Virginia Infantry*, 82-86 & roster..
12. Young, *56th Virginia Infantry*, 82-88 & roster.
13. Hotchkiss, *Virginia,* 686; Driver, *10th Virginia Cavalry*, 40-42.
14. Cross, "Old Soldier Fades Away," 13; Driver, *10th Virginia Cavalry*, 43-45 & roster.
15. Alexander, *Fighting for the Confederacy,* 269-272.
16. Mordecai, "Diary," July 5 & 12, 1863. 62-62; Wallace, *Richmond Howitzers*, 67.
17. Jones, *Rebel War Clerk*, 2:37.
18. Ibid., 2:50, 291, 352-59.
19. Emeline J. Terrell from Charles Francis, July 15, 1863, at camp near Winchester.
20. Emeline J. Terrell from Charles Francis, October 5, 1863, in Orange County.
21. Emeline J. Terrell from B.O. Johnson.
22. Koleszar, *Ashland Light Artillery*, 25.
23. Betty Gray, from James W. Gray, September 22, 1862, at Culpeper.
24. Driver, *10th Virginia Cavalry*, 49 & roster.
25. Botts, *Great Rebellion*, 295-307.
26. Garnett, *Riding with Stuart*, 13.

27. Betty Gray from James W. Gray, November 7, 1863, at camp near Culpeper; November 12, 1863, at camp near Orange Court House.
28. Bell Wiley, *Embattled Confederates*, (NY: Harper, 1964), 178; Botts, *Great Rebellion*, 301; Lyman, *With Grant*, 82.
29. Stiles, *4th Virginia Cavalry*, roster; Trout, *They Followed the Plume*, 26-27; Robert J. Trout. *With Pen and Saber* (Mechanicsburg, PA: Stackpole Books, 1995), 219.
30. Driver, *10th Virginia Cavalry*, 51; Betty Gray from James W. Gray, January 18, 1864.
31. Nicholas, *Courtney Artillery*, 181, 185 & roster; Manarin, *Richmond Volunteers*, 32.

Notes to Chapter 14

1. Alexander, *Fighting for the Confederacy*, 285-86.
2. Ibid., 286-87 & 300.
3. Manarin, *15th Virginia Infantry*, 48-49; Peterkin, "Emmanuel," 12.
4. Hotchkiss, *Virginia*, 615-16; *O.R* 30, pt.2: 603-04 (Jones Report).
5. Emeline J. Terrell from Charles Terrell, undated at Zollicoffer.
6. *O.R.* 30, pt.4: 604-07, 716.
7. Emeline J. Terrell from Charles R. Francis, October 7, 1863, at Petersburg.
8. Emeline J. Terrell from Charles Terrell, October 7, 1863, at Petersburg.
9. Thomas, *Memoirs,* 10.
10. *O.R.* 30, pt 2: 606-07.
11. Ibid.
12. Emeline J. Terrell from Charles Terrell, November 8, 1863, at Blountsville.
13. Alexander, *Fighting for the Confederacy*, 30-32 & 300-01
14. Ibid.
15. Ibid.
16. Thomas, *Memoirs*, 11.
17. Betty Gray from James W. Gray, November 12, 1863, near Orange C. H.; Driver, *10th Virginia Cavalry*, 49-50.
18. Nicholas, *Courtney Artillery, roster;* Wallace, *Richmond Howitzers,* roster; Macaluso, *Morris Artillery;* Lee, *Wartime Papers*, 608-09.
19. Theodore Lyman, *Grant and Meade from the Wilderness* (Lincoln, NB: University of Nebraska, 1994), 58-59.
20. Driver, *10th Virginia Cavalry*, 51.
21. Betty Gray from James W. Gray, January 18, 1864.
22. Manarin, *15th Virginia Infantry,* 53.

23. Emeline J. Terrell from Charles R. Francis, February 8, 1864, near Goldsboro, NC.

24. Emeline J. Terrell from John Thomas Francis & Charles R. Francis, March 10, 1864, near Kinston, NC.
25. Family memorabilia.
26. Edwin W. Beitzell, *Point Lookout Prison Camp for Confederates,* (Abell, MD, 1983): 41, 117-118 & 167.
27. Bailey, *Henrico*, 201-02, 210, 197 & 233.
28. Ibid., 171-74, 183 & 214.
29. Ibid., 97.
30. Ibid., 178-84.

Notes to Chapter 15

1. Ryan, *Cornbread and Maggots,* 99-112.
2. Van Lew, *Yankee Spy, 56-62.*
3. Donald Allison, ed. *Hell on Belle Isle*, (Bryan, OH: Faded Banner Publications, 1997), 18ff.
4. Ryan, *Cornbread and Maggots,* 99.
5. Theodore Lyman, *With Grant and Meade,* (Lincoln, NB: University of Nebraska, 1994), 46.
6. Ibid., 76.
7. Ibid., Virgil Carrington Jones, *Eight Hours before Richmond*, (NY: Henry Holt, 1957), 19 & 34.
8. Jones, *Eight Hours*, 32 & note.
9. Ibid., 27, 41 & 59-60.
10. Swank, *Train Running*, 60-62.
11. Ibid., 62-64.
12. Goldsborough, *Maryland Line*, 188.
13. Jones, *Eight Hours,* 47, 53-54.
14. Ibid., 56, 61-62; *O.R.*, I, 33:184; Mary Elizabeth Davis, "Troubles of the War" – Family memorabilia.
15. Goldsborough, *Maryland Line*, 188-191.
16. Jones, *Eight Hours*, 77-78.
17. Swank, *Train Running,* 68.
18. Ibid., 70-71.
19. Ibid.
20. Ibid., 72-74.
21. Jones, *Eight* Hours, 78-83.
22. Peterkin, "Emmanuel," 12.
23. Ibid.
24. Jones, *Rebel War Clerk*, 2:163.
25. Edward G. Longacre, *Mounted Raids of the Civil War*, (Lincoln, NB: University of Nebraska, 1975), 248-49; Jones, *Eight Hours*, 159n.
26. Jones, *Eight Hours*, 75-76.
27. Longacre, *Mounted Raids, 248*; R.L.T. Beale, *History of the Ninth Virginia Cavalry*, (Richmond: B.F. Johnson, 1899), 180-82.

28. Beale, *Ninth Virginia Cavalry*, 108-111; Jones, *Eight Hours*, 80-82.
29. Van Lew, *Yankee Spy*, 53-58 & 69.
30. Ibid., 70-72.
31. Jefferson Davis, *Private Letters 1823 – 1889. Edited by* Hudson Strode (New York: Harcourt, 1966), 136.
32. *O.R.*, 33: pt. 1, 190-92 (Henry E. Davies).
33. Ibid.
34. Lyman, *With Grant and Meade*, 79; Jones, *Eight Hours*, 140.
35. Van Lew, *Yankee Spy*, 73-85; Jones, *Eight Hours*, 140 & 172n.

Notes to Chapter 16

1. Theodore S. Garnett, *Riding with Stuart*, ed. Robert J. Trout (Shippensburg, PA: White Mane, 1994), 61.
2. J.H. Kidd, *A Cavalryman with Custer* (NY: Doubleday, 1991), 204-205.
3. *Battles and Leaders*, 4:188-89.
4. Ibid., McClelland, *Stuart,* 409.
5. McClelland, *Stuart*, 409-410.
6. Goldsborough, *Maryland Line*, 195-96.
7. Garnett, *Riding with Stuart*, 62; Stiles, *4th Virginia Cavalry*, 47 & roster.
8. Wagman, *Front Page,* from Philadelphia *Inquirer*, May 14, 1864.
9. Gordon C. Rhea, *Battles for Spotsylvania Court House and the Road to Yellow Tavern (*Baton Rouge, LA: Louisana State University, 1997), 192-95.
10. Richard Wheeler, *On Fields of Fury* (New York: Harper, 1991), 159 & 182; Kidd, *Cavalryman,* 201.
11. McClellan, *Stuart*, 410.
12. Ibid.
13. McGuire, *Diary,* 264-65.
14. McClellan, *Stuart*, 409-410; Eric Mink, "The last days of J.E.B. Stuart" in *Hanover County Historical Bulletin*, 63: (Winter 2000).
15. Ibid.; Garnett, *Riding with Stuart*, 63; Robert B. Lancaster, *A Sketch of Early Hanover County* (Richmond, VA: Whittet & Sheppardson, 1976), 44.
16. Burke Davis, *Jeb Stuart the Last Cavalier* (NY: Rinehart, 1957), 393.
17. Garnett, *Riding with Stuart,* 63-65.
18. Rhea, *Spotsylvania*, 195-201.
19. Ibid.
20. Ibid.
21. Douglas H. Pitts, "Landmarks of Sheridan's Raid, *Henrico County Historical Society Bulletin*, 1994 reprint.

22. Robert E.L. Krick, *Staff Officers in Gray* (Chapel Hill, NC: University of North Carolina, 2003), 107-08.
23. Driver, *10th Virginia Cavalry*, roster; "Walkerton" cemetery markers.
24. Memorabilia: Litchfield-Lauterbach, Salmon-Whitaker, Cross-Francis.

Notes to Chapter 17

1. Rhea, *Spotsylvania*, 203.
2. Ibid.
3. Keily, Henrico map.
4. Driver, *5th Virginia Cavalry*, 55, 75-78 & map.
5. Ibid.
6. Garnett, *Riding with Stuart*, 67 & 119n; Driver, *5th Virginia Cavalry*, 77.
7. Kidd, *Cavalrynan with Custer*, 209.
8. Driver, *5th Virginia Cavalry*, 77-78.
9. Garnett, *Riding with Stuart,* 69; Driver, *5th Virginia Cavalry*, roster.
10. Robert J. Driver, *1st Virginia Cavalry* (Lynchburg, VA: H.E. Howard, 1991), 83, 85 & roster.
11. Wheeler, *In Fields of Fury,*161.
12. Ibid., 168.
13. Kidd, *Cavalryman with Custer*, 211; McClellan, *Stuart*, 413; Rhea, *Spotsylvania*, 209; Driver, *1st Virginia Cavalry*, 211.
14. Theo. F. Rodenbough, "Sheridan's Richmond Raid," *Battles & Leaders*, 4:191
15. Driver, *1st Virginia Cavalry*, 84 & roster.
16. Goldsborough, *Maryland Line*, 253.
17. Cross family memorabilia; Chuck Lawless, *Illustrated Encyclopedia of Civil War Collectibles,* (NY: Henry Holt, 1997), 163.
18. Mosby family memorabilia – courtesy Martha Lupton.
19. Mary Powell, to Junius Powell, May 20, 1864.
20. Ibid.
21. Keily, Henrico map
22. Goldsborough, *Maryland Line*, 253; Driver, *1st Virginia Cavalry, 85 & roster.*
23. Eric Mink, "The Last Days of J.E.B. Stuart," *Hanover County Historical Society Bulletin* 63 (winter 2000).
24. Wagman, *Front Pages* – May 13, 1864; Jones, *Ladies of Richmond*, 190.

25. McGuire, *Diary,* 271; Emory Thomas, *Bold Dragoon, the Life of J.E.B. Stuart* (NY: Harper, 1986), 296.
26. Cooke, *Wearing of the Gray*, 114-15.

Notes to Chapter 18

1. Mordecai, "Diary," May 1-6, 1864.
2. Ibid., May 7, 1864; Wallace, *Richmond Howitzers,* 68.
3. Mordecai, "Diary," May 7-8, 1864.
4. Ibid., May 9-19, 1864.
5. Ibid., May 11-12, 1864.
6. Pitts, "Landmarks," 10.
7. Ibid., 12.
8. Ibid., 7.
9. O'Dell, *Inventory of Early Architecture,* 13-225 passim; Pitts, "Landmarks," map.
10. Gordon C. Rhea, *To the North Anna River* (Baton Rouge, LA: University of Louisiana, 2000), 43.
11. Ibid., 40-41.
12. Pitts, "Landmarks," 12 & 14.
13. Mordecai, "Diary," May 12, 1864.
14. Rhea, *North Anna*, 44; Pitts, "Landmarks," 14.
15. Wagman, *Front Pages*, May 13, 1864; Rhea, *North Anna*, 45.
16. Carlton McCarthy, *Detailed Minutiae of Soldier Life* (Richmond: Carlton McCarthy, 1882), 108-09; Rhea, *North Anna,* 45.
17. Pitts, "Landmarks," map; Peterkin, "Emmanuel." 30.
18. Rhea, *North Anna*, 48-50.
19. Ibid.
20. Pitts, "Landmarks," 16.
21. Rhea, *North Anna,* 47, 52, 53, & 62.
22. Pitts, "Landmarks," 16 & 18; Rhea, *North Anna*, 51 & 52.
23. Rhea, *North Anna,* 50; O.R. 36, pt. 1: 814-19.
24. Rhea, *North Anna*, 50, 55 & 56.
25. O.R. 36, pt. 1: 777.
26. Ibid.
27. Wagman, *Front Pages, Richmond Daily Dispatch*, May 13, 1864.
28. O.R. 51, pt. 1: 250.

29. Driver, *5th Virginia Cavalry*, 80 & roster.
30. Hunton, *Autobiography*, 103-111.
31. Ibid; Young, *56th Virginia Infantry*, 89-90.
32. Ibid.
33. Rhea, *North Anna*, 59; Peterkin, "Emmanuel," 41.
34. Mordecai, "Diary," May 12, 1864.
35. Ibid.
36. Ibid.
37. Mary Powell to Junius Powell, May 27, 1864.
38. Ibid.
39. William Glenn Robertson, *Back Door to Richmond* (Newark, NJ: University of Delaware, 1987), 173.

Notes to Chapter 19

1. Stiles, *4th Virginia Cavalry*, 43-45 & roster.
2. Eva Parrish, from Elihu Parrish, in Orange County.
3. Richard Nicholas, *Powhatan, Salem, and Courtney Artillery* (Lynchburg, VA: H.E. Howard, 1997), 186-194.
4. Wallace, *Richmond Howitzers*, 68-69 & roster.
5. Ibid., 96-99.
6. Emily Bingham, *Mordecai, an Early American Family* (NY: Hill and Wang, 2003), 118-121; Mordecai, "Diary," May 14, 1864.
7. Mordecai, "Diary," May 15-18, 1864.
8. G.T. Beauregard, "The Defense of Drewry's Bluff," in *B. &. L.* 4:195-205; William Farrar Smith, "Attack on Drewry's Bluff," in *B. & L.* 4:206.
9. Thomas, *Memoirs,* 12.
10. Manarin, *15th Infantry, 57 & roster;* Massie family memorabilia.
11. LaSalle Corbell Pickett, *Pickett and His Men* (Atlanta: Foote & Davis, 1900), 345.
12. Manarin, *15th Infantry*, 57-59 & roster; William Glenn Robertson, *Back Door to Richmond* (Newark, NJ: University of Delaware, 1987), 191-92.
13. Manarin, *15th Infantry, roster.*
14. Thomas, *Memoirs,* 13; Francis-Terrell memorabilia.
15. *O.R.* 36, pt.2:199-204; Thomas, *Memoir*, 12.
16. Manarin, *15th Infantry*, 91; Lucy Ann Cross, from Charles R. Francis, July 9, 1864, on the south side of the James.
17. Julius Powell from Mary Powell, May 20, 1864, from "Melrose."
18. John D. Imboden, "The Battle of New Market, Va." *B. & L.* 4:481-83.
19. Kidd, *I Rode with Custer, 219.*
20. Ibid., 220-21.

21. Driver, *10th Cavalry*, roster; Betty Gray, from James W. Gray, May 1, 1864, at Picket Post Robertson
22. Alexander, *Fighting for the Confederacy*, 388.
23. Rhea, *North Anna*, 271-73; Driver, *10th Cavalry*, 55; Beale, *Ninth Virginia Cavalry*, 122.
24. Gabbert, *Military Operations*, 68-69; Rhea, *North Anna*, 322-24.
25. Lyman, *Meade & Grant*, 126-29.
26. William Meade Dame, *From the Rapidan to Richmond and the Spotsylvania Campaign* (Baltimore, MD: Green-Lucas, 1920), 190-91.
27. Davis, "Slashes of Hanover," 13.

Notes to Chapter 20

1. Dorothy Francis Atkinson, *King William County in the Civil War* (Lynchburg, VA: H.E. Howard, 1990), 158-170.
2. Goldsborough, *Maryland Line*, 198; Lee, *Wartime Papers*, President Davis, from R.E. Lee, May 23, 1864, at Headquarters ANV, 747
3. Rhea, *Cold Harbor*, 32-34; 41-43.
4. Goldsborough, *Maryland Line*, 198-99.
5. Rhea, *Cold Harbor*, 59-60; Atkinson, *King William*, 171.
6. Harry T. Pollard, "Some War Events in Hanover County," *Hanover County Historical Society Bulletin*, 52, June 1995.
7. Ibid.
8. Ibid.
9. Alexander, *Fighting for the Confederacy*, 395; *O.R.* 36 pt.1:1058.
10. Rhea, *Cold Harbor*, 64, 68, 74 map & 85.
11. Ibid.; Joseph Haw, "Battle of Haw's Shop," *Confederate Veteran,* 33 (1925): 373-76.
12. Ibid.
13. Ibid.
14. Peterkin, "Emmanuel," *26.*
15. Haw, "Battle of Haw's Shop," *Confederate Veteran,* 33, no. 10 (October 1925).
16. Rhea, *Cold Harbor*, 86-87; *O.R.* 36 pt. 1: 821 – Sheridan and Custer's report; Haw, "The Battle of Haw's Shop."
17. Rhea, *Cold Harbor*, 174-76.
18. R.L.T. Beale, *History of the Ninth Virginia Cavalry* (Richmond, VA: B.F. Johnson, 1899), 124.
19. Rhea, *Cold Harbor*, 176-180.
20. Ibid.
21. Ibid.
22. Goldsborough, *Maryland Line*, 200-01.

23. John David Meade, Jr., "Ashland in the Civil War," Ashland *Herald Progress*, October – November, 1964.
24. Rhea, *Cold Harbor*, 218-223; Driver, *10th Virginia Cavalry*, 55.
25. DeWitt Clinton Gallaher, *Diary*, (Charleston, WV: Wade T. Parker, Jr., 1961), 10.
26. Carmichael, *Letcher Artillery*.
27. Wallace, *Richmond Howitzers*, 98.
28. Thomas, *Memoirs*, 13.
29. Manarin, *15th Virginia Infantry*, 61 & roster.
30. Young, *56th Virginia Infantry*, 92.
31. William C. Oates, *The War between the Union and the Confederacy and the Lost Opportunities, with a History of the 15th Alabama*, 340.
32. Kolezar, *Ashland Artillery*, roster; Macaluso, *Morris Artillery*, roster.
33. Wallace, *Richmond Howitzers*, 69; Mordecai, "Diary," June 3, 1864.
34. Mordecai, "Diary," June 4-7, 1864.
35. Ibid.

Notes to Chapter 21

1. Robertson, *Back Door to Richmond*, 241 & 250.
2. Hunton, *Autobiography,* 114-15; Manarin, *15th Virginia Infantry*, 62; Thomas, *Memoirs*, 13; Lucy Ann Cross, from Charles R. Francis, July 19, 1864, on the south side of the James.
3. Driver, *10th Virginia Cavalry*, 56-57.
4. Beale, *Ninth Virginia Cavalry*, 130-31; James W. Gray, from "Aunt Mat", June 20, 1864, at Keysville.
5. Cross family memorabilia. The Gray-Cross cemetery still remains.
6. Koleszar, *Ashland Artillery,* roster.
7. Mordecai, "Diary," June 30, 1864.
8. Ibid., July 4-8, 1864.
9. Driver, *10th Virginia Cavalry*, roster.
10. Gallaher, *Diary*, 6-9.
11. Mordecai, "Diary," June 7, 1864.
12. Frank E. Vandiver, *Jubal's Raid* (New York: McGraw Hill, 1960), 25-26 & 182n.
13. Hotchkiss, *Make Me a Map*, 210-11.
14. Mordecai, "Diary," July 4-7, 1864.
15. Hotchkiss, *Virginia*, 618; Goldsborough, *Maryland Line*, 244-45; Vandiver, *Jubal's Raid*, 163-64.
16. Gallaher, *Diary,* 9, 11-19.
17. Hotchkiss, *Virginia*, 491
18. Mordecai, "Diary," letter to Mrs. D. in Richmond from Mrs. E.P. Lewis September 10, 1864, at "Lynnside."
19. Ibid.
20. Wesley Merritt, "Sheridan in the Shenandoah Valley," *Battles & Leaders,* 4:502-521; Stiles, *4th Virginia Cavalry,* 61-74.
21. Stiles, *4th Virginia Cavalry,* 62-64*; Hotchkiss,* Virginia, 639-640 & 687; Jubal A. Early, "Winchester, Fisher's Hill, and Cedar Creek," *B. & L.* 4: 522-530.
22. Stiles, *4th Virginia Cavalry,* 67 & roster; Early, "Winchester." 524.

23. Stiles, *4th Virginia Cavalry*, 70; Hotchkiss, *Virginia*, 647 & 687.
24. Stiles, *4th Virginia Cavalry*, 70-71 & roster; Hotchkiss, *Make Me a Map*, 235.
25. Mordecai, "Diary," October 12, 1864; Wallace, *Richmond Howitzers, 70.*
26. Wallace, *Richmond Howitzers*, 69-73 & roster.
27. Mordecai, "Diary," October 12, 1864.
28. Gallaher, *Diary*, 19.

Notes to Chapter 22

1. Thomas, *Memoirs,* 14; Lucy Ann Cross from Charles R. Francis, July 7, 1864, on the south side of the James.
2. Mary Elizabeth Davis memorabilia.
3. Emeline J. Terrell from Charles R. Francis, September 14 & 20, 1864, at camp of 15th Virginia Infantry
4. Emeline J. Terrell from Charles R. Franccis, October 26, 1864, at Howlett House.
5. Horace Matthews, ed. "Luther Swank Reports", 44-46; Manarin, *15th Virginia Infantry,* roster.
6. Ibid.
7. Ibid.
8. Driver, *10th Virginia Cavalry,* 57-59.
9. Ibid.; Beale, *Ninth Virginia Cavalry,* 136.
10. Lucy Ann Cross from R.Nathaniel Cross, July 20, 1864, at Camp Henrico; Lucy Ann Cross, from R. Nathaniel Cross, September 23, 1864, in Dinwiddie County.
11. Beale, *Ninth Virginia Cavalry*, 140; Driver, *10th Virginia Cavalry*, 59.
12. Driver, *10th Virginia Cavalry*, roster; James W. Gray from Martha (Priddy?), June 20, 1864, at Keysville.
13. Driver, *10th Virginia Cavalry,* 59 & roster.
14. Ibid., 61 & roster.
15. Lucy Ann Cross from R.N. Cross, September 23, 1864, from Dinwiddie County.
16. Driver, *10th Virginia Cavalry*, 63-64 & roster; Beale, *Ninth Virginia Cavalry*, 137.
17. Mordecai, "Diary," September 13-29, 1864.
18. Ibid., October 5, 1864.
19. Ibid.
20. Trout, *They Followed the Plume*, 119-124.
21. Ibid.; Rhea, *Cold Harbor*. 78.
22. Trout, *They Followed the Plume,* 120-24.

23. Ibid; Helen K. Yates, *Family Graveyards in Hanover County Virginia* (Mechanicsville, VA: Hanover County Historical Society, 2000), I.:4.
24. Macaluso, *Morris Artillery*, 72 & roster; Wallace, *Richmond Howitzers*, 70.
25. Lucy Ann Cross from Bettie (Shepherd), November 12, 1864, in Chesterfield County.
26. Ibid.
27. Golay, *To Gettysburg and Beyond. 246.*
28. Lucy Ann Cross from John Thomas Francis, November 26, 1864 & from Charles R. Francis, November 30, 1864, at Howlett House.
29. Lucy Ann Cross from Charles R. Francis, November 30, 1864; Manarin, *Richmond Volunteers*, 141; Driver, *10th Virginia Cavalry*, roster; Lucy Ann Cross from Charles R. Francis, January 27, 1865, at Fort Gilmer.
30. Lucy Ann Cross from James H. Cross, December 7, 1864, at Fishersville.
31. Lucy Ann Cross from John Thomas Francis, December 8 & 25, 1864.
32. Lucy Ann Cross from James H. Cross, January 1, 1865, at camp near Fishersville.
33. Bailey, *Henrico Home Front*, 26, 117 & 210.
34. Ibid., 216.
35. Ibid., 214 – 17.

Notes to Chapter 23

1. Lucy Ann Cross from Charles R. Francis, November 30, 1864, at Howlett House.
2. William T. Sherman, "The Grand Strategy of the Last Year of the War," *B. & L.* 4:254-55.
3. William Lamb, "The Defense of Fort Fisher," *B. & L.* 4:646; Rowena Reed, *Combined Operations in the Civil War* (Annapolis, MD: Naval Institute, 1978), 320-351.
4. Lamb, "Defense of Fort Fisher," 4:642-654.
5. John Norment Powell, from Junius Levert Powell, January 1, 1865, on S. Ship *Flag*, St. Georgia, Bermuda.
6. Ibid.
7. Ibid., February 10, 1865, at Point Lookout, MD; Wallace, *Richmond Howitzers*, roster.
8. Lucy Ann Cross from R.Nathaniel Cross, January 1, 1865, in Greenville County.
9. Lucy Ann Cross from John T. Francis, January 6, 24 & February 15, 1865; Lucy Ann Cross from Charles R. Francis, January 27, 1865, at Fort Gilmer; Manarin, *15th Virginia Infantry,* 67.
10. Thomas, *Memoirs,* 14; Lucy Ann Cross from Charles R. Francis, January 27, 1865, at Fort Gilmer.
11. Lucy Ann Cross from John T. Francis, February 15, at Fort Gilmer.
12. Thought to be to Lucy Ann Cross from John T. Francis, February 27, 1865.
13. Wallace, *Richmond Howitzers*, 71.
14. Lucy Ann Cross from John T. Francis, January 24, 1865, at Fort Gilmer.
15. Golay, *To Gettysburg and Beyond*, 217 & 247.
16. Emeline J. Terrell from John T. Francis, March 4, 1865, at Camp of Pickett's Division, Guard House near Chester.
17. Manarin, *15th Virginia Infantry*, 68 & 69.

18. Ibid.; Lucy Ann Cross from John T. Francis, March 28, 1865, at Camp of the provost guard near Petersburg.
19. Thomas, *Memoirs,* 15 &16.
20. Manarin, *15th Virginia Infantry*, 69-70; Driver, *10th Virginia Cavalry*, 71.
21. Manarin, *15th Virginia Infantry,* 70 & 71.
22. Ibid. & roster.
23. Driver, *10th Virginia Cavalry*, 69; Manarin, *15th Virginia Infantry*, roster.
24. Freeman, *R.E. Lee*, 4:44-47.
25. Ibid.
26. Thomas, *Memoirs,* 16-18.

Notes to Chapter 24

1. Davis, *To Appomattox*, 38, 39, 100 & 110.
2. Alexander, *Fighting for the Confederacy,* xiii.
3. Friend in the army in North Carolina, in Mordecai "Diary," from Emma Mordecai, April 5, 1865, at "Rosewood."
4. Ibid.
5. Ibid.
6. Ibid.
7. Ibid.
8. Ibid.
9. Ibid.
10. *Old Homes of Hanover County, Virginia*, 72-79.
11. "Diary of Mrs. Thomas Walker Doswell – April 1865," *Hanover County Historical Society Bulletin,* 46 (June 1992).
12. Ibid.
13. Jones, *Ladies of Richmond,* 133-35 & 288-89.
14. Sifakis, *Compendium – Virginia,* 20, 76-78 & 81-83.
15. Ibid., 108, 110, 118-19, 188-190 & 250-51.
16. Freeman, *R.E. Lee*, 4:60-62.
17. John A. Scott, Powhatan Artillery, military records; Scott family memorabilia; *O.R.* 46, pt. 3, 1385.
18. Family memorabilia.
19. Davis, *To Appomattox*, 198.
20. *Seven Fateful Days* (Farmville, VA: The Farmville Herald, 1961), 7-8.
21. Wallace, *Richmond Howitzers*, 71-72.

Notes to Chapter 25

1. "Seven Fateful Days," 5; Freeman, *R.E. Lee*, 81-84..
2. Ibid.
3. Hunton, *Autobiography*, 120-130.
4. Manarin, *15th Virginia Infantry*, roster.
5. Ibid., Thomas, *Memoirs*, 18.
6. Ibid., Manarin, *15th Virginia Infantry*, roster.
7. Driver, *5th Virginia Cavalry*, 109-111 & roster.
8. Wallace, *Richmond Howitzers*, 72-73 & roster.
9. Creed T. Davis, "Prison Diary," *Richmond Howitzer Battalion, Pamphlet 4*, (Richmond: J.W. Randolph, 1886), 3-4.
10. Ibid.
11. Carlton McCarthy, *Detailed Minutia*, 128-151.
12. Ibid.
13. Alexandria, *Fighting for the Confederacy*, 524-25.
14. McCarthy, *Detailed Minutiae*, 128-151; Wallace, *Richmond Howitzers*, 72-73 & roster.
15. Carmichael, *Purcell, Letcher Artillery*, 225-28; Sifakis, *Compendium – Virginia*, 7.
16. Driver, *10th Virginia Cavalry*, 72-74.
17. Ibid., roster; Freeman, *R.E. Lee*, 4:130.
18. "Lee's Report of the Surrender at Appomattox," *B. & L.* 4:724.
19. Thomas, *Memoirs*, 18-19.
20. Freeman, *R.E. Lee*, 4:118; Manarin, *15th Virginia Infantry*, 74; Francis family memorabilia.
21. Driver, *5th Virginia Cavalry*, roster.
22. McCarthy, *Detailed Minutiae*, 155-160.
23. Thomas, *Memoirs*, 19-20.
24. Mordecai, "Diary," April 13, 1865.

Notes to Chapter 26

1. Francis Trevelyan Miller, *Photographic History of the Civil War*, (New York: Review of Reviews, 1912), 7:50 & Appendix A.
2. Macaluso, *Morris Artillery,* roster; 1850 Hanover Census.
3. Ibid.; Cross family memorabilia; Koleszar, *Ashland Artillery*, roster.
4. David B. Tyler, *Delaware, the Bay and the River*, (Cambridge, MS: Cornell Maritime, 1971), 95-111.
5. Ibid.
6. Mauriel P. Joslyn, *Immortal Captives,* (Shippensburg, PA: White Mane, 1996), Appendix; Koleszar, *Ashland Artillery*, roster.
7. J. Ogden Murray, *The Immortal Six Hundred*, (Winchester, VA: Eddy Press. 1905), 42-52 & 71.
8. Ibid., 57-61.
9. Ibid.; J. J. Dunkle, *Prison Life During the Rebellion*, (Singers Glen, VA: Joseph Funk's Sons, 1869), 39-44.
10. Murray, *Immortal Six Hundred*, 84-86.
11. Joslyn, *Immortal Captives,* 170-71.
12. Ibid., 44ff.
13. Ibid., 233-243 & 249.
14. Manarin, 15th *Virginia Infantry*, roster.
15. Ibid.
16. Edwin H. Beitzell, *Point Lookout Prison Camp for Confederates*, (St. Mary's County, MD, 1983), 1-3 &19-23.
17. Peterkin, "Emmanuel," 28.
18. Ibid.
19. *Webster's New Geographical Dictionary,* (Springfield. MS: G. & C. Merriam, 1972), 367; Miller, *Photographic History* (New York: Review of Reviews, 1911), 77, 81 & 149.
20. Driver, *5th Virginia Cavalry*, roster.
21. Koleszar, *Ashland Artillery,* roster.

22. Burke Davis, *To Appomattox, Nine April Days*, (New York: Popular Library, 1959), 319; Driver, *10th Virginia Cavalry*, roster; Peterkin, *Emmanuel*, 31.
23. Wallace, *Richmond Howitzers*, roster; Creed T. Davis, "Prison Diary of Creed T. Davis," *Contributions to a History of the Richmond Howitzer Battalion.* Pamphlet no. 4, (Richmond: J.W. Randolph & English, 1886), 3-8.
24. Davis, "Prison Diary," 9-19.
25. Ibid., 20-30; Wallace, *Richmond Howitzers*, roster.
26. Wallace, *Richmond Howitzers*, roster.
27. Hunton, *Autobiography*, 120-130.
28. Henry Robinson Berkeley, *Four Years in the Confederate Artillery*, 142-43.
29. Lonnie R. Spear, *Portals to Hell*, (Mechanicsburg, PA: Stackpole, 1997), 296 & 325-332.
30. Michael Horigan, *Elmira, Death Camp of the North* (Mechaniscburg, PA: Stackpole, 2002), 164; James Huffman, *Ups and Downs of a Confederate Soldier)*, 95-102.
31. Ibid., 150-163, 180 & 3.
32. Ibid., 74 &194.

Notes to Chapter 27

1. Berkeley, *Four Years with the Confederate Artillery*, 143-45.
2. Ibid.
3. "Diary of Mrs. Thomas Walker Doswell, April 1865." *Hanover County Historical Society Bulletin*, 46, June 1999.
4. Ibid.
5. Wallace, *Richmond Howitzers*, roster; "Diary of Blanche Powell."
6. Koleszar, *Ashland Artillery*, roster.
7. Terrell – Francis family memorabilia.
8. Cross – Francis family memorabilia.
9. Terrell – Francis family memorabilia.
10. "The Mordecais of Rosewood." 46-47.
11. Ibid.
12. Peterkin, "Emmanuel," 22-23.
13. Ibid.
14. Mosby family memorabilia.
15. Ibid.
16. David Sparks, *Inside of Lincoln's Army, the Diary of Marsena Rudolph Patrick*, (New York: Thomas Yoseloff, 1964), 291, 487-89.
17. Ibid., 516.
18. Cross – Francis family memorabilia.
19. Catherine Cross from Joseph Finch Cross, Sept. 5, 1870, at Baltimore, MD.
20. Emeline J. Terrell from Ann E. Terrell, July 19, 1876 – Nov. 15, 1882, at Hinkleville, KY; receipt at "Meadow Farm," Glen Allen, VA.
21. Francis family memorabilia.
22. Ibid.
23. Powell family memorabilia.
24. "The Mordecais of Rosewood," 45-47
25. Ibid.
26. Massie family memorabilia.

27. Emeline J. Terrell, from Mollie G. Terrell, Apr. 26, 1866, at "Locust Row;" Terrell family memorabilia.
28. Emeline J. Terrell, from Barbara O. Johnson, July 2, 1877, at "Montico Hall."
29. Terrell letters, 1874 – 1877.
30. Ibid.
31. Ibid.
32. Joslyn, *Immortal Captives*, 164 & 271.
33. Mrs. Virginia Shepherd, from Hamilton Shepherd. (Meadow Farm Museum)
34. Manarin, *History of Henrico County*, 314-16.
35. "Mt. Olive Baptist Church, Quasquicentennial, 1867-1992. Partners for the Journey," 4; Harry M. Ward, *Richmond in Illistrated History,* (Northbridge, CA: Windsors Publications, 1985), 180-81.
36. "History of St. Peter Baptist Church, Glen Allen, VA," 2005. Courtesy of Rev. C. Diane Mosby.
37. *Hanover County, 1721-1971*, sec. 5, 13; sect. 4, 7.
38. Ibid., sec. 4, 11; "Winn's Baptist Church Records," Virginia Baptist Historical Society.
39. Creed Davis, "Slashes of Hanover," 25-26..
40. Shalf, *Ashland*, 88-92.

NOTES TO EPILOGUE

1. Lewis Terrell, Interview by the author.
2. Martha Hughes Salmon, Interview by the author.
3. Douglas A. Thorpe, "Slave would make history in Henrico," *The County Line*, May 10, 1964.
4. Cocke, *Hanover Chancery Wills and Notes*, 56.
5. Manarin, *Henrico County*, 373 & 382-86; Gary Robertson, "Henrico Plan." *Richmond Times Dispatch*, December 22, 2002, sect. B, 1 &3.
6. David D. Ryan, *Lewis Ginter's Richmond,* (Richmond, VA: Whittet & Shepperson. 1991), 22, 46-47, 56 & 59; Manarin, *Henrico*, 335, 338 & 340.
7. Shalf, *Ashland*, 136.
8. Row, *Emmanuel*, 24-25.
9. "Greenwood Methodist Church, 1874-1999."
10. Ibid.
11. Ibid.
12. "History of Hunton Baptist Church, Glen Allen, Virginia." In Virginia Baptist Historical Society, University of Richmond.
13. "History of Glen Allen Baptist Church, Glen Allen, Virginia." In Virginia Baptist Historical Society, University of Richmond.
14. Alberta Lindsey, "Winn's Baptist Has 190th Anniversary," *Richmond Times Dispatch*. August 7, 1966; Mark H. Cross, "Cross Family History."
15. Herald Progress, *Hanover County, 1721-1971*, sect. 4, 17 (Ground Squirrel); sect. 5, 4 (Independence).
16. Ibid., sect. 4, 7 (Gwathmey), sect. 5, 15 (Cavalry Mission); sect. 5, 6 (St. Paul's).
17. Ibid., sect. 4, 20 (Kenwood).
18. Ibid., sect. 4, 16 (Enon); sect. 5, 3 (Mt. Herman & Forest Grove).
19. Ibid., sect. 5, 3 (Duncan Memorial); sect. 5, 4 (St. Ann's); sect. 5, 7 (St. James).
20. Shalf, *Ashland*, 138.

21. Robert Salmon. Interview by the author.
22. River Road Garden Club, "Henrico Sketches," Henrico, 1977, 36-37; John Cussons, *A Glance at Current History* (Glen Allen, VA: Cussons, May & Co., 1899).
23. Marion Litchfield Lauterbach. Interview by the author.
24. Shalf, *Ashland*, 133-34.

BIBLIOGRAPHY

I – Primary Sources

Alexander, Edward Porter. *Fighting for the Confederacy: the Personal Recollections of General ...* Edited by Gary W. Gallagher. Chapel Hill, NC: University of North Carolina, 1989.

Beale, R.L.T. *History of the Ninth Virginia Cavalry*. Richmond, VA: B.F. Johnson, 1899.

Belo, Alfred Horatio. *Memoirs of ...*Edited by Stuart Wright. Gaithersburg, MD: Old Soldier Books, n.d.

Berkeley, Henry Robinson. *Four Years in the Confederate Artillery*. Edited by Wm. H. Reurge. Chapel Hill, NC: University of North Carolina, 1961.

Bodenstein, Otelia Francis. *Terrell – Francis Family Civil War Letters. Copied by from the originals by ... and Dorothy Francis Atkinson*. Typescript. Crownsville, MD and Hanover, VA:1963.

Botts, John Minor. *The Great Rebellion: Its Secret History, Rise, Progress, and Disastrous Failure*. New York: Harper, 1866.

Coburn, J. Osborn. *Hell on Belle Isle: Diary of a Civil War POW*. Edited by Donald Allison. Bryan, OH: Faded Banner, 1997.

Cooke, John Esten. *Wearing of the Gray*. Baton Rouge, LA: Louisana State University, 1997.

Cussons, John. *A Glance at Current History*. Glen Allen, VA: Cussons, May, & Co., 1899.

Dame, William Meade. *From the Rapidan to Richmond and the Spotsylvania Campaign*. Baltimore, MD: Green Lucas, 1920.

Daniel, Frederick S. *Richmond Howitzers in the War*. Gaitersburg, MD: Butternut Press, 1891.

Davis, Creed T. "Slashes of Hanover." Typescript. Richmond, VA: 1891.

Davis, Jefferson. *Private Letters 1823 – 1889.* Edited by Hudson Strode. New York: Harcourt, 1966.

Dunkle, J.J. *Prison Life During the Rebellion.* Singer's Glen, VA: Joseph Funk's Sons, 1869.

Gallaher, DeWitt Clinton. *A Diary of ... in the War between the States while Serving in the Confederate Army.* Edited by DeWitt C. Gallaher, Jr. Charleston, WV: Wade T. Parker, Jr., 1961.

Garnett, Theodore Stanford. *Riding with Stuart.* Edited by Robert J. Trout. Shippensburg, PA: White Mane, 1994.

Goldsborough, W.W. *The Maryland Line in the Confederate Army 1861-1865.* Gaithersburg, MD: Olde Soldier Books, 1987.

Hotchkiss, Jedediah. *Confederate Military History.* Vol. 3 - Virginia. Edited by Clement A. Evans. Blue and Gray Press, n.d.

Hotchkiss, Jedediah. *Make Me a Map of the Valley.* Dallas, TX: Southern University Press, 1975.

Huffman, James. *Ups and Downs of a Confederate Soldier.* New York: William E. Ridge's Sons, 1940.

Hunton, Eppa. *Autobiography.* Richmond, VA: William Byrd Press, 1933.

Jones, Charles C. *A Catechism for Families and Sabbath Schools, Designed also for Oral Instruction of Coloured Persons.* Philadelphia, PA: Board of Publications, 1852.

Jones, John B. *A Rebel War Clerk's Diary of the Confederate States Capital.* 2 Vols. Philadelphia, PA: J.B. Lippincott, 1866.

Jordan, Wm. C. *Some Events and Incidents during the Civil War.* Montgomery, AL: Paragon Press, 1909.

Joslyn, Mauriel P. *Immortal Captives: the Story of the 600 Confederate Officers and the United States Prisoner of War Policy.* Shippensburg, PA: White Mane, 1996.

Keily, James. *Smith's Henrico County Virginia from Actual Surveys.* Richmond, VA: Robert Smith & Carpenter, 1853.

Map.

Kidd, J.H. *A Cavalryman with Custer.* New York: Doubleday, 1991.

Lee, Captain Robert E. *Recollections and Letters of General Robert E. Lee.* New York: Doubleday, 1924.

Lee, Robert E. *Wartime Papers of …* Edited by Clifford Dowdey. New York: Bramhall House, 1961.

Lyman, Theodore. *With Grant and Meade from the Wilderness to Appomattox.* Edited by George R. Agassiz. Lincoln, NB: University of Nebraska, 1994.

McCarthy, Carlton. *Detailed Minutiae of Soldier Life.* Richmond, VA: Carlton McCarthy, 1882.

McClellan, H.B. *I Rode with Jeb Stuart: the Life and Campaigns of Major General J.E.B. Stuart.* Bloomington, IN: Indiana University, 1958.

McGuire, Judith White. *Diary of a Southern Refugee during the War.* 3rd ed. Richmond, VA: J.W. Randolph, 1889.

Mordecai, Emma. "Diary of … May 1864 – May 1865." Typescript. Southern Historical Collection. Chapel Hill, NC: University of North Carolina.

Mordecai, Samuel. *Richmond in By-gone Days.* 2nd ed. Richmond: Dietz Press, 1946.

Murray, J. Ogden. *The Immortal Six Hundred.* Winchester, VA: Eddy Press, 1901.

Oates, William C. *The War Between the Union and the Confederacy and the Lost Opportunities, with a History of the 15th Alabama Regiment.* New York: Neale, 1905.

Patrick, Marsena Rudolph. *Inside Lincoln's Army, the Diary of …* Edited by David Sparks. New York: Thomas Yoseloff, 1964.

Peterkin, Marian Stewart. "A History of Emmanuel Church, Brook Hill, Virginia." Edited by Kathleen B. Francis. Typescript. Glen Allen, VA: 1986.

Pickett, LaSalle Corbell. *Pickett and His Men.* Atlanta, GA: Foote & Davis, 1900.

Powell, Blanche Norment. "Journal of … January 12, 1862 –

February 12, 1862; October 4, 1862 – February 27, 1863." Typescript. n.d.

Putnam, Sallie Brock. *Richmond during the War.* New York: G.W. Carleton, 1867.

Sheppard, Dr. John M. "Medical Journal." Manuscript.

Swank, Walbrook D., ed. *Train Running for the Confederacy 1861-1865: an Eyewitness Memoir.* Charlottesville, VA: Papercraft, 1990.

Thomas, Joseph Park. *Memoirs of … Richmond, VA: 1919.*

Trout, Robert J. ed. *With Pen and Saber: The Letters and Diaries of J.E.B. Stuart's Staff Officers.* Mechanicsburg, PA: Stackpole, 1995.

Van Lew, Elizabeth L. *A Yankee Spy in Richmond.* Edited by David D. Ryan. Mechanicsburg, PA: Stackpole, 1996.

Wagman, John, ed. *Civil War Front Pages: A collection of 157 Front Pages from the North and South.* New York: Fairfax, 1959.

II – Primary Sources - Articles.

Beauregard, G.T. "The Defense of Drewry's Bluff." *Battles & Leaders,* 4:206.

Burnside, Ambrose. "The Burnside Expedition." *Battles & Leaders,* I:660-69.

Davies, Henry J. "Report – (Kilpatrick's Raid) 1864," *Official Records* 33:190-92.

Davis, Creed T. "Prison Diary." *Richmond Howitzer Battalion,* pamphlet 4 (1886).

Davis, Mary Elizabeth Francis. "Some Troubles of the War," MS. November 1864.

Doswell, Frances Walker. "Diary of … April 1865," *Hanover County Historical Society Bulletin* 46 (June 1992).

Early, Jubal. "Winchester, Fisher's Hill, and Cedar Creek." *Battles & Leaders* 4: 522-30.

Fleming, Vivian Minor. "The last Days of J.E.B. Stuart," ed. Eric Mink. *Hanover County Historical Society Bulletin* 63

(Winter 2000).

Getty, George W. "Report … expedition to the South Anna," *Official Records* 27, pt. 2:837-39.

Haw, Joseph R. "Haw's Shop Community, of Virginia." *Confederate Veteran* 33 (1925): 340-41.

Haw, Joseph R. "The Battle of Haw's Shop." *Confederate Veteran* 33 (1925): 373-76.

Imboden, John D. "The Battle of New Market," *Battles & Leaders* 4:481-83.

Lamb, William. "The Defense of Fort Fisher." *Battles & Leaders* 4:642-54.

Lee, Robert E. "Report of the Surrender at Appomattox." *Battles & Leaders* 4:724.

Merritt, Wesley. "Sheridan in the Shenandoah Valley." *Battles & Leaders* 4:502-21.

Moore, J. Staunton. "1861-1911 – An Address." Williamsburg, VA, May 24, 1911.

Newton, Mary Mann Page. "Letters Cast New Light on the Burial of Latane." ed. Robert E.L. Krick. *Hanover County Historical Society Bulletin* 64 (Summer 2001).

Pollard, Harry T. "Some War Events in Hanover County." *Hanover County Historical Society Bulletin* 52 (June 1995).

Porter, H.B. "General Made Hostage." *Washington National Tribune,* January 21, 1897.

Rodenbough Theodore F. "Sheridan's Richmond Raid." *Battles & Leaders* 4:191.

Sherman, William T. "The Grand Strategy of the Last Year of the War." *Battles & Leaders* 4:254-55.

Shirley, William J. "A Raid of the 11th Pa. Cavalry." *Grand Army Scout & Soldiers Mail,* January 19, 1884.

Smith, William Farrar. "Attack on Drewry's Bluff." *Battles & Leaders* 4:195-205.

Swank, Luther. "Reports." Edited by Horace Matthews.

Tripp, Stephen. "Fighting Them Over." *Washington National Tribune* June 4, 1896.

II – Primary Sources – Regimental Histories, Rosters, and Their Officers.

Carmichael, Peter S. *The Purcell, Crenshaw, and Letcher Artillery*. Lynchburg, VA. H.E. Howard, 1990.
Driver, Robert J., Jr. *1st Virginia Cavalry*. Lynchburg, VA: H.E. Howard, 1991.
Driver, Robert J., Jr. *5th Virginia Cavalry*. Lynchburg, VA: H.E. Howard, 1997.
Driver, Robert J., Jr. *10th Virginia Cavalry*. Lynchburg, VA: H.E. Howard, 1992.
Koleszar, Marilyn Brewer. *Ashland, Bedford, and Taylor Virginia Light Artillery*. Lynchburg, VA. H.E. Howard, 1994.
Krick, Robert E.L. *Staff Officers in Gray*. Chapel Hill, NC: University of North Carolina, 2003.
Macaluso, Gregory J. *Morris, Orange, and King William Artillery*. Lynchburg, VA: H.E. Howard, 1991.
Manarin, Louis H. *15th Virginia Infantry*. Lynchburg, VA: H.E. Howard, 1990.
Manarin, Louis H. *Richmond Volunteers: the Volunteer Companies of the City of Richmond and Henrico County, Virginia*. Richmond, VA: Westover Press, 1969.
Nicholas, Richard L. *Powhatan, Salem, and Courtney Artillery*. Lynchburg, VA: H.E. Howard, 1997.
Sifakis, Stewart. *Compendium of the Confederate Armies, Virginia*. NY: Facts on File, 1992.
Stiles, Kenneth L. *4th Virginia Cavalry*. Lynchburg, VA: H.E. Howard, 1985.
Wallace, Lee A., Jr. *A Guide to Virginia Military Organizations, 1861-1865*. Lynchburg, VA: H.E. Howard, 1964.
Wallace, Lee A., Jr. *The Richmond Howitzers*. Lynchburg, VA: H.E. Howard, 1993.
Young, William A. *56th Virginia Infantry*. Lynchburg, VA: H. E. Howard, 1990.

III – Primary Sources - Church Histories

Glen Allen Baptist Church – Virginia Baptist Historical Society.

Greenwood Methodist Church, 1874-1999.

Herald Progress, Hanover County 1721 – 1971. Sections 4 & 5. Hanover, VA: Herald Progress, 1971.

Hunton Baptist Church – Virginia Baptist Historical Society.

Lindsey, Alberta G. "Winn's Baptist Church Has 190th Anniversary." *Richmond Times Dispatch,* August 7, 1966.

Mt. Olive Baptist Church, 1867-1992, "Partners for the Journey."

St. Peter Baptist Church – courtesy of Rev. C. Diane Mosby.

Slash Christian Church, Disciples of Christ – courtesy of Dianne Jones.

Winn's Baptist Church – Virginia Baptist Historical Society.

IV – Primary Sources - Government Records

Bailey, James H. *Henrico Home Front 1861-1865.* Richmond, VA: Whittet & Shepperdson, 1963.

Cocke, William Ronald, III. *Hanover Chancery Wills and Notes*. Baltimore, MD: Genealogical Publishing, 1978.

Hanover County Chancery Court. Ended File. No. 11, 1860. Davis vs. Francis.

Henrico Chancery Court. File 1861, Cross vs. Cross.

Inman, Joseph F. and Isobel *Hanover County, Virginia: 1850 United States Census*. Richmond, VA: 1974.

United States 1850 Census – "Richmond City, Henrico County." Recorded by S.T. Hulce.

The War of the Rebellion: A Compilation of the Official Records of the Union and Confederate Armies. Washington, D.C., 1880-1901.

V – Primary Sources – Family Memorabilia and History

Anderson family – courtesy Lillian Anderson Baldock.
Cross and Gray families – courtesy the late Catherine Cross, the late Fannie C. Cross, Thomas A. Scott, and Mark H. Cross.
Davis family – courtesy the late Maggie Davis Bowles and Ruth Cross Hawthorne.
Francis family – courtesy the late Cora Francis Bowles and the late Thomas E. Francis.
Kelly family – courtesy the late Hammond Kelly.
Lauterbach, Litchfield family – courtesy Marian Litchfield Lauterbach.
Massie family - courtesy Jayne M. Massie.
Mosby family – courtesy Martha T. Lupton.
Nuckols family – courtesy Thomas A. Scott.
Parrish family – courtesy Lois Cumber and mother.
Powell family – courtesy the late Patsy Taylor.
Salmon family – courtesy the late Martha Hughes Salmon, the late Barbara Salmon Whitaker, and the late Robert Salmon.
Sheppard family – courtesy Meadow Farm Museum and Kim Sicola.
Terrell family – courtesy the late Martha Terrell Durham, the late Lewis Terrell, and Leland Terrell.

VI – Secondary Sources – Books

Alley, Reuben E. *History of the University of Richmond, 1830-1937*. Charlottesville, VA: University Press, 1977.
Atkinson, Dorothy Francis. *King William County in the Civil War*. Lynchburg, VA: H.E. Howard, 1990.
Bailey, Ronald H. *The Bloodiest Day.* Alexandria, VA: Time Life Books, 1984.
Bailey, Ronald H. *Forward to Richmond: McClellan's Peninsular Campaign.* Alexandria, VA: Time Life Books,

1983.

Beitzell, Edwin W. *Point Lookout Prison Camp for Confederates.* St. Mary's County, MD: 1983.

Bingham, Emily. *Mordecai: An Early American Family.* New York: Hill and Wang, 2003.

Carter, Samuel, III. *The Last Cavaliers: Confederate and Union Cavalries in the Civil War.* New York: St. Martin's Press, 1979.

Cormier, Steven A. *The Siege of Suffolk: The Forgotten Campaign, April 11 – May 4,* Lynchburg, VA: H.E. Howard, 1989.

Cross, Katherine Turner. *The Crosses along Falling Creek.* Ashland, VA: 1972.

Dabney, Virginius. *Richmond: The Story of a City.* New York: Doubleday, 1976.

Davis, Burke. *Jeb Stuart the Last Cavalier.* New York: Rinehart, 1957.

Davis, Burke. *To Appomattox: Nine April Days.* New York: Popular Library, 1959.

Downey, Fairfax. *Clash of Cavalry: the Battle for Brandy Station.* New York: David McKay, 1959.

Egerton, Douglas R. *Gabriel's Rebellion.* Chapel Hill, NC: University of North Carolina Press, 1993.

Freeman, Douglas Southall. *Lee's Lieutenants.* Vol. 2. New York: Charles Scribner's Sons, 1943.

Freeman, Douglas Southall. *R.E. Lee: A Biography.* Vol. 4, New York: Charles Scribner's Sons, 1936.

Furgurson, Ernest B. *Chancellorsville, 1863.* New York: Alfred A. Knopf, 1992.

Gabbert, John M. *Military Operations in Hanover County, Virginia, 1861-1865.* Roanoke, VA: Gurther Graphics, 1989.

Golay, Michael. *To Gettysburg and Beyond: The Parallel Lives of Joshua Lawrence Chamberlaine and Edward Porter Alexander.* New York: Crown, 1994.

Griffin, William E., Jr. *Richmond, Fredericksburg & Potomac Railroad: The Capital Cities Route*. Lynchburg, VA: TLC Publishing, 1994.

Hanover County Historical Society. *Old Homes of Hanover County, Virginia*. Hanover, VA: 1983.

Holmes, Oliver W. *Stagecoach East.* Washington, DC: Smithsonian Institute Press, 1983.

Horigan, Michael. *Elmira: Death Camp of the North.* Mechanicsburg, PA: Stackpole, 2002.

Johnston, Angus James, II. *Virginia Railroads in the Civil War.* Chapel Hill, NC: University of North Carolina, 1961.

Jones, Ktharine M. *Ladies of Richmond.* New York: Bobbs-Merrill, 1962.

Jones, Virgil Carrington. *Eight Hours before Richmond.* New York: Henry Holt, 1957.

Lancaster, Robert Bolling. *A Sketch of the Early History of Hanover County. Virginia.* Richmond, VA: Whittet & Shepperson, 1976.

Lawless, Chuck. *Illustrated Encyclopedia of Civil War Collectibles.* New York: Henry Holt, 1997.

Longacre, Edward G. *Mounted Raids of the Civil War.* Lincoln, NB: University of Nebraska, 1975.

McPherson, James M. *Battle Cry of Freedom.* New York: Oxford University, 1988.

Manarin, Louis H. *The History of Henrico County.* Charlottesville, VA: University Press, 1984.

Miller, Francis Trevelyan. *Photographic History of the Civil War.* New York: Review of Reviews, 1911.

Murfin, James V. *The Gleam of Bayonets: Battle of Antietam, September 17, 1862.* Atlanta, GA: Mockingbird Books, 1965.

O'Dell, Jeffrey Marshall. *Inventory of Early Architecture and Historic Sites.* County of Henrico, VA, 1976.

Peters, Margaret T. *Guidebook to Virginia's Historical Markers.* Charlottesville, VA: University Press of Virginia, 1986.

Reed, Rowena. *Combined Operations in the Civil War.* Annapolis, MD: Naval Institute Press, 1978.
Rhea, Gordon C. *The Battles for Spotsylvania Court House and the Road to Yellow Tavern.* Baton Rouge, LA: Louisiana State University, 1997.
Rhea, Gordon C. *Cold Harbor: Grant and Lee, May 26 – June 3, 1864*. Baton Rouge, LA: Louisiana State University, 2002.
Rhea, Gordon C. *To the North Anna River.* Baton Rouge, LA: Louisiana State University, 2000.
Robertson, William Glenn. *Back Door to Richmond: The Bermuda Hundred Campaign April – June 1864.* Newark, NJ: University of Delaware, 1987.
Row, Stephen E. *Emmanuel Church – Brook Hill, 1860-1985.* Richmond, VA: Emmanuel Church History Committee, 1988.
Ryan, David D. *Cornbread and Maggots: Cloak and Dagger.* Richmond, VA: Dietz Press, 1994.
Ryan, David D. *Lewis Ginter's Richmond*. Richmond, VA: Whittet & Shepperson, 1991.
Shalf, Rosanne Groat. *Ashland, Ashland.* Lawrenceville, VA: Brunswick, 1994.
Sidbury, James. *Ploughshares into Swords: Race, Rebellion, and Identity in Gabriel's Virginia 1730-1810.* New York: Cambridge University, 1997.
Speer, Lonnie R. *Portals to Hell: Military Prisons in the Civil War*. Mechanicsburg, PA: Stackpole, 1997.
Stackpole, Edward J. *They Met at Gettysburg*. New York: Crown, 1956.
Thomas, Emory M. *Bold Dragoon, the Life of J.E.B. Stuart.* NewYork: Harper & Row, 1986.
Trout, Robert J. *They Followed the Plume.* Mechanicsburg, PA: Stackpole, 1993.
Turner, Charles W. *Chessie's Road.* Richmond,VA: Garrett & Massie, 1953.

Tyler, David B. *Delaware, the Bay and the River.* Cambridge, MD: Cornell Maritime Press, 1971.
Vallindigham, Edward Noble. *Delaware and the Eastern Shore.* Philadelphia, PA: Lippincott, 1922.
Van Der Heuvel, Gerry. *Crowns of Thorns and Glory: Mary Todd Lincoln and Varina Howell Davis.* NewYork: Dutton, 1988.
Vandiver, Frank E. *Jubal's Raid.* New York: McGraw – Hill, 1960.
Ward, Harry M. *Richmond in Illustrated History.* Northbridge, CA: Windsors, 1985.
Wheeler, Richard. *On Fields of Fury.* NewYork: Harper, 1991.
Wheeler, Richard. *Sword over Richmond.* New York: Harper, 1986.
Wiley, Bell Irvin. *Embattled Confederates.* NewYork: Harper, 1964.
Yates, Helen K. *Family Graveyards in Hanover County, Virginia.* Vol. 1. Mechanicsville, VA: Hanover County Historical Society, 1995.

VII - Secondary Sources – Articles

Cashon, Joan E. "Landscape and Memory and Anti-Bellum Virginia." *Virginia Magazine of History and* Biography 102 (October 1994): 493-96.
Cross, Mark H. "An Old Soldier Fades Away." Typescript. 1996.
Kyle, Joseph D. "The Most Unhappy Contest: Hanover Tavern During the Civil War." *Hanover Tavern Foundation*: 4 (Winter 1977).
Meade, John David, Jr. "Ashland in the Civil War." *Herald Progress,* October - November 1964.
"The Mordecais of Rosewood." *Henrico County Historical Society Magazine.*" 12 (1988).

Pitts, H. Douglas. "Landmarks of Sheridan's Raid." Typescript. 1995.

River Road Garden Club. "Henrico Sketches." Henrico County: 1977.

Robertson, Gary. "The Henrico Plan." *Richmond Times Dispatch, December 22, 2002,* Section B: 1 & 3.

"Seven Fateful Days: The Story of General Robert E. Lee's Retreat from Petersburg to Appomattox, Virginia April 2-9, 1865." *The Farmville Herald and The Times-Virginian of Appomattox.* Reprint. Farmville, VA: 1962.

Stauffer, William H. "Westward from Petersburg to Appomattox." *Farmville Herald,* April 7, 1901. Reprint.

Thorpe, Douglas A. "Slave Would Make History in Henrico." *The County Line*, May 19, 1984.

Trotti, Michael. "Freedmen and Enslaved Soil: A Case Study of Manumission, Migration, and Land." *Virginia Magazine of History and Biography* 104 (Autumn 1996): 458-465.

About the Author

Dorothy Francis Atkinson, the granddaughter of a Confederate veteran, lives in an 18th century farmhouse, "Wyoming," on the Pamunkey River in King William County where Grant crossed some of his troops on the way to Cold Harbor. She graduated with a degree in history from Westhampton College and from Emory University with a degree in library science, served on the library staff of the University of Richmond and the Kanawha County Public Library in West Virginia and as chairman of the board of trustees for the Pamunkey Regional Library. Beginning in 1957, she helped her husband, the late Benjamin Overton Atkinson, operate his family farm and has been for many years a lay speaker in the United Methodist Church. Mrs. Atkinson is the author of *King William County in the Civil War: Along Mangohick Byways.*

www.ingramcontent.com/pod-product-compliance
Lightning Source LLC
LaVergne TN
LVHW010223110826
845148LV00022B/1266

* 9 7 8 0 7 8 8 4 4 1 3 1 8 *